# THE PREHISTORIC SOCIETY

# Neolithic Stone Extraction in Britain and Europe

*an enthnoarchaeological perspective*

# THE PREHISTORIC SOCIETY

# *Neolithic stone extraction in Britain and Europe*
## an ethnoarchaeological perspective

by
Peter Topping

*Prehistoric Society Research Paper No. 12*
*2021*

THE PREHISTORIC SOCIETY
Series Editor: Michael J. Allen
Managing Editor: Julie Gardiner

Oxford & Philadelphia

Published in the United Kingdom in 2021 by
The Prehistoric Society

*and*

OXBOW BOOKS
The Old Music Hall, 106–108 Cowley Road, Oxford, OX4 1JE

and in the United States by
OXBOW BOOKS
1950 Lawrence Road, Havertown, PA 19083

© The Prehistoric Society, Oxbow Books and the authors, 2021

Hardcover Edition: ISBN 978-1-78925-705-2
Digital Edition: ISBN 978-1-78925-706-9 (epub)

A CIP record for this book is available from the British Library

Library of Congress Control Number: 2021946645

All rights reserved. No part of this book may be reproduced or transmitted in any form or by any means, electronic or mechanical including photocopying, recording or by any information storage and retrieval system, without permission from the publisher in writing.

Printed in Malta by Melita Press

For a complete list of Oxbow titles, please contact:

UNITED KINGDOM
Oxbow Books
Telephone (01865) 241249
Email: oxbow@oxbowbooks.com
www.oxbowbooks.com

UNITED STATES OF AMERICA
Oxbow Books
Telephone (610) 853-9131, Fax (610) 853-9146
Email: queries@casemateacademic.com
www.casemateacademic.com/oxbow

Oxbow Books is part of the Casemate Group

*Front cover:* The summit of Pike of Stickle, Langdale, Cumbria, and one of the axeheads from the Belmont hoard (Image P. Topping)
*Rear cover:* Top: Antlers abandoned in one of the side galleries of Greenwell's Pit at Grime's Graves (Norfolk) (photo: author)
*Top right:* Grime's Graves (Norfolk), Late Neolithic–Early/Middle Bronze Age flint mines (photo: author)
*Bottom right:* Mont Viso (Italy), one of the major jade sources in the Alps (photo: author)

Sponsor of this publication
MARC FITCH FUND

# THE PREHISTORIC SOCIETY RESEARCH PAPERS

*The Prehistoric Society Research Papers* publish collections of edited papers covering aspects of Prehistory. These may be derived from conferences, or research projects; they specifically *exclude* the publication of single excavation reports. The Research Papers present the fruits of the best of prehistoric research, complementing the Society's respected *Proceedings* by allowing broader treatment of key research areas.

The Research Papers is a peer-reviewed series whose production is managed by the Society.

Further information can be found on the Society's website (www.prehistoricsociety.org)

### SERIES EDITOR: MICHAEL J. ALLEN
*Editorial Advisory Committee:*

| | | | |
|---|---|---|---|
| N. Ashton | E. Bánffy | G. Barker | H. Fokkens |
| C.A.I. French | A. Gibson | F. Healy | M. Holst |
| K. Mizoguchi | D. Price | R. Risch | N. Sharples |
| A. Sheridan | S. Ulm | G. Warren | |

## THE PREHISTORIC SOCIETY

The Prehistoric Society's interests are world wide and extend from the earliest human origins to the emergence of written records. Membership is open to all, and includes professional, amateur, student and retired members.

An active programme of events – lectures, study tours, day- and weekend conferences, and research weekends – allows members to participate fully in the Society and to meet other members and interested parties. The study excursions cater for all preferences from the relatively luxurious to the more economical, including highly popular student study tours. Day visits to sites are arranged whenever possible.

The Society produces two publications that are included with most categories of membership: the annual journal, *Proceedings of the Prehistoric Society* and the topical newsletter, *PAST*, which is published in April, July and November. In addition the *Prehistoric Society Research Papers* are published occasionally on which members may have discount.

Further information can be found on the Society's website (www.prehistoricsociety.org), or via the Prehistoric Society's registered address: % Institute of Archaeology, University College London, 31–34 Gordon Square, London, WC1H 0PY.

*The Society is a registered charity (no. 1000567)*

# THE PREHISTORIC SOCIETY RESEARCH PAPERS

Other volumes in this series, available from Oxbow Books

No. 1. *From Bann Flakes to Bushmills – papers in honour of Professor Peter Woodman*
eds N. Finlay, S. McCartan, N. Milner & C. Wickham-Jones (2009)

No. 2. *Land and People – papers in memory of John G. Evans*
eds M.J. Allen, N. Sharples & T. O'Connor (2009)

No. 3. *Materialitas: working stone, carving identity*
eds B. O'Connor, G. Cooney & J. Chapman (2010)

No. 4. *Is there a British Chalcolithic? People, place and polity in the later 3rd millennium*
eds M.J. Allen, J. Gardiner, A. Sheridan & D. McOmish (2012)

No. 5. *Image, Memory and Monumentality: archaeological engagements with the material world*
eds A.M. Jones, J. Pollard, M.J. Allen and J. Gardiner (2012)

No. 6. *Settlement in the Irish Neolithic: new discoveries at the edge of Europe*
by Jessica Smyth (2014)

No. 7. *The Beaker People: isotopes, mobility and diet in prehistoric Britain*
eds M. Parker Pearson, A. Sheridan, M. Jay, A. Chamberlain, M. Richards & J. Evans (2019)

No. 8. *First Farmers of the Carpathian Basin: changing patterns in subsistence, ritual and monumental figurines*
by Eszter Bánffy (2019)

No. 9. *Bell Beaker Settlement of Europe: the Bell Beaker phenomenon from a domestic perspective*
ed. Alex M. Gibson (2019)

No. 11. *The Social Context of Technology: non-ferrous metalworking in later prehistory*
by Leo Webley, Sophia Adams & Joanna Brück (2020)

Volumes in production

No. 10. *Re-peopling La Manche: new perspectives on Neanderthals lifeways at La Cotte de St Brelade*
eds Matt Pope, Beccy Scott & Andrew Shaw

No. 13. *Fragments of the Bronze Age*
by Matthew G. Knight

# CONTENTS

List of figures and tables — ix
Author details — xi
Abstract — xii
French language abstract — xiii
German language abstract — xiv
Spanish language abstract — xv
Acknowledgements — xvi
Foreword, by John Kelly — xvii

1. Setting the scene: the Mesolithic prelude and first contact Neolithic — 1
    The Mesolithic prelude in Europe … — 2
    Materiality and placed deposits during the European Mesolithic — 11
    What trends emerge from the Mesolithic data? — 15
    The appearance of Neolithic extraction — 16
    Overall trends during the Mesolithic–Neolithic transition — 20

2. The ethnography of lithic extraction — 23
    Research methodology — 23
    The analysis of 168 ethnographic studies — 25
    Implications for the archaeological record — 34

3. Ethnographic snapshots of traditional extraction practices — 39
    Storied sources — 39
    Ownership or restricted access to extraction sites — 41
    Seasonal use — 42
    Age/sex demographic of extraction site workers — 43
    Evidence for ritualised extraction — 43
    Evidence for ritualised production — 45
    Extraction site product functionality — 46
    The involvement of craft specialists — 49
    Distribution of extraction site products — 50
    The presence of rock art, graffiti, or idols at extraction sites — 51

4. The archaeology of lithic extraction — 53
    Distinctive landscape settings and/or raw material — 54
    Evidence for ownership/restricted access — 56
    Evidence for seasonal use — 57
    The age/sex demographic of extraction participants — 57
    The evidence for ritualised extraction — 57

|   |   | Page |
|---|---|---|
|   | Ceremonialism | 58 |
|   | Product functionality | 59 |
|   | Craft specialist artefact production | 59 |
|   | Produce distribution | 60 |
|   | The use of rock art, graffiti, or idols at or near extraction sites | 60 |
|   | The presence of burials | 61 |
|   | Implications for the interpretation of Neolithic extraction sites in Britain and Ireland | 62 |
| 5. | An ethnoarchaeological analysis of Neolithic extraction sites in Britain and Ireland | 65 |
|   | Landscape setting of extraction sites | 66 |
|   | Evidence for seasonal extraction | 69 |
|   | The practice of stone extraction | 71 |
|   | Site abandonment and rites of renewal | 81 |
|   | A summary of the evidence for ritualised extraction practices | 84 |
| 6. | The products: an ethnoarchaeological analysis of lithic objects from extraction sites | 89 |
|   | Issues | 89 |
|   | The importance of objects | 90 |
|   | The social value of archaeological extraction site products | 94 |
|   | The iconography of the axehead … | 101 |
|   | General trends in pan-European product deposition | 103 |
|   | A brief review of British and Irish depositional trends | 107 |
|   | Conclusions | 112 |
| 7. | Neolithic extraction: a pan-European phenomenon | 113 |
|   | Neolithisation by genome … | 113 |
|   | Extraction practices at the Mesolithic–Neolithic transition | 116 |
|   | Chronology | 117 |
|   | Extraction site locations | 122 |
|   | Extraction technology | 125 |
|   | On-site artefact deposition | 127 |
|   | Shaft fills | 128 |
|   | Burials | 129 |
|   | Hearths | 131 |
|   | Graffiti | 132 |
|   | Exchange networks and artefact distribution | 132 |
|   | Conclusions | 137 |
| 8. | Neolithic stone extraction in Britain and Europe | 139 |
|   | The emergence of Neolithic extraction practices | 140 |
|   | The social context of Neolithic extraction sites | 143 |

| | |
|---|---|
| Bibliography | 151 |
| Appendix: References to excavation reports and archives, listed alphabetically by site | 165 |
| Index | 169 |

# LIST OF FIGURES

## List of Figures

Figure 1.1: Carn Menyn (Pembrokeshire)
Figure 1.2: Pike of Stickle and South Scree
Figure 1.3: Mesolithic axeheads from the Thames
Figure 1.4: Later Mesolithic flake axeheads Zealand
Figure 1.5: Alpine jadeitite axehead Lochearnhead
Figure 1.6: Breton fibrolite axeheads Tumulus Saint-Michel at Carnac
Figure 1.7: Grime's Graves (Norfolk)
Figure 2.1: The Great Hypostyle Hall in the Karnak temple complex
Figure 3.1: Pipestone Quarries: photograph by Samuel Calvin c. 1900
Figure 3.2: Pipestone Quarries: sweat lodges
Figure 3.3: Pipestone Quarries: forked stick set in a small mound
Figure 3.4: Pipestone Quarries: traditional quarrying
Figure 3.5: Pipestone Quarries: rejected Plains type pipe blank
Figure 3.6: Native American tobacco pipe
Figure 3.7: Elaborately hafted New Guinea axe
Figure 3.8: Pipestone Quarries: The Three Maidens glacial erratics
Figure 4.1: Creag na Caillich (Perthshire)
Figure 4.2: Flint Ridge (Ohio)
Figure 4.3: Mont Viso (Italy)
Figure 4.4: Hoshikuso Pass, Nagawa (Japan): Jomon obsidian quarries
Figure 4.5: Hoshikuso Pass, Nagawa (Japan): Kasori B1 pot
Figure 4.6: Two Mississippian chert bifaces, Kaolin Quarries (Illinois)
Figure 4.7: Riebeckite felsite axehead found at Modesty (Shetland)
Figure 4.8: Hopewell bird's head motif copper plate from Mound City (Ohio)
Figure 4.9: Burial mound, Cresent Hills quarries (Missouri)
Figure 5.1: Distribution map of extraction sites mentioned in the text
Figure 5.2: Pike of Stickle (Cumbria)
Figure 5.3: Tievebulliagh (Antrim)
Figure 5.4: Periglacial stripes, Grime's Graves (Norfolk)
Figure 5.5: Le Pinacle (Jersey)
Figure 5.6: Pit 2, Grime's Graves: plan
Figure 5.7: Carved chalk objects South Downs
Figure 5.8: Antlers abandoned in Greenwell's Pit at Grime's Graves
Figure 5.9: Cave Pit, Cissbury
Figure 5.10: Top Buttress, Pike of Stickle: cave-like quarries
Figure 5.11: Pit 2, Grime's Graves: 'sundial' graffito
Figure 5.12: Pit 1, Grime's Graves: Lingwood's section drawing
Figure 5.13: Spatial and temporal distribution of deposits in the English flint mines
Figure 6.1: Grut Wells Hoard (Shetland)
Figure 6.2: Belmont Hoard of Group VI axeheads, Penrith (Cumbria)
Figure 6.3: Orthostat C1 from Petit Mont, Arzon (Morbihon)
Figure 6.4: Menhir de Kerloas at Plouarzel (Brittany)
Figure 6.5: Woodhenge: chalk axeheads (Wiltshire)
Figure 6.6: Hoard from Modesty (Shetland)
Figure 7.1: Shaft 27, Cissbury (Sussex): John Pull's plan
Figure 7.2: Probable routes of migrant extraction site users
Figure 7.3: Easton Down (Wiltshire): plan
Figure 7.4: Plussulien (Côte-du-Nord): Dolerite 'A' quarry
Figure 7.5: Porco supérieur (Italy)
Figure 7.6: Spiennes (Belgium): gallery with a narrow buttress
Figure 7.7: Krzemionki (Poland): charcoal graffito of a possible human figure
Figure 7.8: A typical Spiennes axehead
Figure 8.1: A reconstruction of Neolithic mining activities at Spiennes
Figure 8.2: Mané Hui (Carnac) tomb assemblage
Figure 8.3: Distribution of Group VI Langdale axeheads in Britain

## List of Tables

Table 1.1: The Mesolithic quarries of southern Norway: data
Table 1.2: Relative percentage of Middle and Late Ertebølle artefacts from coastal settlements in Denmark
Table 1.3: Relative importance of Danish Mesolithic axeheads
Table 2.1: Trend data from storied/mythologised sites

Table 2.2: Trend data for the social context of ownership
Table 2.3: Evidence for seasonal use/permanently settled sites
Table 2.4: Attributes associated with ritualised extraction
Table 2.5: Attributes associated with ritualised tool production
Table 2.6: Attributes associated with craft specialists
Table 2.7: Ethnographic product distributions by distance against potentially archaeologically visible features
Table 2.8: Attributes associated with the ceremonial use of extraction sites
Table 2.9: Attributes associated with the use of rock art, graffiti, and idols
Table 2.10: Attributes associated with human burials at extraction sites
Table 4.1: Comparison of ethnographic trends with the archaeological data
Table 4.2: Comparative analysis of ritualised extraction practices
Table 4.3: Comparison of high level ethnographic themes with archaeological features
Table 5.1: Landscape settings of proven Neolithic extraction sites
Table 5.2: Carved chalk objects from British flint mines
Table 5.3: Relative percentages of 21 potential indicators of ritualised practices at extraction sites
Table 6.1: Social context of axehead production and use at the New Guinea Highlands/Lowlands interface
Table 6.2: Grave assemblages in the Netherlands over time
Table 6.3: Relative abundance of products from earlier Neolithic extraction sites in Europe
Table 6.4: Relative abundance of products from Later Neolithic assemblages at extraction sites in Europe
Table 6.5: Relative abundance of products from Early Neolithic assemblages at extraction sites in Britain
Table 6.6: the relative abundance of products from Later Neolithic Assemblages at Extraction Sites in Britain
Table 6.7: Intensity of axehead production from British flint mines
Table 6.8: Jade axehead hoards by context and number
Table 6.9: General trends in jade axehead hoard deposition
Table 6.10: Depositional contexts of Irish stone axeheads by number
Table 6.11: Depositional trends of Irish stone axeheads by number
Table 6.12: Depositional trends of Cumbrian Group VI axeheads found in Ireland by number
Table 6.13: The number of flint implements discovered at English causewayed enclosures
Table 6.14: The contexts of stone axeheads and fragments from Etton (Cambridgeshire)
Table 6.15: Stone axeheads recovered from Early Neolithic enclosures in south-west England
Table 6.16: Flint axehead and adzehead contextual data from Windmill Hill (Wiltshire)
Table 7.1: Crude selective chronology of the introduction of Neolithic extraction practices in Europe
Table 7.2: Changing character of human interment at Gavà (Spain)
Table 7.3: Size range of axeheads from Dutch TRB graves and wetland deposits
Table 8.1: Similarities and differences between Mesolithic and Neolithic extraction practices
Table 8.2: The 'sacred and profane' binary oppositions associated with the origins and use of lithic assemblages from expedient sources compared to those from extraction sites

# AUTHOR DETAILS

PETER TOPPING
School of History, Classics and Archaeology,
Newcastle University,
Newcastle upon Tyne, NE1 7RU
topping.pete@gmail.com

Peter Topping is a Visiting Fellow at Newcastle University, following a career as a landscape archaeologist in RCHME and English Heritage where he researched Neolithic flint mines, causewayed enclosures, henges and the Stonehenge landscape. He has participated in fieldwork led by the US National Park Service in Ohio and Minnesota, and excavated at the Hoshikuso Pass obsidian quarries in Nagawa, Japan. He is currently directing a project on prehistoric quarries in the Northumberland Cheviots.

# ABSTRACT

This research focuses on the introduction of Neolithic stone extraction across Europe and the role of the indigenous foraging communities in the development of what became Neolithic practices. The key questions explored are when, why, and how were these practices adopted and what role did extraction sites and their products play in the creation of Neolithic society.

Neolithic mines and quarries have frequently been linked to the expansion of a Neolithic agro-pastoral economy. However, this ignores the fact that many communities had selectively dug for certain types of stone in preference to others, and many of the products from these sites went unused and were deposited in special places such as rivers, wetlands, enclosures, and pits.

To investigate this question, 168 ethnographic studies from five continents were quantatively analysed, identifying statistically robust trends concerning motivations, extraction practices, the use-life of products, and their residual material signatures. This was tested against excavation evidence drawn from 223 near-global archaeological extraction sites which confirmed a similar material patterning in both data.

Repeated associations emerged from the ethnography between storied or mythologised extraction sites and the form of extraction practices, coupled with the long distance distribution of products. Such activities left behind archaeologically visible empirical evidence. This suggests that we can now *probably* identify mythologised/storied extraction sites, ritualised extraction practices, and the social context underpinning the use-life of extraction site products in the archaeological record. The model can also be used to offer interpretive frameworks and broad trends in extraction practices for many cross-cultural contexts and time periods

The ethnoarchaeological model has primarily been used here to analyse the social context of 79 Neolithic flint mine excavations and those at 51 axe quarries in Britain and Ireland, and to review the evidence for their European origins. This has confirmed the pivotal role played by Neolithic extraction sites in European Neolithisation and that the interaction of indigenous foragers with migrant agro-pastoralists at extraction sites in Britain, Ireland, and Europe led to the development of common extraction practices that became fundamental to the adoption of farming.

*French Language Abstract*

## *Résumé*

Cette recherche porte sur l'introduction de l'extraction néolithique de la pierre à travers l'Europe et sur le rôle des communautés indigènes de chasseurs-collecteurs dans le développement de ce qui est devenu des pratiques néolithiques. Les questions clés explorées sont quand, pourquoi et comment ces pratiques ont été adoptées et quel rôle les sites d'extraction et leurs produits ont-ils joué dans la création de la société néolithique.

Les mines et les carrières néolithiques ont souvent été associées à l'expansion d'une économie agro-pastorale néolithique. Cependant, c'est ignorer le fait que de nombreuses communautés ont creusé de manière sélective pour exploiter certains types de pierre préférentiellement à d'autres, et que beaucoup des produits de ces sites n'étaient pas utilisés et étaient déposés dans des endroits spéciaux tels que les rivières, les zones humides, les enceintes et les fosses.

Pour répondre à cette question, 168 études ethnographiques provenant de cinq continents ont fait l'objet d'une analyse quantitative, identifiant des tendances statistiquement robustes concernant les motivations, les pratiques d'extraction, la durée d'utilisation des produits et leurs signatures matérielles résiduelles. Cette analyse a été confrontée aux résultats des fouilles de 223 sites d'extraction archéologiques à l'échelle mondiale, ce qui a confirmé l'existence d'une structure matérielle similaire dans les deux ensembles de données.

Des associations répétées ont émergé de l'ethnographie entre des sites d'extraction légendaires ou mythologiques et la forme des pratiques d'extraction, associées à la distribution des produits sur de longues distances. Ces activités ont laissé derrière elles des preuves empiriques archéologiquement visibles. Cela suggère que nous pouvons maintenant probablement identifier les sites d'extraction mythologiques/légendaires, les pratiques d'extraction ritualisées et le contexte social qui sous-tend la vie d'utilisation des produits des sites d'extraction dans les vestiges archéologiques. Le modèle peut également être utilisé pour proposer des cadres d'interprétation et des tendances générales dans les pratiques d'extraction pour de nombreux contextes transculturels et différentes périodes.

Le modèle ethnoarchéologique a été principalement utilisé ici pour analyser le contexte social de 79 fouilles de mines de silex néolithiques et de 51 carrières de haches en Grande-Bretagne et en Irlande, et pour examiner les témoins de leurs origines européennes. Cette analyse a confirmé le rôle central joué par les sites d'extraction néolithiques dans la néolithisation européenne et le fait que l'interaction entre les agro-pasteurs migrants et les chasseurs-collecteurs indigènes sur les sites d'extraction en Grande-Bretagne, en Irlande et en Europe a conduit au développement de pratiques d'extraction communes qui sont devenues fondamentales pour l'adoption de l'agriculture.

## Zusammenfassung

Die hier vorgestellten Forschungsarbeiten widmen sich der Einführung des neolithischen Steinabbaus in Europa und der Rolle indigener Sammlergesellschaften in der Ausformung von neolithischen Praktiken. Es werden Antworten gesucht auf die Schlüsselfragen, wann, warum und wie diese Praktiken übernommen wurden und welche Rolle Abbauplätze und ihre Produkte in der Entstehung der neolithischen Gesellschaft spielten.

Neolithische Bergwerke und Steinbrüche wurden häufig mit der Ausbreitung einer neolithischen Agrar- und Viehwirtschaft in Verbindung gebracht. Dabei wird jedoch außer Acht gelassen, dass viele Gemeinschaften selektiv und vorzugsweise nach bestimmten Gesteinsarten gegraben haben und viele der Produkte aus diesen Stätten ungenutzt blieben und an besonderen Orten wie Flüssen, Feuchtgebieten, Grabenanlagen und Gruben deponiert wurden.

Um diesen Fragen nachzugehen, wurden 168 ethnographische Untersuchungen von fünf Kontinenten quantitativ analysiert, wobei statistisch belastbare Trends in Bezug auf Motivationen, Abbaumethoden, Nutzungsdauer der Produkte und deren materielle Signaturen festgestellt wurden. Dies wurde mit Ausgrabungsdaten aus 223 nahezu globalen archäologischen Abbaustätten verglichen, was ein ähnliches materielles Muster in beiden Datensätzen bestätigte.

Die ethnographischen Daten zeigten wiederkehrende Zusammenhänge zwischen traditionsreichen oder mythologisierten Abbauplätzen und der Art der Abbaupraktiken, verbunden mit der Fernverbreitung der Produkte. Solche Aktivitäten hinterließen archäologisch sichtbare empirische Daten. Daraus lässt sich schließen, dass wir nun *wahrscheinlich* mythologisierte/ geschichtsträchtige Abbauplätze, ritualisierte Abbaupraktiken und den sozialen Kontext, der der Nutzung der Produkte von Abbaustätten zugrunde liegt, in den archäologischen Daten identifizieren können. Das Modell kann auch verwendet werden, um Interpretationsrahmen und allgemeine Trends in den Abbaupraktiken für viele kulturübergreifende Kontexte und Zeiträume aufzuzeigen.

Das ethnoarchäologische Modell wurde hier in erster Linie verwendet, um den sozialen Kontext von 79 neolithischen Feuersteinminen und 51 Axtsteinbrüchen in Großbritannien und Irland zu analysieren und die Nachweise für ihre europäischen Ursprünge zu überprüfen. Dies bestätigt die zentrale Rolle, die neolithische Abbaustätten bei der europäischen Neolithisierung spielten, und dass die Interaktion zwischen einheimischen Wildbeutern und zugewanderten agrarischen Viehzüchtern an Abbauplätzen in Großbritannien, Irland und Europa zur Entwicklung gemeinsamer Abbaupraktiken führte, die für die Übernahme der Landwirtschaft von grundlegender Bedeutung waren.

## Resumen

Esta investigación se centra en la introducción de las actividades de extracción mineras durante el Neolítico a lo largo de Europa y el papel de las comunidades indígenas en el desarrollo de lo que llegan a constituir unas prácticas eminentemente neolíticas. Las cuestiones fundamentales que se exploran son el cuándo, el por qué y cómo se adoptaron estas prácticas, qué papel tuvieron estos emplazamientos de extracción y el papel que jugaron sus productos en la creación de la sociedad neolítica. Las minas y canteras neolíticas se han vinculado frecuentemente a la expansión de la economía agropecuaria neolítica. Sin embargo, esto ignora que muchas comunidades excavaron selectivamente cierto tipo de rocas con preferencia sobre otras, y que muchos de los productos obtenidos en estos lugares no fueron usados sino depositados en lugares relevantes como ríos, zonas de humedal, recintos y fosas.

Con el objetivo de abordar estas cuestiones, se han analizado cuantitativamente 168 estudios etnográficos, identificando estadísticamente las tendencias más resistentes en cuanto a las motivaciones, las prácticas de extracción, el uso de los productos y las evidencias materiales residuales. Estos estudios etnográficos se han analizado en contraste con la evidencia arqueológica procedente de 223 canteras arqueológicas de alrededor del mundo que han confirmado un patrón de extracción similar.

La evidencia etnográfica permite observar asociaciones recurrentes entre los sitios de extracción legendarios o mitificados y la forma de las prácticas de extracción, así como en la distribución de productos a larga distancia. Estas actividades quedan plasmadas en una evidencia arqueológica empírica y visible. Esto sugiere que posiblemente podemos identificar los lugares de extracción legendarios o mitificados, las prácticas de extracción ritualizadas, y el contexto social subyacente en la vida útil de los productos documentados en los lugares de extracción del registro arqueológico. Este modelo puede ser igualmente empleado para ofrecer un marco interpretativo y una visión amplia sobre las prácticas de extracción en múltiples contextos culturales y períodos cronológicos.

El modelo etnoarqueológico se ha usado preferentemente para analizar el contexto social de 79 minas de sílex neolíticas y 51 canteras de extracción de rocas orientadas a la producción de hachas en Gran Bretaña e Irlanda, y en la revisión de sus orígenes europeos. Se ha confirmado el papel crucial jugado por los sitios de extracción neolíticos en los procesos de neolitización europeos, en los procesos de interacción de las poblaciones indígenas con las sociedades agrícolas y ganaderas en los lugares de extracción en Gran Bretaña e Irlanda y que el desarrollo de prácticas de extracción comunes en Europa se convirtió en un fenómeno fundamental en el proceso de adopción de la agricultura.

# ACKNOWLEDGEMENTS

The author would like to offer his sincere thanks to the following: Dave Field who read too many drafts of this book and provided so many helpful suggestions; Trevor Pearson who produced most of my illustrations; Mik Markham for providing information from the Implement Petrology Group's Masterlist and producing the distribution map of Group VI axeheads; Sachie Otake who kindly provided a photograph of her excavations at the Hoshikuso Pass obsidian quarries in Nagawa, Japan, and gave the author the opportunity to participate in the excavations; the late Mark Lynott and the Midwest Archeological Center of the US National Park Service who invited the author to undertake fieldwork at the Pipestone Quarries in Minnesota which sparked so much of this research. Gabriel Cooney gave the author the chance to participate in his fieldwork in Shetland; Pierre Pétrequin guided the author around some of the Mont Viso jade quarries; Frances Healy provided a helpful steer on the use of radiocarbon data from the European extraction sites and so much useful information about Grime's Graves; and Gill Varndell also provided helpful information about Grime's Graves from the British Museum's archives. The author would like to thank the anonymous referees for many helpful suggestions which improved the structure and accuracy of the text. Thanks also go to Worthing Museum and Art Gallery for permission to use John Pull's plan of Shaft 27 at Cissbury. A big thank you goes to John Kelly for providing the foreword and guiding me around quarry sites in Missouri and Illinois.

The author would also like to thank Torben Ballin, Martyn Barber, Françoise Bostyn, Hélène Collet, the late Vin Davis, Chris Fowler, Michael Fuller, Julie Gardiner, François Giligny, Charles Le Roux, Hidehisa Mashima, Kyoko Mizusawa, Akira Ono, Noriaki Otake, Yvan Pailler, Hiroyuki Sato, the late Alan Saville, Alison Sheridan, Anne Teather, Tom Thiessen, Takashi Tsutsumi, and Marshall Weisler, who all happily shared their research and helped to shape this study – it was much appreciated. The members of the Neolithic Studies Group, the Prehistoric Quarries and Early Mines Interest Group of the Society for American Archaeology, the UISPP's Commission on Flint Mining in Pre- and Protohistoric Times, and the Implement Petrology Group, all deserve thanks for so much advice and useful information given over many years. Finally, a big vote of thanks goes to Mike Allen, Julie Gardiner, and all at Oxbow for their hard work in producing this book. Any errors or misrepresentations are solely the responsibility of the author.

Peter Topping
July 2021

The Prehistoric Society would like to add thanks in particular to the Marc Fitch Fund but also the Neolithic Studies Group and Implement Petrology Group for their support. We also thank our referees and members of our Editorial Advisory Committee, and our reviewers for their expert advice and opinions. In particular, I would like to offer my thanks to Oxbow Books and Julie Gardiner (Prehistoric Society Managing Editor), for their advice and assistance, and also to Julie Blackmore of Frabjous Books for typesetting yet another of our volumes with skill, proficiency, dexterity, and great speed.

Michael J. Allen

# FOREWORD

Peter's ancestors are from the British Isles, as well as mine, and as archaeologists we have an abiding interest in the ancient past. Peter's research is centred in the British Isles and mine in eastern North America with its rich history of the American Indian. I came to know Peter through our common friend and colleague, the late Dr. Mark Lynott. Mark, who at the time was the Director of the National Park Service's (NPS) Midwest Archaeological Center (MWAC), brought Peter to Cahokia after the Society for American Archaeology meetings that were held in Chicago in late March of 1999. Mark had organised a session on ancient monuments and Peter was invited to participate. In a recent communication, Peter recalled the tour I gave them around Cahokia and the nearby mound group in East St. Louis. Mark also exposed Peter to the rich ancient cultural heritage of the greater Midwest, which included visiting and working in the field at the NPS's earlier Hopewell site, Hopeton, as well as a visit to the Flint Ridge quarry complex. As an important site within the expansive ritualised exchange network across the eastern woodlands of North America, it was here at Flint Ridge that colourful cherts were extracted and used in the production of lamellar blades. A year earlier, Peter had the opportunity to visit the sacred quarry site at Pipestone in southwest Minnesota that entailed Peter surveying some of the quarry pits at this NPS National Monument. His detailed plan became the cover of that year's report on the work at Pipestone.

Although in the interim Peter made several trips back to the United States, he came back to the American Midwest in 2015, a year after Mark's passing. This return visit began when Washington University's Department of Anthropology extended Peter an invitation to visit us and lecture on Stonehenge and the Late Neolithic. In his lecture, he also spoke of his research on stone quarries in the British Isles and their sacred nature and strong connection with the landscape. While in St. Louis we had the opportunity to visit the Mill Creek and Kaolin quarry areas in southern Illinois hosted by Dr. Brian Butler, Director of the Center for Archaeological Investigations at Southern Illinois University at Carbondale.

These sojourns were a unique experience that expanded and reshaped Peter's perspective and thinking on quarrying not just in the British Isles during the Neolithic but more importantly across the globe. The ritualisation of the quarrying at Pipestone by indigenous people in the past and even today, becomes an important analytical datum throughout his book. Peter stresses throughout the volume that quarrying is often more than an economic activity, as previously suggested by many Western economic models. It is the relationship that all our ancestors across the globe have had with the landscape and the manner in which those relationships were an integral part of their cosmos: the heavens, the earth, and the water. It was undoubtedly the journey to Pipestone that opened Peter's eyes to the sacred and symbolic connection between the more ancient past of this continent and the indigenous people who still honour that past and their ancestors today. It is still very much alive today as it was in the past. For comparative purposes Peter discusses throughout the various chapters not only Pipestone but also a number of important extraction sites in North America and in other parts of the world such as New Guinea, Africa and Australia. Many have a long history of use with some – as in the case of the sacred

Pipestone quarry complex – still being actively used and honoured today.

Peter's volume at the outset focuses on his area of expertise of the British Neolithic mines and quarry sites where flint and igneous-metamorphic material was excavated for axeheads. He expands his site sample and draws heavily on stone extraction sites from northern Europe, even extending to relevant sites outside Europe. The volume goes beyond the description and characterization of extraction sites that are detailed in the opening chapters of the book. It attempts to examine the processes of extraction as something more than economic and technological pursuits. As western scholars, and especially following our mentors of the nineteenth and most of the twentieth century, we have regularly interpreted our own ancient past as well as others' in terms of western economic models. Drawing on the rich histories of indigenous people globally and their extraction practices, Peter has shaped a more nuanced approach and developed a perspective on what might have been occurring amongst the Neolithic landscapes of the British Isles and Europe. In order to go beyond the traditional selective use of ethnographic analogy, Peter has employed a quantative analysis of both the archaeological and ethnographic data for a more rigorous comparison and understanding on the nature of stone extraction amongst our ancestors.

The publication of *Neolithic Stone Extraction in Britain and Europe* by the Prehistoric Society, an ancient establishment in the British Isles, will be through Oxbow Books and represents a timely and significant contribution to our understanding of resource extraction by all of our ancestors.

John E. Kelly
Washington University in St. Louis (WUSTL)

*For Joyce, Emma and Lucy*

# 1

# Setting the scene: the Mesolithic prelude and first contact Neolithic

> Production sites may have been studied as evidence of technology and exchange, but these were probably places that possessed a special significance in their own right, and that has still to be investigated
>
> (Bradley 2000, 41)

The European Neolithic was a transformative period that built upon aspects of existing Mesolithic practices and introduced a new lifeway superimposed upon a pre-agricultural landscape which was still inhabited by foragers. First contact during the Mesolithic–Neolithic transition led to a cross-cultural fertilisation which spawned a mature Neolithic, within which extraction sites appear to have played a pivotal role. Radiocarbon dates now suggest that they were some of the earliest sites to appear in the landscape as Neolithic practices spread across Europe.

The emerging scientific and archaeological data record significant social and technological changes that are predicated on an east–west population movement across Europe. This created a complex socio-cultural matrix which combined elements of both Mesolithic and Neolithic lifeways (cf. Brace *et al.* 2019; Cassidy *et al.* 2020; Rivollat *et al.* 2020; ancient DNA will be discussed in Chapter 7). The result was the introduction of a novel subsistence regime based on mixed farming, new types of material culture, a shift in burial customs towards a greater emphasis on cemeteries, the sporadic construction of communal enclosures, and, in terms of the present study, the introduction of deep shaft and galleried mining (eg, Whittle *et al.* 2011; Consuegra & Díaz-del-Río 2018). However, the new Neolithic ideology spread across continental Europe at different speeds and with different levels of adoption, suggesting that a social 'mosaic' of varied levels of subsistence strategies, technology, and community organisation may have occurred (eg, Whittle 1996).

The new technique of deep shaft and galleried mining was essentially an enhancement of Late Mesolithic open-air quarry practices which led to a greater symbolic emphasis being placed on extraction site products and the ways they were used during the Neolithic. This is epitomised by the visually impressive jade objects derived from sources high in the Italian Alps, comprising rare axeheads and rings which were disseminated extensively throughout Europe (Pétrequin *et al.* 2012b; 2017). Much of the raw material from the Neolithic mines and quarries was generally used for producing axeheads. Over the course of the Neolithic period the axehead appears to have been used in two different ways, as an artefact and a symbol, with roles embodying the functionality of a tool alongside non-functional applications in special deposits and artworks. The origin of the raw material also appears to have had considerable significance. Much of the archaeological evidence from non-extraction sites suggests that purely functional tools were normally made from local deposits, whereas those from distant extraction sites were used in non-domestic social practices and deliberately placed in locations such as wetlands, pits, burials, or used as inspiration for motifs in megalithic art. By implication, the cultural value associated with axeheads from extraction sites must have originated at the source of the raw material from which these artefacts were made.

Within Britain and Ireland the archaeological timeframe of the present study concerns the origin and development of extraction processes focused primarily around the 'contact period' between Mesolithic occupants and Neolithic migrants, *c.* 4100–3850 cal BC (eg, Cleal 2004, 181–2), ie, before the widespread construction of monuments, and subsequently of mature Neolithic developments though to *c.* 3000 cal BC. The discussion will also take account of general developments during the remainder of the Neolithic period through to the Early–Middle Bronze Age transition, *c.* 1450 cal BC (Needham *et al.* 2010, 363–73). This will be complemented by a review of the European evidence to describe the introduction and spread of Neolithic extraction across the continent to the Atlantic façade.

Digging for buried lithic resources, rather than the surface collection of loose material, appears to begin during the Palaeolithic period. Survivals of small Palaeolithic quarries have been discovered at I Ciotti (Italy; Negrino *et al.* 2006), with even larger 3.4 m deep shafts at Orońsko II (Poland; Werra & Kerneder-Gubała 2021). However, a more complex picture emerges from the Nile Valley in Egypt where Middle Palaeolithic quarries at Nazlet Safaha and Nazlet Khater 4 used ditches up to 2.0 m deep, shafts, and some had underground galleries or adits, providing some of the earliest evidence of subterranean mining (Vermeersch *et al.* 1995). Other parts of the world also provide evidence of early lithic extraction, such as the Alibates quarries in the Texas Panhandle (USA) where Paleoindian mammoth hunters exploited outcrops of agatised dolomite for finely knapped, fluted Clovis points around 13,500 years ago (Shaeffer 1958). In the Hudson Valley (New York State) XRF studies of Paleoindian assemblages have demonstrated the importance of Normanskill chert within regional networks (Lothrop *et al.* 2018), and evidence suggests obsidian sources were prioritised among the quarries in the Yellowstone region (Wyoming) during the Late Paleoindian period (Davis *et al.* 1995; MacDonald *et al.* 2019). Similar patterns developed on the Japanese Archipelago where, for example, on Honshu in the Central Highlands important obsidian resources were exploited by Upper Palaeolithic hunter-gatherers, who would travel considerable distances from low-lying settlements to highland quarries to exploit stream-bed deposits of obsidian located at 1200–2000 m asl (Otake *et al.* 2020). Arguably the epitome of lithic exotica may have been the dramatic Kozu-Onbase Island obsidian source, which lies 50 km off the east coast of Honshu and required sea travel to secure the raw materials found at many mainland settlements (Ono *et al.* 2016; Shimada *et al.* 2017). On Hokkaido, circulation of Shirataki obsidian varied over time, during the Early Upper Palaeolithic it was moved up to 170 km from the source, whereas by the Late Upper Palaeolithic Stage 3 period it was transported much further, over 700 km (Yakushige & Sato 2014).

Taken together, these examples of various Palaeolithic and Paleoindian extraction sites demonstrate that quarries were often exploited by technically competent users and some (eg, certain Egyptian sites) featured relatively sophisticated precursors of shaft and gallery extraction methods. In addition, the long distance distribution of particular lithics suggests that raw materials could be highly valued and transported over great distances and, because of this, quarries became persistently visited, returned to time and again for their highly prized lithologies even before the advent of the Mesolithic period.

## The Mesolithic prelude in Europe …

During the Mesolithic period quarrying was widely practised by communities occupying the periphery of Europe from the south-east, and around the Atlantic façade to Scandinavia. Extraction was generally by open-air quarries of variable scale and depth, although one east European site (Krumlovský les, Czechia) offers the possibility that deeper niche mines existed before Neolithic galleried mines (see below). The Mesolithic period also saw the exploitation of specific lithic resources which appear to have been highly valued by their users, and more so than expedient materials. This is borne out by the long distance distribution of many products and, importantly, certain extraction sites contained small on-site assemblages of redeposited raw material. Some European sites were located near rock art, suggesting that there

# 1 Setting the scene: the Mesolithic prelude and first contact Neolithic

was some elaboration to extraction practices at this time. Such Mesolithic extraction occurred alongside pit-digging, and a strong interest in natural geological features with subterranean access, such as swallow holes and caves (Field 2011a).

The variety and complexity of Mesolithic pits in England and Ireland has been reviewed recently, suggesting that they could contain waste materials, deliberately placed deposits, possible caching, and sometimes burials. Some even show evidence of re-use or recutting and they can occur in a variety of landscape settings (Blinkhorn *et al.* 2017). Certain pits contained knapping debris and lithics, as at Pendell Farm (Lewis & Pine 2008, 41) and Mercer's Quarry (Hammond 2005, 24), both in Surrey. At Belderrig (Co. Mayo), the lithics discovered within pits were larger than those found amongst on-site assemblages, suggesting caching or deliberate deposition (Blinkhorn *et al.* 2017, 215). Amongst the pits surveyed by Blinkhorn *et al.* (*ibid.*, 215), only six of those in England and one in Ireland produced axeheads. Ireland's only example, at Hermitage, was undoubtedly a deliberately placed deposit (see below), although it is unclear whether the English examples represent this.

The interest in subterranean features and digging into the earth was clearly part of a wider tradition associated with the ordering, categorisation, and explanation of the cultural landscape among Mesolithic communities. Such cosmographic ordering identified locations, topographic features, or raw material deposits that had a cultural resonance, which symbolised shared cultural experiences or cosmological referents, and were often encountered during the rhythmic movements of people through the landscape. The revisiting of specific locations developed into communal traditions through repetition and created tangible relationships between people and the landscape which combined to shape and maintain group identity (eg, Mauss 1979; Ingold 1990; 2000; Bourdieu 1977; 1990). These repetitive practices must have framed extraction sites for Mesolithic hunter-gatherer-fishers.

The role of Mesolithic quarries is well documented in southern Norway where a number of extraction sites have recently been surveyed in detail, providing important new information that helps model their role in social networks and subsistence strategies (Nyland 2015; 2017; 2019; 2020). Mobile hunter-gatherer-fishers had quickly colonised the coastline of Norway following a partial glacial retreat after 9500 BC, and by *c.* 8000 BC the mountainous interior had become ice-free. The mobility of Mesolithic groups created an extensive network of contacts spanning Fennoscandia and the Baltic region, exchanging blade and bone tool technology, and creating rock art. Critically, the technology involved in grinding stone adzeheads was known among these groups in southern Norway during the Middle Mesolithic (*c.* 8000 BC), and this may have stimulated local lithic prospection which led to the appearance of quarrying. By the Late Mesolithic (*c.* 5500 BC) there was a distinctive regionalised adzehead typology which may reflect the use of materiality to underscore cultural identity (Nyland 2015, 59–67; 2019, 5; 2020). Given its importance, the following is a brief review of the Norwegian evidence.

## Norwegian Mesolithic quarries

A small selection of sites will be described to characterise the nature of Mesolithic extraction in southern Norway. One of the more dramatic is Hespriholmen, a heavily exploited greenstone quarry located at 22.5 m asl on a small islet 3 km west of Bømlo at the mouth of the Hardangerfjord. Rock art sites are found on the north-eastern shores of the fjord. This quarry is one of the two largest adzehead quarries on the west coast (the other being Stakalleneset), where imported hammerstones were discovered and charcoal may represent fire-setting. Workshops were located on adjacent islands where roughout adzeheads, preforms, and flakes were found. The superior quality of the greenstone from Hespriholmen ensured it was widely circulated around some 350 km of the western coastline and the quarry was used between the Middle Mesolithic through to the Middle Neolithic (*c.* 8000–3000 BC) (Nyland 2015, 125–8, 179–80; 2019, 67–77).

The Stegahaugen greenstone quarry lies at the foot of Mount Siggjo on Bømlo Island at *c.* 135 m asl. This site also produced hammerstones and evidence of fire-setting. Workshops manufacturing roughout adzeheads, preforms, and flakes lay adjacent to the quarry, which began in the Middle Mesolithic and was exploited into the pre-Roman Iron Age (*c.* 8000 BC onwards). Its similar lithology to Hespriholmen suggests it may have had a comparable coastal distribution in western Norway (Nyland 2015, 132–4).

The quarry at Stakalleneset is situated on a promontory overlooking the Eikefjord, less than 6 km from known contemporary settlements. Rock art is found nearby. This large complex comprised five quarries focused upon a dolerite dyke exploited for adzehead production during the Middle Mesolithic to Middle Neolithic (*c.* 8000–3000 BC). Workshops lie adjacent to the quarries. Excavation of quarry waste dumps discovered debitage and hammerstones alongside the deliberate deposition of imported quartzite lithics, followed during the Early Neolithic by objects of rhyolite. Evidence of Late Mesolithic to Middle Neolithic fire-setting was found (*c.* 5500–3000 BC). The production of roughout adzeheads occurred at the quarries but finishing took place off-site and the Stakalleneset products were distributed up to 50 km from the quarries (Nyland 2015, 100–5, 208).

Kjølskarvet is the largest known quartzite quarry, situated in the mountains at *c.* 1400 m asl on a watershed. The site comprises numerous quarried boulders with adjacent workshops which produced blades, flakes, and bifacial implements. At Site 1 debitage was carefully put beneath tilting boulders creating discrete placed deposits in hidden contexts within the quarried boulder field, similar to the debitage deposits returned to many Neolithic flint mines. Extraction began here during the Middle/Late Mesolithic and continued into the Iron Age (*c.* 8000 BC onwards), and products were distributed up to 50 km from the source (Nyland 2015, 112–16, 208; 2020, 50–4).

The Halsane quartzite quarries lie in the mountains at roughly 1100 m asl in the Hemsedal Valley. Broken hammerstones were discovered and waste dumps contained both cores and debitage from initial testing and reduction at seven workshops. Among surrounding boulder fields small, placed deposits of debitage and large flakes were inserted beneath tilting boulders in a similar manner to Kjølskarvet, providing another example of Mesolithic extraction practice which may have influenced those in the Neolithic. This large quarry produced bifacial tools, blades, and flakes, and appears to have operated from the Middle–Late Mesolithic (*c.* 8000–4000 BC), but with a limited distribution of only 10 km from the source (Nyland 2015, 108–11).

The Rivenes dolerite quarry lies on a peninsula on the south coast overlooking the Søgne archipelago at roughly 5 m asl. Here a dolerite sill was exploited, with adjacent workshops, to produce adzeheads. This Middle Mesolithic (*c.* 8000 BC onwards) quarry was involved in a network circulating products up to 10 km (Nyland 2015, 142–4).

Taken together, the southern Norwegian Mesolithic extraction sites are often near rock art (eg, Walderhaug 1998), or appear to have a distant link with rock art. For example, at Stakalleneset, rock art had been placed on opposing shores of the Eikefjord, at Brandsøy on the northern shore, and Ausevik on the southern, effectively framing the quarry promontory. The Late Mesolithic (*c.* 5500–4000 BC) rock art at Ausevik on the southern shore was found to have dolerite fragments inserted into fissures, probably from the Stakalleneset quarry, suggesting a relationship between the art and the quarry (Nyland 2015, 100–5, 256). In addition, a pointed pick-like hammerstone discovered at the Vingen coastal rock art complex, which lies 40 km north of Stakalleneset quarry, has been sourced to Stakalleneset (Lødøen 2013, 39–41), again demonstrating associations between quarries and rock art panels.

If the location and material associations of the southern Norwegian Mesolithic quarries are considered in detail, patterns of practice and preference emerge (Table 1.1). Adzeheads were only produced at coastal greenstone and dolerite quarries, although these lithologies were also used for flakes, microblades, and cores at some sites. In contrast, the inland quartzite and jasper quarries were exploited to produce microblades, blades, flakes, cores, and bifacials, but apparently no large implements. Only certain coastal sites used imported hammerstones, whereas the other quarries made use of hammerstones of local rock. Similarly, only the coastal and fjord quarries were near rock art panels, whereas the inland quarries were not. Evidence for the use of fire was found at both coastal and inland sites, suggesting fire-setting during quarrying and vegetation clearance. Interestingly, at the long-

Table 1.1: The Mesolithic quarries of southern Norway arranged hierarchically according to the scale of their product distributions (data from Nyland 2016)

| Quarry | Quarry size [l=large; m=medium; s=small] | Coastal | Inland | Placed deposits | Imported hammerstones and/or lithics | Use of fire | Quarry products | Lithology | Rock art found locally | Distribution of quarry products (km) | Quarry used in later periods |
|---|---|---|---|---|---|---|---|---|---|---|---|
| Hespriholmen | L | ■ | | | | ● | Adzeheads, flakes | G | ● | >350 | ✓ |
| Stegahaugen | M | ■ | | | | ● | Adzeheads, flakes | G | ● | >350 | ✓ |
| Stakalleneset | L | ■ | | ● | ● | ● | Adzeheads | D | ● | >50 | ✓ |
| Kjølskarvet | L | | ■ | ● | | | Blades, flakes, bifacials | Q | | >50 | ✓ |
| Flendalen | L | | ■ | | | ● | Microblades, blades, flakes, cores | J | | >50 | ✗ |
| Halsane | L | | ■ | ● | | | Flakes, blades, cores | Q | | >10 | ✓ |
| Stongeskaret | M | | ■ | | | | Blades, flakes | Q | | >10 | ✓ |
| Kreklevatnet 2 | M | | ■ | | | | Blades, cores | Q | | >10 | ✓ |
| Kreklevatnet 3 | M | | ■ | | | | Blades, flakes, bifacials | Q | | >10 | ✓ |
| Skjervika | M | ■ | | | ? | | Blades, flakes, bifacials | J | ● | >10 | ✓ |
| Nautøya | M | ■ | | | | | Flakes, microblades | J | ● | >10 | ✓ |
| Rivenes | M | ■ | | | | | Adzeheads | D | | >10 | ✗ |
| Tømmervigodden | S | ■ | | | ? | | Adzeheads | D | | >10 | ✗ |
| Knapstad | S | ■ | | ● | | | Adzeheads, microblades, cores | D | | >10 | ✗ |
| Ekeberg | M | ■ | | | | | Adzeheads | D | | >10 | ✗ |

*Key to lithology*: D = Dolerite; G = Greenstone; J = Jasper; Q = Quartzite

term quarries at Stakalleneset, Kjølskarvet, and Halsane, placed deposits of debitage and implements or imported material were discovered, suggesting elaborate extraction practices of the type seen later at Neolithic sites.

The products from Norwegian Mesolithic quarries have distinctive distribution patterns. Generally, the smaller quarries in coastal regions and inland areas satisfied local requirements for tools within a crude radius of *c.* 10 km from the source, and these sites had little or no evidence of sophisticated extraction practices such as placed deposits, the use of fire, or links to rock art. Conversely, the larger quarries which mostly specialised in adzehead production, or blades/flaked tools and cores, were generally exploited over longer time periods and incorporated evidence of sophisticated extraction practices and associations with rock art; they also had product distributions stretching up to 350 km from the quarries. Consequently, the Norwegian Mesolithic quarries appear to be ranked in importance, with the larger quarries displaying elaborate extraction practices and witnessing extensive product distributions, in contrast to the smaller quarries that followed comparatively unsophisticated practices with far more restricted product circulation.

The relative importance of Stakalleneset during the Mesolithic period is demonstrated by the fact that from a sample of 1680 adzeheads discovered at coastal and fjordland sites, 54% originated from this quarry (Nyland 2015, 170). During the Late Mesolithic (c. 5500–4000 BC) when there appears to have been a shift towards sedentism in western Norway, the Stakalleneset and Hespriholmen quarries saw intensified activity with adzehead production at secluded workshops coupled to a widespread distribution of their products (Nyland 2015, 255–6). Consequently, during the Late Mesolithic, certain implements from recognised sources appear to have attained a cultural value transcending similar examples made from other lithologies.

Although quarrying occurred in parallel with the expedient use of surface material and beach flint (Nyland 2019, 69–70), these materials do not appear to have achieved the same status as certain quarried lithics. Contrary to functional expectations, lithic quality was not always a primary concern and, in many cases, provenance took precedence. For example, the jasper quarries at Nautøya and Skjervika were repeatedly exploited but it was rarely used for tool production (Nyland 2015, 178). This recalls the situation at the later Early Neolithic flint mines at Blackpatch and Harrow Hill (South Downs), which ignored better quality deposits nearby to target inferior flint located between the Rottingdean and Old Nore Marls (Barber et al. 1999, 24). Similarly, certain quarries at Langdale (Cumbria) were positioned in extremely challenging locations, such as Top Buttress on Pike of Stickle, while ignoring more accessible sources of equivalent quality (Bradley & Ford 1986), and at Krumlovský les (Czechia) Mesolithic extraction sites produced a poor quality chert which was unsuitable for the large implements that were popular at the time but it was still widely circulated as a raw material (Oliva 2010, 383). From the later Mesolithic onwards locations appear to have determined where extraction sites were placed, presumably incorporating cultural referents which created a meaningful interface between communities and their beliefs. The significance of some quarries was heightened by placed deposits of debitage and flakes amongst boulder fields, at Stakalleneset, Halsane, and Kjølskarvet for example, hinting at the existence of specialised extraction practices (cf. Nyland 2015, 108–16).

The long-term quarries at Hespriholmen and Stakalleneset were used into the Early Neolithic period, yet this was a region which apparently did not experience major impacts from incoming migrant agro-pastoralists and seems to have retained many pre-existing traditions. Indeed, much of Norway appears to have been relatively conservative with little significant material change until c. 2300 BC, when two-aisled houses were introduced, although in south-eastern Norway incipient pastoralism and small-scale cultivation had appeared c. 3800 BC, alongside pottery, ground 4-sided flint axeheads, and imported flint nodules that probably originated from the flint mines in Sweden and Denmark. In stark contrast, western Norway witnessed little evidence of external contacts beyond small quantities of pottery and imported axeheads until the introduction of cereals in c. 2300 BC, suggesting a greater adherence to traditional lifeways (Nyland 2017; 2019, 6–8).

During the transition to the Neolithic (c. 4000–3800 BC), the dominance of the greenstone quarries at Hespriholmen was gradually eclipsed by use of the white-veined rhyolite from the quarries on the summit of Mount Siggjo (474 m asl). Here the rhyolite was intensively quarried for tanged points, blade production, scrapers, and other tools, and its products were distributed around 600 km of the west coast of southern Norway. The establishment of the Mount Siggjo quarries heralds the beginning of the Early Neolithic in western Norway (Nyland 2015, 268–9; 2017, 40; 2019, 4; 2020, 54–6). Overall, the Norwegian data shows that quarrying was well established in Norway before the Neolithic, and some Mesolithic quarries continued to provide raw materials into the Neolithic period.

### Elsewhere in northern Europe

In Denmark, lithics are generally presumed to have been knapped from beach flint or material dug from moraines (Price & Gebauer 2005, 139). However, Mesolithic quarrying has been recorded at Hov and Bjerre in north-western Denmark (Weisgerber 1999, 456–68; Strassburg

2000, 345), and at Sallerup-Tullstop and Kvarnby-Södra in southern Sweden (Rudebeck 1998). These coastal Mesolithic communities in north-western Europe resisted Neolithisation by incoming Bandkeramik farmers from central Europe for a considerable period of time. This resistance can be seen particularly in regions such as the Rhine–Waal–Maas Delta and the Ijsselmeer in the Netherlands. Here indigenous Swifterbant hunter-gatherer-fishers in these low-lying wetlands took more than a millennium to fully adopt agricultural practices, despite some colonisation by farming groups from c. 5300 BC (van Gijn 2009; Rowley-Conwy & Legge 2015, 437), and a shift to roughly equal proportions of domesticated and wild resources from c. 4600 BC (Thorpe 2015, 220). One of the earliest material indicators of first contact between indigenous hunter-gatherer-fishers and early agro-pastoralists was the appearance of pottery, and the indigenous Swifterbant communities developed their own S-profile ceramics similar to more northerly Ertebølle styles. Both these communities of successful foragers appear to have continued with their slowly evolving lifeway beyond first contact. In addition, despite the presence of adjacent farming communities on the wetlands and upland interface to the east, Swifterbant communities continued to import certain flint artefacts and raw materials from the south, maintaining their traditional pre-contact lithic procurement networks.

The value placed on certain lithic resources can be seen at the Late Mesolithic seasonal sites on the dunes at Hardinxveld (Netherlands) where, amongst the middens and burials, lay evidence of extensive networks importing Wommersom quartzite, Rijckholt flint tools, and Linearbandkeramik artefacts. Importantly, use-wear analysis established that these objects were little used, suggesting they were imported for non-functional purposes (Louwe Kooijmans 2001a; 2001b; van Gijn 2009; 2010a; 2010b). By implication, their places of origin, ie, the quarries and non-local communities, must also have been considered important or aspirational. These examples also highlight the fact that a number of extraction sites traditionally considered as primarily Neolithic phenomena, such as Rijckholt, clearly witnessed some level of Mesolithic activity.

The protracted Neolithisation of the Netherlands can be seen at the Early Neolithic B site of Brandwijk dating to 4600–4100 cal BC, which was located in a relict riverine landscape. This settlement was part of the southern Swifterbant group, and during its key settlement phase [L50] was contemporary with Early Michelsberg activity. This community practiced an 'extended broad spectrum' subsistence strategy of foraging alongside some domesticated animals and limited access to non-local cereals. Yet despite the novel adoption of a limited range of Neolithic agricultural practices, the settlement continued to import Rijckholt artefacts from the south, but now of typical Michelsberg types. Use-wear analysis has discovered that these artefacts had been imported as used tools, but curiously were not re-used at Brandwijk (van Gijn 2009).

Over time the Swifterbant communities adopted a rather haphazard approach to the adoption of Neolithic practices (Louwe Kooijmans 2007), paralleling the situation in southern Scandinavia where the full range of subsistence and life-style practices did not appear until well into the Neolithic period. In both regions the traditional use of quarries and their products continued unabated.

### Eastern Europe
In eastern Europe at Krumlovský les (Czechia), an extensive mining complex noted for Neolithic and later extraction, has provided indications of Mesolithic activity. A group of four radiocarbon dates suggest that a system of shafts designated I-13-1 date to the Late Mesolithic, although caution is required concerning the possible effects of residuality on sample deposition. However, if the dates are an accurate reflection, the Mesolithic phase of extraction was characterised by shafts 2–3 m deep with horizontal niches at their base projecting 1+ m into the chert-rich layers (Oliva 2010, 355, 467). The Mesolithic chipped stone assemblage from these mines is distinctively different from that of later periods, confirming some form of on-site activity. Curiously, the Krumlovský les chert was relatively poor quality and unsuitable for knapping larger artefacts such as axeheads yet, despite this, it was present in all Mesolithic assemblages within 60 km of the source and achieved long distance circulation from Lower Austria to Bohemia (Oliva 2010, 372–3, 383). This suggests that Krumlovský les chert had acquired a value beyond its local area.

*Figure 1.1: Carn Menyn (Pembrokeshire) summit outcrops, below which lay the later Mesolithic pit which was dug to extract mudstone (photo: author)*

### British Isles

In Britain lithic extraction was well established during the later Mesolithic and exploited a range of lithologies such as meta-mudstone at Carn Menyn (Darvill & Wainwright 2014; Darvill 2019). This quarry lies on the southern flanks of the jagged dolerite summit of the eastern Preseli Hills (south-west Wales) at roughly 330 m asl (Fig. 1.1), comprising a pit 5.0 × 6.0 m and up to 1.2 m deep. The quarry straddles the junction of dolerite and mudstone and contained evidence of fire-setting. The landscape setting of this quarry just below the dramatic skyline dolerite outcrops, suggests it may have been a mythologised location.

In the Scottish Borders a small group of quarry pits on Burnetland Hill are located on a hillslope at 300 m asl and exploited deposits of poor quality blue/grey radiolarian chert. A sample of hazel charcoal returned a date of 4080–3960 cal BC at 85.2% probability (5220±35 BP; SUERC-17876) to provide a *terminus ante quem* for the quarrying, placing this site in the Late Mesolithic–Early Neolithic contact period (although caution is needed with a single radiocarbon date). This tentative date was supported by the chipped stone assemblage, comprising flakes, blades, burins, and scrapers. However, 99.8% of the lithic assemblage was debitage, suggesting this quarry was primarily a procurement site with implements finished elsewhere. Fifteen hammerstones or pounders of greywacke and sandstone were also recovered (Ballin & Ward 2013; Ward 2012). Other Mesolithic quarries also existed in the Scottish Borders at Flint Hill, Kilrubie Hill, and Wide Hope Shank in the Upper Tweed Valley, where production focused on blades (Warren 2007, 146). Most

Figure 1.2: Pike of Stickle, part of the Langdale/Scafell axe quarry complex in Cumbria (photo: author)

chert used in the Borders was quarried, and the expedient use of pebble chert from drift deposits was of secondary importance (Ballin & Ward 2013, 3). At Burnetland Hill the fact that people chose to expend time quarrying chert when it was readily available in drift deposits again suggests deliberate selection and that raw material provenance was an important factor in the choice of lithics.

Considering the Mesolithic interest in swallow holes mentioned above, the excavations at Farnham (Surrey) are particularly informative. This site lay on gravel deposits along the former course of the Blackwater River near Bourne Mill Spring and comprised a series of pits or tree-throws which lay adjacent to a swallow hole (Oakley *et al*. 1939, 67–80). Of particular interest was the ovoid Pit IV which lay roughly 33 m to the north-west of the swallow hole and was 8.2 m NE–SW × 3.9 m transversely, and 0.9 m deep, and contained a substantial lithic assemblage comprising Mesolithic and Neolithic material (Clark & Rankine 1939, 67–8). The stratigraphy suggested that the pit was dug (or revealed as a tree-throw) gravels which were extracted and then processed off-site. The lithic assemblage from the pit totalled 10,709 pieces, including debitage and finished implements, four core tools comprising examples of adzeheads, axeheads and picks, and 3880 burnt flints (Clark & Rankine 1939, 67, 72; Ellaby 1987, 67; Field 2011a, 29). Indeed, the pit/tree-throw group and adjacent swallow hole may have formed a discrete complex of some cultural importance, suggested by the discovery of an assemblage of 12,000+ Mesolithic implements from within the swallow hole itself (Clark & Rankine 1939, 68–70).

A Mesolithic quarry on the summit of Fin Cop (Derbyshire) overlooks the steep-sided valley of the River Wye, with numerous caves in the cliffs below – suggesting the site may have held a cultural resonance for its users. The hilltop quarries targeted grey, coarse-grained chert outcrops amongst the limestone bedrock and excavations produced an assemblage of 2000+ Mesolithic chipped stone artefacts, demonstrating it was another important location for lithic procurement (Waddington *et al.* 2012).

Arran Pitchstone, originating from the eponymous island off the west coast of Scotland, provided raw material from outcrops at Monamore, the Corriegills, and probably coastal outcrops on the island. The products were typically burins and microliths (inf. T Ballin; Affleck *et al.* 1988). Recently Mesolithic pitchstone artefacts have been discovered on mainland Scotland at three sites in Argyll and Dumfries & Galloway (Ballin *et al.* 2018), suggesting that this black, glassy rock had gradually spread to off-island groups through contact networks. By the Early Neolithic pitchstone had become part of an assemblage of exotic artefacts that included other lithologies and carinated bowl pottery (Ballin 2015, 6, 11) and became emblematic of Neolithisation around the Irish Sea (eg, Sheridan 2004; 2007; 2010). This suggests once again that Late Mesolithic materiality contributed directly to Neolithic practices, particularly during first contact when indigenous communities on the west coast of Scotland appear to have co-existed alongside incoming agro-pastoralists (Brace *et al.* 2019, 770).

The exploitation of distinctively coloured or recognisable lithologies appears to have been a recurrent theme during the Mesolithic. On Rhum (west coast Scotland), the source of Rhum Bloodstone is on Bloodstone Hill on the western side of the island. This hill has a dramatic, mesa-like profile with exposed craggy outcrops around its summit and sloping flanks tumbling into the sea. Fieldwork suggested Mesolithic groups exploited the talus slopes or beach nodules (Wickham-Jones 1990, 51–2). Although Bloodstone exists in a range of colours, the major variety is a fine-textured dark green rock with red inclusions and was a key component of the lithic assemblage discovered at the Kinloch Mesolithic settlement at the head of Loch Scresort on the east coast of the island and other mostly coastal Mesolithic sites on Rhum (*ibid.*, 116, 162–4). Importantly, analysis of other Bloodstone sources in western Scotland has suggested that it was Rhum Bloodstone that is found among mainland assemblages (*ibid.*, 151–6). Consequently, the familiar Mesolithic pattern of a topographically distinctive source and/or a recognisable raw material was repeated at Rhum with the use of Bloodstone, which went on to develop a value for off-island communities.

In England, circumstantial evidence of putative Mesolithic quarrying also exists. For example, Group VI Epidotised Tuff was found amongst a Late Mesolithic assemblage at the Stainton West site, a camp located on an island in the River Eden floodplain, although caution is needed as this tuff occurs widely on high ground in Cumbria and may not necessarily represent quarried material. Although the majority of this assemblage comprised beach flint and chert it also produced exotic lithologies ranging from Arran Pitchstone, Scottish chert, and Yorkshire flint alongside the putative Langdale tuff, suggesting extensive networking across some 200 km (124 miles) from the site. Artefacts of tuff consisted of a partly ground adzehead, ground tool fragments, and a fragment of a ground axehead with a characteristic side facet (cf. Davis & Edmonds 2011b, 174), all recovered from beneath an alluvial deposit dated to *c.* 4300 cal BC (Brown *et al.* 2019). These discoveries demonstrate that ground axehead production occurred in pre-Neolithic contexts during the 5th millennium BC, and suggests that the acquisition of Group VI tuff was an established part of lithic procurement strategies during the Late Mesolithic. In addition, classic forms of Mesolithic artefacts made from tuff, such as geometric microliths, have also been discovered at coastal areas of Cumbria such as St Bees, Rottington, and South Cliff (Cherry & Cherry 1973; 1983; Cherry 2009). Although geologically this raw material may have been beach pebbles or glacial drift, it does offer the possibility of pre-Neolithic extraction amongst the upland Scafell/Langdale sources (Fig. 1.2). The evidence for Mesolithic extraction in Cumbria is growing.

In north Wales the surviving quarries at Graiglwyd are ranged along an east-facing outcrop up to 425 m asl, with panoramic views overlooking the coastline, Anglesey, and the Great Orme. A low cairn was excavated 300 m west of the outcrop, comprising both angular and rounded stones alongside some potentially imported hammerstones. Beneath the cairn a compact clayey silt contained large quantities of axe-making debitage and a roughout axehead; charcoal flecks produced a radiocarbon date of 4350–3990 cal BC at 95.4% probability (5330±90 BP; Swan-142; Williams & Davidson 1998, 18–19). Although, as ever, caution is needed with a single radiocarbon determination, this site may represent a Late Mesolithic short-term knapping event fossilised beneath the cairn.

On the Lleyn Peninsula south-west of Graiglwyd lie the Mynydd Rhiw quarries, ranged along a prominent ridge around 260 m asl and overlooking the sweeping expanse of Porth Neigwl (Hell's Mouth Bay) on the southern coastline of the peninsula. This quarry exploited Group XXI Tufaceous Sediments (Burrow 2011, 248) but may have provided raw material during earlier periods too. Excavations on Ynys Enlli (Bardsey Island), lying 13 km off the tip of the Lleyn Peninsula, dated a Late Mesolithic assemblage to 7500–4000 cal BC that included flakes which macroscopic examination suggested were from Mynydd Rhiw (Edmonds *et al.* 2004). The discovery of these putative Mynydd Rhiw lithics adds to the corpus of deliberately sourced materials found around the western seaboard from the Late Mesolithic period which may indicate contemporary quarrying.

### *Ireland*

Mesolithic quarrying at Monvoy (Co. Waterford) in south-east Ireland targeted rhyolite found on a prominent ridge with panoramic views. The rhyolite was used mostly for the production of Late Mesolithic leaf-shaped Bann flakes which do not appear to have travelled further than 3–5 km from the quarry. Curiously, the repertoire of the quarry users included implements which were normally knapped from pebble flint, such as blades and scrapers (Zvelebil *et al.* 1989). It appears that the Monvoy rhyolite serviced a local demand for utilitarian items.

Overall, the evidence presented here suggests extraction was a widespread phenomenon in Mesolithic Europe and was not a Neolithic innovation. The key points which emerge from this growing body of evidence is that Mesolithic extraction often took place on prominent landforms or targeted distinctive lithologies, occasionally debitage or implements formed placed deposits on-site rather than as casually strewn wastage, while most sites were linked to extensive distribution networks. In some regions there was a link to rock art. These practices are all found at Neolithic sites.

## Materiality and placed deposits during the European Mesolithic

One of the traditional indicators of Neolithisation is the appearance of ground and polished stone tools. For clarity, all these tools, whether from pecked or flaked preforms, have had their form modified by grinding, some in addition were burnished to provide a distinctive sheen. In a number of European regions this technology existed during the Mesolithic period. For instance, in southern Norway and Sweden the production of ground stone axeheads appeared around 8000 BC, when it was introduced alongside a new blade tradition, distinctive rock art motifs, and new bone tool-working methods (Nyland 2016, 59; 2019, 71). In neighbouring Denmark several forms of distinctive Mesolithic ground stone artefacts developed, particularly the Trindøkse and Limnhamnøkse types of greenstone axehead (Price & Gebauer 2005, 70).

Ground stone technology also existed in Ireland during the Mesolithic period, as can be seen at the Early Mesolithic site at Lough Boora (Co. Offaly). This was located on a gravel ridge on the lough shore and comprised several hearths and assorted burnt animal, bird, and fish remains, suggesting a temporary hunting camp. Amongst the lithic assemblage of some 200 microliths, *c.* 400 blades and many cores, were three complete ground stone axeheads and a number of axehead fragments. Although only a single date of 7550–7180 cal BC (8350±70 BP, UB 2200) was returned from charcoal from a hearth, the presence of microliths and the fact that the site was buried beneath a peat inundation dated to *c.* 6000 BC confirm a Mesolithic date (Ryan 1980; Costa *et al.* 2005). Other examples of Mesolithic ground implements from Ireland occur at Mount Sandel, where an assemblage of ground axeheads was discovered in a pit in one of the earliest Mesolithic settlements (Woodman 1985; Bayliss & Woodman 2009, 116–17). Another, which may be the earliest example of a ground adzehead in Europe, was discovered in a cremation pit at Hermitage on the banks of the River Shannon (Co. Limerick) and dated by association with the cremation to 7530–7320 cal BC (8350±40 BP, Beta 214236; Little *et al.* 2017). Consequently, ground stone technology was well established in the Irish Mesolithic at both settlements and in burials.

In Wales, the Nab Head II site (Pembrokeshire) produced a 6th millennium lithic assemblage which included four ground dolerite axeheads and a radiocarbon date of 7310–6700 cal BC (8070±80 BP, OxA-1497) provided a *terminus post quem* for the axeheads (David & Walker 2004; David 2007, 135–55). The presence of ground stone technology on both sides of the Irish Sea demonstrates that close pre-Neolithic cultural connections existed between communities around this archipelagic seascape.

### Deposition of Mesolithic ground axeheads

The deposition of ground axeheads was carefully considered in many cases. In southern Norway, for example, large numbers of ground axeheads have been discovered placed amongst scree slopes, under flagstones or boulders, beside outcrops, in wetlands, and in the sea along the Mesolithic coastline, all demonstrating a clear purpose within Mesolithic depositional practices (Bradley 2010; Lødøen 2013, 42). There was also a particularly strong correlation between hoards of dolerite axeheads and large earthfast boulders overlooking fjords in western Norway, such as Lusterfjord where three axeheads were deposited beside a prominent boulder with panoramic views over the fjord (Lødøen 2013, 44–5). Other contexts included the Late Mesolithic settlement of Bökeberg III (Scania), which produced an imported axehead set in a ditch; a second ditch contained another axehead which had been burnt and set upright while a third unused axehead and an antler point were discovered in a midden, all suggesting deliberate deposition (Bradley 1998, 28). Scandinavian burials also featured axeheads, as in Graves II and IV at Skateholm II (Larsson 1988), and the age demographic of some burials suggests that they were associated with individuals who were either too old or too young to have used them, implying that they were deposited as symbolic objects (Strassburg 2000, 203).

In Britain, Mesolithic wetland deposition appears to follow pan-European traditions (Chatterton 2006, 103). Surveys by Wymer (1977), Care (1979), and Field (1989) have recorded at least 549 tranchet axeheads and 48 picks which have been recovered from the Thames river network, alongside human remains and antler and bone implements (Fig. 1.3). Although various explanations for this deposition have been proposed, mostly suggesting accidental loss or foreshore erosion (eg, Saville 1977; Jacobi 1987), when viewed from a European perspective, and considering the number of Thames artefacts which cluster in locations where accumulations of ground axes (usually attributed to the Neolithic) also occur (Adkins & Jackson 1978), it is difficult to accept accidental loss or casual discard as adequate explanation for such a large number of implements. Rather, this suggests a widespread cultural practice of wetland deposition – especially as many of these implements are of comparatively large size compared to those found at settlements. In addition, many riverine axeheads had never been used as tools, implying that they were manufactured for special purposes and not mundane uses (however, caution is needed as it is often difficult to identify whether resharpened tranchet axeheads had been previously used; Rankine 1956; Care 1979). This mirrors the situation in southern Sweden, for example, where imported stone axeheads were deliberately deposited in rivers and bogs (Karsten 1994).

One of the most remarkable Irish discoveries occurred at Hermitage (mentioned above), on the banks of the River Shannon (Co. Limerick). Here a group of three pits was excavated near a possible ford. Pit A was a modest 0.6 m in diameter and up to 0.3 m deep, and had held an upright timber post marking the location of a cremation burial. Resting against the post and buried in the pit was a ground stone adzehead set vertically with its cutting edge downwards. Two microliths completed the assemblage. Microwear analysis suggested that the adzehead had been manufactured for deposition with the cremation, with only minor edge damage suggesting it was deliberately blunted during funerary rites, perhaps symbolically paralleling the death of the individual it accompanied. The pan-European trend for riverine deposition sketched above, is continued at Killaloe, upstream from the Hermitage site, where an astounding assemblage of 750 stone axeheads and adzeheads have been discovered (Collins & Coyne 2003). These examples from the

*1 Setting the scene: the Mesolithic prelude and first contact Neolithic*

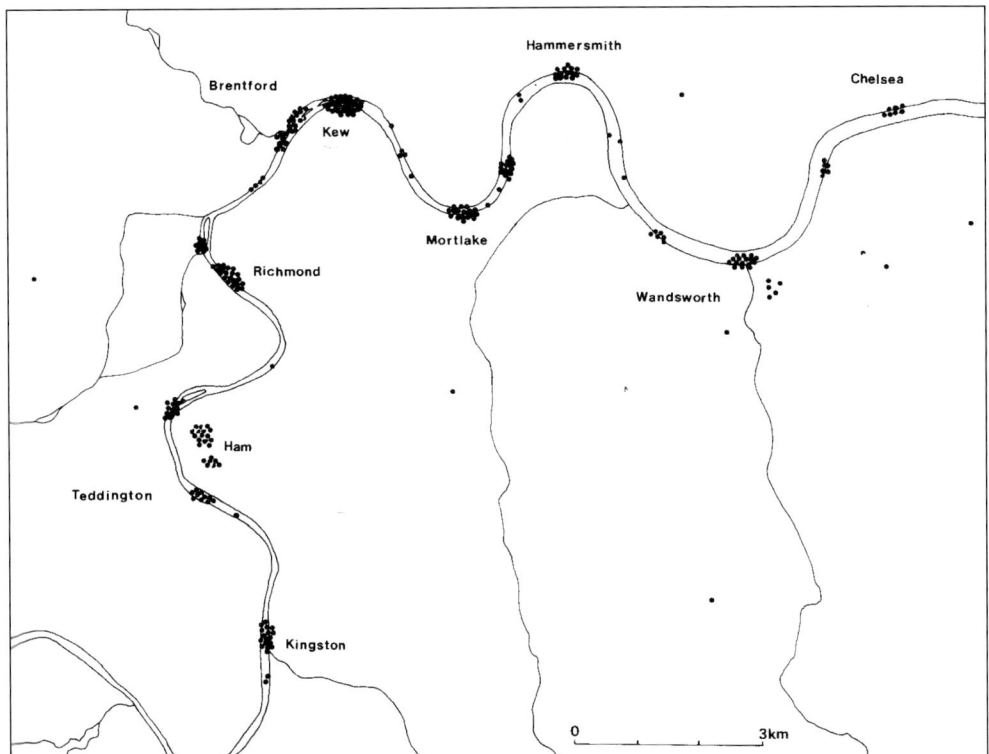

*Figure 1.3: The distribution of Mesolithic axeheads from the Thames (© Dave Field)*

River Shannon again illustrate the strong trend for wetland deposition in Mesolithic Ireland (O'Sullivan 1998), presaging Neolithic wetland practices.

A further trend in the Irish Mesolithic was the deliberate caching of axeheads, portending Neolithic practices in Britain. At Ferriter's Cove (Co. Kerry), a coastal site in south-west Ireland, a hoard of five ground stone axeheads was found juxtaposed with domesticated cattle bones lying amongst hearths and middens (Woodman *et al.* 1999). The Ferriter's Cove cache has similarities with other Irish sites, particularly those in the Bann Valley to the north, where a number of caches of unused ground axeheads have been recorded (Woodman 1978, 114). These caches have been considered evidence of practices underpinning social reproduction through the use of lithic technology (Warren 2006, 28). This is lent weight by pits containing debitage in later Mesolithic Ireland, alongside the structured deposition of non-axehead lithics at sites such as Dalkey Island, Glendhu, and Newferry (Woodman 1978; Warren 2006). These patterns of use and deposition imply that particular lithic implements, especially certain axeheads and adzeheads, were treated in different ways to everyday functional objects, creating a distinctive artefact biography appropriate to their specialised roles in society. By implication, the extraction sites which produced these artefacts must also have been regarded as culturally important, as illustrated by the practices and deposits at many of the extraction sites discussed above. Indeed, as Chatterton (2006, 119) has observed, 'certain stone sources were revered, returned to again and again and the stone therefrom dispersed over large areas'.

Similar deposits occurred in Scandinavia. In Denmark, for example, the later Mesolithic Ertebølle assemblages provide useful data concerning the relative importance of different implement types (Table 1.2). The most common tool was the unretouched flint blade (Price & Gebauer 2005, 139) but at 50% of Mesolithic sites, such as Braband, Dyrholmen II, and Fiskerhuset, the 'flake axehead' was the dominant tool type, suggesting that these artefacts were used for a variety of roles ranging from subsistence tasks to more symbolic uses (Table 1.3). The latter is suggested by an analysis of flaked flint axeheads from the Zealand archipelago, which discovered that four contemporary but distinctively different

*Figure 1.4: Later Mesolithic flake axehead groups in Zealand (Denmark), which suggest that large implements were used in the creation of identity, often alongside other non-local objects (after Price & Gebauer 2005, 34; illustration: T. Pearson)*

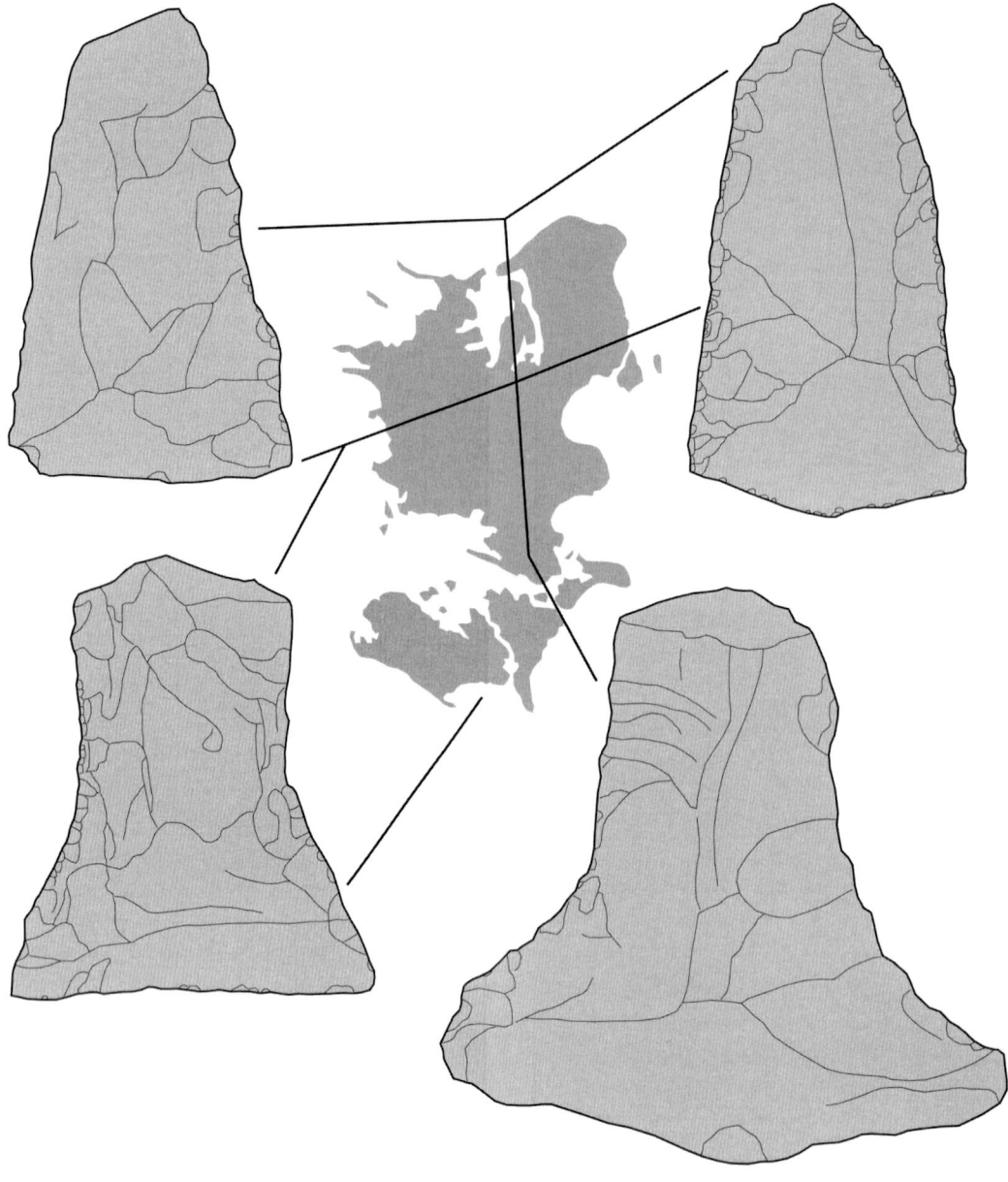

axehead types were recovered from four discrete areas (Fig. 1.4). Other artefacts such as decorated pottery vessels, T-shaped antler axeheads, and bone artefacts, were also found to have characteristic distributions (Price & Gebauer 2005, 33–5). These distinctive Ertebølle assemblages demonstrate that material culture was an increasingly important element in defining status and identity amongst these communities on the periphery of European Neolithisation. The presence of imported Michelsberg and Rössen shaft-hole axeheads in southern Scandinavia during the Late Mesolithic, particularly in the eastern islands of the Danish archipelago, demonstrates contact between indigenous foragers and encroaching agro-pastoralists. These axeheads, generally associated with the central European Neolithic, were crafted from amphibolite, possibly from Poland, Bulgaria, or even Brittany (cf. Pailler 2012a; 2012b), and suggest seaborne networks operating around the Atlantic/North Sea littoral, paralleling the situation in the Irish Sea and English Channel (eg, Sheridan 2004). Clearly axeheads in Scandinavia played an important role in social networks, either as aspirational objects, identity markers, or part of the materiality of status or wealth.

*1 Setting the scene: the Mesolithic prelude and first contact Neolithic*

| Site | Flaked axeheads | Core axeheads | No. other implements | Total no. items in assemblage | All axeheads as a % of assemblage |
|---|---|---|---|---|---|
| Bjørnsholm | 47 | 63 | 97 | 207 | 53 |
| Bloksbjerg | 38 | 55 | 219 | 312 | 30 |
| Braband | 225 | 35 | 106 | 366 | 71 |
| Dyrholmen II | 571 | 93 | 639 | 1303 | 51 |
| Fiskerhuset | 889 | 74 | 897 | 1860 | 52 |
| Norslund 1 | 19 | 5 | 21 | 45 | 53 |
| Norslund 2 | 28 | 7 | 184 | 219 | 16 |
| Ølby Lyng | 67 | 20 | 476 | 563 | 15 |
| Smakkerup Huse | 30 | 19 | 406 | 455 | 11 |
| Vejlebro | 101 | 11 | 719 | 831 | 13 |
| | | | | | Average = 36.5 |

(based on data from Price & Gebauer 2005, 125–36)

*Table 1.2: The relative percentage of major artefact types discovered at Middle and Late Ertebølle coastal settlements in Denmark*

| Site | Total no. all axehead types | No. second most numerous implement type in assemblage |
|---|---|---|
| Bjørnsholm | 110 | 38 scrapers |
| Bloksbjerg | 93 | 122 points |
| Braband | 260 | 69 scrapers |
| Dyrholmen II | 664 | 310 scrapers |
| Fiskerhuset | 963 | 480 points |
| Norslund 1 | 24 | 13 points |
| Norslund 2 | 35 | 155 points |
| Ølby Lyng | 87 | 376 points |
| Smakkerup Huse | 49 | 365 points |
| Vejlebro | 112 | 530 points |

(based on data from Price & Gebauer 2005)

*Table 1.3: The relative importance of Danish Mesolithic axeheads compared to the second most numerous implement type in each site assemblage*

## What trends emerge from the Mesolithic data?

A number of trends are evident from the ways Mesolithic people used extraction sites and their products. First, there is good evidence to suggest that Mesolithic communities had a strong interest in adopting prominent rock outcrops or recognisable topographic settings as persistent places, as well as locations with a subterranean character. Caves were a particular focus for habitation, burials, and the deposition of special materials and objects. Swallow holes like Fir Tree Field (Cranborne Chase, Dorset) (Green & Allen 1997) contained animal bones juxtaposed with microliths. Pits held special lithic deposits at many sites such as Pendell Farm and Belderrig. Indeed, it may have been pit digging to obtain cobbles that led to the development and adoption of more sustained quarrying. Rock from prominent locations was often sought and quarried, and these sites appear to have been used over many generations. Quarries such as Carn Menyn, situated close to dramatic topographic features, had deposits of debitage or roughouts placed on-site. Curiously, certain quarries appear to have targeted inferior lithologies, and some (eg, Burnetland Hill) were dug when more accessible alternatives were available. In addition, circumstantial evidence suggests that extraction may have begun during the Mesolithic at some major upland quarries such as Langdale/Scafell and Graiglwyd, unless the evidence represents surface collection. Alongside this, the site of Krumlovský les offers the possibility that small shafts with niches were used during the Mesolithic, creating a precursor for the Neolithic development of deep shaft, galleried mines.

Many of the products from Mesolithic quarries were distributed over long distances, particularly where the stone was unusually

The growing body of evidence demonstrates that quarries existed in many regions of Europe during the Mesolithic – extraction sites were *not* a Neolithic introduction. Many Mesolithic quarries had extensive product distributions, and some had elaborate extraction practices which included on-site placed deposits. Alongside this, ground stone technology was clearly in use across much of Europe from at least 8000 BC, so another traditional Neolithic trait must be reconsidered. Overall, the archaeological record shows clearly that stone extraction and ground stone technology were well established practices during the Mesolithic period in many regions of Europe … the question now is exactly how did these practices influence extraction during the onset of the Neolithic period?

## The appearance of Neolithic extraction

At present the earliest Neolithic mining in Europe is found around the Mediterranean and the Iberian Peninsula (see Chapter 7). The Defensola A mine complex on the Gargano Peninsula (Italy) operated between 5870 and 4600 cal BC based upon median date ranges, the start date being consistent with ceramics found in the mine. However, abandonment appears to fall within the period 5470–5310 cal BC, thus exploitation may have been of considerably shorter duration than initially indicated (Consuegra & Díaz-del-Río 2018). On the Iberian Peninsula the Early Neolithic mines at Casa Montero (Madrid) are located on a prominent bluff overlooking the confluence of two major rivers. This large site comprised 3794 shafts up to 9.2 m deep with a mean diameter of 1.15 m, but without galleries; six open-air quarries were also recorded. Shafts were sunk here between 5380 and 5320 cal BC and abandoned 5290–5180 cal BC, suggesting they were used for 30–170 years, and their main product was large blades. Chronologically, the Casa Montero mines coincided with the earliest evidence of Neolithic practices in central Iberia (Consuegra & Díaz-del-Río 2018; Consuegra *et al.* 2018).

Arguably one of the most influential extraction phenomena was the high-altitude Alpine jade quarries on Mont Viso and Mont Beigua in the north Italian Alps which operated around 5300–4900 cal BC and produced

*Figure 1.5: An Alpine jadeitite axehead discovered at Lochearnhead (Perthshire) and now curated in the National Museums of Scotland (photo: author)*

distinctive, and some distinctive axeheads (eg, those from Scandinavia) appear to have formed part of the way people used material culture to express their identity. Depositional practices were important, with pit and riverine/wetland deposition two of the most common forms of treatment for axeheads, predominantly in major rivers such as the Thames and Shannon, but also the bogs and wetlands of Europe.

*1 Setting the scene: the Mesolithic prelude and first contact Neolithic*

*Figure 1.6: Breton fibrolite axeheads discovered in the Tumulus Saint-Michel at Carnac (Morbihan), and now curated at Carnac Museum (photo: author)*

lustrous green ground and highly polished axeheads (Fig. 1.5) and other items, which were initially found in local contexts. However, by 4900–4500 cal BC, the distribution of these Alpine objects expanded dramatically across central Europe. By 4600–3900 cal BC the Morbihan region (Brittany), with its massive earthen monuments and elaborate megalithic architecture, had become a key area in the use and circulation of these axeheads, particularly larger examples (Pétrequin *et al.* 2012a; 2017). The value placed on these exotic axeheads is shown at Tumulus St-Michel in Carnac which contained 11 Alpine jade axeheads amongst an assemblage of 39 stone axeheads, 135 variscite beads, pottery, and burnt bones, all discovered in a centrally-located trapezoidal cist. Some axeheads were set vertically, blades upwards, and two had been deliberately broken, suggesting elaborate burial ceremonialism (Le Rouzic 1932; Cassen *et al.* 2012a). The circulation of these exotic, high-quality Alpine axeheads may have stimulated axehead production more generally and led to the creation of imitations in new raw materials such as Breton Fibrolite (Fig. 1.6). This source of Fibrolite was excavated from small quarries such as those at Plouguin from *c.* 4800 cal BC, and it was used for large axeheads which, when ground and polished, attained a jade-like green colour with brown mottling (Y. Pailler pers. comm.; Pailler 2012a; 2012b).

The influence of jade was even felt in Britain during the earliest stages of Neolithisation. Early finds, such as the Glastonbury-type axehead discovered in a deposit at the Sweet Track in the Somerset Levels (dated by dendrochronology to 3807 or 3806 BC), may originally have been manufactured sometime between 4500 and 4200 cal BC, at a time when British communities were Mesolithic in character (Coles *et al.* 1974; Pétrequin *et al.* 2008, 269). The fact that this axehead was found alongside Carinated Bowl pottery and a flint axehead attributed to the South Downs flint mines, suggests that the Sweet Track jade axehead was in circulation for a number of centuries before it was deposited beside this wooden trackway crossing a wetland. It is generally thought that it was imported soon before deposition but it could equally have arrived much earlier. The introduction of green axeheads into Britain may have stimulated a search for similar lithologies at the upland axe quarries such as Scafell/Langdale (Groups VI & XI) or the Cornish Group I quarries (A. Sheridan pers. comm.; Clough 1988). Such lithic prospection was part of a Europe-wide phenomenon in the Early Neolithic, which was focused upon sourcing green lithologies including variscite from the mines at Gavà (Barcelona) which was used for high-status objects such as beads and jewellery (Borrell & Estrada 2009). While mining and quarrying was product driven, the search for exotic lithologies fulfilled a cultural need for distinctive raw materials which was generally not satisfied by expedient surface resources.

The erratic course of Neolithisation in the Low Countries led to a piecemeal adoption of Neolithic practices (Louwe Kooijmans 2007). Considering the topography, wetland settlement appears to have been a deliberate choice by many transitional Swifterbant communities of the Rhine–Waal–Maas estuary and the Ijsselmeer, despite their close proximity to incoming farmers (Rowley-Conwy & Legge 2015, 437). These Swifterbant communities focused equally on wild and domesticated subsistence resources from *c.* 4600 BC onwards until around 4000 BC when mainstream farming practices finally spread into the Low Countries and southern Scandinavia (Rowley-Conwy & Legge 2015, 437–9; Thorpe 2015, 220). Yet despite the fluctuations in subsistence practices, lithics played a major role in everyday life. This is seen in the range of imported implements such as LBK shoe-last axeheads and Alpine jade axeheads in these regions (Klassen 2004), alongside large Scandinavian axeheads and Grand Pressigny daggers, presumably influenced by contact with the early Bandkeramik farmers who had arrived in Limburg. At the riverine settlement at Brandwijk, referred to above (4600–4100 cal BC), the lithic assemblage included large numbers of imported Michelsberg tools such as ground blades and end-scrapers fashioned from Rijckholt flint. Use-wear analysis suggests that these were imported as used tools and were not re-used or resharpened at Brandwijk. Clearly the Swifterbant communities valued these particular lithics, perhaps as part of defining a new identity during the onset of the Neolithic. In contrast, indigenous flint technology used small surface-collected nodules for everyday tools. This dichotomy in lithic sourcing had a long tradition in the Rhine–Meuse Delta, where Wommersom quartzite and Rijckholt flint were found at Late Mesolithic sites such as Hardinxveld and De Bruin, demonstrating well-established traditions of sourcing exotic lithics from distant places (van Gijn 2009).

The Rijckholt flint mines (Netherlands) appear to have been sunk around 4000 BC, and the data suggest their major period of use was during the first half of the 4th millennium BC when Rijckholt flint is found in Belgium, the Netherlands, and eastern Germany (de Grooth *et al.* 2011). However, at present it is difficult to differentiate Rijckholt flint from that of the major Belgian source at Spiennes. The Spiennes mines were exploited from *c.* 4350 BC until around 2300 BC for the production of axeheads, blades, and large flakes, some of which have been recovered 160 km from the mines (Collet *et al.* 2016). Considering the technical difficulties in provenancing flint, it is possible that the product distribution of these two major complexes may have originally been more extensive than presently indicated.

The Paris Basin became a major centre of flint mining in northern France in the regional Middle Neolithic when the first mines were excavated and flint axeheads became numerous. Chronologically, these mines overlap in date with those in the Low Countries. In the north-west part of the Paris Basin the mines at Flins-sur-Seine and Jablines exploited Bartonian flint, while Bretteville targeted secondary deposits, illustrating the range of lithologies being exploited. Surprisingly, despite the presence of at least 15 mines in this part of the Paris Basin, the local communities still imported axeheads from the Armorican Massif, the Alps, the Vosges, the Massif Centrale, and the Ardennes

# 1 Setting the scene: the Mesolithic prelude and first contact Neolithic

to use alongside their own regionally sourced flint implements (Bostyn & Lanchon 1992; Giligny *et al.* 2009; Giligny 2011; Giligny & Bostyn 2016).

Scandinavia, located on the periphery of Neolithisation, had a similar timeline to the British and Irish evidence. Over time, Scandinavia witnessed increasing contact with farming communities. In Norway many Mesolithic quarries remained in use but some, like Hespriholmen, were eclipsed by new quarries such as Mount Siggjo on Bømlo island, where rhyolite was quarried for blades and flakes and distributed over 600 km around the western coastal regions of southern Norway (Nyland 2015; 2019). Impacts were felt elsewhere, with changes to extraction practices seen on Thy (Denmark) at Hov and Bjerre (Weisgerber 1999, 456–68; Strassburg 2000, 345), and in southern Sweden at Sallerup-Tullstop and Kvarnby-Södra (Rudebeck 1998), where open-air quarries were superseded by deep galleried shafts, showing a technological shift in lithic procurement after first contact with migrant agriculturalists. Material culture played a major role in these social transformations too, particularly in Denmark and southern Norway where the new extraction techniques stood alongside the importation of LBK shaft-hole adzeheads, T-shaped antler axeheads, and small numbers of Alpine jade axeheads (Fischer 2002; Klassen 2002; 2004; Klassen *et al.* 2012). These transformations can be seen at the coastal Scanian site of Löddesborg, where domesticated cattle remains are juxtaposed with Ertebølle pottery with cereal impressions dated to *c.* 4050 BC, suggesting a community in flux, or possibly the co-existence of two culturally-different communities (Fischer 2002).

The appearance of early agro-pastoralists in southern Britain around *3980–3720 cal BC* (modelled date) (Brace *et al.* 2019, 768), coincided with the relatively 'sudden' introduction of deep shaft mining around 4000–3700 cal BC on the South Downs and Wessex as recorded by radiocarbon chronologies (Healy *et al.* 2011b, 257–62; Edinborough *et al.* 2019). However, sampling bias may be distorting this as it is possible that some of the shallow undated pits amongst the South Downs and Wessex mines (eg, Easton Down B1A, B 19, B45 & B67) may actually be Mesolithic in origin and represent traditional indigenous extraction at the time of first contact. The fact that these early mines rarely produce ground implements among their assemblages, which comprise largely flaked axeheads with Mesolithic-like profiles along with tranchet axeheads, eg, Easton Down (Stone 1931) and Cissbury (eg, Park Harrison 1878), suggests that the earliest 'Neolithic' mining and axehead production may have occurred at Mesolithic extraction sites where flint was traded between indigenes and newcomers (D. Field pers. comm.). Subsequently, these sites may have become collaborative ventures as acculturation occurred between communities, ultimately leading to the introduction of deep shaft, galleried mines. This mirrors the sequences in Iberia, Italy, and possibly Czechia, where the appearance of Neolithic agro-pastoralism coincided with the introduction of deep shaft mining. The presence of deep shaft *galleried* mines in southern Britain suggests that the technology probably came from northern France and the Low Countries where galleried mining was well established before its appearance in Britain (Felder *et al.* 1998; Healy *et al.* 2011b, 257; Collet *et al.* 2016; Giligny & Bostyn 2016).

The corpus of Neolithic flint mines in Britain and Ireland currently stands at 17 and they are located on chalk downs or in regions where glacially-derived secondary deposits of flint nodules are found (Britain: Blackpatch, Buckenham Toft, Church Hill, Cissbury, Den of Boddam, Durrington, Easton Down, Grime's Graves, Harrow Hill, Long Down, Martin's Clump, Nore Down, Skelmuir Hill, Stoke Down; Ireland: Ballygalley Hill, Goodland, Black Mountain; data from Bell & Bennett (1923); Case (1973); Barber *et al.* (1999)). In contrast, the number of quarries for igneous rocks may be as high as 36, situated in upland regions or on islands (V. Davis pers. comm.; Clough 1988). As suggested above, some of these extraction sites may have originally been established by Mesolithic foragers.

Current chronological models for mines and quarries suggest that in Britain and Ireland extraction generally began around 4100–3700 cal BC, with the possibility of earlier phases at Easton Down, Martin's Clump, Blackpatch, and Church Hill. Certain sites, such as Grime's Graves (Fig. 1.7), Church Hill, Long Down, and Langdale also witnessed late phases of activity

*Figure 1.7: Grime's Graves (Norfolk), Late Neolithic–Early/Middle Bronze Age flint mines (photo: author)*

(Healy *et al.* 2018; Edinborough *et al.* 2019). The South Downs and Wessex Groups of mines appear to pre-date the construction of most causewayed enclosures and long barrows (Whittle *et al.* 2011, 261, 853). The earliest quarries are Graiglwyd (Wales) and Lambay Island (Ireland) may represent the persistence of Mesolithic outcrop quarrying. The only dates available for the major porcellanite quarries at Tievebulliagh (Ireland) relate to a phase of woodland clearance which *might* correlate with episodes of extraction and parallel those from Lambay Island. The Mynydd Rhiw quarries (Wales) date from the second half of the Early Neolithic and overlap with Creag na Caillich (Scotland) which was used intermittently into the Early Bronze Age when it was abandoned. During the Late Neolithic the Den of Boddam flint quarries remained in use and were joined by Grime's Graves – all overlapping chronologically with Creag na Caillich. However, when extraction came to an end at these sites, around 2100–2000 cal BC, following a hiatus of several centuries, mining resumed at Grime's Graves when the so-called 'primitive pits' were dug during the Middle Urn/Arreton Phase of the Early Bronze Age, and were used until around the Middle Bronze Age transition when mining finally came to an end (Needham *et al.* 2010; Whittle *et al.* 2011; Healy *et al.* 2014, 55–8; 2018).

## Overall trends during the Mesolithic–Neolithic transition

Although Mesolithic quarries existed throughout Europe, the Neolithic innovation of deep shaft, galleried mining allowed the exploitation of more deeply buried lithic deposits. This coincided with a gradual and, at times, erratic intensification of land-use brought about by the introduction of agro-pastoralism by migrant communities. The use of vertical shafts, often with subterranean workings, opened up a new range of lithologies for artefact production. Many Mesolithic practices, such as the focus on distinctive locations and/or unique raw materials, deliberate on-site deposition of raw material and lithics, modest long distance product distributions, and the occasional use of rock art/graffiti, were adopted into Neolithic extraction practices. Technologically, Neolithic extraction went beyond the Mesolithic model by developing deeper mining and practices such as placed deposits became more complex incorporating a wider range of artefacts, animal remains, on-site graffiti, and rare human remains. Certain Neolithic artefacts achieved a pan-European distribution. As the millennium proceeded, some of the practices and deposits found at contact period extraction sites occurred at communal monuments such as causewayed enclosures and long barrows, suggesting they were part of a wider and long-lived continuum. Throughout Europe indigenous Mesolithic groups clearly influenced Neolithic extraction practices but cultural and technical differences existed between the two traditions and the growing sophistication of Neolithic extraction practices must reflect the dynamics of shifting populations, first contact, and social transformations.

The fundamental question to be considered is what motivated people to dig for stone and flint in the first place when in many cases the same raw material was often readily available amongst adjacent surface deposits? It is this observation that a critical use of ethnography can help to address.

# 2

# The ethnography of lithic extraction

Ethnography has often been used to provide fresh insights into pre-industrial, traditional practices which might correlate with material evidence in the archaeological record. To this end, a large sample of ethnographic data recording extraction practices, their social settings, and the use-life of products has been reviewed. The sample was drawn from communities in five continents comprising Africa, Australasia, Oceania, Europe, and the Americas. This ethnography was analysed to identify trends and produce robust statistics which establish a near-global, cross-cultural assessment of extraction practices. Statistically, these data provide a more reliable interpretive guide to extraction practices than that previously employed by earlier commentators using only a limited amount of ethnography (eg, Torrence 1984; 1986; Edmonds 1995; 2012). As Torrence (1986, 1–2) has noted, the potential divergence between interpretation and archaeological reality can be bridged by 'research conducted in the present where the relationship between behaviour and its material correlates can be observed directly', ie, by understanding the practices recorded by ethnography that document the procurement, use and deposition of material culture.

The 'ethnoarchaeology' of the 1970s onwards often produced potentially flawed hypotheses because they were generally based upon loose analogies with

> little consideration for sampling or formal comparison', consequently such '[a]d hoc analogies provide no support at all for the argument at hand. The fact that some human group somewhere in the world did something vaguely similar to what you are claiming for your archaeological case does not in fact support your claim. (Smith 2015)

Ethnography will provide a parallel to fit any proposed model.

Although it has become a cliché, ethnographic data has to be used with care to avoid the danger of circular arguments becoming self-fulfilling prophecies by continually citing the same social constructs such as 'bride wealth', etc. Such paradigms often restrict consideration of other possibilities such as the roles of material culture in building status, creating identity, and maintaining cosmographic order. Just as robust chronological models cannot be built upon single radiocarbon determinations, the same is true for archaeological hypotheses built upon a single or limited number of ethnographic 'parallels'. Consequently, as with radiocarbon dates, secure contexts, material patterning, and bulk sampling provide a much more solid foundation for an ethnoarchaeological model.

## Research methodology

The over-arching aim of this study was to gain an understanding of the probable motivations behind prehistoric extraction and its impact on society through the careful use of ethnographic analogy. This approach was founded upon the presumption that an interpretive guide can be obtained from an ethnographic model which has analysed the social contexts of extraction and the material patterning of its practices, product manufacture and use. To create this model, 168 ethnographic case studies were analysed to produce high-level aggregated trend data which identified material patterning by context (spatial, temporal, and social). Not every ethnographic record documented every trend, consequently these results have a bias, not unlike taphonomic processes in the archaeological record. Nevertheless, by analysing a larger ethnographic sample the new data has the capacity to identify strong trends in practices by aggregating many fields of data to produce a cross-cultural *probability analysis* with a near global perspective. In addition, the model has incorporated appropriate social and anthropological theories to explain content, variability, spatial patterning, and social context to inform the interpretation of the archaeological record (eg, Gero 1989; 1991; Bourdieu 1990; Godelier 1999; Gosden & Marshall 1999; Pétrequin & Pétrequin 2020) and is testable (Schiffer 1988; Popper 2002).

This study has used a 'flow model' approach (cf. Schiffer 1972; Fogelin & Schiffer 2015), similar in concept to the *chaîne opératoire*, to sketch the various stages of extraction practice and its outcomes from initiation to source identification, exploitation, product manufacturing, to product use and final deposition. This ethnoarchaeological model has the potential to explain why and how extraction site products became objects of significance and the nature of their roles in social networks (Hodder 1982b; 2012), and how they can influence society (Rathje 1979; Marshall 2008). The ethnography has provided information on ritualisation within extraction practices and product manufacturing, and its impacts upon communities who use these extraction site products (cf. Bell 1997; Spielmann 2002; Insoll 2004; 2011).

Although this study has not reviewed *all* available ethnography, it has accessed a far larger sample than the norm, and it offers a more nuanced understanding of traditional practices from a range of socio-technological contexts drawn from five continents. For example, New Guinea has a rich and varied ethnography of stone extraction which is often missed by archaeologists who only use a small number of easily accessible sources from the region (eg, Chappell 1966; Burton 1984; McBryde 1984) which inevitably restricts interpretation. As Hampton (1997, 79) has observed, the contiguous communities inhabiting the New Guinea highlands, although superficially similar, 'have significant differences' including a complex series of language groups, different materialities and varied socio-cultural settings. Critically, it is the role of materiality, and in particular stone tools and other significant lithic objects, which are central to the 'ideological reproduction of these communities of forest farmers' (Pétrequin & Pétrequin 2012, 27) – a situation reminiscent of Neolithic Europe.

The rigorous quantification and analysis of this large ethnographic dataset has provided new robust insights concerning the identification of motivations, actions, and their material signatures. As with radiocarbon analysis, by adopting a clear focus on material culture deposited in archaeologically visible contexts, robust trend data has emerged which suggests potential reasons underpinning archaeological deposition. By using a large aggregated, statistically significant data sample this has provided a far stronger assurance that the emerging themes and trends will provide meaningful results.

The analysis of the 168 ethnographic examples indicates that cosmological or ritual motives underpin extraction for many traditional societies, offering an interpretive steer for the apparently non-functional artefacts and assemblages often found in the archaeological record. In addition, 120 studies recorded the use of artefacts sourced from locations which had mythological associations and were used in social networks for various transactions, or to demonstrate identity, power, status, or wealth. The objects linked with prestige and status often rely upon such storied associations, as can be seen in the often-cited extravagant potlatch ceremonies amongst North-west Coast Native Americans (Boas & Hunt 1921; Mauss 1988; Godelier 1999), or the 'kula' exchange system of Melanesia, both designed to increase renown and prestige through ritualised actions and extravagant gift giving (Malinowski 1922; Godelier 1999).

The ethnographic sample was sifted to assess the presence or absence of 14 attributes or themes:

- Raw material
- Storied/mythologised sources
- Ownership/restricted access to sites
- Seasonality
- Age/sex demographic of extraction teams

## 2 The ethnography of lithic extraction

- Ritualised extraction
- Ritualised tool production
- Extraction site product typology
- Extraction site product functionality
- Involvement of craft specialists
- Distribution of extraction site products
- Ceremonial use of sites
- Rock art/graffiti/idols at extraction sites
- Human burials at extraction sites

As noted above, not all themes are documented in the ethnography, consequently the number of records can be variable and is shown in brackets in the tables below, eg, [89 cases out of 120 records], but all are drawn from the total corpus of 168 records. Negative data is also registered.

## The analysis of 168 ethnographic studies

### *Raw material type [stone=124; metals=29; minerals=15 records]*

The ethnography records extraction of a range of raw materials: stone, primarily for tool manufacture; minerals for personal adornment, burial practices, artefact production; and metal ores for a variety of uses. If this data is analysed by raw material type, the trend data is similar for all. Many sites are mythologised and have stories and legends associated, particularly locations where stone and metals are extracted. Metal sources are more likely to be owned, and only a small percentage of sites will be permanently settled. Seasonal use is most prevalent at lithic sources. The age/sex demographic of extraction teams is predominantly male at lithic sites, whereas metals and minerals have a greater demographic mix. Ritualised extraction practices are well represented at stone and mineral sites, and generally associated with mythologised/storied locations. Products are often highly valued and distributions are normally supra-regional, particularly those from locations which have storied associations. The after-use of many extraction sites is also noteworthy, which adds to the creation of a sense of place and the symbolism of products.

In the case of minerals, it appears that fewer sources had storied associations or were owned by groups or individuals. Extraction teams were generally male or mixed sexes, and ritualised extraction occurred in roughly half of the studies. Minerals were used for both ritual and functional purposes and were generally distributed over long distances. However, mineral extraction sites are used less as ceremonial arenas, rarely feature rock art, and none has burials on-site, suggesting they were perceived differently from stone and metal extraction sites.

### *Storied/mythologised sources [120=present; 9=negative; 39 no data]*

Most extraction sites have storied associations incorporating mythology, cosmology, religious beliefs, and/or community history, often to legitimise ownership or exploitation, or as an explanation of the origin of the raw material to underpin product biography (Kopytoff 1986; Bourdieu 1990; Godelier 1999; Gosden & Marshall 1999). Such associations operate at a variety of scales, either as part of an embodied entity such as a deified earth (eg, Inka, South America), or as a symbolic material given to a community by an ancestor or spirit (eg, Lakota/Dakota, USA; Dani, New Guinea; Aboriginal Australians). The data records 93% [120 of 129] of communities have storied extraction sites (Table 3.1; note: 93% is arrived at from the data sub-set of 120 records of presence and 9 records of absence, thus 129 in total, therefore, 120 is 93% of 129; 39 records provided no data so were not included in this calculation).

The ethnography does not always document topographic settings of storied sites or the precise nature of the raw material, but where this data exists many of these places are locally prominent or distinctive landforms or comprise unusual or atypical deposits which are visually different in scale, texture, or colouration to the landscape around them. It is the extraordinary character and topographic setting of storied deposits which sets them apart from the norm. The differences stimulated mythologisation, creating links with the cultural narratives of the community. These associations objectify the raw materials – often in tandem with ritualised extraction – and the products go on to fulfil roles in social transactions, the creation of identity, and the definition of status.

The nature and scale of storied materials varies, ranging from the earth as an engendered entity to specific mountains, exposed rock strata, rivers, individual boulders, nodules, down to fine minerals. The global scale is epitomised by the Inka (South America), who viewed the earth as a female entity, *Pachamama*,

Table 2.1: The trend data from storied/mythologised sites

| STORIED SOURCES [n=120 of 168]<br>(Note: 9 records provided negative data; 39 no data)<br>Attributes | 93%<br><br>% of key attributes in data sub-set | 120<br><br>No. of records in data sub-set [n=120] |
|---|---|---|
| Storied/mythologised source | 93 | 120 |
| Ownership/restricted access | 50 | 60 |
| Seasonal use of the resource | 54 | 65 |
|     Permanently settled | 5 | 6 |
| Age/sex demographic of the extraction site workers: | | |
|     Adult men | 62 | 75 |
|     Women | 1.5 | 2 |
|     Men, women & children | 12 | 15 |
| Evidence for ritualised extraction | 52 | 62 |
| Evidence for ritualised reduction | 48 | 58 |
| Extraction site artefact/product functionality: | | |
|     Functional/ritual | 71 | 85 |
|     Functional | 10 | 12 |
|     Ritual | 5 | 6 |
|     Wealth/status objects | 1.5 | 2 |
| Involvement of craft specialists in product manufacturing | 74 | 89 |
| Distribution of extraction site products: | | |
|     Supra-regional 200+km | 76 | 91 |
|     Regional 100–200 km | 12 | 15 |
|     Local >100 km | 12 | 14 |
| Evidence for the ceremonial use of extraction sites | 44 | 53 |
| The presence of rock art/graffiti/idols at extraction sites | 37 | 44 |
| The presence of burials at extraction sites | 25 | 30 |

but the mountains with their storied raw materials were considered *Apu*, or male 'lords', thus constructing an engendered male–female dichotomy replicating human fertility. Inkan storied raw materials were often exploited via caves or mines, which were considered portals to the underworld and were treated reverentially through the use of idols, offerings, rock art, and ritualised practices (Dean 2010). In the Ozarks (United States), Native Americans also considered caves and rock shelters as origin places and entrances to the underworld and many storied locations were exploited for flint clay extraction for the production of ceremonial objects, especially figurines (Emmerson & Hughes 2000).

Mountains can reveal unusual surface materials such as the northern Californian volcanic obsidian flows, where glass-like deposits are starkly different to underlying country rock, leading many Native American communities to view them as having *atiswin*, a transferrable supernatural power (Robinson 2004). Exposed lithologies also occur on the Plains, where pipestone (Catlinite) in Minnesota was exposed in the foreground of a locally prominent cliff face and became mythologised by many Plains tribes (Hughes & Stewart 1997). The Hidatsa sought toolstone from the higher buttes west of the Missouri because of their association with the springtime Big Bird ceremony (Bowers 1992).

Smaller storied sites can comprise individual boulders, such as those of nephrite used by the Maori who believe them to be the fossilised bodies of fish that had travelled with the first Maori settlers (Field 2012). River cobbles are storied for many New Guinea highland communities, who believe they are the remains of supernatural beings, or significant ancestors, and are therefore treated reverentially by ritual specialists to 'free' the tool within them. At the Yeineri quarries the storied locations along the Kembe River comprise boulders and outcrops which are controlled by the spirit *Elogor*, who has to be appeased before quarrying can begin (Hampton 1997, 695). Similarly, at the Ngilipitji quarry in Arnhem Land, Aboriginal Australians view quartzite nodules as supernatural 'eggs' from the Dreamtime, which are shown deference with ritual practices (Brumm 2011).

Minerals can also be storied. The Aboriginal Australian Wilgie Mia quarries also have Dreamtime associations and the ochre is believed to be the liver and gall of an ancestor known as *Mondong* and was highly valued (Flood 1995).

Overall, the raw materials from storied sites are generally visually distinctive. The associations appear to operate on two levels: first, those linked to the body of an omnipresent entity or, secondly, as materials curated by an ancestor/spirit who needs to be appeased to gain access to the resource to allow extraction.

One recurrent feature of cosmological associations with raw materials is that they are often female engendered, such as *Pachamama*, the Earth Mother of the Inka (Dean 2010, 36–9, 68). This female-gendered principle provides a 'global-scale' platform for many cosmologies, which is manifested on a local scale by focusing on specific landscape features for separate and/or complementary embodiment. In cases where ancestral or supernatural figures are recorded, female characters also predominate. For example, at the Pipestone Quarries in Minnesota, *Buffalo Calf Woman* is credited with providing the red pipestone for the Plains tribes which institutionalised smoking rituals (Matthiessen 1989, 432; Hall 1997, 77–85). In New Guinea the Una, who operate the Langda quarries, revere a mythical woman known as *Alim Yongnum* who "gives birth" to the stones in the Ey River and controls their availability' (Stout 2002, 704), while *Murbilik Kue*, a male spirit, owns the toolstone (Hampton 1997, 747–56). The Wano (New Guinea) invoke the *Mother of Axes* to assist in freeing stone from the quarry-face (Pétrequin & Pétrequin 2011; 2012). Consequently, a female-engendered cosmology can be viewed as the ideological affirmation of female fecundity and its role in the provision of valuable toolstone, metal ores, and important minerals, which are then often procured by ritualised practices. The counterpoint to such female engenderment of resources is that it is generally adult men who form extraction teams (62% [75 of 120]) and then create objects which carry a biography, transforming a female-derived substance into a symbol of male power (Table 2.1).

Consequently, the ethnography suggests that if Neolithic mines and quarries were in distinctive locations or extract unusual raw materials, we might expect to find evidence of seasonality, ritualised extraction (mostly by men), craft specialists, supra-regional product distribution, some ceremonialism, some rock art/graffiti, and rare burials.

### Ownership, or restricted access to extraction sites [75=owned; 36=not owned; 57=no data]

The ethnography records that 68% [75 of 111] of sites are owned, ranging from individual ownership (eg, village headman, New Guinea), to clans (eg, Aboriginal Australia) or tribes (eg, Lakota/Dakota). Ownership is recorded as: unspecified = 29 examples; tribal = 22; clan = 15; village = 4; an elder = 3; and an individual = 2. The data suggest corporate, group, or village ownership is most common.

Ethnography generally describes the control of resources by elders or hereditary officers who licence access, normally in a trans-egalitarian social network. The hereditary officers are often clan elders or ritual specialists who have paramount authority over the extraction sites. In contrast, open access extraction is documented amongst Plains peoples in North America (Lakota/Dakota, Mandan, Cheyenne, Sac and Fox, Pawnee, Kiowa, Ponca), Navajo in the American South-west, the Western Dani and Wano in New Guinea, and the Mata'are of the Cook Islands.

Occasionally owned sites were/are permanently occupied (eg, Mt William, Australia; Yeineri, New Guinea) but are more often located 1–5 days march from the users (eg, North America, Australia, highland New Guinea). At all owned sites access is restricted and procurement has to be negotiated and paid for. As Childs and Killick (1993, 333) have observed '[t]echnology is not a monolithic force that is somehow separate from people, but is the product of complex ideology, careful social negotiations and manipulations, and the vagaries of local resources'. Ownership is documented in all geographic regions (Table 2.2).

Consequently, if Neolithic mines and quarries were owned, indicators would include evidence of seasonality or permanent settlement, ritualised extraction, craft specialists, supra-regional product distribution, evidence of ceremonialism, rare rock art, graffiti, or burials. The strongest archaeologically visible evidence for ownership would be the occurrence of topographically distinctive settings coupled to long distance (200+ km) product distributions.

Table 2.2: The trend data for the social context of ownership

| Attribute | % of key attributes in data sub-set | No. of records in data sub-set [n=75] |
|---|---|---|
| OWNERSHIP/RESTRICTED ACCESS [n=111] (Note: 36 sites not owned; 57 provided no data) | 68% | 75 |
| Storied/mythologised source | 79 | 59 |
| Ownership/restricted access | 68 | 75 |
| Seasonal use of the resource | 36 | 27 |
| Permanently settled | 11 | 8 |
| Age/sex demographic of the extraction site workers: | | |
| Adult men | 63 | 47 |
| Women | 0 | 0 |
| Men, women & children | 21 | 16 |
| Evidence for ritualised extraction | 31 | 23 |
| Evidence for ritualised reduction | 35 | 26 |
| Extraction site artefact/product functionality: | | |
| Functional/ritual | 60 | 45 |
| Functional | 25 | 19 |
| Ritual | 7 | 5 |
| Wealth/status objects | 1 | 1 |
| Involvement of craft specialists in product manufacturing | 76 | 57 |
| Distribution of extraction site products: | | |
| Supra-regional 200+km | 75 | 56 |
| Regional 100–200 km | 17 | 13 |
| Local >100 km | 7 | 5 |
| Evidence for the ceremonial use of extraction sites | 21 | 16 |
| The presence of rock art/graffiti/idols at extraction sites | 8 | 6 |
| The presence of burials at extraction sites | 5 | 4 |

### Seasonal use [74=seasonality; 8=permanently inhabited sites; 1=no access; 85=no data]

In some cases, eg, parts of North America and New Guinea, climate determined when extraction was possible, and seasonality became a pragmatic response to it in 90% [74 of 82] of studies. In contrast, only 5% [8 of 168] of sites were/are permanently settled by controlling clans (eg, highland New Guinea) or quarry custodians (eg, Australia) (Table 2.3).

If Neolithic extraction sites were used seasonally, the data suggest they would likely be storied locations, witness ritualised extraction, involve craft specialists, have supra-regional product distribution, evidence of ceremonialism, and a few feature rock art, graffiti, and rare burials.

### Age/sex demographic of extraction site users [108=male teams; 21=mixed sex and children; 2=female teams; 37=no data]

Extraction site users are predominantly adult males (North America, Australia, Europe, New Guinea), with mixed gender teams at a minority of sites (Africa, New Guinea, New Zealand), and female-only enterprises are rare (Africa, Australia). Certain male teams and most of the mixed sex teams feature children in support roles, usually male apprentices.

The extraction team demographic is recorded in 131 of 168 studies. Of these 82.5% [108 of 131] were male teams, 16% [21 of 131] comprised mixed sex teams with children, and 1.5% [2 of 131] were female-only teams; 37 studies provided no data.

The rare examples of female users occur in Africa amongst the Konso, where stone procurement and tool manufacture are considered female activity (Arthur 2010), and in Tasmania, where Tiwi women mined ochre (Plomley 1966). Consequently, although exceptional cases, women do demonstrably undertake extraction in certain social contexts.

Age/sex roles are important aspects of extraction teams: male only groups generally practice ritualised extraction and produce extensively distributed symbolic implements. Mixed age/sex groups, often involving children, are less likely to practice ritualised extraction and products frequently have a ritual/functional duality but are also widely distributed. Finally, female groups can use ritual practices and some products are extensively distributed (eg, ochre; Plomley 1966).

The determination of the age/sex demo-

## 2 The ethnography of lithic extraction

Table 2.3: The evidence for seasonal use/permanently settled sites

| SEASONAL USE [n=82]<br>(Note: 8 permanently inhabited sites; 1 no access; 85 no data)<br>Attribute | 90%<br>% of key attributes in data sub-set | 74<br>No. of records in data sub-set [n=74] |
|---|---|---|
| Storied/mythologised source | 88 | 65 |
| Ownership/restricted access | 36 | 27 |
| Seasonal use of the resource | 90 | 74 |
| Permanently settled | 11 | 8 |
| Age/sex demographic of the extraction site workers: | | |
| Adult men | 70 | 52 |
| Women | 1 | 1 |
| Men, women & children | 3 | 2 |
| Evidence for ritualised extraction | 70 | 52 |
| Evidence for ritualised reduction | 47 | 35 |
| Extraction site artefact/product functionality: | | |
| Functional/ritual | 82 | 61 |
| Functional | 11 | 8 |
| Ritual | 5 | 4 |
| Wealth/status objects | 0 | 0 |
| Involvement of craft specialists in product manufacturing | 76 | 56 |
| Distribution of extraction site products: | | |
| Supra-regional 200+km | 70 | 52 |
| Regional 100–200 km | 13 | 10 |
| Local >100 km | 7 | 5 |
| Evidence for the ceremonial use of extraction sites | 49 | 36 |
| The presence of rock art/graffiti/idols at extraction sites | 49 | 36 |
| The presence of burials at extraction sites | 32 | 24 |

graphic of work groups in Neolithic sites is problematic as the archaeological evidence comprises formal burials, casual interments, or body parts, which are often difficult to confidently contextualise socially without detailed skeletal analysis. Does the skeletal data represent site users or non-users, and if the latter, what level of association did they have with the site?

### Evidence for ritualised extraction
### [67=present; 6=absent; 95=no data]

Ritualised extraction practices are recorded in 92% [67 of 73] of the ethnography (six studies recorded they were absent). The greatest concentration occurs in North America [32], followed by New Guinea [16], Australia [14], Europe [3], and South America [2], demonstrating that this phenomenon was not restricted geographically.

The North American data is found among the Lakota/Dakota, the Mandan, Hidatsa, Athna, Dena'ina, Yakutat, Oglala, Cheyenne, Sac and Fox, Pawnee, Kiowa, Ponca, and Navajo, spanning communities in the Midwest, Plains, North-west and South-west. In New Guinea, ritualised extraction occurred among highland tribes including the Tungei, Kawelka, Tipuka, Palke, Tumalke, Okimeni-Kisingambka, Make, Wano, Western Dani, Una, Kimyal, Dani, and Ormu. In Australia the Yolngu, Jawoyn, Wardaman, Nunggubuyu, Tiwi, Ngawayil, Kakadu, Warramungu, Yir Yoront, Wiradjuri, and Gunwinggu peoples use ritualised extraction. Taken together, this demonstrates that ritualised extraction occurs in many regions and unrelated cultural contexts, and is not an isolated practice, it is a mechanism which connects procurement to the cosmology and ideologies of indigenous communities (Table 2.4).

Table 2.4 lists attributes associated with records of extraction rituals. From this we might expect that if Neolithic extraction sites followed similar ritualised practices they would be storied locations, incorporate placed deposits in the workings, involve craft specialists, have supra-regional product distribution, provide evidence of ceremonialism, and some sites will feature rock art, graffiti, and rare burials.

### Ritualised tool production [68=present; 9=absent; 91=no data]

Ritualised tool manufacture is recorded in 88% [68 of 77] of studies (nine studies recorded it was absent). This practice is generally

Table 2.4: The attributes associated with ritualised extraction

| RITUALISED EXTRACTION [n=73] (Note: 6 negative data; 95 no data) Attribute | 92% % of key attributes in data sub-set | 67 No. of records in data sub-set [n=67] |
|---|---|---|
| Storied/mythologised source | 93 | 62 |
| Ownership/restricted access | 34 | 23 |
| Seasonal use of the resource | 78 | 52 |
| Permanently settled | 0 | 0 |
| Age/sex demographic of the extraction site workers: | | |
| Adult men | 73 | 49 |
| Women | 0 | 0 |
| Men, women & children | 0 | 0 |
| Evidence for ritualised extraction | 92 | 67 |
| Evidence for ritualised reduction | 52 | 35 |
| Extraction site artefact/product functionality: | | |
| Functional/ritual | 79 | 53 |
| Functional | 10 | 7 |
| Ritual | 3 | 2 |
| Wealth/status objects | 0 | 0 |
| Involvement of craft specialists in product manufacturing | 72 | 48 |
| Distribution of extraction site products: | | |
| Supra-regional 200+km | 76 | 51 |
| Regional 100–200 km | 13 | 9 |
| Local >100 km | 9 | 6 |
| Evidence for the ceremonial use of extraction sites | 55 | 37 |
| The presence of rock art/graffiti/idols at extraction sites | 57 | 38 |
| The presence of burials at extraction sites | 37 | 25 |

designed to appease supernatural forces during production and can also objectify the artefact, as exemplified by the Sabarl axehead with its 'richly layered iconography' incorporating human physiology and reproduction (Battaglia 1990, 133–4; Table 2.5).

The symbolism of ritualised production operates at different levels. In Africa, for example, 'complicated technologies are made comprehensible by analogy to other natural or social processes. Metallurgy in Africa is explained by analogy to human physiology and to theories of social structure and social process' (Childs & Killick 1993, 325). Consequently, ritualised production forms part of social renewal and the reaffirmation of shared beliefs. Additionally, the ritualised 'modification of stone … can sometimes be seen not so much as a creative activity, but instead as a release of entities already residing in the stone' (Boivin 2004, 5), a process which harnesses supernatural powers within material culture for specific purposes in society (cf. Brumm 2004, 157).

*Extraction site product functionality [156=records of functionality; 12=no data]*
Extraction site products have a range of uses from mundane functionality to ceremonialism. However, an important caveat is that functional objects can be converted by appropriate rituals into ceremonial items during their use-life (Hampton 1997, 279; Topping 2017, 81–90).

The ethnography records that 75% [117 of 156] of extraction site products had a ritual/functional duality; 19% [29 of 156] were purely functional; 4% [7 of 156] were purely ritual objects; 2% [3 of 156] were wealth/status objects; 12 of 168 records provided no data.

Archaeological indicators of functionality include evidence/absence of use-wear, context and juxtaposition with other objects in an assemblage, and deposition in hoards/caches. As a general rule, absence of use-wear must indicate curation and use in non-functional activities such as wealth, status or identity displays, in burials, or in ritual performances.

## 2 The ethnography of lithic extraction

Table 2.5: The attributes associated with ritualised tool production

| RITUALISED TOOL PRODUCTION [n=77]<br>(Note: 9 negative data; 91 no data)<br>Attributes | 88%<br>% of key attributes in data sub-set | 68<br>No. of records in data sub-set [n=68] |
|---|---|---|
| Storied/mythologised source | 85 | 58 |
| Ownership/restricted access | 38 | 26 |
| Seasonal use of the resource | 51 | 35 |
| Permanently settled | 3 | 2 |
| Age/sex demographic of the extraction site workers: | | |
| Adult men | 60 | 41 |
| Women | 0 | 0 |
| Men, women & children | 24 | 16 |
| Evidence for ritualised extraction | 51 | 35 |
| Evidence for ritualised reduction | 88 | 68 |
| Extraction site artefact/product functionality: | | |
| Functional/ritual | 79 | 54 |
| Functional | 15 | 10 |
| Ritual | 6 | 4 |
| Wealth/status objects | 0 | 0 |
| Involvement of craft specialists in product manufacturing | 99 | 67 |
| Distribution of extraction site products: | | |
| Supra-regional 200+km | 76 | 52 |
| Regional 100–200 km | 3 | 2 |
| Local >100 km | 12 | 8 |
| Evidence for the ceremonial use of extraction sites | 60 | 41 |
| The presence of rock art/graffiti/idols at extraction sites | 37 | 25 |
| The presence of burials at extraction sites | 37 | 25 |

### Involvement of craft specialists
*[118=presence; 6=absence; 44=no data]*

Craft specialists can operate from a variety of locations. Many begin preliminary production at the extraction site with finishing off-site (eg, New Guinea, Australia), whereas others remove unaltered raw material to off-site workshops (eg, Pipestone Quarries).

The ethnography records craft specialists in 95% [118 of 124] of studies; 95 cases record the age/sex demographic and of these 94% [89 of 95] were male, 4% [4 of 95] were mixed sex, and 2% [2 of 95] female. As with extraction teams, craft specialists are predominantly male. Occasionally children undertake support roles or apprenticeships (eg, New Guinea, Africa; Table 2.6).

The identification of craft specialist production at Neolithic extraction sites is problematic and often inferred from subjective assessments of knapping expertise. However, ethnography records that even relatively mundane objects such as scrapers can be manufactured by recognised craft specialists but they may not exhibit great production skill – unlike certain over-sized ceremonial axeheads. Yet both types of object were produced by people recognised as craft specialists by their communities. Consequently, although archaeology can assess technical skill, without recourse to direct witness evidence it is difficult to identify definitively the work of a craft specialist.

### Distribution of extraction site products
*[146=evidence; 22=no data]*

One hundred and forty-six of 168 studies recorded the scale of extraction site product distribution, and 22 provided no data. The greatest distances of 200+ km from source were recorded in 73% [107 of 146] of studies, 19% [28 of 146] recorded distances of 100–200 km, and 8% [11 of 146] were within 100 km of the extraction site. Ethnographically, the highest value is placed on objects which have travelled the greatest distances and originate from culturally important sources.

If we consider the general context of these distributions against six archaeologically visible characteristics (Table 2.7), the data demonstrates that only 200+ km corresponds

Table 2.6: The attributes associated with craft specialists

| INVOLVEMENT OF CRAFT SPECIALISTS [n=124] (Note: 6 negative data; 44 no data) Attributes | 95% % of key attributes in data sub-set | 118 No. of records in data sub-set [n=118] |
|---|---|---|
| Storied/mythologised source | 82 | 97 |
| Ownership/restricted access | 52 | 61 |
| Seasonal use of the resource | 49 | 58 |
| Permanently settled | 7 | 8 |
| Age/sex demographic of the extraction site workers: | | |
| Adult men | 66 | 78 |
| Women | 2 | 2 |
| Men, women & children | 17 | 20 |
| Evidence for ritualised extraction | 40 | 47 |
| Evidence for ritualised reduction | 56 | 66 |
| Extraction site artefac/product functionality: | | |
| Functional/ritual | 70 | 83 |
| Functional | 22 | 26 |
| Ritual | 4 | 5 |
| Wealth/status objects | 2 | 2 |
| Involvement of craft specialists in product manufacturing | 95 | 118 |
| Distribution of extraction site products: | | |
| Supra-regional 200+ km | 70 | 83 |
| Regional 100–200 km | 16 | 19 |
| Local >100 km | 9 | 11 |
| Evidence for the ceremonial use of extraction sites | 36 | 43 |
| The presence of rock art/graffiti/idols at extraction sites | 25 | 30 |
| The presence of burials at extraction sites | 24 | 29 |

Table 2.7: Ethnographic product distributions by distance against potentially archaeologically visible features (no data: n = 22 of 168)

| Distance | Storied sites | Owned sites | Ritualised extraction | Ceremonial after-use | Rock art/graffiti/idols | Human burials |
|---|---|---|---|---|---|---|
| 200+km = 73% [n=107 of 146] | 85% [n=91] | 50% [n=54] | 48% [n=51] | 49% [n=52] | 41% [n=44] | 27% [n=29] |
| 100–200 km = 19% [n=28 of 146] | 50% [n=14] | 61% [n=17] | 32% [n=9] | 0 | 0 | 0 |
| <100 km = 8% [n=11 of 146] | 73% [n=8] | 55% [n=6] | 55% [n=6] | 9% [n=11] | 0 | 0 |

with all six. Additionally, this data establishes the fact that mythologised/storied extraction sites and ritualised extraction practices were important at all levels of product distribution.

'Unlike settlements, quarries are unique because … these sites are likely to have been the only component of the exchange system which had a link to every other locality where the stone was made, used and discarded' (Torrence 1986, 91). 'Down-the-line' systems (cf. Renfrew 1975; 1993) are common, although ethnography often records socio-political situations which can affect distributions and be difficult to identify in the archaeological record (cf. Godelier 1999). One of the most common phenomenon associated with down-the-line exchange is a decrease in abundance with increasing distance from the source, which may be the impact of consumers periodically retaining traded goods during onward transit, thus decreasing availability (Chappell 1987, 72–3). However, the ethnographic data presented above suggests this may be too simplistic a model, and 200+ km distribution is most prevalent, which may be seen in the archaeological record with Groups I and VI axeheads (Clough & Cummins 1988; Cooney & Mandal 1998), or those of Alpine jade (Pétrequin et al. 2012a).

## 2 The ethnography of lithic extraction

| CEREMONIAL USE OF EXTRACTION SITES [n=58]<br>(Note: 3 negative data; 110 no data)<br>Attribute | 95%<br>% of key attributes in data sub-set | 55<br>No. of records in data sub-set [n=55] |
|---|---|---|
| Storied/mythologised source | 96 | 53 |
| Ownership/restricted access | 29 | 16 |
| Seasonal use of the resource | 67 | 37 |
| Permanently settled | 0 | 0 |
| Age/sex demographic of the extraction site workers: | | |
| Adult males | 47 | 26 |
| Women | 0 | 0 |
| Men, women & children | 27 | 15 |
| Evidence for ritualised extraction | 67 | 37 |
| Involvement of craft specialists in product manufacturing | 78 | 43 |
| Evidence for ritualised reduction | 74 | 41 |
| Extraction site artefact/product functionality: | | |
| Functional/ritual | 93 | 51 |
| Functional | 2 | 1 |
| Ritual | 4 | 2 |
| Wealth/status objects | 0 | 0 |
| Distribution of extraction site products: | | |
| Supra-regional 200+ km | 94 | 52 |
| Regional 100–200 km | 0 | 0 |
| Local >100 km | 2 | 1 |
| Evidence for the ceremonial use of extraction sites | 95 | 55 |
| The presence of rock art/graffiti/idols at extraction sites | 67 | 37 |
| The presence of burials at extraction sites | 45 | 25 |

Table 2.8: The attributes associated with the ceremonial use of extraction sites

### Evidence for the ceremonial use of extraction sites [55=present; 3=absent; 110=no data]

Some extraction sites have secondary roles as ceremonial venues, generally linked to cultural renewal and rites of passage. An example is the Pipestone Quarries (Minnesota) where burial mounds are located on-site, and a sundance circle and sweat lodges provide arenas for rituals and ceremonialism (Hughes 1995; Hughes & Stewart 1997; Scott *et al.* 2006).

The ethnography records 95% [55 of 58] of sites host pre- or post-extraction ceremonies. The greatest number occur in North America [25], associated with the Lakota/Dakota, the Mandan, Cheyenne, Sac and Fox, Pawnee, Kiowa, and Ponca peoples. Africa has the second largest number [15], mostly associated with metal workers, and Australia provides evidence from 12 communities. Only three sites were definitively recorded as not being used for ceremonial purposes, and 110 provided no data (Table 2.8).

Archaeologically, pre- or post-extraction ceremonialism can leave behind evidence of hearths, structures and assemblages in the immediate environs of the site, or in the abandonment sequence of a site; rock art/graffiti is likely.

### Rock art, graffiti, or idols at extraction sites [46=present; 122=no data]

Rock art, graffiti, or the use of idols is recorded in 27% [46 of 168] of the ethnography. North America provides 26 records, Australia 19, and South America 1. However, 73% [122 of 168] of ethnography provided no data, consequently it is possible this trend is under-represented (Table 2.9).

The data indicates that the strongest associations between sites featuring rock art, graffiti and idols is related to seasonal use, ritualised extraction, and long distance (200+ km) product distribution.

### Human burials at extraction sites [30=present; 138=no data]

The ethnography documents human burials in 18% [30 of 168] of studies (North America = 25; Australia = 5). In North America the Pipestone Quarries are the major record, where Plains tribes buried their dead in small earthen mounds adjacent to the quarries, as depicted by George Catlin in 1836–37 (cf. Pratt & Troccoli 2013, 150–1) and recorded by archaeology

Table 2.9: The attributes associated with the use of rock art, graffiti and idols

| ROCK ART/GRAFFITI/IDOLS AT EXTRACTION SITES [n=168] (Note: 122 no data) Attributes | 27% | 46 |
|---|---|---|
|  | % of key attributes in data sub-set | No. of records in data sub-set [n=46] |
| Storied/mythologised source | 96 | 44 |
| Ownership/restricted access | 13 | 6 |
| Seasonal use of the resource | 78 | 36 |
| Permanently settled | 0 | 0 |
| Age/sex demographic of the extraction site workers: |  |  |
| Adult males | 63 | 29 |
| Women | 0 | 0 |
| Men, women & children | 0 | 0 |
| Evidence for ritualised extraction | 85 | 39 |
| Evidence for ritualised reduction | 54 | 25 |
| Extraction site artefact/product functionality: |  |  |
| Functional/ritual | 78 | 36 |
| Functional | 0 | 0 |
| Ritual | 6 | 3 |
| Wealth/status objects | 0 | 0 |
| Involvement of craft specialists in product manufacturing | 65 | 30 |
| Distribution of extraction site products: |  |  |
| Supra-regional 200+ km | 98 | 45 |
| Regional 100–200 km | 0 | 0 |
| Local >100 km | 0 | 0 |
| Evidence for the ceremonial use of extraction sites | 80 | 37 |
| The presence of rock art/graffiti/idols at extraction sites | 27 | 46 |
| The presence of burials at extraction sites | 65 | 30 |

(Scott *et al.* 2006). In Australia the Yolngu, Yir Yoront, Mimi, Mara-larr-mirri and Gurrka-larr-mirri Aboriginal communities interred burials at extraction sites. However, 82% [138 of 168] of the ethnography provided no data, raising the question of how representative this small sample may be (Table 2.10).

The data suggests that if applied to archaeological sites, extraction sites which feature burials may be linked to storied locations, seasonal use, ritualised extraction, use craft specialists, be involved in long distance product distribution (200+ km), employ sites for ceremonial use of sites, and feature rock art/graffiti.

## Implications for the archaeological record

Several trends are apparent from this ethnographic sample. Despite conventional expectations that extraction is generally driven by economic forces and functional requirements, the ethnography provides a substantial body of evidence that documents other motivations. This is particularly true of ritualised extraction practices which generally lead to the provision of objects which can produce significant societal outcomes. The strongest evidence of ritualisation occurs at lithic and metal-producing sites where roughly twice as many are mythologised/storied locations compared to those producing minerals. Mythologisation and the role of cosmographic ordering in explaining cultural origins are often associated with extraction, so that the act of procurement goes beyond the functional and into the sacred. Consequently, socially sanctioned extraction is thus generally ritualised, whereas expedient procurement for functional requirements is not.

If the aggregated ethnographic data is synthesised from the 168 studies it provides the following trends:

- **95%** [55 of 58] **ceremonial use of sites** [55 present; 3 absent; 110 no data] (95% is arrived at by adding 55 records of presence to 3 definitive records of absence, thus 58 in total. Therefore 55 is 95% of 58. 110 records provided no data so were not included in the calculation)
- **95%** [118 of 124] **craft specialists** [118 present; 6 absent; 44 no data]

## 2 The ethnography of lithic extraction

| BURIALS AT EXTRACTION SITES [n=168]<br>(Note: 138 no data)<br>Attributes | 18%<br><br>% of key attributes in data sub-set | 30<br><br>No. of records in data sub-set [n=30] |
|---|---|---|
| Storied/mythologised source | 100 | 30 |
| Ownership/restricted access | 13 | 4 |
| Seasonal use of the resource | 80 | 24 |
| Permanently settled | 0 | 0 |
| Age/sex demographic of the extraction site workers: | | |
| Adult males | 97 | 29 |
| Women | 0 | 0 |
| Men, women & children | 0 | 0 |
| Evidence for ritualised extraction | 83 | 25 |
| Evidence for ritualised reduction | 83 | 25 |
| Extraction site artefact/product functionality: | | |
| Functional/ritual | 76 | 23 |
| Functional | 0 | 0 |
| Ritual | 7 | 2 |
| Wealth/status objects | 0 | 0 |
| Involvement of craft specialists in product manufacturing | 97 | 29 |
| Distribution of extraction site products: | | |
| Supra-regional 200+ km | 97 | 29 |
| Regional 100–200 km | 0 | 0 |
| Local >100 km | 0 | 0 |
| Evidence for the ceremonial use of extraction sites | 83 | 25 |
| The presence of rock art/graffiti/idols at extraction sites | 100 | 30 |
| The presence of burials at extraction sites | 18 | 30 |

Table 2.10: The attributes associated with human burials at extraction sites

- **93%** [120 of 129] **storied/mythologised associations** [120 present; 9 negative; 39 no data]
- **92%** [67 of 73] **ritualised extraction** [67 present; 6 absent; 95 no data]
- **90%** [74 of 82] **seasonal use** [74 present; 8 permanently inhabited sites; 1 no access to sites; 85 no data]
- **88%** [68 of 77] **ritualised tool production** [68 present; 9 absent; 91 no data]
- **73%** [107 of 146] **product distribution 200+ km**; **19%** [28 of 146] **100–200 km distribution**; **8%** [11 of 146] **<100 km distribution**; 22 of 168 no data
- **68%** [75 of 111] **evidence of ownership** [75 present; 31 not owned; 5 communities no access to sites; 57 no data]
- **64%** [108 of 168] **male-only extraction teams**; **13%** [21 of 168] featured **mixed age/gender teams**; **1%** [2 of 168] recorded **female-only teams**; 37 of 168 provided no data
- **27%** [46 of 168] **rock art/graffiti/idols**; 122 of 168 provided no data
- **18%** [30 of 168] **burials**; 138 of 168 provided no data

One of the strongest correlations lies between mythologised/storied locations and long distance product distributions (200+ km), which is found associated with 78% [94 of 120] of sites. In these examples extraction teams are predominantly male, and the site/raw material is often gendered female. The men involved are often specialists brought together by relatives or clan/kinship affiliates, and many undergo apprenticeships or initiations. Political power and status can rest upon access/ownership of the sacred power embodied in extraction site products. Importantly, some artefacts can be transformed from an original functional purpose into sacred/wealth/status objects at a later time by ritual interventions, and there is some connection between certain products and bodily symbolism (eg, Battaglia 1990; Hall 1997). As a result, extraction practices are repeatedly intertwined with social conventions, and form part of the creation of identity, status, and power for many communities.

The potential of this new ethnoarchaeological model is lent weight by briefly testing it against two examples. In Pharaonic Egypt, where prehistory meets recorded history, the

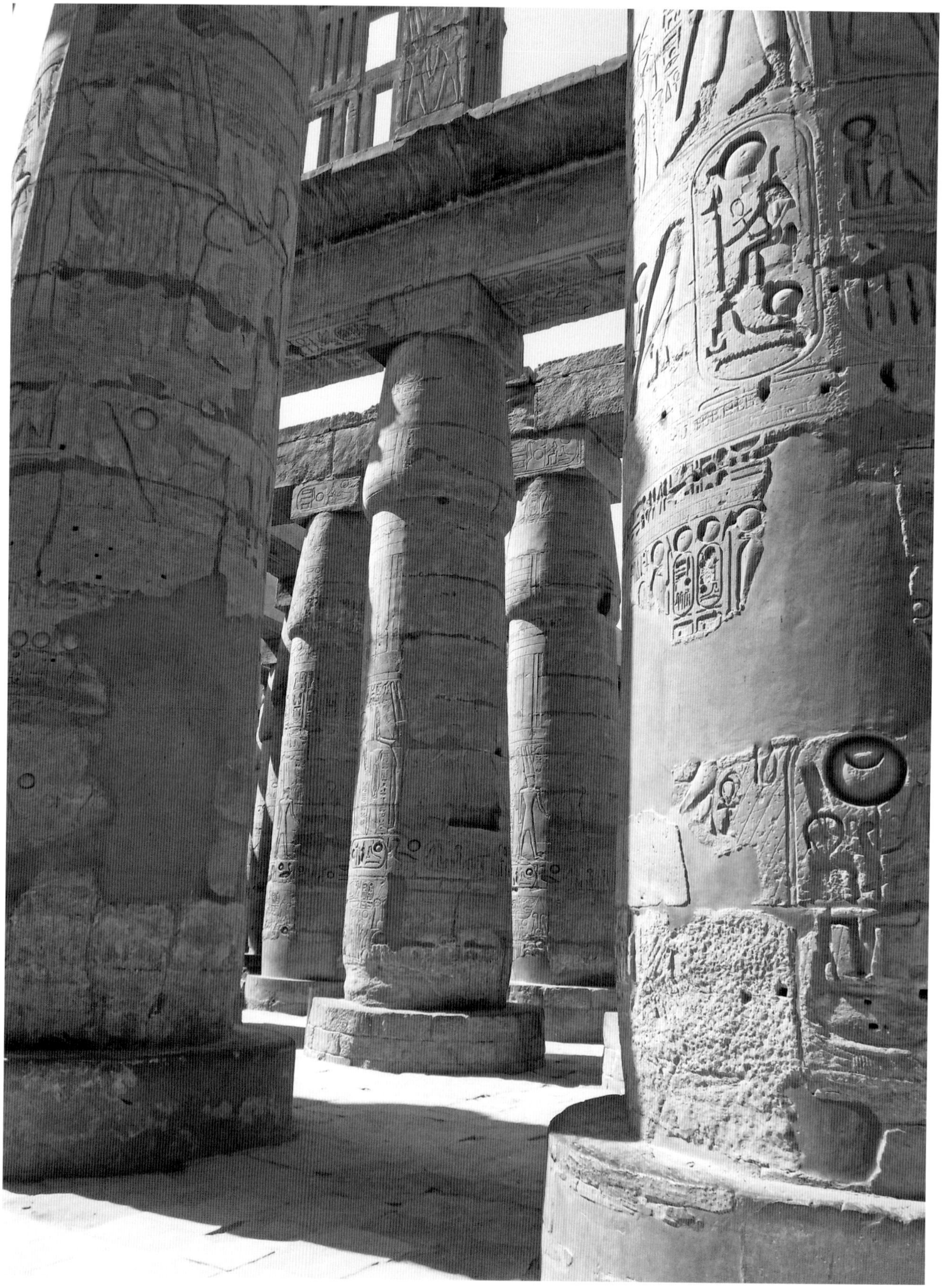

18th Dynasty quarries at Gebel el-Silsila (lying on both banks of the Nile), was an important quarry that provided sandstone for temples at Karnac (Fig. 2.1), Luxor, Amarna, Medinet Habu, Kom Ombo, and the Ramesseum (Kucharek 2012; Nilsson *et al*. 2015). The quarries are located where the Nile narrows at a place where the annual inundation of the river was celebrated. Consequently, the quarry location had a strong link with agricultural fertility engendered by the Nile floods, which underpinned the choice of this stone for the construction of important temples. The quarries had an association with Egyptian cosmology by being dedicated to the crocodile god *Sobek* who controlled the river, and they were decorated with graffiti. Stelae defined the quarry boundaries, and shrines were constructed near the river where they were the first point of contact for visitors. Gebel el-Silsila is one of many Egyptian quarries with evidence of storied associations and ritualised practices (eg, Harrell & Storemyr 2009; Bloxam 2015), demonstrating how stone extraction was used to maintain ideologies and people's links with specific places and events. In addition to construction materials, some Dynastic quarry products had important spiritual uses. One of the most notable was the 'Opening of the Mouth' ritual from the Book of the Dead, when a ceremonial axe was touched against the mouth of a mummy to re-animate the body and allow the deceased to recover the ability to eat, drink, and talk during its journey through the afterlife. This ritual is depicted on the wall paintings in Tutankhamun's burial chamber, for example (Shaw 2014, 169–73).

In South America, late 19th century Spanish sources recorded Inka quarries which were considered sacred, and the raw material was used as a metonym for origin stories (Dean 2010, 50–4). Gold and silver mines excavated into the flanks of 'animate' mountains were believed to lie at the interface between the Upper and Lower Worlds. Rituals were conducted before mining took place to petition the mountain to surrender its mineral wealth. These were focussed on the *huaca*, an idol embodying the spiritual essence of the mountain and crafted from a block of stone which included the metals or minerals being sought. These idols were revered, petitioned, and toasted with appropriate drinks to release the metals. The practice of extraction thus became a ritualised interaction with mountain spirits (Saunders 2004, 126). In parallel, the Inka also excavated subterranean tunnels to communicate directly with the Lower World of the Ancestors and *Pachamama*, and these were decorated with graffiti (Dean 2010, 90–1).

If these observations are applied to archaeological sites, it suggests that Neolithic extraction was probably not driven by economic imperatives or market forces. Instead, other motivations linked to cosmology, power relations, ideology, indebtedness, inequality, identity, and status – which all feature in ethnography – probably also lay behind much of the stone extraction in European prehistory.

*Figure 2.1: (opposite) The Great Hypostyle Hall in the Karnak temple complex, built during the 18th–20th Dynasties using stone sourced from quarries along the banks of the Nile (photo: author)*

# 3

# Ethnographic snapshots of traditional extraction practices

This chapter provides a series of snapshots of traditional extraction practices ranging from prospection to procurement, and from production to use and deposition, drawn from the 168 case studies consulted for this research. It illustrates the rich cultural diversity that exists in the ethnographic record, much of which can be inferred from the material remains surviving in the archaeological record. These snapshots are arranged under the ethnographic trends identified in Chapter 2.

## Storied sources

The Red Pipestone Quarries in Minnesota have a far-reaching ideological significance for many Plains tribes who believe the Great Spirit and/or *Buffalo Calf Woman* created the pipestone and bequeathed the sacred pipe and smoking rituals to the Plains communities (Hall 1997, 77–85). Symbolically, the red pipestone embodies the Native American ethos, as epitomised by an encounter in 1836 between George Catlin and Plains tribes when he was told 'You see (holding a red pipe to the side of his naked arm) that this pipe is a part of our flesh. The red men are a part of the red stone' (Matthiessen 1989, 432). Consequently, the pipestone quarries centre indigenous ideologies directly to a specific place in the landscape, creating physical links between the Plains peoples and their spiritual beliefs through the procurement and use of a raw material which carried a strong cultural biography (Fig. 3.1).

The Hidatsa of the Mid-western Plains practised ritualised flint procurement and tool production. The flint was sourced from the higher buttes and uplands west of the Missouri,

*Figure 3.1: Pipestone Quarries (Minnesota). A photograph taken by Samuel Calvin around 1900 of Native Americans using traditional methods to quarry through overlying Sioux Quartzite to expose the red pipestone (photograph courtesy of the Calvin Collection, Department of Geoscience, University of Iowa (Lantern slide 2566: Photograph No. 258))*

and quarrying was initiated at the springtime Big Bird ceremony by sacred bundle keepers who controlled procurement and knapping activities (Bowers 1992, 166, 370). As a result, flint extraction for the Hidatsa became symbolically linked to cosmology and tribal ceremonialism and was facilitated by ritualised extraction and production.

Around the Great Lakes the Ojibwe believed a spirit entity known as *Mishebeshu* (the Underwater Manitou) controlled both food availability and access to copper resources:

> It gave copper to the Indians, who cut the metal from the being's horns as it raised them above the surface of the water ... Those who attempted to take the copper without offering proper payment met severe punishment from the Underwater Manitou. It was a creature to inspire terror and awe, as well as reverence. (Vecsey 1983, 74–5, quoted in Clark & Martin 2005, 118–19)

For the Ojibwe, offerings to the Underwater Manitou were an essential preliminary to copper procurement which ensured success and maintained a balance with the supernatural world.

'In the South American Andes, in the fifteenth and early sixteenth centuries, the Inka (Inca) framed, carved, sat on, built with, revered, fed, clothed, and talked to certain rocks' (Dean 2010, 1). In Inka cosmographic ordering many topographic features were kratophanic, places where humans could interact directly with powerful numina. These could be natural landforms, man-made structures, or a combination of both, but Andean spirits rarely inhabited representational statuary. The Inka believed that supernatural essence was trans-substantial and independent of form, therefore the varied morphology of stone was also considered trans-substantial and represented a living entity whose animacy has temporarily been 'paused'. The Inkan relationship with stone was aniconic, and considered lithic forms endowed with meaning, and such anicons could embody entities, ideas, or actions. Consequently, stone as a substance could be both sacred and profane and was capable of actively participating in the natural environment and in human society. However, the embodiment of landscape features did not include all rocks. The cosmology was selective and only rocks deemed special were revered. It was the *potential* animacy of a rock or landform rather than any superficial appearance that created significance to the Inka. These rocks/landforms became foci for ritual activity and offerings, which included llamas or even children, and were part of communal legitimisation. Interestingly, the special nature of embodied rock allowed it to transfer 'essence' to different places as a portable metonym. Indeed, in Inka stories soil and rock are metaphors for flesh and bone, consequently much of the landscape was considered parts of a procreative 'body' (Dean 2010, 1–22, 62, 75, 177).

Landscape features were important to the Inka. Mountains, for example, were considered sacred, and believed to be *Apu* (lords) who were powerful male entities that watched over communities and controlled weather patterns. In contrast, other Andean cultures personified the rugged highlands as *Mama Quqa* (Mother Rock), and certain powerful rocks could be engendered as female. Although female gendering is common, this example demonstrates that adjacent contemporary communities can adopt different gender schemes for the cultural landscape. Caves were believed to be portals to the underworld or the supernatural, places where worlds converged. Caves and crevices were considered feminine origin places from where ancestors first emerged to populate the world, and rock art was used to decorate these trans-dimensional portals to symbolise transition and orchestrate encounters with the supernatural (Dean 2010, 27–34, 55–61, 73, 95).

Brumm (2011, 92) states that 'The evidence from [Australian] Aboriginal myths, whilst incomplete, seems to hint at the importance of stone axes in the creation of the Kulin landscape by powerful Ancestral Beings'. The sourcing and production of stone axeheads and minerals in Aboriginal Australia played a pivotal role in maintaining Dreamtime beliefs (Taçon 2004) and particular stones and minerals are associated with the body parts/emissions of Ancestral Beings as they travelled across the continent (Boivin 2004, 7). At the Wilgie Mia ochre mine (Western Australia), the ochre deposits represent the place a great kangaroo was slain by an Ancestor known as *Mondong* (Flood 1995, 271–3). Here the kangaroo's blood became fossilised as red ochre, its liver became yellow ochre, and its gall turned into green ochre. The final leap of the kangaroo took it beyond Wilgie Mia to an adjacent hill known as Little

Wilgie, which was also mined for ochre. The embodied ochre from these mines was highly valued for rituals, particularly the red ochre, and lengthy expeditions were undertaken to procure it. Similarly, supernatural forces at the Ngilipitji blade quarry (Arnhem Land) encourage quartzite nodules to grow in the ground 'like a living thing' and this 'pregnancy' leads to the birth of 'baby stones' or 'eggs' of toolstone (Brumm 2011, 92).

The western and central desert Aboriginal communities travelled great distances to procure Dreamtime-associated raw materials:

> some quarries occur at or near sacred sites – that is, totemic 'dreaming' places. People who believe themselves to be descended patrilineally from the particular totemic being at one of these sites will make special trips to the quarry to secure stone there. A man places a high value on stone from a site of his dreamtime totem. Stone like this is often transported over long distance (as much as 500 km) and is given to distant kinsmen of the same patrilineage ... [b]ecause of his patrilineal relationship to the site, a man sees the stone as part of his own being ... (Gould 1977, 164)

As Brumm (2010, 179) has observed regarding the Mount William axeheads '[a] detailed consideration of the ethnohistorical evidence highlights the embeddedness of axe technology in cultural perceptions of landscape and the belief systems of Aboriginal people', and the interrelatedness between communities and their cultural landscape. Consequently, certain stones and minerals are an integral part of 'being' Aboriginal, and a material representation of their Dreamtime identity.

The Dani and other communities of the New Guinea highlands believe that the Ancestors emerged from caves or crevices; consequently, they are considered sacred and used for ritual observations (Hampton 1997, 54–5). Origin myths describe how the first Ancestor was created from earth and rock: 'Rock is hard and is for man. Earth (or soil) is soft and adds flexibility' (*ibid.*, 55); stone artefacts became associated with origin myths and the Ancestors. The wider cultural landscape is believed to be animate which, although not conscious, is inhabited by Ancestral (derived from humans) and non-Ancestral (mythical) spirits, creating an embodied landscape of the seen and unseen. Consequently, highlanders are highly respectful of the omni-present spirit world and actively placate it with rituals led by the Big Man at pig festivals designed to prevent malevolent supernatural actions (*ibid.*, 52–9).

Unusual rock formations are one of the most potent locations inhabited by supernatural entities, many of which are decorated with pictographs that are ritually re-activated every 4–5 years by ceremonies involving rites of passage (*ibid.*, 75).

Ideologically, the stone artefacts of New Guinea highland communities are believed to pre-exist within the toolstone, which is believed to be the remains of denizens of origin myths. In the Yeleme massif the toolstone is understood to be the fossilised remains of a Primordial Giant who emerged from a cave at the dawn of time but was killed by the Wano tribe and eaten. This mythologised source requires interaction from ritual specialists who use fire-setting to release the toolstone, then set about to 'free' axeheads from the quarried material. It is the supernatural power and ceremonialism employed by these ritual specialists which enables the axeheads to successfully emerge from the bedrock. If, however, fire-setting fails, the quarry face is rubbed with pig fat to solicit assistance from the *Mother of Axes*. The Una also appeal to several female spirits for help to release adzeheads (Pétrequin & Pétrequin 2011, 339–40; 2012, 32). The involvement of female deities in many cultural contexts (eg, North America, New Guinea) is a recurrent theme in the ethnography of extraction, creating male and female dichotomies, with the male role often being fulfilled by the quarry teams and the female role being implicit in the ideologies linked to the extraction sites – the practice of extraction therefore arguably mirroring human procreation.

Amongst the Maori, green nephrite sources were linked to origin myths and considered sacred. The nephrite boulders are believed to be the fossilised bodies of fish which journeyed to New Zealand with the first Maori settlers, and when crafted into meres (axeheads/adzeheads) are used in ritual roles by the community (Field 2012, 58).

## Ownership or restricted access to extraction sites

Native American sites have a range of ownership contexts. For example the Clear Lake (California) obsidian source was considered open access (Bryan 1950, 34). In contrast, the Pipestone Quarries (Minnesota) have a complex history of ownership. Although the

Lakota (Sioux) claimed possession during the 19th century, the Omaha, Mandan, the Sac and Fox had all claimed ownership previously (Hughes 1995, 17). George Catlin recorded in the 1830s that 'tribes have visited this place freely in former times; and that it has once been held and owned in common, as neutral ground, amongst the different tribes who met here to renew their pipes' (Matthiessen 1989, 435). It is possible that the shift from open access to single tribal ownership was stimulated by contact with westernised concepts of land ownership.

The Mount William axe quarries (Australia) were located in the Kulin clan territory and managed by a hereditary senior male clan leader known as a *Ngurungaetas*, who oversaw axehead-manufacturing and distribution networks. The *Ngurungaetas* were normally reputed songmakers with religious knowledge who were part of the political hierarchy. The *Ngurungaetas* had free passage through distant clan territories and their role meant that '[t]hese powerful and influential figures controlled the religious knowledge for the quarry and, hence, ultimately determined its significance to others' (Brumm 2011, 94). The status of the *Ngurungaetas* allowed them to create biographies for Mount William axeheads to enhance the power and desirability of these implements. If Aboriginal quarry custodians neglected their duties they could face disgrace or death; their responsibilities included complete control over access to sacred quarries (Boivin 2004, 11). Elders also controlled access to the Wilgie Mia ochre mine, and non-initiates could not enter certain areas which were often identified by small stone cairns within the workings (Flood 1995, 271–3).

The Yeineri quarries in the New Guinea highlands lie near the interface with the lowland Dismal Swamp. They are operated by the Wano, who control access through an on-site settlement which is subdivided into residential kinship segments, each providing quarry teams. Some 240 adults plus children inhabit this settlement, which was larger in pre-contact times. The Yeineri ('Source-of-the-Axe-Rock-River') clan of the Wano are the controlling group in consensus with the most influential Big Man in an egalitarian system. Each team independently quarries raw material and has direct ownership over all products, tool production, and distribution. Interestingly, the implements produced at this quarry are considered profane, even outsized 'Ye-Yao' blades, and hardness and colour are key criteria in establishing the value of the stone. Distant relatives can be given permission to quarry but they must have their products inspected by quarry leaders. On rare occasions members of other tribes such as the Dani, Damal, and Moni were allowed to quarry under supervision of Wano quarry leaders (Hampton 1997, 686–98, 723–4).

The Tagime quarries (New Guinea) are ranged along a 3–4 km stretch of the Tagime River and exploit river cobbles used at a number of hamlets along the river. Unlike the Yeineri quarries (above), Tagime has unrestricted access for the tribe, although non-tribal members are prohibited from collecting raw material. Apprentices exist at Tagime (generally related adolescent males) who receive on-site training (Hampton 1997, 725–32, 741).

The Langda quarries (New Guinea) are ranged along a 17 km stretch of the Ey River drainage. The quarrying rights are owned by 11 hamlets of the Una tribe who each exploit their own section of the river for raw material for adzeheads and knives. In contrast, a small quantity of stone for outsized ceremonial axeheads is sourced from hillside outcrops. The Una hamlets have a typical New Guinean socio-political system centred upon a Big Man, but no one Big Man has ever controlled all contiguous quarry zones. The quarrying rights to each stretch of the river are owned by a single hereditary head quarryman within each quarry hamlet, whose authority is passed down through patrilineal inheritance, and the roles of head quarryman and local Big Man can reside in a single individual. The head quarryman sanctions access, and occasionally grants permission for supervised visits by outsiders. Similar traditions exist at the Sela quarries (Hampton 1997, 750–5).

## Seasonal use

During treks to obsidian sources in California, Wintu[n] groups fasted for the duration of the journey to and from the quarries, creating a 'semi-religious' experience (Dubois 1935; Robinson 2004, 97).

Amongst Aboriginal Australians many groups undertook long distance expeditions to the Wilgie Mia ochre mine to procure ochre for ceremonial purposes (Flood 1995, 271–3).

Shorter journeys occurred too: the Dieri tribe from Cooper's Creek collected ochre from the Flinders Range quarries, making a 500 km trek annually, and returning with individual loads of 30 kg (Taçon 2004, 34).

In New Guinea certain quarry expeditions were led by warrior 'entrepreneurs' who were motivated by the rapid accumulation of wealth and power (Pétrequin & Pétrequin 2011, 342). The time/distance travelled ranged from 1 day's march for the Wano to 4–5 days' for the Dani (*ibid.*, 338). Although the Wano live on-site at some quarries, they continuously prospect for new lithic sources within a range of 2–3 days' walk. If the prospecting is successful, then *Elogor*, spirit owner of the land, is given offerings of food at 'special places' (Hampton 1997, 696).

The Yeineri complex comprises nine quarries located along 15 km of the Ye River drainage, with the lowest at Diarindo at 645 m asl and the highest at Awigowi lying at 1500 m asl. The hub of the complex is the eponymous Yeineri hilltop settlement which controls access and initiates quarry expeditions. The settlement lies only *c.* 200 m from its two closest quarries, three others are 3–6 hours' walk away, and the remainder 2–7 days' walk. Quarrying expeditions are stimulated by the needs of the quarryman or his relations and the exchange value of implements. The economic base of the quarry owners (Wano) means they are stone rich but pig poor, whereas the neighbouring Dani are potato and pig rich but stone poor, creating the perfect symbiotic relationship between tool producers and forest farmers (Hampton 1997, 715–18).

> 'The timing of the expeditions is entirely regulated by social demands, ... the regularity of ceremonial exchanges between partner villages, undertaken to pay funerary compensation at the end of a war (blood payments), for the re-establishment of peace, or for new marriage alliances' (Pétrequin & Pétrequin 2011, 340)

It is during social events that roughout axeheads were exchanged, and in return producers received wealth and prestige objects such as pigs, marine shells, and new wives. Such transactions were pivotal in building or maintaining kinship links, alliances, and exchange partnerships.

On South Island (New Zealand), the Maori from the Poutini Coast undertook sea journeys every 20–30 years to the greenstone sources at Anita Bay on the north coast of North Island, a sea-crossing of several hundred kilometres (Coutts 1971, 65).

## Age/sex demographic of extraction site workers

In the New Guinea highlands quarry workers are predominantly men. The role of women is largely restricted to support tasks such as food preparation and the transportation of stone and roughouts. Although there are no clear taboos preventing participation in extraction, women rarely quarry and deliberately remain at a distance from the quarry and tool production areas (Hampton 1997, 715–18, 806). At the Tagime quarries apprentices observe tool grinding processes and provide support roles (Hampton 1997, 741).

Amongst quarries in the Yeineri complex, work groups comprise 5–10 men who spend up to 3 days procuring sufficient stone for 10–15 over-sized Ye-yaò blades. Although these quarries are generally not considered sacred, women rarely visit them and remain off-site with the food cache. Generally, quarry expeditions are organised by quarry leaders and the local Big Man, and each team participates in ritual performances before and after each expedition to ensure success and appease the spirit world (Hampton 1997, 698–718).

## Evidence for ritualised extraction

Mining and entering the earth is considered fraught with supernatural dangers by the Diné (Navajo) of the American South-west, who follow traditional lore and 'treat the land and each other with respect ... The Diné become sick upon entering mines that burrow beneath the earth's surface unless they say prayers for protection' (McPherson 1992, 42).

Extraction at the Pipestone Quarries (Minnesota), is highly ritualised and traditionally begins with purification rituals at a sweat lodge which last 3 days (Fig. 3.2), and involves prayers and pipe smoking. Offerings are placed near the quarry pit (Figs 3.3), or at the nearby Three Maidens shrine which is the residence of the quarry guardian spirits and decorated with rock art (Holmes 1919, 31; Winchell 1983, 15–18; Scott *et al.* 2006, 148–9). Quarrying is undertaken using only traditional hand tools which have been purified with sage smoke and

*Figure 3.2: Pipestone Quarries (Minnesota). A group of sweat lodges located roughly 30 m from the quarries. Photographed in 1998 (photo: author)*

prayers (Fig. 3.4) (Holmes 1919, 21–7; Hughes 1995, 44–5). Following extraction further purification rituals occur (Hughes 1995, 44–5). Taboos prevent groups undertaking subsistence tasks near the quarries, and they could not camp within 3.2 km (2 miles) of the quarries to maintain the sanctity of the location (Hughes & Stewart 1997, 9).

In California many Native American communities consider obsidian to be toxic; consequently extraction and handling followed practices designed to counteract negative effects. An example of a protective deposit is provided by an animistic cache comprising abalone shells and the upper mandible of a raven's beak discovered in a remote Chumash microblade quarry (Robinson 2004, 97).

In the Andes certain potters annually sacrificed children to the deities who controlled the clay mines, sealing them alive within deep shaft tombs (Boivin 2004, 6). Ritualised extraction at Wilgie Mia ochre mine (Australia) focused on *Mondong*, an Ancestral Being who slew a kangaroo on this spot and protects the mines. Certain areas of the workings were marked by small stone cairns to signal that only initiates could pass. Tradition stipulated that mining tools had to remain in the workings and, when leaving, miners had to retreat backwards while dusting away any footprints so that *Mondong* could not track and kill them (Flood 1995, 271–3).

Ritualised extraction was not confined to traditional societies but can be found in pre-industrial contexts amongst the 18th and 19th century tin mines of Cornwall where mythical creatures known as 'knockers' inhabited the deepest workings and had to be appeased to ensure success and safety. Although the knockers were generally considered benevolent, they demanded respect and expected offerings of food or tallow to be left for them otherwise dire consequences could ensue (Bottrell 1873, 186).

At Ormu (New Guinea) a large, sacred hammerstone is believed to be an oracle which has the power to authorise new quarry workings (Pétrequin & Pétrequin 2011, 340). However, at the Yeineri quarries the Wano quarrymen conduct rituals before and after extraction to placate the powerful, omnipresent spirit *Elogor* who owns the land and must be given offerings of tobacco or foodstuffs to ensure success and safety (Hampton 1997, 695, 715–18). Similarly, clan groups at the Tagime quarries also conduct rituals at both the beginning and end of quarrying to propitiate the spirits and ensure high quality stones are discovered (Hampton 1997, 726–32).

The Una, who own the Langda quarries (New Guinea), also provide offerings and prayers to spirits associated with quarrying. Much of this ceremonialism focuses on ancestral skulls which are curated in the men's house and are believed to possess 'great spirit power' with the ability to mediate with the spirit world to negotiate access to good toolstone. This reached a peak during a major ceremony known as *Yowali*, occurring roughly every 5 years, when prayers were offered to the Ancestral skulls for permission to quarry and for a guide to the best toolstone (Hampton 1997, 755–6, 780, 799–803). Traditionally, a Langda shaman from each quarry hamlet conducts rituals to seek permission to quarry. Vegetable offerings, and occasionally a pig, are provided for a female spirit called *Alim Yongnum*, who owns the land surrounding the river, and to a male spirit known as *Murbilik Kue* who owns the toolstone. Prayers are also offered for good weather. At the outset of quarrying the head quarryman, who is also the quarry owner, bathes in the Ey River during which he will quietly murmur incantations to the spirits. The gendering of the land and the toolstone as female and male respectively, again symbolically links extraction to human reproduction.

The Langda pig rituals provide sanctified pig fat for use in quarrying, which is used to anoint selected boulders to beautify them and appease the spirits who inhabit them at the end of quarrying. The Tungei (New Guinea) attribute their quarrying success to ritual purity and the use of the correct axehead-making magic (Boivin 2004, 11–12).

## Evidence for ritualised production

Following ritualised extraction at the Pipestone Quarries (Minnesota), pipestone is crafted into distinctive tribal types of tobacco pipe, thus embodying identity into portable artefacts (Murray 1983, 84–5; 1993, 5–11). If breakages occur during manufacturing, the fragments are returned to the quarry as an act of renewal (Fig. 3.5); general pipestone waste is treated similarly. Pipe making takes roughly 8 days and each pipe was purchased directly from the craft specialist (Hughes 1995, 90).

*Figure 3.3: Pipestone Quarries (Minnesota). A forked stick set in a small mound close to the sweat lodges festooned with tobacco-tie offerings. Photographed in 1998 (photo: author)*

*Figure 3.4: Pipestone Quarries (Minnesota). Traditional quarrying using hand tools. Photographed in 1998 (photo: author)*

*Figure 3.5: Pipestone Quarries (Minnesota). A rejected Plains type pipe blank returned to a quarry for renewal purposes. Photographed in 1998 (photo: author)*

Hidatsa flint knappers of the Midwestern Plains lived alone because of the secrecy surrounding the ritualised nature of their activities, which were sanctioned by the keeper of the sacred arrow bundle. Knapping was undertaken in a closed earthlodge by the light of a central hearth, and the flint was stored in covered cache pits around the perimeter of the earthlodge to maintain moisture and maximise workability. Solitary knapping was practised because the Hidatsa believed that if the process was observed the flint would not knap correctly (Bowers 1992, 166). The Maidu (California) also practised ritualised knapping (Robinson 2004, 97).

The Wano (New Guinea) practise ritual acts at various stages of axehead production to appease *Elogor* and other spirits for favourable conditions for axehead manufacturing, and to maintain equilibrium with the spirit world (Hampton 1997, 695). Similar rituals occur at both the Tagime and Langda quarries (Hampton 1997, 732, 755–6).

In Indonesia stone beaters for use in barkcloth production are manufactured solely by the To Onda'e, a tribe of quarry specialists and tool makers who barter their products with lowland cloth producing communities. The To Onda'e use axes to quarry serpentinite, and the finished beater is scored with grooves before being 'cooked' in water containing plants with 'soul-stuff' to infuse strength into the implement. Following this the beater is rubbed with wax while warm to make it smooth and shiny (Kennedy 1934, 237). Similarly, on Hawai'i axe-makers soaked preforms in a special liquid squeezed from the juices of plants which were thought to soften the toolstone, following which roughouts were produced by flaking and grinding (Malo 1951, 51–2).

Moriori adze-makers (Chatham Islands) alleviated the 'laborious and tedious' nature of grinding by singing a song which included an appeal for assistance to *Hine-tchu-wai-wanga*, the goddess traditionally associated with adze production (Smith 1892, 81).

## Extraction site product functionality

The Hidatsa crafted ceremonial flint knives for use in hunting rituals which were deposited at two locations, first a turtle effigy built on the northern bank of the Missouri, and secondly a snake effigy constructed from glacial boulders, west of Independence. The ceremonies at the turtle effigy included 'offerings to the turtle … Some left … the flint knife … for the flint was a sign of the big birds who go with the turtle and the other gods in the Missouri and the creeks around' (Bowers 1992, 370). These ceremonial knives were crafted by ritually-sanctioned knappers during important spring ceremonies.

The Cheyenne curated four Sacred Arrows in a special medicine bundle considered to be the 'supreme tribal fetish', believed to have been given to the Cheyenne by the mythological hero *Sweet Medicine* (Hoebel 1960, 7). These embodied artefacts hold power over buffalo, people, and particularly enemies of the tribe, and played a key role in renewal ceremonies. Similar empowered artefacts occur among the Ho-Chunk (Winnebago) tribe, who curate Seven Sacred Stones which were given to the tribe by 'little people' for ritual use and appear to have been recently rediscovered buried at the foot of a rock art panel featuring a serpentine motif. This cache of seven projectile points had been placed in a large clamshell (Stanley 1999).

Arguably the most iconic Plains artefact is the tobacco pipe, pivotal to smoking rituals. The design reflects tribal identity: disk pipes are typical of Iowa, Oto, and Osage; elbow pipes are associated with northern and eastern Plains tribes (Fig. 3.6); the micmac pipe is linked with the Blackfoot, Cree, Chippewa, and Ojibwe; the Sioux pipe was found amongst the Dakota; and the Sioux variant pipe was common amongst the Mandan and Arikara (Murray 1983, 84–5; 1993, 5–11). The ritualisation of pipe smoking was/is a central element of tribal ceremonialism, with the empowerment of the pipe as part of tribal identity.

The Puebloan *tchamajillas* (slate and siltstone hoes) superficially appear to be functional but are embedded in Hopi ceremonialism, particularly the snake dance where they form part of the altar equipment:

> '[a] long pile of stone implements, regularly arranged, were placed at the back of the altar, and almost upon the green corn-stalks. These were all of green stone and slate, and ... were all agricultural implements, such as hoes, trowles [sic], etc'. When this record was made in 1881 Bourke noted that such 'agricultural implements' had long since gone out of use and were restricted to 'religious ceremonies'. (Bourke 1984, 125, 178–9)

These implements are owned by clans within Puebloan communities. Puebloan Indians also believe that white flint arrowheads can bestow the power of clairvoyancy on the owner, and that obsidian was an elixir capable of defeating diseases (Gunnerson 1998, 242–3).

Greenstone axeheads from the Mount William quarry (Australia) were preferred to others of similar quality because of traditional links between the quarry and Kulin tribal mythology. The quarry custodian was a song-maker who communicated between the Ancestors, the Dreamtime, and his community (McBryde 1979; 1984). Stone axeheads were generally empowered as masculine and age-related, normally belonging to older men, who could lend them to younger men or women as a mechanism to maintain status and power (Boivin 2004, 9). In addition, stone axeheads played roles in burial ceremonies, the construction of sacred Bora Ring enclosures, in increase ceremonialism, and as totemic symbols (Brumm 2004, 150).

Robinson, writing between 1829 and 1834, describes alongside the functionality of stone tools on Tasmania their use in 'affording relief to the afflicted body', recording their role in traditional medicine (Plomley 1966, 190).

In New Guinea many communities have sacred power objects which originated as mundane items but were subsequently withdrawn from secular use and transformed into sacred paraphernalia by ritual practices (Hampton 1997, 279). Consequently, 'functional' appearance can be deceptive. In certain areas ceremonial axeheads share the same characteristics as everyday work axes, particularly those originating from the Abiamp quarry (Chappell 1987, 79–81), thus axehead morphology is not always an accurate indicator of the significance of an axehead. This is illustrated by the over-sized 'Ye-yao' blades which emerge from a quarry initially for profane use, but the owner can later choose to convert the implement into a sacred power object. The ritualisation of objects is believed to be a practice inherited from the Ancestors (Hampton 1997, 468–9).

The criteria for the transformation of artefacts can be social or political necessity, or the rarity of the raw material. Transformations occur at significant events which create a biography, and

> [t]he exchange of ownership by public display and presentation of the display-exchange stones [Ye-yao] not only fuels the economy by the repayment of debts and the establishment of new obligations, but it appeases the ghosts and ancestral and other spirits of the unseen world that are observing and listening to the proceedings. The many formal displays of these stone items of wealth before distribution also establish social prestige.

These transformative rituals seek to domicile ancestors or powerful spirits within the axeheads, who can then be manipulated at ceremonies to maintain social networks and underpin ideologies. The ancestral spirits are drawn from within the individual's patrilineage, with powerful leaders in life being most favoured. Although highlanders have female ghosts and spirits, only male spirits are installed into the sacred axeheads. Taboos prevent sacred axeheads from being identified, discussed, or used functionally (Hampton 1997, 468–76, 542–4).

Amongst highland communities sacred objects are owned by individual adult men but curated and worshipped within small socio-religious groups comprising 6–11 men who share a common patrilineage. All adult men belong to a men's group and each individual owns at least one sacred stone with supernatural powers which provides the focus

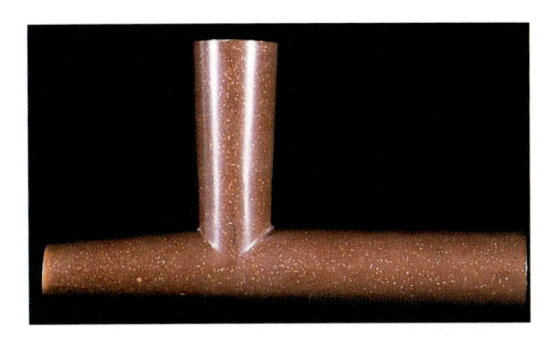

*Figure 3.6: A Native American tobacco pipe made from red pipestone or Catlinite sourced from the Pipestone Quarries (Minnesota) (photo: author)*

*Figure 3.7: An elaborately hafted New Guinea axe, now curated in Manchester Museum (photo: author)*

The Kimyal, Yali and Una of highland New Guinea use 'power stones' at significant events such as harvests or during the creation of new garden plots. These stones have been empowered by a shaman and include non-functional adzeheads and knives (some withdrawn from secular uses and subsequently ritualised), which are then planted among crops to stimulate growth. Other power stones are placed beside domestic hearths where they were prayed to for success with crops or are carried to help the owner discover good toolstone. These stones also protect against aggression, or when placed strategically within a house roof they ward off destructive weather events (Hampton 1997, 649–84).

New Guinea axeheads and adzeheads also signify that owners have undertaken initiation into adult male society (Pétrequin & Pétrequin 2011, 343), and different methods of hafting identify regional affiliations (Fig. 3.7) (cf. Sillitoe 1988). When the axeheads and adzeheads are combined with other paraphernalia (ie, shells, exotic feathers, hunting bows) the complete assemblage signals both status and identity (Pétrequin & Pétrequin 2011, 343). Strathern (1969, 321) has observed that the unusually long, thin Mount Hagen ceremonial axeheads were 'deliberately fashioned as objects of beauty' and mounted in elaborately carved hafts. In contrast, and paralleling the findings of Vial (1941), Strathern also discovered that bride-price axeheads were predominantly oversized with less surface finish, although they were still considered wealth or status objects.

Within New Guinean funerary compensation practices axeheads can symbolically represent a human life. However, as wealth/status objects, a collection of axeheads can become the property of a dominant lineage, rather than an individual, and are consequently curated in a special house within the village. These axeheads are considered sacred objects that have been created by Ancestral Beings and are inalienable (Pétrequin & Pétrequin 2011, 344). Certain ancestral axeheads were thought to fly during the night but could be attracted back to earth with pig fat (Pétrequin & Pétrequin 1993).

The most potent and valuable New Guinea implements are the oversized, non-functional 'Ye-yao' axeheads which can be up to 900 mm in length and are used in ceremonies, ritual exchanges, and in social networks. These blades

for personal Ancestor worship, for defence against malevolent spirits, and for sun worship. Taboos prevent all females and uninitiated boys from interacting with sacred objects (Hampton 1997, 478–9, 542). Consequently, embodied axeheads are considered sentient 'Ancestral Beings', which are treated with respect to placate and manipulate their powers, and repeated rituals feed, beautify, and worship the implements to revitalise their spirit power (Hampton 1997, 545). In addition, certain types of artefact have specific symbolic roles. Stone chisels from the Yeineri quarries are used by the Dani as representations of slain warriors in war ceremonies, and in their healer's kits, and the same tools are used in the Baliem Gorge to protect healer's equipment from malevolent spirits (Hampton 1997, 617).

Conversely, the hereditary chiefs of the Sentani (New Guinea) use special axeheads crafted from rare, highly polished stones in public ceremonies. These axeheads are carefully curated to avoid dulling the polish and are packed in organic cases. Some are covered in latex to enhance their sheen, and they are not hafted but held in the hand as symbols of status and power. It is object biography which enhances the social value of these objects, restricting circulation and use to the local elites (Pétrequin & Pétrequin 2011, 343–4).

are crafted from greenschist or amphibolitic schist, which emits a green glow in the dark, and is quarried from secret locations at Awigobi (the 'River of the Night'), which is believed to be the route used by the Ancestors when searching for luminous Ye-yao. Some communities believe the Ye-yao are splinters from *Yeli*, the Sacred Tree, which grew at the beginning of the world. These highly-charged objects are carefully crafted and polished, and often dressed in miniature tree-kangaroo fur skirts and draped with pendants to transform them into 'women' of stone. Some Ye-yao are considered so powerful that they rarely enter the social arena and are kept strictly secret (Hampton 1997, 468–9; Pétrequin & Pétrequin 2011, 344–6).

In the Grand Valley (New Guinea) a large Ye-yao of 700+ mm in length may be worth a large pig – axehead production being roughly equivalent to the time involved in pig rearing. Ye-yao blades are used in funerary displays, payments, war indemnity payments, bride-wealth transfers, for trade, and for transformation into ritual objects. While circulating as profane objects, blades can be stored openly in the men's house and, when not displayed, wrapped in bark coverings. Ye-yao can be carried to ceremonies by women – or when being traded. Some men restrict trade of these implements to affinal groups and consider them primarily reserved for ritual or ceremonial uses (Hampton 1997, 453–5).

The Maori (New Zealand) believe that nephrite is 'ensouled', and individual objects are animate and embody community histories, thus creating 'documents' which provide evidence of legitimacy (Brumm 2004, 146; Field 2012). The Maori selectively use raw materials, and in some communities obsidian was reserved for cutting tools, whereas basalt was used for adzehead manufacturing (Jones 1984, 251).

On the island of Malaita (Solomon Islands) flaked chert adzeheads are associated with ancestor worship, and priests and community leaders carry them for status and legitimacy, and traditional healers use them to draw pain from the body. Stone adzeheads are believed to have been created during storms and represent the 'teeth of the thunderbolt', responsible for striking down men and trees. 'Thunderbolt' adzeheads are driven into the ground by the force of the storm, where they 'cool' and eventually rise to the surface to be discovered by men, who must treat them with respect as magical objects and not use them for mundane tasks. In pre 19th-century contexts, warriors considered these implements as sacred weapons which would make the bearer invincible (Ross 1970, 416).

## The involvement of craft specialists

The Konso (Ethiopia) provide a rare example of female craft specialists. Culturally, tool production is considered a female task, whereas men 'build things' or farm. The women of this community can quarry stone and are skilled knappers who have undergone lengthy apprenticeships. The Konso 'women procure high-quality stone from long distance, produce formal tools with skill, and use their tools efficiently' (Arthur 2010, 228). Importantly, the Konso female craft specialists are dependent upon tool-making for their livelihood. Consequently, in extraordinary cases such as this and the Tiwi women in Tasmania, who mined ochre, it is females who complete the *chaîne opératoire*, not men (Plomley 1966; Brumm 2004).

The Hidatsa (Midwestern Plains) purchase knapping rights from the sacred bundle keeper (an elder who had purchased these rights from his elders), who also provides training to initiates. Such controls restrict specialist knowledge to elders, which ensures that they receive payments during old age from the next generation (Bowers 1992, 120). The Mandan flint knappers had similar conventions, with knapping rights being purchased from the keeper of the Snowy Owl bundle (Bowers 1950, 283–5). Amongst the Cheyenne, flint knappers were generally older men who could gain great prestige for the quality of their work (Grinnell 1923, 178). At the Pipestone Quarries, tobacco pipes were traditionally manufactured by craft specialists who had been sanctioned by their tribe or had obtained supernatural permission during a vision quest (DeCory & DeCory 1989, 18).

Knappers at the Njillipidji quarry (Arnhem Land) were clan members with traditional and exclusive rights to the quarry through ancestral links. Their principal product was the spearhead, which once crafted was wrapped in paperbark and promptly passed into the ceremonial exchange network; tradition prevented the knappers from using the spearheads themselves (Torrence 1986, 52–3).

Many axehead producers in the New Guinea highlands only manufacture roughouts, and the consumer has to grind, polish, and finish the implement (Pétrequin & Pétrequin 2011, 343), a practice also found amongst the Maori (New Zealand) where certain artefacts are worked upon by the community to embed a biography (cf. Field 2012). Consequently, some craft specialists are only involved in the preliminary stages of production.

In New Guinea craft specialists only exist among communities exploiting the harder, non-laminar rocks, such as Langda, Sela, and Suntamon. However, craft specialisation is not a full-time activity and adzehead makers in Langda are also forest farmers *and* participate in tribal warfare (Pétrequin & Pétrequin 2011, 338–9). At the Yeineri quarries all roughouts are taken to settlements for finishing, and as no local sources of sandstone occur, imported grinders are used. Informants reported that it could take between 1.5–3.0 years to produce a high-quality 250–400 mm long axehead (Hampton 1997, 715–18). The Tagime quarry toolmakers regard themselves as expert grinders who fashion water-rounded cobbles sourced from the Tagi River. Occasionally some flaking is required to complete the preform, followed by 5 weeks of grinding and shaping and, in the case of the oversized blades, more than one grinder could be involved (Hampton 1997, 733–4, 744).

Craft specialists are recorded amongst several Polynesian societies. In the Hawai'ian archipelago axehead makers were highly esteemed as their products enabled tree clearance and facilitated farming (Malo 1951, 51), as were the Samoan adzehead makers (Green 1974, 254). Conversely, in the Cook Islands, adzehead manufacturing was undertaken by a group of 'artisans' who were considered mundane and appear to have gained little prestige from their activities (Cleghorn 1984, 400). However, amongst the Maori craft specialism was embedded in social structures:

> It is worthy of special note ... that Maori life occupations were to some extent specialised, and the knowledge descended from father to son. So that in a tribe ... there might be a family whose hereditary skill and knowledge constituted them makers of axes and implements to the clan. (Best 1912, 21)

The hereditary transference of stone working skills amongst the Maori involved male-dominated patrilineal apprenticeships.

## Distribution of extraction site products

The petrological identification of greenstone axeheads has transformed understanding of distribution patterns in Australia, particularly regarding long distance exchange. This is epitomised by Mount William greenstone quarry which produced axeheads that were transported 300+ km in preference to locally sourced axeheads because of their greater cultural value (Brumm 2011, 87). Large-scale meetings of Aboriginal communities facilitated the exchange of these Mount William greenstone axeheads, and their lack of variation in size, irrespective of distance from the quarry, demonstrates their value to these communities in an unaltered state (McBryde 1979; 1984)

It was not just toolstone that was highly prized among Aboriginal communities. Wilgie Mia ochre with its Dreamtime associations was so important for rituals that communities travelled great distances to procure this pigment which was distributed across the whole of southern Australia (Flood 1995, 271–3).

Pacific ethnography also records trade networks spanning huge distances, all facilitated by seaborne travel. For example, two Polynesian networks distributed fine-grained basalt adzeheads over distances of up to *c.* 4000 km. A western network was focussed upon quarries located on Tutuila Island (Samoa), and an eastern network was centred upon the Eiao quarries located in the Marquesas Islands (Weisler 2008, 540).

The central highland New Guinea exchange networks operate on both sacred and profane levels. Trade normally occurs between men from a single patrilineage, with a smaller number of transactions between unrelated male friends. There are no professional traders. The typical distance for trading transactions between kinsmen was 35–45 km. Everyday transactions are carried out in private and without ceremony, the focus being on material benefit rather than socio-political gain. In contrast, ceremonial exchange underpins rituals and various aspects of cultural interaction. It is traditionally an open-ended transaction through the use of inalienable objects which creates indebtedness between individuals/clans and transforms status and prestige rather than introducing material gain. These transactions generally occur between relatives and are instigated by the Big Man who conducts the proceedings in public with appropriate ceremony. In general the highlands exchange system continually trades objects onwards so that extraction site products were in a continuous state of circulation within the network. The 'customary' value of an object was set by the producers before the product left the extraction site, and it was this set value which was used during later transactions (Hampton 1997, 804–6, 808, 824).

A major aspect of secular axehead distribution is/was symbiotic exchange between axehead producers and those without access to good toolstone. Consequently highlanders traded birds of paradise, decorated woven bags, pigs, tobacco, vegetables, and axeheads to stone-poor lowlanders in return for laurel wood bows, marine shells, sago palm flour, pottery, and dog's teeth (Pétrequin & Pétrequin 2011, 342). However, warfare can disrupt these exchange networks and in certain areas it is only stopped following the payment of large numbers of oversized Ye-yao axe blades (Hampton 1997, 468–9). Trade goods moved in a series of chain-like stages from producers to consumers via contiguous community networks which, when necessary, can divert products to circumvent enemy territories during any outbreaks of hostilities. Normally axehead producers rarely travel beyond the first two interconnecting stages of a trading network because of enemy threat (Hampton 1997, 806, 816).

In highland New Guinea two mutually exclusive distributions of ground stone tools have developed. In Grand Valley and the West Region distinctive axeheads, adzeheads, knives, and chisels are manufactured and traded throughout the area by the Yeineri and Tagime quarries. In contrast, different styles of adzeheads and knives are produced by the Langda-Sela quarries for the adjacent Yali and East Region. These two separate trading networks correlate with separate language boundaries which are reflected in the different forms of stone tools but, curiously, not in other objects and materials traded across the cultural boundary (Hampton 1997, 421, 743). It appears that stone tools can embody cultural identity in a way that other objects/materials do not, thus their circulation is restricted by social conventions whereas non-lithic materials are not. The range of individual movements within these exchange networks covered relatively short distances (Chappell 1987, 88–9).

## The presence of rock art, graffiti, or idols at extraction sites

The Pipestone Quarries (Minnesota) feature rock art panels created on a group of glacial erratics known as the Three Maidens (Fig. 3.8), which are believed to be the residence of the quarry's guardian spirits. Offerings are placed beside the rock art, as recorded by George Catlin (1830s), 'humbly propitiating the guardian spirits of the place, by sacrifices of tobacco, entreating for permission to take away a small piece of the red stone for a pipe' (Matthiessen 1989, 430). The rock art comprises anthropomorphs, animals, and geometric/abstract shapes; the predominant motifs are human figures and turtles (Holmes 1919, 264; Winchell 1983, 15–18).

*Figure 3.8: Pipestone Quarries (Minnesota). The Three Maidens, the home of the guardian spirits of the quarries. These glacial erratics are decorated with rock art and are another location for offerings. Photographed in 1998 (photo: author)*

# 4

# The archaeology of lithic extraction

The important question is how well does the ethnographic model equate with data in the archaeological record? To test this, the ethnographic model has been compared with a sample of archaeological extraction site records drawn from five continents. This near-global archaeological data comprises 223 studies: 9 from Africa; 54 from the USA; 15 from South America; 3 from Asia; 3 from Australia; 1 from the Middle East; 1 from New Zealand; 7 from the Pacific; and 130 from Europe; the European data comprises multi-period flint, stone, copper, tin, quartz, and gunflint sites. This has created a substantial body of quantified evidence which can be compared with the ethnographic data to provide robust probability statistics and detect trends (cf. Topping 2017). The archaeological data was analysed against 13 high level themes which are comparable to the ethnographic themes identified in Chapter 2 (see Table 4.1).

The comparative analysis has used the same 'flow model' methodology as Chapter 2 (Schiffer 1972; Fogelin & Schiffer 2015), which has identified common material patterning by context between the two data sets. As before, this analysis relies upon positive/negative records in both data sets, and no presumption of presence has been applied to the calculations.

Although there are some differences between the ethnographic and archaeological data, by comparing like-for-like contexts and assemblages, aggregating traits, and using relational analogy, robust trend data emerges. The analysis recognised correlations in material patterning of practices from prospection,

*Table 4.1: The comparison of ethnographic trends with the archaeological data*

| Ethnographic sample: trends | Archaeological sample: comparable features and trends |
|---|---|
| Whether extraction sites and their raw materials were storied or mythologised | Characterisation of the landscape setting and lithology of the extraction site |
| Ownership or restricted access to the extraction site | The presence of on-site structures |
| Seasonal use of the extraction site | Evidence for seasonality |
| Sex/age demographic of extraction teams | Age/sex demographic of skeletal material from extraction sites |
| Empirical evidence of ritual practices at extraction sites | Non-functional assemblages at extraction sites |
| Inputs from craft specialists | Evidence of craft specialisation |
| Ritual associated with artefact production | Elaborate reduction sequences for lithics |
| The production of signature artefacts | Signature products |
| The functional or specialised use of the artefacts | Inferred use of products |
| The scale of circulation of extraction site products | Maximum distribution of artefacts |
| The secondary use of extraction sites for ceremonial activities | After-use of extraction sites |
| The presence of rock art, graffiti or idols | Rock art, graffiti and idols at extraction sites |
| The interment of human remains | Human burials or body parts |

*Figure 4.1: (opposite) The dome-shaped topography of Creag na Caillich (Perthshire), source of Group XXIV axeheads (photo: author)*

*Figure 4.2: (opposite) Flint Ridge (Ohio), one of the quarry pits with mounded waste dump behind (photo: author)*

extraction, to product manufacture, use, and discard.

The strength of the new interpretative model lies in the closeness of the correlations between the ethnography and the archaeological record, which suggests in many cases the materiality of the archaeological record may have been produced by similar practices and social motivations to those documented by the ethnography. Although it would be naïve to expect to identify every motivation or practice undertaken at extraction sites to create a meta-narrative for prehistoric society, it is possible to construct a meaningful social narrative which identifies the general trends, and some of their details, to develop a greater understanding of what Lewis-Williams and Pearce (2005, 9) have characterised as 'the universal foundations of diversity'. The use of robust, quantifiable, and testable ethnographic data to formulate these new interpretations – and restrict bias as far as possible – leads to a novel 'deconstruction' of current archaeological models by an ethnographic paradigm.

## Distinctive landscape settings and/or raw material

The ethnography recorded 93% of extraction sites as storied/mythologised locations, many anchored upon locally distinctive landforms or associated with unusual lithologies. The extraordinary nature of these sites has prompted mythico-religious associations to explain origins and maintain social transactions. Thus, locally prominent landforms or locations with distinctive deposits where there is archaeological evidence of extraction might fall into this category. For example, Pike of Stickle (Britain), Tievebulliagh (Ireland), and Creag na Caillich (Britain) (Fig. 5.1) are all dome-shaped mountains; Harrow Hill and Cissbury (Britain) are amongst the highest points on the chalk downland; Rijkholt (Netherlands), Sélèdin (France), Valle Sbernia (Italy), Mill Creek (Illinois), Kaolin (Illinois), and Crescent Hills (Missouri) are all ranged along prominent summits of major river valley scarps.

Dramatic or isolated extraction sites can also be seen along the ridgetops of Flint Ridge (Ohio; Fig. 4.2), crests or mountain/mesa summits such as Scafell Pike (Britain), Casa Montero (Spain), Alibates (Texas), and Obsidian Cliffs (Wyoming); volcanoes at Hoshikuso Pass (Honshu, Japan) and Manau Kea (Hawai'i); caves such as Wyandotte (Indiana) and Mammoth (Kentucky); lake settings at Isle Royale (Great Lakes); and islands like Lambay and Rathlin (Ireland), Heligoland (Germany), Shetland (Britain), and Henderson (Pacific). Most of these sites also had secondary deposits of detached raw material that were more accessible, but these expedient sources were frequently ignored in favour of the more challenging deposits which must have had a greater value, irrespective of increased logistical costs. An extreme example of acute logistical investment is provided by the 3rd Unnamed Cave in Tennessee where archaeological fieldwork discovered that Native Americans had crawled a kilometre through underground tunnels to quarry chert in a 'dark zone' cave chamber decorated with rock art (Simek *et al.* 1998). However, only a small number of caves in the Tennessee Appalachian Plateau had evidence of mining, most were reserved as ritual arenas during the Archaic, Woodland, and Mississippian periods (Simek in lecture). These archaeological examples probably all represent storied places.

The archaeological data records 64% [142 of 223] of sites located upon unusual and/or locally prominent landforms, whereas 93% of ethnography recorded storied associations across all forms of site. This discrepancy arises from the fact that the ethnography records oral evidence whereas prehistoric archaeology cannot and has to rely upon inference and empirical evidence. Consequently, the ethnography suggests that most prehistoric extraction sites were probably considered storied places by their users and mythologised.

The ethnography of storied extraction sites records that 50% have restricted access or ownership, over half are exploited seasonally, 92% practice ritualised extraction, 74% involve craft specialists, 64% of storied site products are distributed over 200+ km, almost half of these sites host ceremonialism, over a third feature graffiti/rock art, and 25% contain human burials or body parts.

In comparison, 39% of the archaeological sites provide empirical evidence of ritualised extraction, taken here as features not functionally associated with extraction, such as small structures (eg, chalk platforms, 'caves'), the presence of non-extraction artefacts (eg,

4  *The archaeology of lithic extraction*

*Figure 4.3: Mont Viso (Italy), one of the major jade sources in the Alps (photo: author)*

pottery, carved chalk objects, etc), graffiti, human remains, and possibly hearths. One of the key ethnographic observations is that storied sites are invariably associated with long distance product distribution (200+ km), a pattern well attested in archaeology where, for example, Alpine jade axeheads, Breton fibrolite axeheads, Groups VI and IX axeheads from Langdale (Britain) and Tievebulliagh (Ireland) respectively, obsidian bifaces from the American Rockies, and obsidian implements from quarries in Honshu and Hokkaido (Japan), were all extensively distributed lithologies. Similarly, the presence of rock art/graffiti and human burials is recorded in similar ratios in both data, suggesting strongly that these sites may originally have been storied locations.

## Evidence for ownership/restricted access

The ethnography records that 68% of extraction sites were in ownership or had restricted access, a factor which can be difficult to identify archaeologically without documentary evidence. However, some archaeological evidence does exist, such as shrines used by elite-sponsored craft specialists at the Manau Kea quarries, Hawai'i (McCoy *et al.* 2011), and rare buildings inhabited by quarry custodians on Mount William in Australia (McBride 1984; Brumm 2011). Therefore, certain types of structural evidence can, with suitable caution, be a potential indicator of ownership or restricted access.

Ethnography suggests that rock art is often used to signpost a culturally important site and indicate ownership. Archaeologically, rock art is carefully positioned in and around important cave extraction sites in Africa, Australia, the USA, and South America (eg, Flood 1997; Robbins *et al.* 1996; Simek *et al.* 1998; Brady & Rissolo 2006; Crothers 2012), it is juxtaposed with upland and mountain extraction sites such as Manau Kea on Hawai'i (McCoy *et al.* 2011), Krumlovský les in Czechia (Oliva 2010; Fig. 4.4), Graiglwyd (Warren 1921), Creag na

Caillich, and Langdale (Sharpe 2008; 2015; Bradley *et al.* 2019). Different motifs on panels at the Pipestone Quarries in Minnesota appear to reflect changes in tribal ownership of the quarries (Hughes 1995, 17). However, archaeologically, the contemporaneity of rock art with extraction can be difficult to demonstrate and caution is needed when drawing associations between the two.

A comparison of the data illustrates a number of correlations. Ethnographically, the Aboriginal Australian quarry custodian at Mount William was central in managing the extraction, valourisation, and distribution of axeheads across vast tracts of south-eastern Australia (Brumm 2011). Consequently, ownership and restricted access can form part of a mechanism which embedded a cultural value in extraction products and led to significant distribution networks, as seen archaeologically with a number of Neolithic axehead types, many obsidian implements from Japan and the North American Rockies, or Flint Ridge chert from Ohio.

To summarise, candidate archaeological indicators of ownership or restricted access include:

- On-site shrines
- Small buildings on-site
- Rock art/graffiti

## Evidence for seasonal use

The ethnography records that 90% of extraction sites were used seasonally. While seasonal use is difficult to identify archaeologically, circumstantial evidence from 13% of sites could indicate seasonality (eg, Topping 2005; 2011).

Location is a major constraint, and topography and climate can restrict activity. High altitude sites such as the obsidian quarries in the Rockies, jade sources in the Italian Alps (Fig. 4.3), high altitude obsidian sources in Japan, and the Lake District Fells, are all snow-covered and often inaccessible during the winter/spring periods. Similarly, island sites such as Rathlin, Henderson, or Heligoland may also have operated seasonally, particularly during equinoctial and winter sea conditions. Consequently, many extraction sites by the nature of their location may have been subject to some degree of enforced inaccessibility.

The data comparison provides a close correlation between ethnographic sites used seasonally which have storied associations, and archaeological sites in locally prominent locations. However, seasonal extraction also correlates with many activities which can leave material evidence in the archaeological record and should be expected where extraction formed part of a range of subsistence tasks.

## The age/sex demographic of extraction participants

Ethnography often records the age/sex demographic of extraction participants, but archaeology can only interpret this from human remains found at extraction sites and these are rarely analysed for evidence of actual participation in extraction (see Chapter 7 regarding Gavà (Spain)). Consequently, this creates a conundrum: do the human remains found at, for example, the Cissbury flint mines, represent the burial of mine users or of people with strong associations with the mines, or are they of expedient interments. As a result, this study will rely upon the burial record (see below) to cautiously sketch the demographic and associations of those interred at extraction sites.

## The evidence for ritualised extraction

Of the ethnography, 92% records ritualised extraction practices, and 94% of those records occur(ed) at storied/mythologised sites, demonstrating a strong link between these trends.

The ethnography records preliminary purification rituals preceding ritualised extraction, generally on-site artefact production, and often post-extraction renewal rites (eg, Hampton 1997; Stout 2002; Clark & Martin 2005; Dean 2010). Such practices leave behind material evidence retrievable in the archaeological record (Table 4.2; Figs 4.4–4.6), comprising both functional and non-functional artefacts, and structured assemblages which are not casual discard.

In ethnography ritualised extraction generally occurs at storied/mythologised sites, involves craft specialists, objectifies artefacts, long distance product distribution, and was often associated with on-site ceremonialism and, to a lesser extent, human burials. Most

*Figure 4.4: Hoshikuso Pass, Nagawa (Japan). These Jomon period obsidian quarries comprise a cluster of 195 pits, some revetted with 100–200 mm diameter timbers. Near the centre foreground is a recycled digging stick with a carbonised tip used to prop the revetment. Other digging sticks were left in the workings, and a deer antler, small fragments of lacquerware, and three deliberately broken Kasori B1 pots were thrown into the workings at abandonment (Otake et al. 2020; S Otake pers. comm) (photograph © S. Otake)*

of these activities can be retrieved by archaeology. In ethnographic reality, ritualised extraction practices are designed to provide meaningful objects for social transactions such as alliance building, kinship networks, house societies, status, identity, ideologies, and ceremonialism. The material evidence in the archaeological record may also represent such interactions.

## Ceremonialism

The ethnography documents on-site ceremonialism in 95% of studies, generally performed following procurement. Such activities form part of ritualised extraction practice and produce structural and material remains which can be retrieved archaeologically. Post-extraction ceremonialism is normally linked to rites of renewal, the reaffirmation of group

*Table 4.2: A comparative analysis of ritualised extraction practices and their potential material remains in the archaeological record*

| Ethnographic events | Ethnographic evidence | Possible archaeological correlates |
| --- | --- | --- |
| Purification rituals | Sweat lodges; hearths; use of substances to purify people and tools | Hearths or charcoal in or near workings, but separate from quarry surfaces (ie, not fire-setting) |
| Pre- and post-extraction offerings or rituals | Rock art/graffiti; curated animal remains; human burials and sacrifices; food stuffs; feasting; consultation of ancestral remains; evidence of ceremonialism | Rock art/graffiti near or on-site; placed deposits; carved chalk objects; pottery; curated animal remains; human remains; structures (eg, chalk platforms, 'Cave Pit' Cissbury, 'caves') |
| Ritualised extraction | Extraction tools remain on-site; special tools; substances used to anoint workfaces | Tools abandoned on-site; tool caches; unusual or non-local tools |
| Rites of renewal/ abandonment | Broken artefacts, rejects and production debris returned to site; debitage left on-site; human remains | Broken artefacts, rejects and debitage returned to workings; human remains; structured deposits in backfill of extraction site |

(based on Topping 2017, 127, table 4.8, with amendments)

## 4 The archaeology of lithic extraction

identities, and the maintenance of social networks such as kinship links (eg, Gould 1977; Hall 1997; Hughes & Stewart 1997; Brumm 2010).

Overall, the two data sets show similar emphases, suggesting that archaeology is recognising appropriate comparators.

### Product functionality

The interpretation of artefact functionality can be problematic. This is particularly true as ethnography records that in certain cases functionality can be changed as artefacts accumulate a biography, or social conventions dictated, which can then lead the object into alternative social trajectories. Indeed, ritual action can transform mundane objects into ceremonial or status items (eg, Chappell 1987, 79–81). However, some artefacts, such as over-sized axeheads in New Guinea (Vial 1941; Hampton 1997), which may parallel certain Neolithic Alpine jade axeheads (Pétrequin *et al.* 2012a), or others in Shetland (Ballin *et al.* 2017), for example, are too large for practical use so functionality is not an issue. Unfortunately, some of the finer nuances of certain ethnographically recorded trajectories such as marriage/bride wealth or compensatory payments (eg, from warfare), may be beyond the reach of archaeological analysis, as evidence might easily be confused with displays of wealth, status, or identity.

For archaeology, use-wear analysis can also play a role in identifying artefacts which were active tools, compared to those with a non-utilitarian role in society.

### Craft specialist artefact production

The involvement of craft specialists in the *chaîne opératoire* of tool production occurs in 95% of ethnography and can be inferred from 43% of archaeological examples. Clearly this disparity may reflect differences in the evidential base between the disciplines, or the interpretation of the archaeological evidence. In addition, proficiency in craft technology is relative. Individuals can be considered craft specialists by their community even when they are involved in the production of comparatively mundane tools (eg, Arthur 2010). Consequently, the identification of the work of craft specialists in the archaeological record becomes problematic because it relies on the subjective assessment of the quality of artefact production which may under-represent the presence of craft specialists (Fig. 4.7). It remains salutary that ethnography records over twice as many examples of craft specialists as is suggested by archaeology. Perhaps raising awareness of this issue may lead to a finer nuancing of archaeological interpretive frameworks in the future. In addition, the process of mining and quarrying is in its nature a learned craft specialisation in most ethnographic studies, thus extraction teams should equally be considered as craft or technical specialists.

In ethnography 82% of storied sites record the involvement of craft specialists in tool production, whereas 64% of archaeological examples of locally prominent sites are associated with well-crafted products. Both ethnography (70%) and archaeology (49%) record long distance artefact distribution (200+ km) is the most common association.

*Figure 4.5: Hoshikuso Pass, Nagawa (Japan). One of the three deliberately broken Kasori B1 pots found in the Jomon period obsidian workings (photo: author)*

*Figure 4.6: (above) Two Mississippian chert bifaces, rejected or deliberately returned to the Kaolin Quarries (Illinois), probably representing aspects of renewal rituals (photo: author)*

*Figure 4.7: (right) A finely ground riebeckite felsite axehead (Group XXII) found at Modesty in Shetland and one of a hoard discovered at a possible timber hall. Axehead now curated at the National Museums of Scotland (photo: author)*

Drawing the evidence together, locally prominent extraction sites with rock art/graffiti, human remains, and long distance product distribution may all indicate the presence of craft specialists.

## Product distribution

The distribution of extraction site products has been analysed at three different scales: (1) within 100 km of the source; (2) between 100 km and 200 km; and (3) long distance circulation at 200+ km. The archaeological data uses correlations between proven extraction sites in distinctive topographic settings and artefact distributions documented by petrological analysis.

The less than 100 km product distribution shows a close correlation between ethnography at 6% and archaeology at 5%, and the 100–200 km scale data are also comparable, with ethnography recording 17% and archaeology 19%. Long distance distribution of 200+ km is most numerous in both data, accounting for 64% in ethnography and 60% in archaeology.

The presence of robust petrological analysis gives the archaeological data validity. The fact that the majority of provenanced extraction site products fall into the 200+ km category (Fig. 4.8) (eg, Clough & Cummins 1988; DeRegnaucourt & Georgiady 1998; Pétrequin *et al.* 2012a; Yakushige & Sato 2014) suggests the probability that archaeological items that entered long distance networks originated from storied sites and carried significant biographies to far-flung communities.

## The use of rock art, graffiti, or idols at or near extraction sites

The use of rock art, graffiti, and idols at extraction sites is recorded in 27% of ethnographic cases, but at only 13% of archaeological sites.

*4 The archaeology of lithic extraction*

Ethnography records art at extraction sites such as the Pipestone Quarries (Minnesota; eg, Holmes 1919; Winchell 1983) and in South America, where art and idols are used by several cultures (eg, Dean 2010). Archaeologically, the 3rd Unnamed Cave (Tennessee) featured rock art (Simek *et al*. 1998), the Copt Howe rock art panels (Cumbria) lie on the valley floor below the Langdale quarries (Sharpe 2015; Bradley *et al*. 2019), panels are found below the Creag na Caillich quarries (Perthshire), and rock art has been discovered in the Pô Valley located strategically below the jade sources in northern Italy (Pétrequin & Pétrequin 2012, 257), all of which may be signposting the extraction sites. However, caution is always needed in demonstrating contemporaneity between the art and the extraction site, which can often only be shown by the presence of motifs contemporary with the stone procurement.

Both data sets show links between the use of art and storied/distinctive sites, the use of ritualised extraction, craft specialists, long distance product distribution, ceremonialism, and the presence of human burials.

## The presence of burials

Human burials at extraction sites have been recorded in 18% of ethnography and in 19% of excavations, both as interments within the workings and as adjacent burial monuments. The strong correlation between data sets may suggest that social practices at archaeological extraction sites included ritualised interment linked to the maintenance of identity and demonstrated group legitimacy in relation to stone procurement.

A number of extraction sites feature monumentalised burials. Examples include the Pipestone Quarries (Minnesota) where at least seven mounds existed in the quarry environs (Scott *et al*. 2006, 112–13, 180–3), and Flint Ridge (Ohio) featured at least four mounds (Holmes 1919), one of which was the Hazlett Mound covering a square flint-built tomb with a hearth and two extended inhumations accompanied by Hopewell grave goods (Mills 1921). The Crescent Hills quarries (Missouri) also have evidence of mounds on the ridge top directly above the extraction zones (Fig. 4.9; Holmes 1919). Mounds also existed at

*Figure 4.8: A Hopewell bird's head motif plate made from copper sourced from mines around Lake Superior and discovered during excavations at Mound City (Ohio) by Mills and Shetrone in 1920–1921. The copper had been transported over 1450 km (900 miles) and was one element of a range of exotic imported items drawn into Ohio from the Rockies, the Gulf Coast, and the Appalachians. The copper plaque is now curated at the Hopewell Culture National Historical Park, Ross County, Ohio (photo: author)*

*Figure 4.9: A burial mound on the crest of the valley scarp above the Crescent Hills quarries in Missouri (photo: author)*

Blackpatch in southern Britain (Pull Archive, Worthing Museum; Barber 2005), some of which were contemporary with mining from the evidence of stratigraphy, context, and assemblages.

## Implications for the interpretation of Neolithic extraction sites in Britain and Ireland

The preceding analysis has identified common trends present at both ethnographic and prehistoric extraction sites. The key archaeologically visible indicators are:

- *Location*. Ethnography documents many storied/mythologised sites are generally locally prominent landforms and/or unusual raw materials, which compares well with archaeological extraction sites located in distinctive topographic settings, suggesting that similar conventions are likely to have occurred in the archaeological past.
- *Restricted access*. This can be difficult to identify archaeologically. However, shrines or on-site buildings can indicate control by custodians, clans, or craft specialists.
- *Seasonality*. Seasonal working is often a pragmatic response to climate and can be indicated in the archaeological record by site locations at high altitudes and the presence of seasonal faunal indicators stratified in the workings.
- *Ritualised extraction*. This practice is well documented in 92% of ethnography, and is often associated with storied locations, craft specialists, and ceremonialism.

# 4 The archaeology of lithic extraction

- *Ceremonialism/burials.* This generally comprises human and animal remains, some built structures for ceremonial performance, and is generally associated with storied locations where ritualised extraction is practised.
- *Rock art, graffiti, and idols.* Rock art sometimes signposts a storied extraction site and graffiti can adorn the workings, both media designed to impart messages. The use of idols is rare.
- *Long distance product distribution.* Products distributed 200+ km from their source generally originate from storied sites where ritualised extraction was practised, craft specialists were involved, and where there is evidence of ceremonialism.

These statistically validated indicators are considered to be the most archaeologically visible, and those which can deliver a more nuanced interpretation of the social context of prehistoric extraction. To reiterate, one of the strongest and most recurrent correlations in the data is between prominent locations and long distance product distribution (200+ km).

To sketch the comparability between the ethnography and archaeological data each of the broad ethnographic themes has been re-assessed for its archaeological visibility (Table 4.3). Each theme has had its likely archaeological material analogues grouped together by context, alongside related ethnographic themes. In archaeological terms, the presence of combinations of indicators can provide clearer insights into the potential complexity of the social context of prehistoric extraction.

These broad ethnographic themes can now be used to analyse the social context of the structures and material evidence found at Neolithic extraction sites.

| High level ethnographic themes ranked by percentage importance [n=168] | Potential archaeological analogues [n=223] [note: strongly linked ethnographic themes shown in italics] |
|---|---|
| [95%] ceremonial use of extraction sites | Rock art/graffiti in workings<br>Rock art/graffiti near workings [<5 km]<br>Portable art<br>Non-domestic structures<br>*Mythic or storied associations*<br>*Evidence of ritualised extraction*<br>*Product circulation 200+ km* |
| [93%] mythic or storied associations | Locally prominent/unusual topographic setting<br>Distinctive raw materials<br>Human remains in/at workings<br>*Ceremonial use of extraction sites*<br>*Evidence of ritualised extraction*<br>*Product circulation 200+ km* |
| [92%] evidence of ritualised extraction | Extraction tools abandoned in workings<br>Imported extraction tools in/at workings<br>Hearths on shaft floors/galleries<br>Charcoal deposits in workings<br>Non-functional objects in workings<br>Placed deposits in workings<br>Structures in workings<br>Animal remains, articulated, in workings<br>Hearths in backfill<br>Human remains in workings<br>Rock art/graffiti/portable art<br>Rock art/graffiti near workings [>5 km]<br>*Ceremonial use of extraction sites*<br>*Mythic or storied associations*<br>*Seasonal use*<br>*Product circulation 200+ km* |

Table 4.3: The comparison of high level ethnographic themes with potentially equivalent archaeological features and assemblages, arranged by ethnographic priority

| High level ethnographic themes ranked by percentage importance [n=168] | Potential archaeological analogues [n=223] [note: strongly linked ethnographic themes shown in italics] |
|---|---|
| [90%] seasonal use | Shaft fills containing stabilised horizons, placed deposits, and hearths<br>Animal remains, articulated, in workings<br>Migrant wild animal species (e.g. Bats) in open workings indicating seasonal abandonment<br>*Mythic or storied associations*<br>*Evidence of ritualised extraction*<br>*Ceremonial use of extraction sites*<br>*Product circulation 200+km* |
| [68%] evidence of ownership | Shrines<br>Small-scale on-site settlement<br>*Mythic or storied associations*<br>*Product circulation 200+ km* |
| [64%] product circulation 200+km | Distribution of site products 200+ km<br>*Mythic or storied associations*<br>*Evidence of ritualised extraction* |
| [27%] presence of rock art/graffiti | Rock art/graffiti in workings<br>Rock art/graffiti near workings [>5 km]<br>*Mythic or storied associations*<br>*Evidence of ritualised extraction*<br>*Ceremonial use of extraction sites*<br>*Product circulation 200+ km* |
| [18%] burials at extraction sites | Human remains in workings<br>Human burials at or adjacent to sites<br>*Mythic or storied associations*<br>*Evidence of ritualised extraction*<br>*Ceremonial use of extraction sites*<br>*Product circulation 200+ km* |

(Based on Topping 2017, 169, with revisions)

# 5

# An ethnoarchaeological analysis of Neolithic extraction sites in Britain and Ireland

Mortimer Wheeler famously stated that archaeology was about people, not 'things'. So to address this fundamental issue and gain a better understanding of the social context of Neolithic stone extraction the ethnoarchaeological model has been applied to the analysis of 79 excavations at 11 flint mine complexes (Ballygalley Hill, Blackpatch, Church Hill, Cissbury, Den of Boddam, Durrington, Easton Down, Goodland, Grime's Graves, Harrow Hill, Stoke Down), and 51 excavations at nine axe quarries (Creag na Caillich, Graiglwyd, Lambay Island, Langdale, Mynydd Rhiw, Le Pinacle, Rathlin Island, Shetland, Tievebulliagh) in Britain and Ireland (Fig. 5.1).

The analysis of the structures and assemblages discovered at these sites was compared with 21 categories of empirical evidence drawn from the ethnographic data:

- topographically distinctive locations or extraordinary lithologies;
- accessibility;
- debitage/lithics in workings;
- debitage/lithics in post-extraction contexts;
- stabilised horizons/hearths in post-extraction contexts;
- tools in workings;
- imported tools in workings;
- knapping tools in workings;
- hearths in workings;
- charcoal deposits in workings;
- non-extraction objects in workings;
- placed deposits in workings;
- structures in workings;
- animal remains, articulated;
- animal remains, disarticulated;
- human burials;
- human body parts;
- rock art/graffiti in workings;
- rock art/graffiti within 5 km of workings;
- settlement at workings;
- distribution of products.

The analysis of this aggregated data has provided an extremely detailed assessment of common trends in assemblage patterning, contexts and structures found at mines and quarries. As a result, it is now possible to infer a more nuanced explanation of the motivations lying behind Neolithic extraction practices based upon a comparison of the archaeological record with the material evidence documented in the ethnoarchaeological model. This provides an opportunity to go beyond typologies and quantification studies and get closer to the probable social contexts and practices of the people who used extraction sites during the Neolithic period.

To improve the flow of the text and avoid repetitive referencing, references to excavation accounts are listed in the Appendix, where they are collated alphabetically by site.

Figure 5.1: The location of extraction sites mentioned in the text (illustration: T. Pearson)

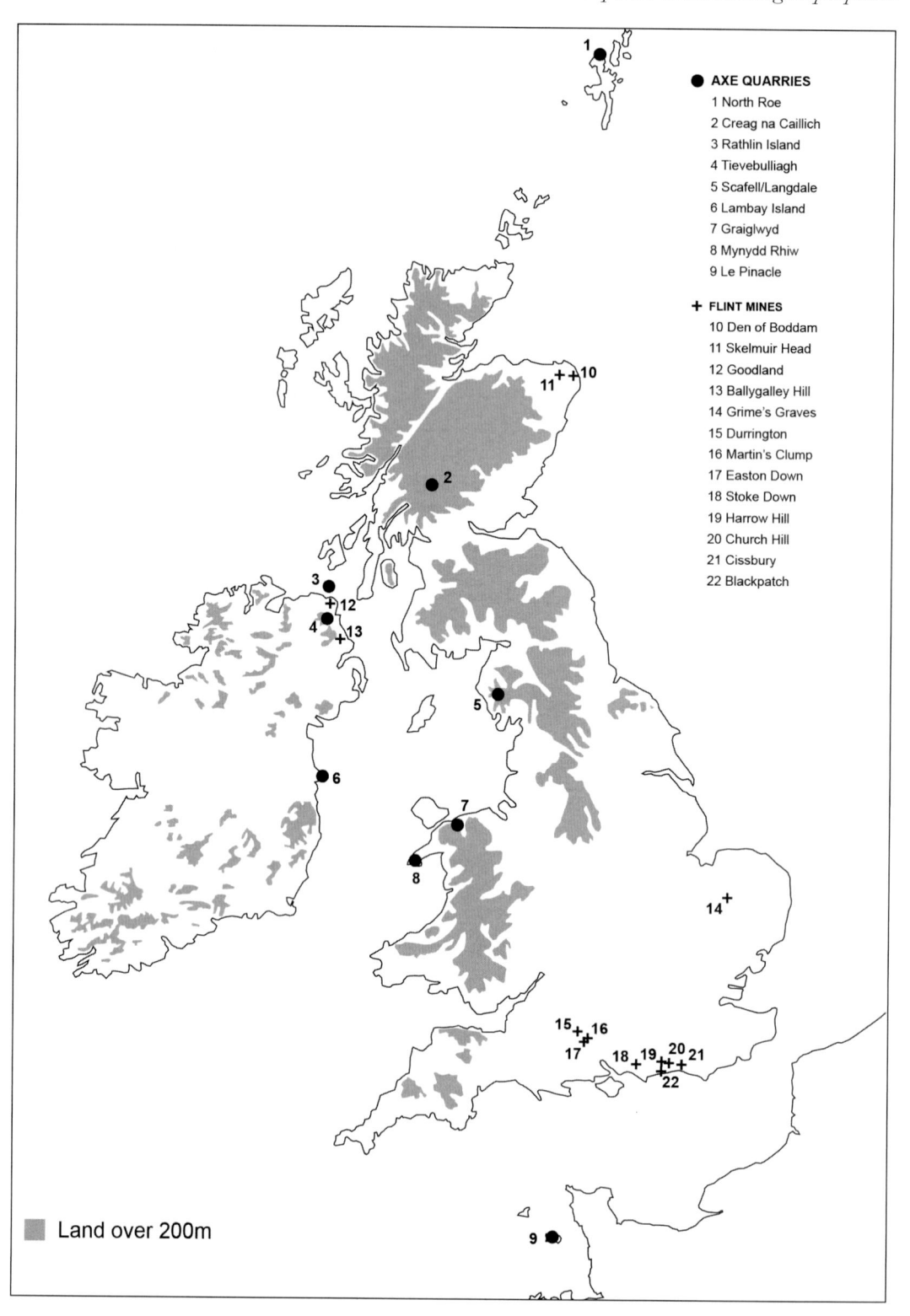

● AXE QUARRIES
1 North Roe
2 Creag na Caillich
3 Rathlin Island
4 Tievebulliagh
5 Scafell/Langdale
6 Lambay Island
7 Graiglwyd
8 Mynydd Rhiw
9 Le Pinacle

+ FLINT MINES
10 Den of Boddam
11 Skelmuir Head
12 Goodland
13 Ballygalley Hill
14 Grime's Graves
15 Durrington
16 Martin's Clump
17 Easton Down
18 Stoke Down
19 Harrow Hill
20 Church Hill
21 Cissbury
22 Blackpatch

Land over 200m

## Landscape setting of extraction sites

When the ethnoarchaeological model is applied to the landscape settings of extraction sites in Britain and Ireland, several themes emerge which suggests they were probably storied or mythologised places where ritualised procurement was practised (Table 5.1). First, location was important, with summits or false-crests preferred, often irrespective of raw material quality. In terms of distinctive topography, many of the axe quarries favour dome-shaped mountains, eg, Pike of Stickle (Fig. 5.2); Creag na Caillich; Tievebulliagh (Fig. 5.3), while the flint mines generally lie on or near rolling downland crests, some within view of the Channel. The fact that toolstone quality was not always the main motivation is demonstrated at Blackpatch and Harrow Hill (South Downs) where inferior toolstone was targeted despite better quality deposits being present nearby (Barber *et al.* 1999, 73; Topping 2005, 84). This is paralleled at Langdale where it was discovered '[t]he larger, more conspicuous outcrops were preferred to those which were easier to reach, even when more accessible sites had equally suitable raw material' (Bradley & Ford 1986, 127). Clearly in these examples it was raw material from a particular location which was more important than toolstone quality. The ethnoarchaeological model suggests that these were likely to have been storied or mythologised locations with strong links to communal beliefs.

Despite prominent locations, however, woodland and vegetation may have restricted visibility to and from some sites (Allen & Gardiner 2012). However, recent research in Wessex suggests that drainage, grazing animals, and human impacts on the chalk downs inhibited woodland succession (Richards 1990; French *et al.* 2007; Field & McOmish 2016, 42–5; Allen & French 2020), and a similar pattern might be expected elsewhere on other similar lithologies (Field 2008, 26–7). Consequently, some southern British flint mines may have been highly visible. Conversely, the environmental data from the upland quarries

*Figure 5.2: The dome-shaped profile of Pike of Stickle (Cumbria) (photo: author)*

*Figure 5.3: The dome-shaped profile of Tievebulliagh (Antrim) (photograph © D Field)*

*Figure 5.4: The periglacial stripes defined by different vegetation at Grime's Graves (Norfolk), which surround the northern parts of the site. Similar glacial features may have existed around the South Downs flint mines (cf. Field & McOmish 2016, 45) (photo: author)*

at Creag na Caillich and Langdale/Scafell, and the mines at Grime's Graves, all suggest the presence of woodland. The upland quarries were probably near the treeline, overlooking woodland with a patchwork of clearings (eg, Pennington 1991; Bradley & Edmonds 1993). However, lowland Grime's Graves appears to have been located in open woodland, with the mines encircled by prominent unploughed periglacial stripes which may have enhanced cultural perceptions of the site, suggesting possible links to mythologies or cosmological beliefs (Fig. 5.4; Topping 2019b, 214). Similar periglacial effects may have originally been visible around the South Downs mines before later agricultural activity removed them, and such features clearly influenced the building of Stonehenge and its Avenue (Allen *et al.* 2016).

By their location, island extraction sites had their own differences created by separation from the mainland. Sites such as Le Pinacle (Jersey; Patton 1991; 1993; Fig. 5.5), Lambay Island (Ireland; Cooney 2005) and Rathlin Island (Ireland; Cooney 2004; 2017), were all located in island-hopping locations in the southern and western seaways used by incoming migrants during Neolithisation. The same seaways were overlooked by the mainland quarries at Graiglwyd (Wales; Williams & Davidson 1998), Scafell (Cumbria), Ballygalley Hill (Ireland; Collins 1978), and Tievebulliagh (Ireland; Mallory 1990), demonstrating that the sea routes to new lands often incorporated stone procurement strategies.

The use of rock art or graffiti is an integral part of ritualised extraction for many cultures and the model suggests that Neolithic examples were used both to signpost sites and form arenas for offerings and ceremonies during ritualised practices. In addition, almost 40% of all British and Irish Neolithic sites had an association with burial monuments, such as the long barrow at Martin's Clump, built some 300 years after mining began, or certain barrows at Blackpatch, created from mining debris (Barber *et al.* 1999, 36, 45; Barber 2005). The colocation of burial monuments added a layer of complexity and cultural meaning to these extraction sites.

The lack of permanent settlement at British and Irish sites could be explained from the ethnography as evidence of taboos preventing on-site domestic activity, as at Pipestone and several New Guinea quarries, for example, adding weight to the suggestion of exclusive use. However, in these cases pragmatic reasons such as climate, high altitude, and in some instances lack of water, will also have played a part.

Finally, the ethnographic data links long-distance product distribution (200+ km) in almost every case to storied/mythologised locations where ritualised extraction was practised to produce highly valued products, a trend reflected in the archaeological record where data from provenanced axeheads is available (see below).

The data collated in Table 5.1 records high percentages of quarries, and to a lesser extent mines, positioned in locally-distinctive settings, thus providing a strong parallel with the cross-cultural trends identified in the ethnography, suggesting the probability that the majority were storied locations. This is supported by similar percentages of human remains in the two data sets, strong parallels with rock art/graffiti and long-distance product distribution, all features indicative of storied sites.

Consequently, the ethnoarchaeological model suggests that this archaeological evidence implies that 60–90+% of extraction sites probably had storied or mythologised associations. In addition, the liminality of many extraction sites required users to journey through structured, monumentalised landscapes where rock art and burial mounds may have created a staged interface between areas considered sacred and profane, where living communities could reconnect with supernatural forces to procure special materials.

## Evidence for seasonal extraction

Seasonality can be both a choice and/or a practical constraint imposed by location and climate. The ethnography records seasonal working in 90% (74 of 82) of studies, and of these 89% (66 of 74) were storied/mythologised locations. The archaeological record has evidence of periods of stasis at extraction sites which can be interpreted as indications of seasonality or temporary abandonment. This comprises natural wind-blown silts within the workings, stabilised and compacted horizons in backfill, and the remains of events (eg, hearths, deposits of debitage, placed deposits, animal remains placed upon stabilised layers, etc.). Circumstantial evidence consisting of bat skeletons in galleries at Grime's Graves (Pit 1, galleries 1 & 8; Pit 2, galleries 1, 3, 5 & 6; Clarke 1915, 55, 58, & 90) suggests these mines remained open during winter hibernation (October–March) and were deserted, which encouraged roosting by these timid, nocturnal creatures (Topping 2011).

Migratory species such as the skull of a shorebird of the genus phalarope that had been carefully placed in Greenwell's Pit (Grime's Graves), may have been the symbolic deposition of a species only present during migration, which could indicate commemorative seasonal events (Topping 2011). Another 'possible' bird bone recorded in Shaft 27 (Cissbury; Pull Archive, Worthing Museum), hints at similar practices, but importantly suggests links between practices found at mines with those at long barrows where migrant bird species were deposited with mortuary assemblages (Field 2006, 131–2).

The migratory species discovered at extraction sites suggests they were a symbolic part of belief systems associated with extraction. The apparent disappearance of migrant species in the autumn may have defied rational explanation for Neolithic communities and come to symbolise otherworldly links because of their unexplained absence. When species such as the phalaropes reappeared during spring migration, they may have been viewed as supernatural harbingers that triggered expeditions to extraction sites in much the same way as the Big Bird ceremony, linked to migrating raptors, initiated Hidatsa quarry expeditions in North America. Consequently,

*Figure 5.5: Le Pinacle (Jersey), a massive granite stack located on the northwest coast of the island where dolerite was quarried for axeheads from sills around the site (photo: author)*

| Context/trend | Sites | % of sites displaying trend |
|---|---|---|
| *Axe quarries* | | |
| ① quarries located on/near skyline | Langdale/Scafell/Glaramara; Creag na Caillich; Graiglwyd; Shetland; Mynydd Rhiw; Hyssington; Fairfield; Carrock Fell; Tievebulliagh; Lambay Island; Rathlin Island; Le Pinacle | 100 [12 of 12] |
| ② quarries located on distinctively shaped landforms | Langdale/Scafell/Glaramara; Graiglwyd; Creag na Caillich; Hyssington; Fairfield; Tievebulliagh; Lambay Island; Rathlin Island; Le Pinacle | 75 [9 of 12] |
| ③ quarries lie beyond permanent settlement | Langdale/Scafell/Glaramara; Creag na Caillich; Graiglwyd; Shetland; Mynydd Rhiw; Hyssington; Fairfield; Carrock Fell | 67 [8 of 12] |
| ④ burial monuments or standing stones juxtaposed with quarries | Shetland; Graiglwyd; Mynydd Rhiw; Lambay Island; Rathlin Island | 42 [5 of 12] |
| ⑤ quarries near rock art/graffiti | Hyssington; Langdale/Scafell/Glaramara; Creag na Caillich | 25 [3 of 12] |
| ⑥ quarry products distributed <200 km | Mynydd Rhiw; Shetland; Carrock Fell; Le Pinacle | 33 [4 of 12] |
| ⑦ quarry products extensively distributed 200+km | Langdale/Scafell/Glaramara; Fairfield; Graiglwyd; Creag na Caillich; Hyssington; Tievebulliagh; Lambay Island; Rathlin Island | 67 [8 of 12] |
| *Flint mines* | | |
| ① mines located on/near skyline | Blackpatch; Harrow Hill; Cissbury; Church Hill; Stoke Down; Long Down; Skelmuir Hill | 50 [7 of 14] |
| ② mines located on distinctively shaped landforms | Grime's Graves; Cissbury; Harrow Hill; Church Hill; Blackpatch; Skelmuir Hill | 43 [6 of 14] |
| ③ mines may occur beyond permanent settlement | Blackpatch; Church Hill; Cissbury; Easton Down; Grime's Graves; Harrow Hill; Long Down; Martin's Clump; Stoke Down; Nore Down; Buckenham Toft; Den of Boddam; Skelmuir Hill | 93 [13 of 14] |
| ④ burial monuments juxtaposed with mines | Blackpatch; Long Down; Stoke Down; Martin's Clump; Skelmuir Hill | 36 [5 of 14] |
| ⑤ mines associated with graffiti | Cissbury; Harrow Hill; Grime's Graves; Church Hill | 29 [4 of 14] |
| ⑥ mine products distributed <200 km | ? | ? |
| ⑦ mine products extensively distributed 200+km | South Downs axeheads are found in East Anglia and Wessex (Craddock et al. 2012) | c. 50 [?7 of 14] |

The 12 axe quarries are those proven to be the source of specific groups of axeheads: Carrock Fell (Grp XXXIV; cf. Davis *et al.* 2007); Creag na Caillich (Grp XXIV); Fairfield (Grp XI; cf. Davis & Quartermaine 2007); Graiglwyd (Grp VII); Lambay Island (Grp XXXV; Cooney & Mandal 1998); Langdale/Scafell/Glaramara (Grp VI); Le Pinacle (Patton 1991); Mynydd Rhiw (Grp XXI); Rathlin Island (Grp IX); Shetland (Grp XXII); Tievebulliagh (Grp IX); and Hyssington (Grp XII; Jones & Burrow 2011). The 14 flint mines are those ratified by Barber *et al.* 1999: Blackpatch, Church Hill, Cissbury, Durrington, Easton Down, Grime's Graves, Harrow Hill, Long Down, Martin's Clump, Stoke Down; the putative mines at Nore Down and Buckenham Toft; and two Scottish sites at Den of Boddam and Skelmuir Hill (Saville 2005; 2006 for the Scottish sites)

*Table 5.1: Landscape settings of proven Neolithic extraction sites*

the symbolism and reappearance of spring migrants may have been associated with renewal rituals at Neolithic extraction sites, designed to ensure future supplies of the raw materials. The deposition of bird and animal remains may also indicate totemism and represent aspects of identity.

At Graiglwyd, Trenches 3 and 5 provided evidence of sequential workings, some cutting through redeposited scree, which suggests lengthy periods of abandonment if not seasonality (Williams & Davidson 1998). Similarly, at Langdale, excavations at Site 98 (Pike of Stickle) discovered sequences of quarrying and axehead production which may represent seasonal working (Bradley & Edmonds 1988; 1993). Lambay Island featured a number of pits at the quarry, one of which contained a complex series of deposits and was subsequently covered by a low cairn, alongside stone settings, suggesting episodic if not seasonal activity (Cooney 2000; 2005).

Amongst the British and Irish archaeological data, natural silts, stabilised horizons, and placed deposits are recorded in 53% (42 of 79) of the mines and 33% (17 of 51) of quarries.

The stabilised and compacted surfaces suggest at least a temporary halt to backfilling, if not seasonality. Examples range from primary silts containing scapulae, antler picks, and debitage at Easton Down Pit B49 (Stone 1933), to the natural silts which buried structures such as the chalk platform on the floor of the 1971 Shaft at Grime's Graves that displayed a pair of rare, internally-decorated Grooved Ware bowls, indicating the shaft had remained open long enough for wind-blown silts to accumulate before a sequence of dumps of chalk occurred up to 1.5 m deep interspersed with bands of silt (Mercer 1981a, 20, figs 17–18). These examples suggest temporary delays between the deposition of separate dumps of chalk which allowed silts to accumulate, and this may indicate seasonal abandonment, or at least episodic backfilling.

## The practice of stone extraction

The ethnography outlined in Chapter 2 records ritualised practices in 92% (67 of 73) of data, of which 92.5% (62 of 67) occurred at storied/mythologised sites, demonstrating that cosmology and ritualisation were entangled.

Of course, the inference of ritual has to be treated with caution, particularly as ritualised practices can be obscured amongst mundane activities in the ethnography. For example, the apparently 'functional' deposits of abandoned extraction tools found *in situ* at most extraction sites, may result from taboos preventing removal – as recorded at the Wilgie Mia mines in Aboriginal Australia, amongst others (Flood 1995, 271–3; Taçon 2004, 32).

Overall, the archaeological record contains material evidence which fits the patterning in the ethnoarchaeological model, and this forms the basis for the interpretations presented below.

### Ritualised preparations

Extraction is generally initiated after appropriate purification rituals have occurred, comprising offerings, prayers, and the creation or veneration of rock art/graffiti/idols at many sites. The ethnography also records the occasional slaughter of animals as offerings or for feasting, and more rarely humans as sacrifices (eg, South America).

Evidence from archaeological sites indicates such preparations. The nature of the archaeological record can make it difficult to differentiate between preparatory acts from those linked to renewal/abandonment rituals. However, context can provide a steer as to the nature of the deposits. The presence of non-functional assemblages such as carved chalk objects in Shaft 7 at Blackpatch, the carved chalk objects and animal remains in Tindall's 1874 Shaft at Cissbury, carved chalk objects, pottery, and animal remains in Pit 2 at Grime's Graves, or the elaborate pit groups at Lambay Island, all demonstrate that offerings formed part of extraction practice and were repeatedly located in similar contexts.

### Hearths

Evidence for the purification of individuals and extraction tools as described in the ethnography involving fire and smoke may be represented in the archaeological record by hearths or charcoal deposits. Hearths are present in 29% (23 of 79) of flint mines and 10% (5 of 51) of axe quarries, and smaller random charcoal deposits at 29% (23 of 79) of mines and 30% (15 of 51) of quarries.

Hearths were discovered on shaft floors of Shaft 5 at Blackpatch, the Cave Pit at Cissbury, Pit B49 at Easton Down, Pit 21 and Shaft III at Harrow Hill, and Pits 1, 2 (Fig. 5.6), 15, and the 1971 Shaft at Grime's Graves, which do not appear to have been used for light, warmth, cooking, or hardening antler picks. A group of hearths was discovered on Floor B at Graiglwyd, integrated within the quarry workings; another was found at the axehead production site at Thunacar Knott at Langdale; none appears to be domestic in nature. A similar hearth was discovered at Ballygalley Hill (Ireland) adjacent to a debitage deposit immediately upslope from the quarry.

Site 98 at Langdale produced a 'considerable quantity of charcoal' against the quarry face which was interpreted as fire-setting. Similarly, the cave-like Site 95 at Langdale produced substantial deposits of charcoal, again interpreted as fire-setting. At Le Pinacle (Jersey), a series of hearths and midden deposits were ranged around the quarry at the foot of a coastal stack, suggesting evidence of feasting during artefact production – but without settlement evidence (Patton 1991; 2001). A hearth found at the Lambay Island (Ireland) quarries appears to be associated with the closure of the Phase 1 pits before they were

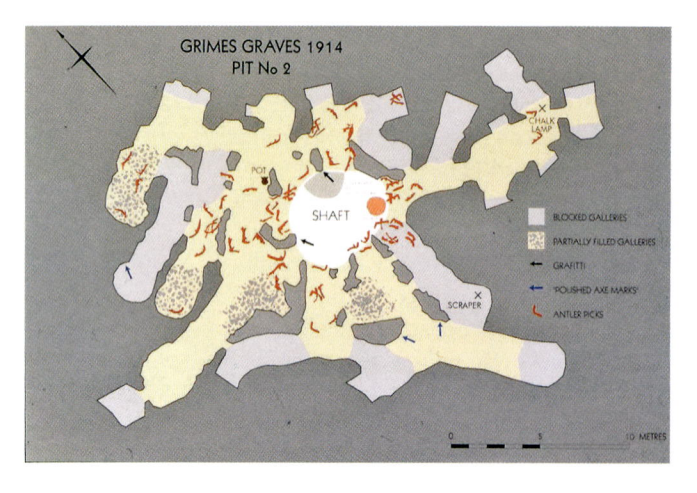

*Figure 5.6: Pit 2 at Grime's Graves (Norfolk) showing the hearth at the base of the shaft, and the distribution of abandoned antler picks and other artefacts (illustration: T. Pearson)*

buried beneath a large mound of quarry debris. The contexts of these various hearths and the lack of associated settlement suggest that they were part of extraction practice, rather than subsistence related.

Fire-setting at axe quarries can be a major issue in this context. The presence of scorched quarry surfaces with adjacent quantities of charcoal provides strong evidence of fire-setting. However, where fire-damaged quarry faces are absent other explanations are needed.

### Deposits of charcoal

Small random deposits of charcoal were discovered in galleries in Shaft V and the Cave Pit at Cissbury, and Greenwell's Pit, the 1971 Shaft, and Pit 15 at Grime's Graves, which may be the remains of burnt floral or vegetable material. However, 'soot stains on roof fragments' were discovered in the 1971 Shaft, which suggested to the excavator the use of torches in these galleries (Mercer 1976, 107). However, there is generally little evidence to support the use of torches in the mines, as no definitive soot residues were discovered on gallery ceilings, apart from in the 1971 Shaft. The female skeleton found at the base of Shaft 27 at Cissbury had charcoal in her right hand, and further unspecified deposits of charcoal were discovered at the base of the Large Pit at Cissbury.

Small deposits of charcoal discovered in the workings at Creag na Caillich were not considered to be evidence of fire-setting. Deposits of charcoal were also recovered at Stake Beck at Langdale and in Trench 1 at Mynydd Rhiw in Gwynedd. At Graiglwyd (Gwynedd) Site F, Test Pit I, a thin layer of charcoal was discovered juxtaposed with small amounts of debitage. Overall, these small deposits may represent the burning of herbs or similar vegetable matter as part of ritualised practice.

### Offerings

In tandem with preparatory activities, the archaeological record provides evidence of offerings.

- At Blackpatch, Shaft 2, Gallery III produced a 'shell deposit' and carved chalk object; Shaft 5 contained charcoal and pig bone fragments in the shaft and galleries; Shaft 7 produced an unfinished carved chalk ball from Gallery I, and other chalk objects and animal bones from the shaft fill; Chipping Floor 2 featured a hearth juxtaposed with ox, pig, sheep, and human bones and pottery fragments (also an intrusive cremation deposit); the shallow pit known erroneously as 'Barrow 2' contained a carved chalk object adjacent to a human skull near the pit floor; 'Barrow 4', a shallow pit, produced an ox tooth, lithics and a disarticulated adult male inhumation.
- At Cissbury, Tindall's 1874 Shaft contained two ox skulls, a faunal assemblage comprising stag, otter, wild boar, and roe deer, and four carved chalk objects from basal deposits; the Large Pit produced a carved chalk cup in basal deposits; the Skeleton Shaft contained a female skeleton discovered lying head-first in the shaft and resting upon lower silts among the remains of four pigs, ox, goat, fox, roe deer, shrew, mice, voles, toads, and snails (the latter smaller species probably accidental pit fall victims); a quartzite fragment was found in Gallery E in the Cave Pit.
- At Easton Down, Pit B1(A) contained a dog skull in the middle fills of this shallow pit.
- At Goodland (Ireland) the workings included a large number of pits, some containing randomly collected and redeposited pottery sherds and lithics from off-site sources.
- At Grime's Graves, Greenwell's Pit contained a dog skeleton in Gallery II, and in another gallery the aforementioned phalarope skull lying between two antler picks and a Cornish stone axehead; Pit

1 produced carved chalk objects and Grooved Ware from the shaft base and galleries; Pit 2 contained a chalk 'lamp' at the end of Gallery 5; Pit 4 contained a chalk 'cup' on the basal silts; Pit 15 held a contentious group of carved chalk objects on the shaft floor; the 1971 Shaft contained a carved chalk object lying beside a chalk platform upon which lay two internally decorated Grooved Ware bowls.
- At Harrow Hill, Pit 21 contained a portable chalk block scratched with seven parallel lines placed next to a hearth and debitage deposit.

Many of the carved chalk objects found in the flint mines are clearly non-functional offerings, and include balls, phalli, and inscribed blocks (Fig. 5.7). The analysis of the small cup-shaped chalk 'lamps' has provided no evidence that they contained oils or fats and experiments have shown that if they had been used as lamps they would have had a very short burn time (Tanimoto *et al.* 2011). The general lack of soot-staining in galleries implies they formed part of ritual paraphernalia.

If the presence and number of carved chalk objects from flint mines is considered over time (Table 5.2), none was discovered at Easton Down, arguably the earliest site (Edinborough *et al.* 2019), which may reflect an unmodified indigenous extraction practice. However, as other sites appeared across the South Downs over successive generations carved chalk objects appear in increasing quantities, paralleling the evidence from causewayed enclosures such as Windmill Hill where cups, phalli, putative figurines, and inscribed blocks were also discovered (Smith 1965, 130–4). This suggests that extraction practice had begun to diverge from the indigenous norm, as also seen in Europe where carved limestone 'lamps' were discovered in the Early Neolithic mines of Defensola 'A' (Italy; Di Lernia *et al.* 1995, 126–8). Carved chalk objects clearly became an increasing part of extraction practice as the Neolithic progressed in Britain, peaking quantitatively at Grime's Graves during the Late Neolithic–Early/Middle Bronze Age. It

*Figure 5.7: Various carved chalk objects discovered in the flint mines of the South Downs (Sussex) and now curated in Worthing Museum (photograph: © D. Field)*

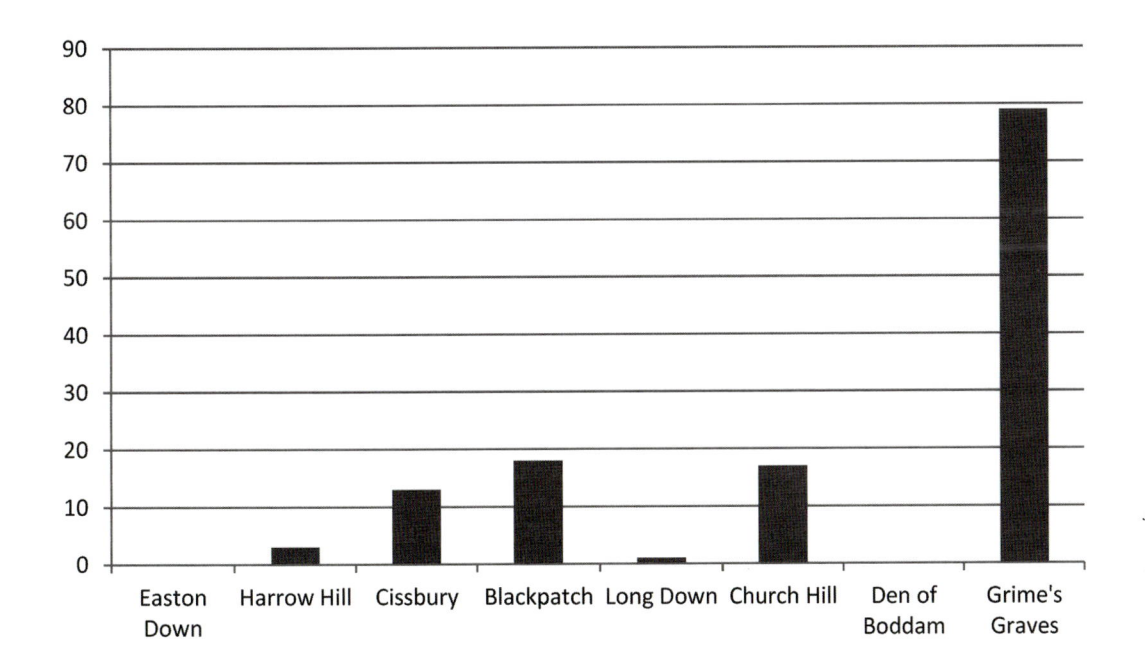

*Table 5.2: The number of carved chalk objects from British flint mines (the large quantity of Middle Bronze Age post-mining worked chalk is excluded)*

is possible, however, that excavation bias may have distorted the size of the corpus at Grime's Graves which remains the most extensively investigated site in Britain. The negative result from the Den of Boddam may reflect the lack of soft lithologies on-site. The presence of carved chalk objects and other non-functional artefacts suggest that ritualisation increased in sophistication over time as Neolithic beliefs took hold.

Evidence of offerings can also be inferred at axe quarries.

- At Graiglwyd, Site F, Test Pit E, contained two roughout axeheads placed in the corner of a quarry; Site F, Test Pit C, sampled a chipping floor which included a quartz nodule.
- At Langdale, the South Scree 'Cave' contained two roughout axeheads placed on a deposit of silt and debitage.
- At Shetland, the Working Gallery (Beorgs of Uyea) produced a schist disc of 63 mm diameter.
- At Lambay Island, a series of pits contained assemblages of pottery, debitage, hammerstones and rubbers, the pits were sealed by low cairns and a hearth, all buried beneath a cairn of quarry debris with an axehead hoard and jasper pendants juxtaposed.

These examples of probable offerings demonstrate that extraction practices in the quarries also involved non-functional events.

### Rites of renewal

Certain deposits may represent renewal rites, following the ethnography from sites such as the Pipestone Quarries where waste material and broken/rejected artefacts were returned to the quarry for this purpose. At British and Irish archaeological sites this can be inferred with redeposited debitage and lithics discovered in dark, subterranean workings which were unlit and where knapping could not have comfortably taken place.

- At Blackpatch, Shaft 2, debitage in Galleries V and VII; Shaft 5, debitage and 'waste' nodules in galleries and niches.
- At Church Hill, Shaft 1 contained a carved chalk object midway down the shaft, and animal bones and axeheads in the upper fills; Shaft 4 had axeheads, various lithics, charred fragments of a wooden bowl, and intrusive later pottery in the upper fills; Shaft 5A had an axehead, lithics, and ox bones in the upper fill of the shaft; Shaft 6 contained a sequence of debitage deposits and roughout axeheads in the shaft fills; Shaft 7 had a sequence of debitage deposits in the shaft; Pit A had debitage, axeheads, and lithics in the backfill.
- At Cissbury, Willett's 1874 Shaft contained lithics on the shaft floor; at the Cave Pit, two roughout axeheads and a quartzite fragment lay in Gallery E, and Gallery F produced debitage; Shaft 24, produced two flint knives in West Gallery; Shaft 27 had lithics on the shaft floor, Gallery 1 produced a flint knife, Gallery 2 flakes, blades, and a knife, North Gallery flakes, nodules, a core, an endscraper and blade.
- At Den of Boddam, Pit 46 contained a substantial deposit of rejected cobbles and debitage, cores, flakes, chips, and a small number of retouched pieces.
- At Durrington, Shaft 5 had a petit tranchet derivative arrowhead on the floor of the South Gallery.
- At Goodland, certain pit deposits contained lithics and debitage from off-site sources.
- At Grime's Graves, Greenwell's Pit produced roughout axeheads and a Cornish greenstone axehead from its galleries; Pit 1, a pile of nodules in Gallery 1; Pit 2, lithics and a roughout axehead from the shaft floor; Pit 15, a pile of flint nodules at the entrance to Gallery 7; 1971 Shaft, debitage on the shaft floor, four pristine axeheads in the upper fills.
- At Harrow Hill, Pit 21 contained debitage on the shaft floor and in Galleries 1 and 2; Shaft III produced an unknown number of roughout axeheads from the shaft floor.
- At Stoke Down, Shaft 1 featured lithics on the shaft floor.

The axe quarries had similar deposits.

- At Creag na Caillich, the East Quarry (Site 1) contained a compact deposit of debitage >250 mm thick with small charcoal deposits beneath flakes and further deposits of charcoal; the West Quarry (Site 2) produced a sequence of debitage deposits juxtaposed with charcoal and isolated flakes.
- At Graiglwyd, Floor B comprised a massive deposit of debitage with a sequence of hearths commingled with scree slope

exploitation; Trench 3 produced flakes from all contexts, and four roughout axeheads from secondary quarrying; Trench 5 contained debitage from tertiary workings; Site F, Test Pit E, discovered debitage in a quarry overlying two well-finished roughout axeheads placed carefully in one corner; Site F, Test Pit G, recovered flakes and debitage in a quarry; Site F, Trench M/Mound 3077, lay on the outcrop summit and was constructed of debitage with a vestigial kerb but no evidence of human remains or charcoal; Site F, Trenches J and R/Mound 3078, comprised weathered debitage heaped into a cairn and encircled with stone blocks; Site F, Trench K and Test Pit P/Mound 3079, contained debitage and quarried blocks with two roughout axeheads, but no kerb; Site F, Pit 550e/570n, produced a deposit of debitage with a broken roughout axehead; Site F, Cairn 65, sealed a pit containing an upright ?anvil stone in a fill of debitage, charcoal flecks and coarse sherds; Site F, Cairn 67, produced debitage and a roughout axehead beneath the cairn.

- At Pike of Stickle, South Scree Cave contained two roughout axeheads placed upon a deposit of debitage; Dungeon Ghyll quarries produced debitage from the Phase 2 workings; Site 98 had alternating sequences of debitage, charcoal, and quarry debris adjacent to the quarry face; Site 95, 'cave' extraction contained successive tips of debitage, silts, and charcoal.
- At Mynydd Rhiw, Site B comprised a quarry scoop filled with debitage, lithics, and hearths; Site G produced debitage in a quarry; Trench 1 contained quarry debris and small deposits of charcoal; Trench 2 quarry contained a deposit of debitage.
- On Shetland, the Working Gallery (Beorgs of Uyea) contained debitage and lithics.
- At Tievebulliagh, numerous roughouts and lithics were abandoned amongst quarry debris.
- On Lambay Island, pits near the quarries contained debitage, hammerstones, rubbers, and sherds of bowl pottery.

Overall, the assemblages found in subterranean workings, on shaft floors, and abandoned at quarries, are strongly reminiscent of renewal rites as recorded in ethnography.

### Tools found in workings

Another ritualised practice found in ethnography is the custom of deliberately leaving extraction tools in the workings to satisfy ideologies (eg, Aboriginal Australian mine of Wilgie Mia; Flood 1995, 271–3). The archaeological data records that 65% (52 of 79) of flint mines and 27% (14 of 51) of axe quarries contained extraction tools in the workings. This was recorded at flint extraction sites at Ballygalley Hill, Black Mountain, Blackpatch, Church Hill, Cissbury, Den of Boddam, Durrington, Easton Down, Goodland, Grime's Graves (Fig. 5.8), Harrow Hill, and Stoke Down. Among the quarries, tools remained in workings at Beorgs of Uyea, Creag na Caillich, Graiglwyd, Lambay Island, Langdale, Le Pinacle, Mynydd Rhiw, and Tievebulliagh.

Although expediency or casual discard could explain some of these deposits, the juxtaposition of other apparently ritualised deposits suggests other explanations are needed. For example, on the shaft floor of Pit 15, Grime's Graves, a chalk platform held seven antler picks (Longworth & Varndell 1996, 51); similarly at Shaft V, Cissbury, a chalk platform lying against the western shaft wall held three antler tines. These examples appear to be deliberate and not casual discard, implying that at least some tools were curated in prescribed ways, as epitomised by the placed deposit in Greenwell's Pit of two inward-facing antler picks grouped with a bird skull and Cornish stone axehead. In addition, Pit 3 at Grime's Graves, dating from the Early Bronze Age, produced a bone pick made from a human femur amongst others of animal bone (Legge 1992, 69–70). Overall, the abandonment of extraction tools within workings seems to be a deliberate act of extraction practice.

### Imported extraction tools

Another aspect of extraction practice revealed by archaeology was the use of imported extraction tools which could have had symbolic undertones associated with the differently sourced materials. As mentioned above, imported granite hammerstones have been recorded at the Langdale quarries (Bradley & Suthren 1990), which could imply extraction by different groups, and indirectly indicate the origin of the site users. The closest granite sources to Langdale are Wasdale Head and mid-

*Figure 5.8: Antler picks abandoned in one of the side galleries of Greenwell's Pit at Grime's Graves (Norfolk) (photo: author)*

Eskdale, which might suggest a westerly route to the quarries, possibly from the Cumbrian coast and from sites such as Ehenside Tarn (Darbishire 1874) or Furness (Robinson *et al.* 2020). Imported hammerstones were also discovered at Graiglwyd, in this case water-worn cobbles derived from riverine or coastal deposits no more than 2 km distant (Williams & Davidson 1998, 12–16). At Mynydd Rhiw both local dolerite hammerstones and imported beach cobbles were used (Houlder 1961), possibly from the bay at Hell's Mouth, 2 km to the south-east – which may indicate the quarry users arrived at this site via a coastal route. The Working Gallery at the Beorgs of Uyea (Shetland) produced a number of hammerstones, including seven granite water-rolled cobbles derived from off-site riverine or coastal sources roughly 2 km away (Scott & Calder 1952). The use of imported hammerstones may represent the expedient use of the nearest suitable toolstone but, alternatively, may reflect group identity and legitimisation. However, the combination of imported hammerstones with other more definitive evidence of ritualised practices suggests they were probably part of a suite of ritualised practices.

Grime's Graves provides another example of an imported implement in the form of the Cornish greenstone axehead discovered in Greenwell's Pit 'in the first gallery, 4 feet from the entrance', which may have been used to produce the rare concave axe marks on the gallery walls (Greenwell 1870). Further concave axe marks were recorded in galleries in Pit 1 and Pit 2 (Clarke 1915), suggesting ground axeheads played a role in extraction, even if only symbolically. A second Cornish axehead was found amongst the assemblage on Floor 15 (Peake 1917).

The sourcing of extraction tools for flint mines is problematic as isotopic analysis has not yet been applied to provenancing antler picks. However, deer biology provides some clues to likely resource exploitation. Red deer shed antlers between March and May, and the study of picks from Grime's Graves revealed that 80+% were shed compared to <20% sourced from hunted stags, demonstrating that the majority had been expediently collected (Clutton-Brock 1984, 13, 16). This may have been facilitated by stags shedding antlers in the same place each year (Clason 1981, 122), introducing a degree of predictability for collecting strategies. However, each stag inhabits a territory of roughly 10 ha of semi-open forest, so the population can be dispersed. If the assemblages collected at Grime's Graves are an approximate guide to the quantities of antler picks required for mining, then excavation data suggest an average of 140+ antler picks were used per mine (Topping 2011). Consequently, the catchment for antler collection for each mine would be a *minimum* area of 7 km², or 1400 ha (allowing for two antlers per 10 ha) of forest – and that only if the stag territories were contiguous. However, considering the familiarity of Neolithic communities with animal husbandry, it is equally possible that deer herding could have occurred and supplied the requisite numbers of antlers needed for mining (Clutton-Brock 1984, 13, 16; D. Field pers. comm.). Overall, whichever antler procurement strategy was used, it must have been a considerable time-commitment each year before mining could begin.

It may be noteworthy that of around 78,500 antler picks that were estimated to be required for digging up to 239,133 m³ of chalk to construct Silbury Hill (Wiltshire), relatively few were found discarded during excavations (Worley in Leary *et al.* 2013, 95), suggesting that they were removed for use elsewhere. This provides contrast with the subterranean process of mining, where antler picks could have similarly been taken away but indicates instead that tools were left behind in the galleries for non-practical purposes.

### Built structures

Structures were discovered at 10% (8 of 79) of flint mines and 10% (5 of 51) of quarries. Some are reminiscent of the small cairns found underground in the Wilgie Mia Aboriginal Australian mines which created boundaries to areas closed to non-initiates (Flood 1995, 271–3).

- At Blackpatch, Shaft 1, a putative chalk platform lay in the centre of the shaft floor.
- At Cissbury, an artificial 'cave' was constructed around Gallery F in the Cave Pit (Fig. 5.9); in Shaft V a chalk platform holding three antler tines abutted the western wall on the shaft floor.
- At Goodland, 171 pits were discovered, containing quarry debris, debitage, lithics, and pottery, some covered by low cairns.
- At Grime's Graves, Pit 1 had a chalk platform juxtaposed with hearths, extraction tools, lithics, and Grooved Ware; in Pit 2, a platform lay adjacent to the Gallery 6 entrance; at Pit 15 an 'ogive-shaped' platform of mined flint occupied the north-western part of the shaft floor with seven antler picks placed upon it; while the 1971 Shaft floor featured a hearth overlain by a platform of flint and chalk blocks, upon which lay two Grooved Ware bowls and flint debitage, a small burnt area overlay part of the platform.

All structures were located upon shaft floors or in gallery entrances, all key access points to the underground workings.

Structures differed at the axe quarries.

*Figure 5.9: The Cave Pit at Cissbury (Sussex), showing the chalk block structure built on the shaft floor (from Park Harrison 1877a & b)*

*Figure 5.10: Top Buttress, Pike of Stickle (Langdale, Cumbria); one of the cave-like quarries below the summit of the mountain (photo: author)*

- At Graiglwyd, Mound 3077 lay on the summit of the outcrop and was constructed of axe-making debitage; Mound 3078 was also built of debitage some 15 m west of the outcrop; Mound 3079 comprised debitage and lithics and was located near Mound 3078; Cairn 65 covered a pit containing a putative anvil and axe-making debris; Cairn 67 was constructed over debitage and a roughout axehead.
- At Lambay Island, pits containing pottery, debitage, hammerstones, and polissoirs were sealed by stone settings and a hearth, juxtaposed with maceheads and axeheads, then all buried beneath a low cairn of quarry debris.
- At Langdale, the South Scree Cave may have been purposefully quarried to contain the placed deposits described above; Site 95 was another quarried cave containing placed deposits and charcoal (Fig. 5.10).
- On Shetland, the Working Gallery at the Beorgs of Uyea is a roofed structure abutting a felsite dyke; quarries on Midfield and the Beorgs of Uyea have small walled structures abutting felsite boulders, small cairns and 60+ standing stones >0.7 m high.

The built structures at quarries monumentalise the extraction sites and aspects of extraction practice, particularly rites of renewal through the deposition or mounding of debitage. In addition, middens facing the quarries at Le Pinacle, and arguably some of the midden-like deposits in the mines, may also be material expressions of extraction practice. Midden material is particularly fecund, notably used for soil enrichment during cultivation. It was often deposited, apparently symbolically, in funerary contexts such as the long barrow at Skendleby (Lincolnshire), in the chambers of West Kennet (Wiltshire) long barrow, and in burial chambers on the Isles of Scilly, and ditches of causewayed enclosures such as Whitehawk (Sussex) (McOmish *et al.* 2010, 86).

## Human remains

Human remains are found in a small number of sites, although excavation bias and taphonomic processes need to be considered, especially at quarries where acidic upland soils are not conducive to bone preservation. Consequently, human remains discussed here are from chalkland mines. The ethnography records burials in 18% (30 of 168) of studies, particularly in Aboriginal Australia and North America. Amongst British and Irish mines/quarries, excavated burials have been discovered at 12% (9 of 79) of sites.

- At Blackpatch, 'Barrow' 2, a small pit contained an extended adult male inhumation with a 'serrated lump of chalk' near the skull, an unrelated skull fragment in the upper fill, and an intrusive Saxon burial; at 'Barrow' 3, a small niche pit, two successive crouched inhumations were accompanied by lithics and animal bones buried beneath a mound of reconfigured mining debris with an intrusive and disturbed unaccompanied cremation; at 'Barrow' 4, a small pit contained a disarticulated adult male inhumation accompanied by lithics and an ox tooth; at 'Barrow' 12, a remodelled waste dump covered a primary and unaccompanied inhumation followed by a secondary adult male inhumation with carved chalk objects and lithics, a third disarticulated burial was scattered throughout the mound (and three intrusive Saxon interments occurred in the upper fills).
- At Church Hill, Shaft 1 produced a secondary cremation in the upper fills accompanied by lithics, a bone tool, and sherds of Beaker and Collared Urn.
- At Cissbury, the Skeleton Shaft contained a near-vertical female skeleton, head down 0.76 m above the shaft floor, juxtaposed with animal bones; at Shaft VI a crouched adult male inhumation lay roughly midway down the shaft surrounded by chalk blocks and nodules, accompanied by lithics and a carved chalk object; in Shaft 27 an adult female extended inhumation was discovered on the lower shaft fills with 'charcoal' in her right hand and juxtaposed with two chalk objects and a 'fossil-like worm'.
- At Grime's Graves, Pit 2, mid-way down the shaft lay a disarticulated skeleton below a sequence of two hearths adjacent to animal bones and lithics.

Body part deposition occurs at 10% (8 of 79) of sites.

- At Blackpatch, Shaft 4, a child's mandible and adult femur were discovered in the upper fills; Chipping Floor 2, western hearth, was juxtaposed with human and animal bones, an intrusive cremation was associated with Beaker sherds; 'Barrow' 2 contained an extended inhumation below a mound of mined waste which featured a secondary skull fragment in the upper fills; 'Barrow' 12 was a remodelled waste dump containing a tertiary disarticulated inhumation above a sequence of two crouched inhumations;
- At Church Hill, Shaft 6 produced a single human fibula on or close to the shaft floor; Chipping Floor 4 featured a hearth with unspecified human bone.
- At Grime's Graves, Pit 1, the middle shaft fills contained a human skull wedged between chalk blocks 50 mm above an ox bone; Pit 3 produced a pick crafted from human bone from the lower fills.

The human remains discovered at flint mines suggest they represent formal or semi-formal interments designed to associate the deceased with the site and raw material, as recorded in the ethnography of the Yolngu (Morphy 1995) and Mara-larr-mirri (Taçon 1991) Australian Aboriginal communities, or various North American Plains Tribes (Hughes 1995), for example. Both burials and body parts are predominantly found in the lower half of shaft fills or buried beneath remodelled waste dumps which have been converted into *ersatz* burial mounds. However, the later pits at Grime's Graves have an absence of human remains, implying a shift in practices, epitomised by Pit 3 where a human femur was now being used as a pick.

*Figure 5.11: Pit 2, Grime's Graves (Norfolk); the 'sundial' graffito discovered near a gallery entrance (illustration: T. Pearson)*

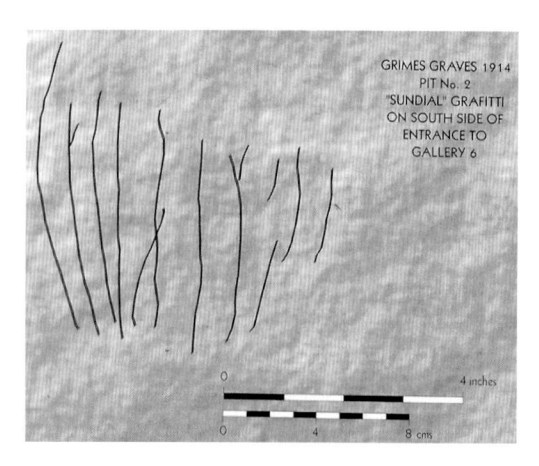

If the human remains recovered from the flint mines are representative of those who worked these sites then, unlike the predominantly male-orientated teams of ethnography, the archaeological record suggests that mixed gender teams, possibly with children, operated on the South Downs. The picture is less clear at Grime's Graves and the axe quarries.

### Graffiti/rock art

There is a small corpus of graffiti or rock art at or near some extraction sites, comprising graffiti at gallery entrances in flint mines, and rock art panels in valley floor locations below certain axe quarries. Ethnography records that rock art/graffiti was created for purposes of legitimisation, for cosmological reasons, and to provide a setting for rituals and offerings. Ethnographic accounts document rock art/graffiti in 27% (46 of 168) of studies, predominantly in the Americas and Australia.

In Britain and Ireland 14% (11 of 79) of flint mines feature on-site art/graffiti compared to just 2% (1 of 51) of axe quarries. However, if rock art/graffiti within a catchment of 5 km of a site is considered, then the flint mines provide no evidence, whereas 61% (31 of 51) of quarries are located within 5 km of rock art panels – generally on low-lying valley floors. However, a general lack of suitable surfaces for art near the flint mines may explain this absence. In addition, the issue of whether extraction sites and rock art panels are contemporary needs to be considered (cf. Bradley *et al.* 2019).

Flint mine graffiti comprises:
- At Church Hill, Shaft 4 has a putative graffito above a gallery entrance.
- At Cissbury, Willett's 1874 Shaft featured a lattice-like graffito in the East Gallery; No. 2 Escarp Shaft had two lattice graffiti above gallery entrances; the Cave Pit contained two graffiti above the entrances to the East-south-east Gallery and Gallery B; Shaft VI had a graffito above a gallery entrance.
- At Grime's Graves, Pit 2 contained two graffiti, the 'Sundial' above the Gallery 6 entrance (Fig. 5.11) and 'Tally Marks' between entrances to Galleries 4 and 7; in addition, in Greenwell's Pit, Pit 1 Galleries 2, 6, 7, 11, 12, 13, and in Pit 2 Galleries 1–2, 5, and 11, unusual and rare impact marks from a ground axe were discovered on gallery walls where the usual extraction tool was an antler pick, and these marks may have had a similar symbolic resonance to graffiti for the miners.
- At Harrow Hill, Pit 21 had seven graffiti near gallery entrances and scratched upon portable chalk blocks; Shaft 13 had graffiti placed near entrances to Gallery 13-III and Shaft 13G.

The axe quarries generally use rock art/graffiti in different ways. At Graiglwyd, Floor B produced the only recorded example of portable art found at a quarry (Hazzeldine Warren 1921, 194), comprising a stone plaque inscribed with geometric designs reminiscent of Grooved Ware, Passage Grave motifs and the chalk plaques from Amesbury (Wiltshire) Harding 1988). Its context close to hearths and discarded axehead roughouts parallels the portable art in flint mines (eg, Pit 21, Harrow Hill). However, rock art located within 5 km of a quarry is more common, occurring at Creag na Caillich and Langdale, where rock art panels occur on nearby valley floors and are intervisible with the quarries, potentially creating viewpoints to the sites if the art were contemporary.

Overall, the graffiti in flint mines is generally found above gallery entrances at the main entry points to subterranean workings. In contrast, rock art near quarries appears to route-mark sites or provide viewpoints. The inscribed chalk blocks from mines, and the Graiglwyd stone plaque, all suggest portable artworks also played a role in extraction practices.

# 5 An ethnoarchaeological analysis of Neolithic extraction sites in Britain and Ireland

## Site abandonment and rites of renewal

The abandonment of many extraction sites appears to follow deliberate, staged sequences of backfilling, paralleling ethnographic trends of post-extraction ceremonialism in 33% (55 of 168) of studies. The archaeological backfilling events comprise natural silts and stabilised layers which are often overlain by hearths, debitage, lithics, pottery, extraction tools, animal remains, and rare human remains within the confines of the extraction arena. These assemblages occur at 53% (42 of 79) of mines and 35% (18 of 51) of quarries, demonstrating common abandonment practices incorporating a range of materials. Such evidence was recorded at flint extraction sites at Blackpatch, Church Hill, Cissbury, Easton Down, Harrow Hill, Goodland, Grime's Graves, and Stoke Down, and quarries at Creag na Caillich, Den of Boddam, Graiglwyd, Lambay Island, Langdale, and Mynydd Rhiw. The chronological range of these sites spans the entire Neolithic period into the Early/Middle Bronze Age transition, demonstrating the longevity of episodic backfilling events.

Examples of staged deposits can be seen in the Sussex mines:

- At Blackpatch, in Shaft 7, lower fills incorporated carved chalk objects. A third of the way up the shaft lay a 'large floor … [comprising] bushels of flakes and fine splinters in places piled 4ins [101 mm] thick. Along the shaft wall on the northern edge of this floor was a huge pile of raw flint nodules … [A]nimal bones, principally ribs of oxen, were littered about on this floor …' (Pull 1932, 49), all buried by chalk blocks. When approximately two-thirds backfilled, cremated human bone was deposited accompanied by a flint axehead, flint knife, scraper, and 'a curious charm of worked chalk' (ibid., 58), all buried by dumps of chalk debris. However, the epitome of elaborate abandonment deposits at Blackpatch occurred in the upper fills of Shaft 1, where a large deposit of debitage, charcoal, ox and pig bones, and a 'central pile' of 12–15 lower sheep mandibles was surrounded by burnt stones, 'an ovate and a beautifully finished celt' and red quartzite hammerstone (ibid., 40; Pull Archive, Worthing Museum). Clearly such a carefully constructed assemblage was not casual discard and must represent ceremonialism incorporating feasting, offerings, and renewal rites at the closure of the mine.
- At Cissbury, the Cave Pit sequence began with cultural deposits 1.2 m above the shaft floor in this 6.09 m deep shaft (Park Harrison 1877b; 1878). Here, comingled with chalk backfill were debitage, roughout axeheads, lithics, charcoal, and antler picks were found in successive layers, arguably referencing extraction practice and its products. In Shaft VI (Park Harrison 1878) the stratigraphy recorded at least 13 separate depositional events, alternating between chalk rubble with comingled lithics, debitage, 'four masses of iron pyrites', a hearth with an ox bone and lithics, and mid-way down a formal crouched inhumation with further deposits of lithics and animal bones. Similar staged fills occurred in Shaft 24 where sequences of hearths, debitage, lithics, and animal bones were discovered (Pull Archive, Worthing Museum; Russell 2001, 176–7). However, arguably the most elaborate sequence was found in Shaft 27 (ibid., 178–89; Topping 2005), with a minimum of 12 separate deposits. Primary deposits comprised debitage, roughouts, a broken axehead and charcoal, all sealed beneath dumps of chalk debris. Roughly 1 m above the shaft floor lay an adult female inhumation juxtaposed with carved chalk objects, charcoal and the 'fossil-like worm' (see above), followed by layers incorporating a near complete ox skeleton, pig bones, and lithics. The upper half of the shaft comprised mostly silts containing roughout axeheads, lithics, and animal bones, suggesting deposits continued as the shaft naturally filled with wind-blown material.
- At Harrow Hill, in Pit 21 (Curwen & Curwen 1926), alternating bands of chalk rubble were juxtaposed with charcoal deposits, debitage, and lithics, again referencing extraction practice and its products. Similarly, in Shaft III although the shaft stratigraphy is not described, an assemblage of 33 axeheads was recovered, including a broken refitted example with one part found at the base of the shaft and the other at the top (Holleyman 1937,

242–3), strongly suggesting deliberate deposition referencing the place of origin.

- At Stoke Down, redeposited material was taken to extremes in Shaft 2 where a substantial amount of flint was discovered in the shaft, arguably more than this mine had actually produced (Wade 1923; Barber & Dyer 2005, 47). This suggests that the flint in Shaft 2 had been deliberately curated for deposition, which the ethnoarchaeological model would indicate was linked to rites of renewal. The fill of this shaft also produced a saddle quern found at a depth of 2.13 m, which may parallel deposits seen at causewayed enclosures such as Windmill Hill (Wiltshire) and Etton (Cambridgeshire), creating links between mines and practices at other types of site.

Overall, the abandonment events found in the South Downs mines are similar, often beginning when shafts were roughly one-third full and comprising deposits of extraction tools, faunal remains, rare human remains and products in various stages of manufacture.

Similar practices were recorded at the Wessex mines:

- At Easton Down, in Pit B1 (Stone 1931), deposits of chalk rubble contained scapulae, antler picks, rakes, tines, animal bones, lithics, and roughout axeheads, seemingly reference extraction practices. A large deposit of chalk silt filled the top of the shaft incorporating lithics, animal bones, antler tines, and a roughout axehead, all partly overlain by Chipping Floor 1. Pit B1(A), a shallow prospecting pit, contained debitage, lithics, and axeheads on its floor but remained open, allowing silts to accumulate containing flakes, lithics, a roughout axehead, a broken axehead, antler tines, and a dog skull. This suggests that natural backfilling was interspersed with deposition. The curated dog skull hints at symbolism, possibly totemism, reminiscent of the later dog skeleton found in Greenwell's Pit at Grime's Graves (see below). In Pit B49, a two-phase pit was backfilled with chalk blocks and extraction tools for a depth of around one third, followed by silts containing five ox scapulae, 3 broken antler picks, charcoal, and debitage. The sequence was completed with chalk rubble and another larger deposit of silt containing molluscs, coarse pottery, five roughout axeheads, a broken antler pick, and a possible flint pick. Again, the Easton Down sequences, like other Wessex mines, clearly reference extraction practice through placed deposits of digging tools and cultural material in a series of staged deposits as part of the backfill of the pit.

- At Grime's Graves, the abandonment of Greenwell's Pit began in the galleries with the placed deposit of the phalarope skull, antler picks, and a Cornish stone axehead discussed above, and then progressed to backfilling the shaft with dumps of chalk debris containing mining tools, carved chalk objects, hearths, 'numerous' animal bones, scatters of debitage, and two deposits of wind-blown silts, suggesting at least seven distinct backfilling events in the 12 m deep shaft (Greenwell 1870; Longworth & Varndell 1996). In a gallery linking Greenwell's Pit and Shaft A and placed upon a dump of mining debris, lay the curled-up skeleton of a dog, carefully buried beneath chalk blocks which probably began the abandonment sequence in Shaft A. In Pit 1 (Fig. 5.12) (Clarke 1915) the shaft was initially filled with dumps of chalk rubble incorporating extraction tools, lithics, debitage, and Grooved Ware, all sealed beneath a stabilised deposit of 'fine' chalk rubble, which was followed by a substantial deposit of wind-blown silts which incorporated lithics, nodules, and antler picks, marking a hiatus in backfilling. Following this, a series of chalk deposits featured hearths, a human skull wedged between two chalk blocks, debitage, hammerstones, and assorted animal bones, suggesting a minimum of ten abandonment events. Pit 2 had a similar sequence and assemblages but in this case the mine contained a disarticulated skeleton half-way down the shaft juxtaposed with assorted animal bones. The 1971 Shaft contained a sequence of 20+ layers of alternating chalk debris and silts, with the penultimate silt containing four axeheads in 'fresh condition', suggesting structured deposition (Mercer 1976, 106). These examples contrast markedly with later Early/Middle Bronze Age extraction on-site (Healy et al. 2014; 2018), where Pit 3 (Armstrong 1923) contained a few bone

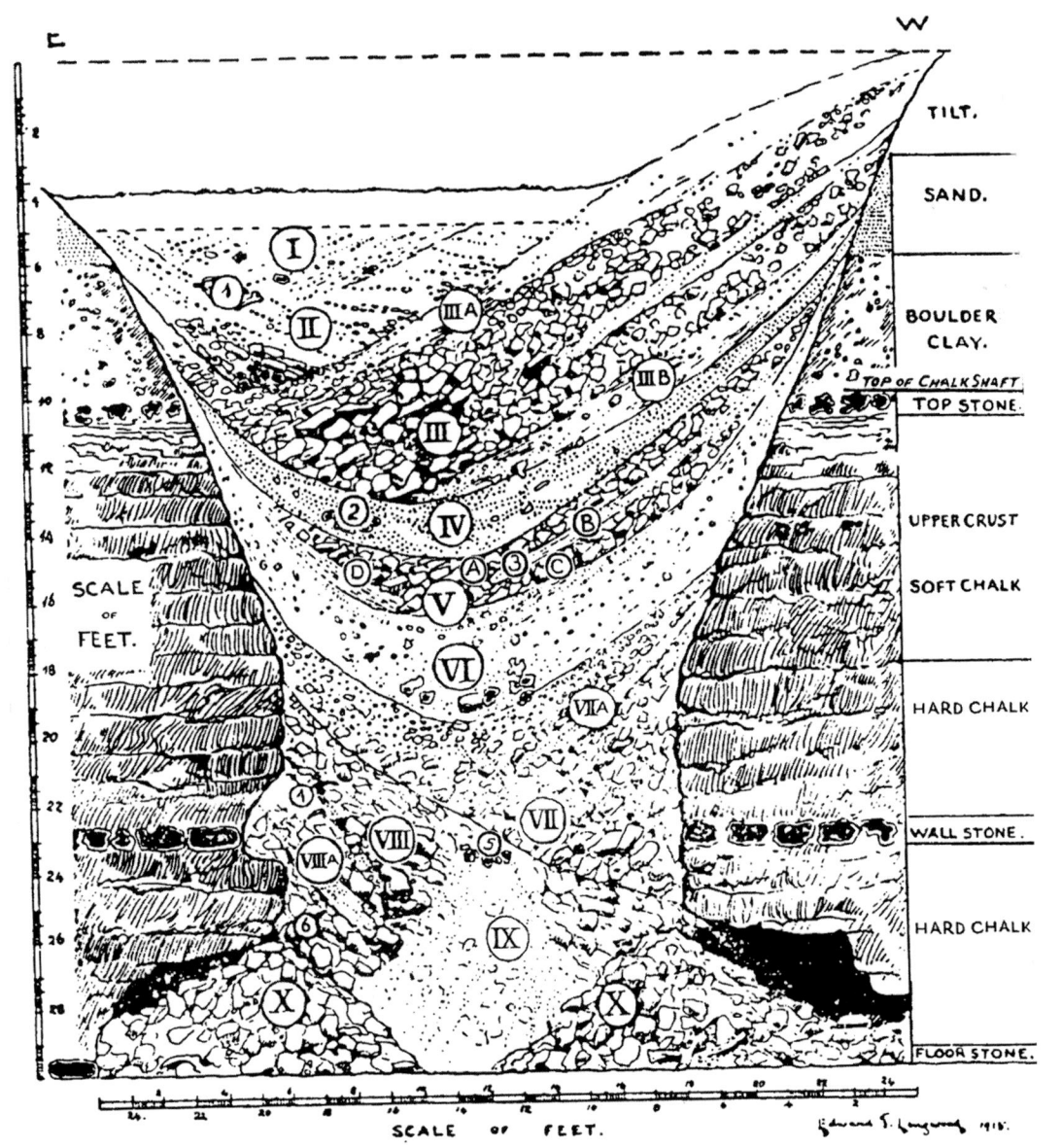

## 5 An ethnoarchaeological analysis of Neolithic extraction sites in Britain and Ireland

*Figure 5.12: Pit 1, Grime's Graves (Norfolk), E.T. Lingwood's drawing of the shaft fills, showing the sequence of deposits (from Clarke 1915)*

picks, one made from human bone; parts of Pit 15 were active, but with little of the former richness in artefact deposition, all suggesting that abandonment practices had changed significantly. Pit extraction had become the norm and extraction was no longer a secluded, subterranean activity. The hiatus between Late Neolithic and Early/Middle Bronze Age mining at Grime's Graves saw a move away from ritualised practices to a more mundane approach to extraction with little material deposition.

- At Goodland (Case 1973), a U-shaped, ditched enclosure with outcropping flint nodules on its south-eastern perimeter encircled 171 pits which contained nodules, debitage, sherds, and lithics, with some covered by low cairns. Although abandonment practices differed from the English mines, the composition of the pit deposits was similar. Comparable features occurred at the Lambay Island quarries (Cooney 2005; 2009), suggesting that pit deposition at extraction sites may have been an indigenous Irish practice.

The quarries had similar sequences of quarry waste, debitage and extraction tools.

- At Creag na Caillich, East Quarry (Site 1) (Edmonds *et al.* 1992), the primary backfill comprised quarry debris with deposits of charcoal, sealed by compacted debitage and charcoal up to 250 mm thick, followed by humic soil incorporating flakes, quarry debris, charcoal, and a granite hammerstone. The West Quarry (Site 2) had an almost identical sequence, suggesting the deliberate deposition of quarry debris and debitage at its source.
- At Graiglwyd, Floor B, an area of scree quarrying created a substantial 'floor' of 'cubical blocks of stone' (Hazzeldine Warren 1921, 170) on which was placed a large hearth 6.1 m in diameter and smaller satellite hearths. Huge quantities of debitage, flakes and 'imperfect axes' were discovered, including 400+ broken axehead roughouts, 'some 1,100 specimens ... [belonging] ... to the axe and adze group' were collected, alongside a stone plaque decorated with linear and geometric motifs (*ibid.*, 194). A 'few [unidentified] scraps of bone' were found (*ibid.*, 195). The Graiglwyd evidence suggests extraction practice comprised the on-site management of scree-working debris, the use of hearths, bones implying offerings/feasting, and the deliberate deposition of axeheads at their place of origin. Trench 3 (Williams & Davidson 1998) produced flakes and four roughout axeheads amongst quarrying episodes.
- At Lambay Island occur some of the most elaborate sequences (Cooney 1998; 2000; 2004; 2005; Cooney *et al.* 2011), where shallow scoops containing pottery, lithics, and roughout axeheads are located near the quarry face, juxtaposed with pits containing debitage, hammerstones, and grinders which were sealed by stone slabs. A hearth lay near the centre of these features. The scoops, pits, and hearth were then buried beneath a mound of quarry waste and beach gravel 8 m in diameter and 1 m high. This pit group to mound sequence references extraction practice and tool production by symbolically returning tools to the earth while incorporating the use of fire, then monumentalising these events with an overlying cairn of quarry debris.
- At the Langdale quarries, the South Scree Cave (Fell 1951) was excavated into the side of Pike of Stickle and contained a deposit of compacted silts and debitage 530 mm in depth. Lying on top of this were two roughout axeheads, suggesting a structured deposit of chipping debris and quarry products in a shrine-like structure which echoes practices common in New Guinea (Hampton 1997). A secondary phase of extraction at the Dungeon Ghyll quarries (Bradley & Edmonds 1988; 1993) saw the redeposition of debitage and hammerstones within the workings, rather than expediently dumped downslope. Again, extraction tools and debitage were carefully curated on-site. Site 95, Pike of Stickle (*ibid.*), was another cave-like quarry with a stratigraphy recording episodic working which culminated in a sequence of dumped flakes and hammerstones reminiscent of the South Scree Cave.

Apart from Lambay Island, most quarries do not have the rich array of artefacts found in the mines. Most are open to the elements and often on steep slopes where items would easily become dispersed. However, they do follow the custom of curated deposits of debitage, structured deposits of artefacts, and the retention of extraction tools on-site.

## A summary of the evidence for ritualised extraction practices

The assemblages in the archaeological record strongly parallel the material evidence in the ethnographic data, suggesting that ritualised extraction practices, perhaps to varying degrees, probably occurred at most sites discussed – and arguably others (Table 5.3). Preparatory activities appear to be indicated by hearths and charcoal deposits which generally cannot easily be explained in functional terms. The tools recorded in both extraction and post-extraction contexts, alongside structures, placed deposits, and rock art/graffiti, occur at most sites. In addition, on-site redeposition of debitage and broken or rejected implements parallels ethnographic renewal rites. The often elaborate and episodic nature of backfilling at many sites and the presence of rare human remains imply that abandonment was generally a structured and formalised series of events. It is noteworthy that core elements of ritualised extraction practice are represented at both mines and quarries.

The assemblages from the mines and quarries illustrate a number of trends:

- human remains only occur in mine shafts and not galleries;
- pottery was only found in flint mine shafts and at the Irish quarries at Ballygalley Hill (Collins 1978), Goodland (Case 1973), and Lambay Island (Cooney 1998; 2000; 2005);
- hearths are only discovered on shaft floors or stabilised layers in shafts and adjacent to quarry workings;
- hearths are discovered in shafts, on working floors, or on stabilised horizons and adjacent to quarry workings;
- placed lithics and debitage occur throughout the workings;
- graffiti is sometimes found above gallery entrances in the mines, and some sites feature portable art.

Many assemblages are located at access points, suggesting that they targeted the first and last places experienced by users. The presence of lithics and debitage in dark galleries was a deliberate act of redeposition, as noted above, as the lack of evidence for artificial lighting suggests that they were not knapping locations. However, it was the shafts which witnessed the majority of activity, ranging from the use of hearths, through to assemblages of artefacts, human remains, and animal bones, suggesting elaborate but episodic backfilling practices in the mines and, to a lesser extent, at the quarries.

The role of artefacts at extraction sites was often mnemonic, designed to aid the memory and stimulate an appropriate response at particular locations during ritualised extraction practices. Placed deposits reinforced and maintained belief systems and cosmographic ordering, building upon Mesolithic precursors, but subverting them in new ways as society redefined itself and adopted the new Neolithic lifeway. This occurred during a comparative explosion of Neolithic art-forms [n=75] in Europe compared to those of the preceding Mesolithic [n=12] (Robb 2015, 643), demonstrating a dramatic increase in the materiality of cultural expression. The ethnographic data suggests that on-site assemblage deposition was part of a mitigation strategy, designed to appease supernatural forces who oversaw or were believed to own the raw material, or it formed part of renewal rites.

### The flint mines

The ethnoarchaeological model comprises 21 material indicators of potential ritualised extraction practices (Table 5.3). The data indicate that 19 flint mines combine the commonest features, and are located at four sites: Blackpatch, Church Hill, Cissbury (all Sussex) and Grime's Graves (Norfolk). The 19 mines are: Pit 2 (Grime's Graves); Greenwell's Pit (Grime's Graves); Shaft 27 (Cissbury); The Cave Pit (Cissbury); 1971 Shaft (Grime's Graves); Pit 15 (Grime's Graves; Willet's 1873 Shaft (Cissbury); Shaft V (Cissbury); Shaft 24 (Cissbury); The Large Pit (Cissbury); Shaft 4 (Blackpatch); The Skeleton Shaft (Cissbury); No2 Escarp Shaft (Cissbury); Pit 7 (Grime's Graves); Shaft 3 (Blackpatch); Shaft 3A (Blackpatch); Shaft 8 (Blackpatch); Shaft 3 (Church Hill); No 1 Escarp Shaft (Cissbury).

Among the mines, Pit 2 at Grime's Graves featured the greatest number with 16 [80%] of 21 indicators, closely followed by Greenwell's Pit and Pit 1 at Grime's Graves both with 15 [75%]. In comparison, Shaft 27 at Cissbury contained the most indicators among the southern mines with 13 [65%]. Generally, the South Downs Group range between three and 12 indicators, whereas the Wessex Group has fewer with 3–7. In the later pits at Grime's Graves only 3–6 indicators are recorded. This suggests that ritualised practices changed over time, may have had regional characteristics, and reached their apogee at Grime's Graves in the Late Neolithic deep-shaft, galleried mines before dramatically diminishing afterwards (Fig. 5.13).

### The axe quarries

The nine axe quarries which exhibit the commonest indicators of ritualised practices (Table 5.3) comprise: Pike of Stickle Site 98, Creag na Caillich Site 1, Graiglwyd Site F Test Pit E, Pike of Stickle Site 95, Creag na Caillich Site 2, Graiglwyd Floor B, Pike of Stickle South Scree Cave, Graiglwyd Trench 3, and

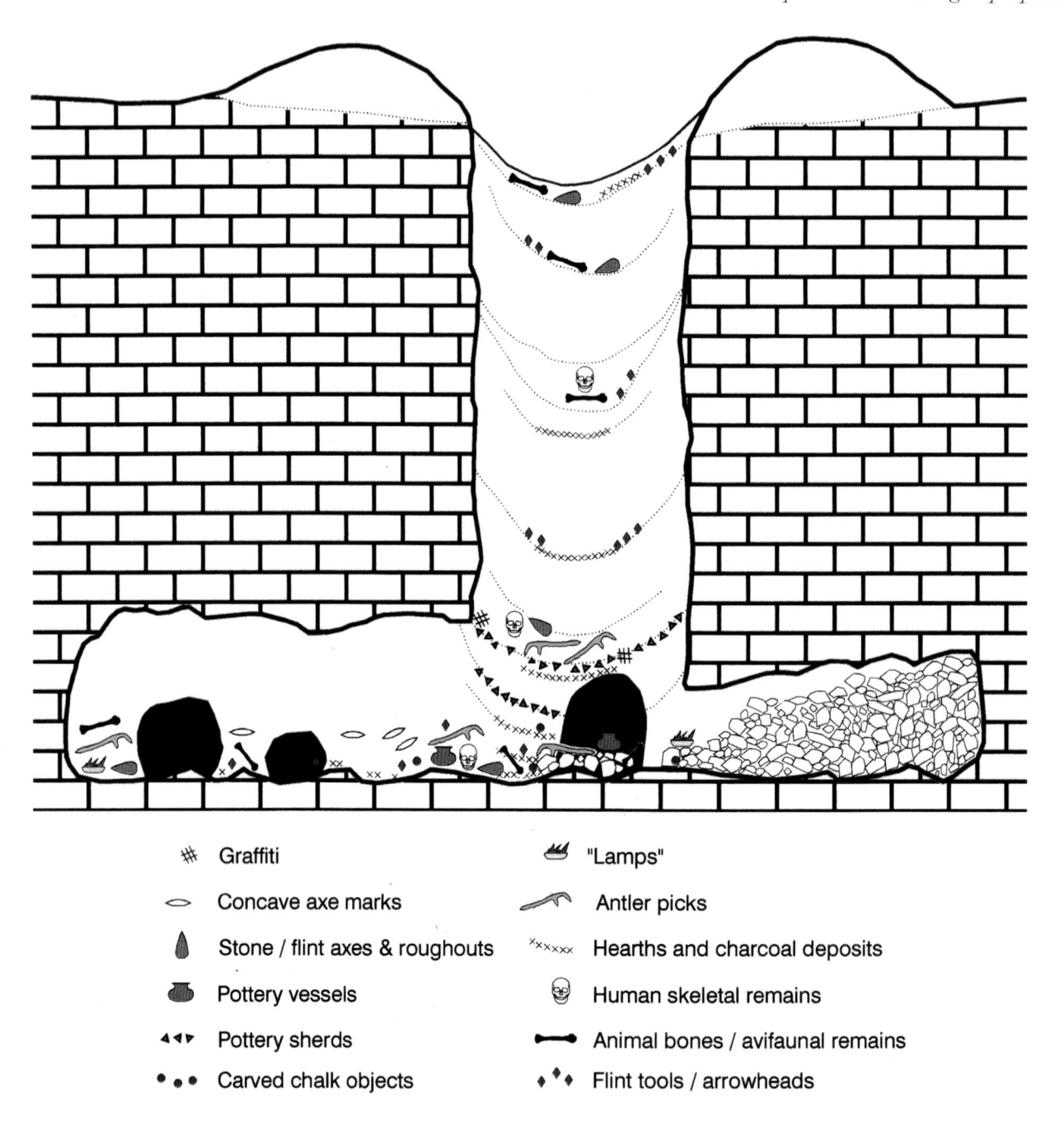

*Figure 5.13: The spatial and temporal distribution of deposits and events in the English flint mines (illustration: P. Topping & T. Pearson)*

| Symbol | Meaning | Symbol | Meaning |
|---|---|---|---|
| # | Graffiti | "Lamps" | "Lamps" |
| ⌒ | Concave axe marks | ⌒ | Antler picks |
| ◊ | Stone / flint axes & roughouts | xxxxx | Hearths and charcoal deposits |
| 🏺 | Pottery vessels | 💀 | Human skeletal remains |
| ◂▸ | Pottery sherds | — | Animal bones / avifaunal remains |
| • • • | Carved chalk objects | ♦ ♦ ♦ | Flint tools / arrowheads |

Graiglwyd Trench 5. As with the flint mines, the geographical distribution and chronology of these sites demonstrates that common extraction practices existed during the Early Neolithic, with only Creag na Caillich (and possibly Graiglwyd) operational in the later Neolithic period (Edinborough *et al.* 2020).

Overall, the empirical evidence presented above and in Table 5.3 suggests that ritualised extraction took place at most mines and quarries during the Neolithic period but had almost disappeared at the latest workings ascribed to the Early–Middle Bronze Age transition. The sites which recorded strong evidence for ritualisation include Ballygalley Hill, Blackpatch, Cissbury, Church Hill, Goodland, Grime's Graves, and Harrow Hill, and the quarries at Creag na Caillich, Graiglwyd, Lambay Island, Langdale, Le Pinacle, and Shetland (Beorgs of Uyea). Consequently, it can be concluded that ritualised extraction practices were widespread in Britain and Ireland.

## 5 An ethnoarchaeological analysis of Neolithic extraction sites in Britain and Ireland

| Flint mines [n=79 excavations] | % | Axe quarries [n=51 excavations] | % |
|---|---|---|---|
| Grime's Graves Pit 2 | 80 [16] | | |
| Grime's Graves Greenwell's Pit | 75 [15] | | |
| Grime's Graves Pit 1 | 75 [15] | | |
| Cissbury Shaft 27 | 65 [13] | | |
| Cissbury Cave Pit | 60 [12] | | |
| Blackpatch Shaft 1 | 60 [12] | Lambay Island Eagle's Nest | 60 [12] |
| Cissbury Shaft VI | 55 [11] | | |
| Cissbury Willet's Shaft | 55 [11] | | |
| Goodland | 55 [11] | | |
| Grime's Graves 1971 Shaft | 55 [11] | | |
| Grime's Graves Pit 15 | 50 [10] | | |
| | | Langdale Pike of Stickle Site 98 | 50 [10] |
| Blackpatch Shaft 2 | 50 [10] | | |
| Blackpatch Chipping Floor 2 | 50 [10] | | |
| Cissbury Willet's Shaft | 45 [9] | | |
| Cissbury Shaft V | 45 [9] | Le Pinacle | 45 [9] |
| Cissbury Pull Shaft 24 | 45 [9] | | |
| Harrow Hill Pit 21 | 45 [9] | | |
| Blackpatch Shaft 5 | 45 [9] | | |
| Church Hill Shaft 1 | 45 [9] | | |
| Cissbury Large Pit | 40 [8] | | |
| | | Langdale Pike of Stickle Site 95 | 40 [8] |
| Cissbury Tindall's Shaft | 40 [8] | | |
| | | Shetland Beorgs of Uyea Gallery | 40 [8] |
| Ballygalley Hill | 40 [8] | Creag na Caillich East Quarry Site 1 | 40 [8] |
| Church Hill Shaft 4 | 40 [8] | Graiglwyd Site F Test Pit E | 40 [8] |
| Church Hill Shaft 5A | 40 [8] | Mynydd Rhiw Site B | 40 [8] |
| Harrow Hill Shaft 13 | 40 [8] | Graiglwyd Site F Test Pit I | 40 [8] |
| | | Graiglwyd Site F Cairn 65 | 35 [7] |
| Blackpatch Shaft 7 | 35 [7] | | |
| Church Hill Shaft 6 | 35 [7] | | |
| Easton Down Pit B49 | 35 [7] | | |
| Blackpatch Barrow 1 (dump of Shaft 3) | 35 [7] | Creag na Caillich West Quarry Site 2 | 35 [7] |
| | | Graiglwyd Site F Test Pit S | 30 [6] |
| Church Hill Chipping Floors 1–11 | 30 [6] | | |
| | | Langdale South Scree Cave | 30 [6] |
| | | Graiglwyd Floor B | 30 [6] |
| Harrow Hill Shaft III | 30 [6] | Langdale Thunacar Knott | 30 [6] |
| | | Mynydd Rhiw Trench 1 | 30 [6] |
| Grime's Graves Pit 12 | 30 [6] | Graiglwyd Site F Cairn 67 | 30 [6] |
| Church Hill Chipping Floor 14 (cut by Shafts 6 & 7) | 30 [6] | | |
| Stoke Down Shaft 2 | 30 [6] | | |
| Black Mountain | 30 [6] | Graiglwyd Site F Mound 3079 | 30 [6] |
| Blackpatch Barrow 3 | 30 [6] | | |
| Blackpatch Barrow 12 | 30 [6] | | |
| Church Hill Pit C (IA/Med?) | 30 [6] | | |
| Easton Down Pit B1 & Floor B1 | 30 [6] | | |
| Easton Down Pit B1(A) & Floor B2 | 30 [6] | | |
| Grime's Graves Pit 3 | 30 [6] | | |
| Blackpatch Shaft 4 | 25 [5] | | |
| | | Shetland Beorgs of Uyea/Midfield | 25 [5] |
| | | Tievebulliagh [Discovery] | 25 [5] |
| Cissbury Skeleton Shaft | 25 [5] | | |
| Easton Down B67 | 25 [5] | Langdale Harrison Stickle | 25 [5] |

Table 5.3: (continued overleaf) The relative percentages of the presence of 21 potential indicators of ritualised practices recorded at Neolithic to Early/Middle Bronze Age extraction sites, ranked in descending order with greatest number first. The number of indicators is shown in brackets [n=21]

| Flint mines [n=79 excavations] | % | Axe quarries [n=51 excavations] | % |
|---|---|---|---|
| Grime's Graves Pit 8 | 25 [5] | | |
| | | Graiglwyd Trench 3 | 25 [5] |
| | | Graiglwyd Trench 5 | 25 [5] |
| Church Hill Chipping Floor 12 | 25 [5] | | |
| Church Hill Shaft 7 | 25 [5] | | |
| Grime's Graves Pit 9 | 25 [5] | | |
| Grime's Graves Pit 10 | 25 [5] | | |
| Grime's Graves Pit 14 | 25 [5] | | |
| Stoke Down Shaft 3 | 25 [5] | | |
| Blackpatch Chipping Floor 4 | 25 [5] | Creag na Caillich East Working Floor Site 3 | 25 [5] |
| Blackpatch Barrow 2 | 25 [5] | Creag na Caillich West Working Floor Site 4 | 25 [5] |
| Blackpatch Barrow 4 | 25 [5] | Langdale Dungeon Ghyll | 25 [5] |
| Grime's Graves Pit 4 | 25 [5] | | |
| Grime's Graves Pit 5 | 25 [5] | | |
| Stoke Down Shaft 1 | 25 [5] | | |
| Cissbury 2 Escarp Shaft | 20 [4] | | |
| Grime's Graves Pit 7 | 20 [4] | | |
| | | Mynydd Rhiw Site G | 20 [4] |
| | | Langdale Stake Beck | 20 [4] |
| Blackpatch Shaft 6 | 20 [4] | Graiglwyd Site F Test Pit C | 20 [4] |
| Grime's Graves Pit 11 | 20 [4] | Mynydd Rhiw Trench 2 | 20 [4] |
| Blackpatch Chipping Floor 1 | 20 [4] | | |
| Church Hill Pit A | 20 [4] | | |
| Durrington Shaft 5 | 20 [4] | | |
| Blackpatch Chipping Floor 3 | 20 [4] | | |
| Blackpatch Shaft 3A | 15 [3] | Rathlin Island | 15 [3] |
| Blackpatch Shaft 8 | 15 [3] | | |
| Church Hill Shaft 3 | 15 [3] | | |
| Blackpatch Shaft 3 | 15 [3] | | |
| Church Hill Shaft 2 | 15 [3] | | |
| Church Hill Chipping Floor 13 | 15 [3] | | |
| Cissbury 1 Escarp Shaft | 15 [3] | | |
| | | Graiglwyd Site F Mound 3077 | 15 [3] |
| | | Graiglwyd Site F Mound 3078 | 15 [3] |
| | | Graiglwyd Site F Test Pit N | 15 [3] |
| | | Graiglwyd Site F Test Pit Q | 15 [3] |
| | | Graiglwyd Site F Test Pits B & F | 15 [3] |
| | | Graiglwyd Site F Test Pit 550e/570n | 15 [3] |
| Grime's Graves Pit 6 | 15 [3] | | |
| Easton Down B19 | 15 [3] | | |
| Easton Down B45 | 15 [3] | | |
| | | Langdale Loft Crag Site DS87 | 15 [3] |
| Den of Boddam | 15 [3] | | |
| Church Hill Pit B (?IA) | 15 [3] | Graiglwyd Site F Test Pit G | 15 [3] |
| | | Graiglwyd Site F Test Pit H | 15 [3] |
| | | Tievebulliagh Trench 1 | 15 [3] |
| | | Tievebulliagh Trench 2 | 15 [3] |
| | | Tievebulliagh Trench 6 | 15 [3] |
| | | Tievebulliagh Trenches 4a & 4b | 10 [2] |
| Church Hill Chipping Floor 5 | 10 [2] | | |
| Stoke Down Pit D1 | 10 [2] | | |
| | | Tievebulliagh Trench 3 | 10 [2] |
| | | Tievebulliagh Trench 5 | 10 [2] |
| | | Graiglwyd Site F Test Pit L | 10 [2] |
| | | Graiglwyd Site F Test Pit O | 10 [2] |
| | | Tievebulliagh Trench 7 | 10 [2] |
| | | Tievebulliagh Trench 8 | 10 [2] |
| | | Tievebulliagh Trench 9 | 10 [2] |

# 6

# The products: an ethnoarchaeological analysis of lithic objects from extraction sites

Ethnography records the complex relationships people have with extraction sites and their products and demonstrates the pressing need to consider a more rounded view of the social context of extraction. This is especially true as there is a considerable amount of empirical evidence in the archaeological record which the ethnoarchaeological model suggests can indicate more esoteric motivations regarding the sites and product use and provides a more balanced view of the probable role of lithic procurement in Neolithic society.

## Issues

The study of lithic artefact distributions is constrained by the state of research relating to raw material sourcing. This is especially true of flint, where technical difficulties have prevented the precise identification of sources. Current techniques are largely restricted to the identification of regional groups of mines rather than individual sites because of difficulties with the chemical signature of the raw material. To add further complexity, some flint sources, such as Great Massingham in Norfolk, share similarities with those in the South Downs, further clouding source identification. However, some regional signatures of flint sources have emerged from the small number of samples analysed (Craddock *et al.* 1983; 2012), with indications that individual mine complexes such as Cissbury, Blackpatch, Church Hill, and Grime's Graves can be identified from within regional groupings (Thompson *et al.* 1986; Craddock *et al.* 2012). Nevertheless, research into flint artefacts remains severely handicapped through these difficulties with provenancing and the lack of precise distributions of products.

In total contrast, the sourcing of igneous rocks has benefitted from many decades of petrographic analysis captured in the publications of the Implement Petrology Committee (eg, Clough & Cummins 1979; 1988) and the work of the Implement Petrology Group (eg, Davis & Edmonds 2011a). Currently 36 general sources have been identified in Britain and Ireland (one in Brittany), which provided lithologies mainly for axehead production. Of these, 11 have been located with some precision and linked to specific quarries, and the remainder have been identified as broader regional groupings – much like flint. An increase in the use of rapid, non-destructive techniques such as pXRF – used so successfully in the Italian Alps (Pétrequin *et al.* 2012a; 2017) and Shetland (Cooney *et al.* 2014) – may well lead to the identification of other quarries in Britain and Ireland. The precision such technologies provide will be especially useful in heavily exploited areas such as the Langdale/Scafell complex where currently 700+ quarries have been identified (Vin Davis pers. comm.). In the Italian Alps pXRF made it possible to associate axeheads with specific quarries or jade boulders, creating a far better understanding of the mechanics of extraction and its social outcomes.

## The importance of objects

Artefacts can attain a degree of value and cultural importance through processes of objectification, whereby an artefact is given a biography during its sourcing, production, or use which can create a meaningful narrative for society. Clear parallels exist between the temporal development of biographies of people and the constructed biographies of objects, materials, and substances. Communities characterise their place in the world through the use of objects, and these objects (as with people) have agency and the capacity to play significant roles in society (Gell 1998). Miller (2010, 60) has summarised the theoretical context as 'the idea that objects make us, as part of the very same process by which we make them ... ultimately there is no separation of subjects and objects' – a situation akin to cyclical symbiosis, one process leading to the creation of the other before repeating the cycle when necessary. To play a role in society, objects first need to have a cultural value to the human community (often through associations with cosmology such as origin stories) before they can become objectified and embody individual or communal self-knowledge. The objectified artefact thus becomes a material embodiment of cultural concepts, temporally spanning the past, present, and future, thus empowering it to interact with social practices. An objectified artefact can thus be an agent for tradition and stability or, alternatively, an initiator of change.

Ethnography documents the roles of objectified artefacts in social processes such as the creation of identity and knowledge transfer, the underpinning of social networks, value systems, and political relationships (eg, Kopytoff 1986; Gell 1998). In New Guinea, for instance, many communities have sacred power objects which were originally mundane, functional items that were withdrawn from secular use and ritually transformed into sacred paraphernalia that enabled them to manipulate supernatural forces and provide access to wealth and power (Hampton 1997, 279; Godelier 1999, 162). Consequently, the 'functional' appearance of an object can be deceptive and not necessarily reflect its true role in society.

Objectified artefacts can encapsulate histories, origin myths, and cosmologies (cf. Best 1912; Boas & Hunt 1921; Malinowski 1922) and through these associations legitimise social constructs such as kinship networks, political relations, gift-giving, indebtedness, obligations, and create deliberate inequalities (Mauss 1954; Godelier 1999). Although these artefacts can be enabling and a powerful device within society, they can also fuel rivalries, competition, and antagonism, as seen in the often cited potlatch ceremonies of the North-west Coast Native American communities (Boas & Hunt 1921; Mauss 1954, 31–45; Godelier 1999, 56–78), or the Kula exchange network amongst Trobriand Islanders (Malinowski 1922; Mauss 1954, 18–31; Godelier 1999, 78–95).

A comparison of the Hagen and Wiru, two New Guinea communities, is an informative example of the contrasting ways similar material culture can be used to enable or frame different forms of social interaction (Chappell 1966; Strathern 1969). Here, two societies indirectly linked by the same exchange network have different cultural practices while using the same types of objects, especially axeheads – some of which carry biographies (Table 6.1). The two communities are separated by a distance of roughly 65 km (40 miles), the Hagen live in the Western Highlands close to axe quarries in the Jimi, Wahgi, and Chimbu Valleys (Strathern 1969, 314) whereas the Wiru inhabit the Southern Highlands south of Hagen territory, at the interface of the uplands and lowland swamps and only have limited access to poor quality locally sourced stone (*ibid.*, 320). Both communities trade slightly different exchange items and use axeheads in different ways. As a result of the different levels of access to quarries, the toolstone rich Hagen obtain a greater range of luxury items compared to the toolstone poor Wiru. The intervening territory between the Hagen and the Wiru is inhabited by two culturally separate communities, the Kauil and the Imbonggu, who complete the pan-tribal exchange network.

The toolstone rich Hagen are recognised as expert quarrymen and axehead makers. Their stone implements, including large axeheads, span the everyday requirements of forest dwellers alongside the needs of ceremonial

# 6 The products: an ethnoarchaeological analysis of lithic objects from extraction sites

Table 6.1: The social context of axehead production and use at the New Guinea Highlands/Lowlands interface inhabited by the Hagen and Wiru tribal communities

| Hagen [highland forest dwellers; direct access to quarries] | Spatial, socio-economic and cultural filters | Wiru [lowland grassland dwellers; no direct access to quarries] |
|---|---|---|
| Subsistence: Pigs; Sweet potato<br>Variables: taro; yam; banana; sugar cane; beans | Spatial (65 km/40 miles) and cultural separation by intervening Kauil and Imbonggu communities<br><br>Indirect trade links between Hagen and Wiru<br><br>Distance from, and access to, high quality lithic raw materials<br><br>• • • | Subsistence: Pigs; Sweet potato<br>Variables: taro; yam; banana; sugar cane; beans |
| Segmentary group structure, especially clans;<br>Women banned from participation in exchanges and rarely dance;<br>Stone axes solely a male tool | | Formerly segmentary group structure, now village dwellers with village as active unit;<br>Only males display stone axes;<br>Both males and females use work axes |
| Ceremonial exchange determines prowess:<br>Axes = bridewealth, compensation and funeral payments, gifts to ritual specialists | | Ceremonial exchange determines prowess:<br>Axes = bridewealth, exchange with maternal kin, funeral payments, gifts to ritual specialists |
| Exchange items: pigs, shells, plumes, stone axes, salt, oil | | Exchange items: pigs, shells, plumes, stone axes, salt, sugar cane |
| Public transactions = shells and pigs | | Public transactions = sugar cane and cooked vegetables |
| Primary exchange items = salt, oil, shells | | Primary exchange items = pigs, foodstuffs, sugar cane |
| Hagen produced stone axes as wealth or ceremonial objects, not just for subsistence tasks; participated in extensive multi-directional trade networks | | Wiru in poor trading position, produced no major commodity, did not have access to high quality lithic raw materials; were not middlemen; restricted trade network |
| Near quarries in Jimi, Wahgi, and Chimbu valleys | | Distant from quarries; only poor quality toolstone found locally |
| Axes LARGE [130–150 mm]<br>Axes circulate as wealth objects;<br>Classify axes into *c.* 15 types;<br>Good quality axes plentiful<br><br>STONE AXES, ALL PURPOSE TOOL | | Axes SMALL [50–75 mm]<br>Axes circulate as wealth objects;<br>Classify axes into 2 types;<br>Good quality axes few, thus wooden replicas used<br><br>NO LONGER USE STONE AXES (STEEL NOW USED) |
| Flake tools have no exchange value;<br>Flake tools simple, no secondary retouch;<br>Raw material widespread;<br><br>NO LONGER USE FLAKE TOOLS | | Flake tools have no exchange value;<br>Flake tools simple, no secondary retouch;<br>Raw material widespread<br><br>FLAKES = ALL PURPOSE TOOLS |
| Ceremonial and work axes manufactured by Hagen<br>Ceremonial axes worn on special occasions<br>Ceremonial axes could be used in warfare | | No axe types manufactured by Wiru<br>Ceremonial axes held during dances<br>Ceremonial axes *not* used in warfare |

(data extrapolated from Strathern 1969 and Chappell 1966)

life. For the Hagen, stone axes are exclusively a male tool and only men are involved in their trade. In contrast, the toolstone poor Wiru no longer use stone work axes, now preferring steel which can be used by both men and women. Consequently, the Wiru are reliant upon trade for what are invariably smaller stone axeheads, which like the Hagen are used for display and restricted to male use. Interestingly, the Wiru overcome their lack of high quality stone axeheads by crafting skeuomorphic wooden replicas for ceremonial use, a situation reminiscent of Neolithic examples (see below).

Overall, these two subtly contrasting but indirectly linked communities illustrate the ways social practices and materiality can differ over relatively short distances and between culturally similar groups. This emphasises the importance that access to lithic resources plays in the maintenance of cultural traditions and the transformative influence of the two intervening communities who act as cultural filters between the Hagen and Wiru. Consequently, this example could have an important bearing upon the interpretation of artefact distribution during the Neolithic, suggesting that we should expect cultural differences, even if only subtle, between contiguous or interlinked communities. This is particularly true concerning the use and meaning of extraction site products once they have crossed cultural boundaries. The difficulty, as always, is to identify Neolithic cultural boundaries in the archaeological record (cf. Brophy & Barclay 2009).

Although New Guinea has become something of a cliché in the archaeological literature, it does provide another useful example. Here, many communities have sacred power objects which originated as everyday, functional items but which have been withdrawn from secular use and ritually transformed into sacred paraphernalia to enable them to manipulate supernatural forces (Hampton 1997, 279). Consequently, the 'functional' appearance of an artefact can be deceptive, particularly among ceremonial axeheads which share the same characteristics as everyday work axes from the Abiamp quarry (Chappell 1987, 79–81). As a result, morphology is not always an accurate indicator of the use-life of an axehead. In addition, the over-sized Ye-yao axeheads, which surprisingly emerge from the quarry as profane objects, also have the potential for conversion into sacred power objects at a later time. Such ritual transformations are believed to have been inherited from the Ancestors (Hampton 1997, 468–9).

The criteria for artefact transformation can be social or political necessity or to acknowledge the rarity of the raw material. Ritual transformation occurs at significant events to objectify the artefacts involving public displays for debt repayment or the creation of new debts, all observed by the spirits and ancestors from the 'unseen world'. The redistribution of axeheads fuels the economy and establishes the donor's credentials to both his community and the spirit world. Importantly, these transformative rituals domicile ancestors or powerful spirits within the axe blades, who can then be ceremonially manipulated to maintain social order. The ancestral spirits are drawn from the individual's patrilineage, with powerful leaders being most favoured. Although the highlanders have female ghosts and spirits, only male spirits are installed into these sacred objects (Hampton 1997, 468–76, 542–4).

Summarising a range of ethnography, Godelier (1999, 168) observed that

> [m]atters are all the more complicated because a single type of object can often function first as a (valuable) commodity, then as a gift-object, and then as a treasure … [consequently] objects … little by little take on human attributes, or those of persons more powerful than humans – deities, nature spirits, mythic ancestors - … [l]ike human or supernatural persons, they acquire a name, an identity, a history, and powers … [and can] circulate as substitutes for persons, living … or dead …, or serve as instruments in the reproduction of the social, kinship, and power relations …

In New Guinea taboos prevent sacred axeheads from being identified, discussed, or used functionally (Hampton 1997, 468–76, 542–4).

Among highland communities sacred objects are owned by individual adult men but curated and worshipped within small socio-religious groups comprising 6–11 men from the same patrilineage. Each individual owns at least one sacred object to provide the focus for personal Ancestor worship, for defence against malevolent spirits, and for sun worship. Taboos prevent women and uninitiated boys from using sacred objects (Hampton 1997, 478–9, 542). As a result, embodied New Guinean axeheads are considered sentient 'Ancestral Beings', which are treated respectfully to placate and manipulate their powers, ritually fed, beautified, and worshiped to revitalise their spirit power (Hampton 1997, 545). Some axeheads amongst the Sentani are covered in latex to enhance sheen, curated in organic cases, and are not hafted but held in the hand as symbols of status by local power elites (Pétrequin & Pétrequin 2011, 343–4). In addition, some artefacts have specific symbolic roles. The Dani use chisels from the Yeineri quarry as representations of slain warriors in war ceremonies and in healer's kits; in the Baliem Gorge these chisels are used to protect healer's equipment from malevolent spirits (Hampton 1997, 617).

The Kimyal, Yali, and Una of the New Guinea highlands use their 'power stones' to stimulate, maintain, or augment significant events such as harvests, or the creation of new garden plots. Here, small Yeineri or Tagime-style adzeheads and stone knives, which are never used as functional tools, are planted amongst crops to stimulate growth. This form of deposition could explain the apparently random discoveries of Neolithic axeheads in non-settlement contexts, possibly amongst former Neolithic fields, or some caches of axeheads (Pitts 1996, 339–41). Other New Guinean power objects are placed beside domestic hearths as a focus for prayers for successful crop growth, others are carried as diviners to discover good toolstone. These stones also protect the individual against aggression or, when placed strategically within the house, they can ward off extreme weather. Such contexts are reminiscent of the deposits in the Ronaldsway Neolithic house (Isle of Man), where an assemblage of 11 axeheads, many 'uniform in character and unweathered', may have held similar symbolic roles (Bruce *et al.* 1947, 143; Topping 1996, 166–7), or the hoard of axeheads and Shetland knives from the putative house at Modesty (Shetland) (Sheridan 2012, 12–17). Such symbolic protection of Neolithic houses may also be represented by deposits placed in foundation trenches, pits, and post-holes of Irish houses, comprising axeheads, arrowheads, potsherds, beads, lithics, and bone remains (Smyth 2014, 57–62).

The possession of New Guinean axeheads and adzeheads signifies that owners have been initiated into adult male society (Pétrequin & Pétrequin 2011, 343), and different methods of hafting identify regional affiliations (cf. Sillitoe 1988). When these blades are combined with other paraphernalia (ie, shells, exotic feathers, and hunting bows) the total assemblage signals both status and identity (Pétrequin & Pétrequin 2011, 343). Strathern (1969, 321) has observed that the unusually long, thin Mount Hagen ceremonial axeheads were 'deliberately fashioned as objects of beauty' and mounted in elaborately carved hafts; in contrast, and paralleling the findings of Vial (1941), Strathern also discovered that bride-price axeheads were predominantly oversized but less well finished, although this did not affect their acceptance as wealth or status objects.

New Guinean transactions concerning funerary compensation or marriage payments demonstrate that axeheads (and pigs) can symbolically represent a human life. In terms of wealth and status, a group of axeheads can become the property of a dominant lineage, rather than an individual, and are consequently curated in a special house within the village (another possible explanation for the Ronaldsway or Modesty house assemblages). Such axeheads are considered inalienable sacred objects that were created by Ancestral Beings to legitimise status and group identity (Pétrequin & Pétrequin 2011, 344). Some ancestral axeheads were considered embodied, living entities that can fly at night but could be attracted back to earth with pig fat (Pétrequin & Pétrequin 1993).

The most potent and valued New Guinean artefacts are the over-sized, non-functional 'Ye-yao' axe blades, some 0.90 m long, which are created for ceremonial uses, ritual exchanges, or to fulfil obligations. As discussed previously, these greenschist or amphibolitic schist blades emit a green glow in the dark and are quarried from secret locations at Awigobi ('River of the Night'), believed to be the route used by Ancestors when prospecting for toolstone. Some communities view Ye-yao as splinters from *Yeli*, the Sacred Tree which grew at the beginning of the world. These highly charged objects are carefully crafted and polished, then dressed in miniature clothing and draped with pendants to transform them into 'women' of stone. In addition to their ceremonial value, certain Ye-yao are considered so powerful they rarely enter the social arena and are kept strictly secret (Hampton 1997, 468–9; Pétrequin & Pétrequin 2011, 344–6).

The Ye-yao axeheads are graded by characteristics:

1. The longest are the most valuable, but their width is less important.
2. Rock type and colour preferences exist.
3. Multiple items traded together can increase the value of an axehead.
4. Miniature clothing does not enhance an axehead's value.

In the Grand Valley a Ye-yao axehead of 700+ mm in length can be worth a large pig, as the timescales for blade production and pig rearing are comparable. Ye-yao blades are used in funerary displays, war indemnity payments, bride-wealth transfers, trade, and can be transformed into ritual objects (Hampton 1997, 453–5).

While nowhere near reaching the size of those in New Guinea, large axeheads are found in Neolithic contexts in Europe, most notably the jade examples from the Italian Alps that were distributed up to 1800+ km from their source, but others occur on Shetland amongst the Grut Wells Hoard on North Roe (Fig. 6.1), for example, where one roughout axehead was 421 mm long (Ballin *et al.* 2017). Like those in New

*Figure 6.1: The Grut Wells Hoard (Shetland), comprising a large roughout axe/adzehead, a smaller roughout axe/adzehead and a roughout Shetland knife. These objects were discovered downslope from the felsite quarries in an erosion scar. Scale = 0.3 m (photo: author)*

*Figure 6.2: The Belmont Hoard of Group VI axeheads discovered near Penrith (Cumbria) around 1867 (cf. Davis & Edmonds 2011b) (photo: author)*

Guinea, jade axeheads (generally up to 500 mm in length) were carefully curated and deposition suggests they were valued by axehead using elites, particularly around the Gulf of Morbihan (Pétrequin *et al.* 2012c; 2017).

In Britain large axeheads occur amongst Group VI products from the Langdale/Scafell quarries which have a size range of 150–450 mm in length, although those above 230 mm in length are more rare (Fig. 6.2; Davis & Edmonds 2011b; D. Field pers. comm.). These particular axeheads were distributed throughout Britain (Fell & Davis 1988) and Ireland (Cooney & Mandal 1988, 81–2). Taken together, the contexts of large axeheads in Britain, Ireland, and Europe demonstrate specialised roles with final deposition in meaningful locations.

## The social value of archaeological extraction site products

As outlined above, material culture can play significant roles in social transactions and the creation of identity. Indeed, as Miller (2010, 67) has observed 'it is the circulation of things that creates society', as we have seen in Native American, Aboriginal Australian, and Pacific ethnography – a view endorsed by other research (eg, Mauss 1954; Bourdieu 1977; 1990; Godelier 1999; Boivin 2008). Significant raw materials crafted into meaningful artefacts can be given a biography and used in social interactions. For instance, Whittle (2003, 47) has observed that the majority of Linearbandkeramik (LBK; *c.* 5500–5000 BC) site assemblages contain imported axeheads and adzeheads. The densely settled Aldenhovener Platte (northwest Germany) saw LBK settlements import raw materials and finished lithic artefacts from the Dutch Limburg, such as the mine at Rijckholt, 40+ km to the west; a lithic source that also supplied LBK sites as distant as Baden-Württemberg and Hesse more than 400 km to the east (Zimmerman 1995). At the Late LBK settlement at Hienheim (Bavaria) the inhabitants used local cherts for everyday tools but preferred non-local amphibolite for adzeheads (de Grooth 1997), demonstrating the selective use of lithic materials.

Among the Villeneuve-Saint-Germain Culture (VSG) in the Paris Basin (*c.* 5100–4700 BC), which overlaps with, but mostly follows the LBK, lithic material was chosen for the type of artefact to be produced. Secondary flint sources were used for mundane flake production, whereas better quality Bartonian flint was favoured for longer (>200 mm) blades which were probably produced by craft specialists and distributed widely from the Armorican massif in the west to the Ardennes in the east. Consequently, Bartonian blades appear to have been more valued than those chipped from secondary lithologies (Bostyn 1997; Giligny 2011). Only small numbers of Alpine or Armorican axeheads have been recovered and LBK shoe-last adzeheads and perforated wedges are rare (Giligny & Bostyn 2016, 276), implying that VSG communities may have had difficulty obtaining exotic axeheads from long-distance networks and had to rely upon Bartonian flint for important implements.

In the Paris Basin catchment another regional network was centred upon the Île-de-France and produced quartzite sandstone axeheads in workshops on the Stampian Hills from the beginning of the Neolithic. These axeheads circulated alongside imported examples, comprising roughly 20% Alpine jade, 45% Armorican dolerites, metadolerites, and hornfels, and small numbers of Caen Plain flint axeheads (Giligny & Bostyn 2016, 278). This example, which was contiguous with the VSG, demonstrates that different material traditions existed between near neighbours as seen above in the ethnographic study of the Hagen and Wiru in New Guinea.

It was not until the Chasséen and Michelsberg Cultures (*c.* 4150–3450 BC; Middle Neolithic II) appeared in the Paris Basin that the important flint mines at Jablines (Bostyn & Lanchon 1992) and Ri (Marcigny *et al.* 2011) began operating. Following this, axeheads of local flint occurred alongside exotic imported axeheads. By the end of the French Neolithic flint axeheads are recovered from settlements, as grave goods in burials, and some tombs such as Gavrinis (Larmor-Baden) and Petit Mont (Arzon) feature walls decorated with axe depictions (Fig. 6.3) (Shee Twohig 1981; Cassen & Grimaud 2020), suggesting that culturally the axe had achieved iconic status. In the Paris Basin the greatest number of axeheads was recovered from flint mines [18%], followed by workshops [11%], settlements [3%], and burials [1%] (Giligny & Bostyn 2016, 276). A notable grave assemblage discovered at *La porte aux Bergers* in Vignely, playing on the iconography of axeheads, comprised the crouched inhumation of a child accompanied

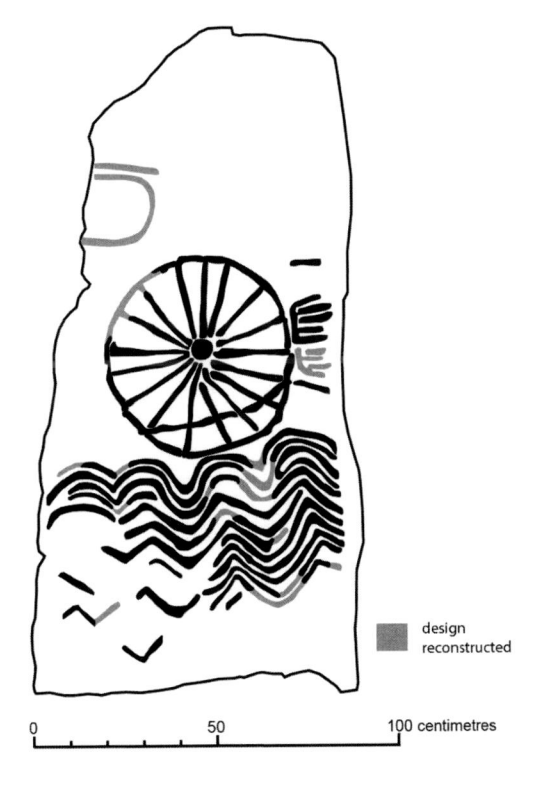

*Figure 6.3: Orthostat C1 from Petit Mont, Arzon (Morbihan), showing a wheel-like motif which has been interpreted as depicting a circular setting of axeheads in a manner recorded locally amongst certain hoards (after Cassen & Grimaud 2020; illustration: T. Pearson)*

*Table 6.2: The composition of grave assemblages in the Netherlands over time*

|  | LBK | Early–Middle Neolithic | TRB | Single Grave Culture | All-Over-Ornamented | Bell Beaker |
|---|---|---|---|---|---|---|
| Axeheads |  |  | ● | ● | ● |  |
| Blades | ● |  |  | ● | ● |  |
| Daggers |  |  |  | ● | ● | ● |
| Arrowheads | ● | <No data> |  | ● | ● | ● |
| Strike-a-lights |  |  | ● |  |  |  |
| Scrapers |  |  |  |  |  |  |
| Sickles | ● |  | ● |  |  |  |
| BB-knife |  |  |  |  |  | ● |
| Flakes |  |  | ● | ● | ● | ● |

(Based on van Gijn 2010b, 226)

*Table 6.3: The relative abundance of products from earlier Neolithic extraction sites in Europe*

| Site | No. | % of assemblage | Axeheads & associated types as % of total assemblage |
|---|---|---|---|
| JABLINES Lithics (data from Bostyn & Lanchon 1992) | | | |
| Axeheads >300 mm long | 81 | 16 | 16 [81] |
| Axeheads >160 mm long | 216 | 42 | 42 [216] |
| Cores [flake] | 25 | 5 | |
| Cores [blade] | 2 | 0.5 | |
| Blades | 34 | 6.5 | |
| Scrapers | 38 | 7 | |
| Preforms [retouched] | 10 | 2 | |
| Flakes [retouched] | 110 | 21 | |
| Total assemblage | 516 | 100 | 58 [297] |
| FLINS-SUR-SEINE Lithics (data from Giligny & Bostyn 2016) | | | |
| Axeheads, polished | 3 | 0.3 | 0.3 [3] |
| Preforms & roughouts | 595 | 70 | 70 [595] |
| Tranchet axeheads | 39 | 5 | 5 [39] |
| Picks | 5 | 0.6 | 0.6 [5] |
| Scrapers, end | 71 | 8 | |
| Scrapers | 13 | 1.5 | |
| Denticulate | 27 | 3.1 | |
| Notched tool | 2 | 0.2 | |
| Backed edge | 1 | 0.1 | |
| Splintered piece | 2 | 0.2 | |
| Chisel | 14 | 1.6 | |
| Point | 1 | 0.1 | |
| Bifacial piece | 17 | 2 | |
| Large tools | 43 | 5 | |
| Borers | 7 | 0.8 | |
| Multi-tool | 10 | 1.1 | |
| Cores | 4 | 0.4 | |
| Total assemblage | 854 | 100 | 75.9 [642] |
| RIJCKHOLT-ST GEERTRUID Lithics (data from Felder *et al.* 1998) | | | |
| Picks & pick fragments | 14,217 | 99.1 | 99.1 [14,217] |
| Cores | 58 | 0.4 | |
| Other implements | 37 | 0.3 | |
| Miscellaneous | 21 | 0.2 | |
| Total assemblage | 14,333 | 100 | 99.1 [14,217] |

by a partially ground axehead and chisel, a roughout axehead, and a flint flake, all Bartonian flint and probably from the Jablines mines (Giligny & Bostyn 2016, 264). The distribution of Jablines products spans 200+ km, overlapping with those from the north from the broadly contemporary Spiennes (Hainault) mining complex (Collett & Bostyn 2011). However, by *c.* 2700 cal BC during the Single Grave Culture (SGC) in the Netherlands (Table 6.2), these distribution networks were eclipsed by that of Grand-Pressigny (Indre-et-Loire) whose long flint blades were preferred for SGC burials, having been transported roughly 800 km from the French source to the Dutch burial mounds (van Gijn 2010b, 19). This situation demonstrates the changing values of certain exotic lithologies over time and the importance of long-distance networks.

In contrast with the examples cited above, most flint imported to the north-eastern Netherlands during the TRB period [*c.* 4300–2800 BC] was from north Germany or southern Scandinavia and this ranged from nodules to large numbers of finished axeheads (see below; Midgeley 1992, 232–302; van Gijn 2010b, 20;). Additionally, there appears to have been a rigid distinction between flint destined for domestic use and that deposited in hoards, wetland deposits, or burial assemblages. Domestic tools were produced on poor quality local morainic flint whereas imported flint implements are largely absent from settlement assemblages. However, the imported large axeheads from the north were deposited in wetlands or graves, suggesting that they played a role in belief systems (Wentink 2006; 2008). Wetland deposition may have been associated with animistic beliefs, or rites designed to maintain a balance in the world. The grave assemblages diverge from these practices and appear to be linked to identity, specifically that of the farmer, symbolised by imported axeheads, strike-a-lights linked with slash and burn agriculture, and sickles used for harvesting crops (van

Table 6.4: The relative abundance of products from later Neolithic assemblages at extraction sites in Europe

| Site | No. | % of assemblage | Axeheads & associated types as % of total assemblage |
|---|---|---|---|
| KRUMLOVSKÝ LES, CZECHIA: Late Lengyel. Lithics (data from Oliva 2010) | | | |
| Axeheads | 0 | 0 | 0 |
| Primary cores | 91 | 23 | |
| Prepared cores | 1 | <1 | |
| Bifacial/flat cores | 20 | 5 | |
| Flake cores | 40 | 10 | |
| Blade cores | 1 | <1 | |
| Core fragments | 43 | 11 | |
| Non-cortical flakes | 186 | 48 | |
| Parallel-sided flakes | 5 | 1 | |
| Blades | 2 | <1 | |
| Ventrally thinned flakes | 1 | <1 | |
| Total assemblage | 390 | 100 | 0 |
| LOMA DE ENMEDIO-REALILLO, SPAIN. Lithics (data from Domínguez-Bella *et al.* 2011) | | | |
| Axeheads | 0 | 0 | 0 |
| Cores | 44 | 24 | |
| Blades | 114 | 68 | |
| Retouched tools | 16 | 8 | |
| Total assemblage | 164 | 100 | 0 |

Gijn 2010b, 220–7). Consequently, TRB communities appear to have reserved exotic imported lithics for non-domestic purposes to satisfy the needs of belief systems, identity, and status.

During the earliest part of the Neolithic axeheads were the major products of many European extraction sites. This occurred against a backdrop of population movements which transformed most communities demographically (Brace *et al.* 2018; 2019; Olalde *et al.* 2018), leading to a shift in subsistence strategies and an increasing reliance upon agro-pastoral activities. Traditionally it was the ground axehead which enabled and epitomised much of this subsistence realignment and came to feature prominently in the lithic repertoires of extraction sites. Once associated with forest clearance and linked to slash-and-burn agricultural practices, the axehead became synonymous with European mines and quarries during the Early Neolithic. However, woodland clearance would have built upon Mesolithic precedents, including the use of ring-barking and fire to create breaks in the canopy, therefore the role of the axehead in woodland management may have been overstated. In addition, some axeheads – especially larger examples – were clearly not used for forest clearance and, like many miniature implements, were not put to practical use. They were created for special purposes and/or deposition in particular contexts as non-utilitarian objects. Consequently, the preponderance of axeheads from mines needs further explanation.

In Europe (Tables 6.3 & 6.4) the preference for axeheads – as opposed to other implements – can be seen at Jablines where they comprised 58% of the tools in the excavated assemblage (Bostyn & Lanchon 1992), 75.9% at Flins-sur-Seine (Giligny & Bostyn 2016), and 99.1% at Rijckholt-St Geertruid (Felder *et al.* 1998). In Britain the situation was similar, but with some variation in tool preferences (Table 6.5). The chemical analysis of a small sample of flint axeheads from southern Britain found that they had been manufactured from mined flint (Craddock *et al.* 2012), suggesting it may have been preferred for axehead production. According to recent radiocarbon determinations (Edinborough *et al.* 2020) Easton Down may be the earliest British mine (although caution is needed as this is based upon one date) where 82.1% of the published tool assemblage comprised axeheads. However, if this early date is combined with the suggestion that Neolithic practices came relatively late to parts of Wessex (Healy *et al.* 2011a), it offers the possibility that Easton Down represents indigenous Mesolithic pit extraction and did not initially involve Neolithic migrants whose presence is not seen until more elaborate deposits occur in the pits. In

Sussex, the early site at Cissbury produced 76.8% axeheads from the total tool assemblage (including tranchet types, again possibly indicating a Mesolithic presence), Harrow Hill peaks at 90%, followed by a gradual decline at the later sites at Long Down with 19.4%, and Church Hill with 16.5%.

During the later Neolithic (Table 6.6) in

*Table 6.5: (continued opposite) The relative abundance of products from Early Neolithic assemblages at extraction sites in Britain*

| Site | No. | % of assemblage | Axeheads & associated types as % of total assemblage |
|---|---|---|---|
| **EASTON DOWN. Lithics (data from Stone 1931a; 1931b; 1933)** | | | |
| Axeheads | 35+ | 44.9+ | 44.9+ [35+] |
| Choppers | 5+ | 6.4+ | 6.4+ [5+] |
| Adzeheads | 2 | 2.5 | 2.5 [2] |
| Tranchet axeheads | 1 | 1.3 | 1.3 [1] |
| Axe fragments | 20 | 25.7 | 25.7 [20] |
| Picks | 1 | 1.3 | 1.3 [1] |
| Roughouts | 'Abundant' | ? | ? |
| Cores | 2 | 2.5 | |
| Flakes/blades | Not quantified | ? | |
| Scrapers | 5 | 6.4 | |
| Planes | 2 | 2.5 | |
| Points | 1 | 1.3 | |
| Awls | 1 | 1.3 | |
| Combination tools | 1 | 1.3 | |
| Chisels | 1 | 1.3 | |
| Leaf-shaped arrowheads | 1 | 1.3 | |
| Total assemblage | 78+ | 100 | 82.1+ [64] |
| **HARROW HILL. Lithics (data from Russell 2001)** | | | |
| Axeheads | 152 | 88 | 88 [152] |
| Picks | 2 | 1 | 1 [2] |
| Choppers | 1 | 1 | 1 [1] |
| Cores | 7 | 4 | |
| Retouched flakes | 5 | 3 | |
| Scrapers | 2 | 1 | |
| Chisels | 2 | 1 | |
| Arrowheads | 1 | 1 | |
| Total assemblage | 172 | 100 | 90 [155] |
| **CISSBURY. Lithics (data from Russel 2001)** | | | |
| Axeheads | 948 | 69 | 69 [948] |
| Miniature axeheads | 46 | 3 | 3 [46] |
| Picks | 36 | 2.5 | 2.5 [36] |
| Tranchet axeheads | 20 | 1.5 | 1.5 [20] |
| Choppers | 4 | 0.5 | 0.5 [4] |
| Adzes | 2 | 0.3 | 0.3 [2] |
| Cores | 79 | 6 | |
| Retouched flakes | 78 | 6 | |
| Scrapers | 45 | 3 | |
| Chisels | 43 | 3 | |
| Fabricators | 18 | 1 | |
| Knives | 17 | 1 | |
| Laurel Leaves | 8 | 0.7 | |
| Arrowheads | 6 | 0.6 | |
| Borers | 6 | 0.6 | |
| Plano-convex knives | 4 | 0.5 | |
| Sickles | 3 | 0.3 | |
| Slugs | 3 | 0.3 | |
| Tranchet tool | 1 | 0.1 | |
| Rod | 1 | 0.1 | |
| Total assemblage | 1368 | 100 | 76.8 [1056] |

| Site | No. | % of assemblage | Axeheads & associated types as % of total assemblage |
|---|---|---|---|
| BLACKPATCH. Lithics (data from Russell 2001) | | | |
| Axeheads | 134 | 48 | 48 [134] |
| Picks | 11 | 4 | 4 [11] |
| Choppers | 10 | 3 | 3 [10] |
| Miniature axeheads | 2 | 1 | 1 [2] |
| Thames Pick | 1 | 0.5 | 0.5 [1] |
| Polished axehead | 1 | 0.5 | 0.5 [1] |
| Cores | 35 | 12 | |
| Miscellaneous | 27 | 9.5 | |
| Retouched flakes | 19 | 7 | |
| Scrapers | 12 | 4 | |
| Planes | 11 | 4 | |
| Knives | 6 | 2 | |
| Fabricators | 3 | 1 | |
| Borers | 3 | 1 | |
| Slugs | 2 | 1 | |
| Chisel | 1 | 0.5 | |
| Discoidal knife | 1 | 0.5 | |
| Laurel Leaf | 1 | 0.5 | |
| Total assemblage | 280 | 100 | 57 [159] |
| LONG DOWN. Lithics (data from Salisbury 1961) | | | |
| Axeheads, picks & roughouts | 103 | 19.4 | 19.4 [103] |
| Knives | 278 | 52.2 | |
| Points & Borers | 21 | 4 | |
| Scrapers | 58 | 11 | |
| Saws | 8 | 1.5 | |
| Cores | 18 | 3.3 | |
| Miscellaneous | 34 | 6.4 | |
| Sickles | 2 | 0.4 | |
| Fabricators | 1 | 0.2 | |
| Planes | 9 | 1.6 | |
| Total assemblage | 532 | 100 | 19.4 [103] |
| CHURCH HILL. Lithics (data from Russell 2001) | | | |
| Axeheads | 64 | 16 | 16 [64] |
| Choppers | 1 | 0.5 | 0.5 [1] |
| Flakes/blades | 266 | 65 | |
| Scrapers | 45 | 11 | |
| Cores | 9 | 2 | |
| Borers | 9 | 2 | |
| Knives | 6 | 1.5 | |
| Serrated flakes | 6 | 1.5 | |
| Arrowheads | 2 | 0.5 | |
| Total assemblage | 408 | 100 | 16.5 [65] |

north-eastern Scotland, the Den of Boddam produced no axeheads at all (probably reflecting raw material quality), and at Grime's Graves only 9% of the tool assemblage was axeheads, the main product being points (26% of total, although nearly all points and rods were recovered from late 2nd millennium contexts at Grime's Graves). This suggests an overall decline in axehead production at extraction sites during the latter part of the Neolithic, a factor seemingly borne out by the lack of axeheads at Late Neolithic sites such as henges. If the data in Table 6.7 is compared to the new radiocarbon chronology, it would appear that the major phase of axehead production spanned *c.* 4100–3200 cal BC. It should, of course, be noted that these percentages may reflect an excavation bias, so require caution, although the general trends should be broadly accurate.

Table 6.6: The relative abundance of products from later Neolithic assemblages at extraction sites in Britain

| Site | No. | % of assemblage | Axeheads & associated types as % of total assemblage |
|---|---|---|---|
| DEN OF BODDAM. Lithics (data from Saville 2011) | | | |
| Axeheads | 0 | 0 | 0 |
| Piercers | 11 | 6 | |
| Scrapers | 5 | 2.5 | |
| Rods | 2 | 1 | |
| Edge-trimmed flake | 1 | 0.5 | |
| Miscellaneous retouched pieces | 170 | 90 | |
| Total assemblage | 188 | 100 | 0 |
| GRIME'S GRAVES. Lithics (data from Mercer 1981b; Longworth et al. 2012) | | | |
| Axeheads | 374 | 9 | 9 [374] |
| Points | 1015 | 26 | |
| Miscellaneous | 779 | 20 | |
| Scrapers | 490 | 12 | |
| Utilised blades | 351 | 9 | |
| Flakes | 326 | 8 | |
| Rods | 249 | 6 | |
| Discoidal knives | 200 | 5 | |
| Bulbar segments | 104 | 3 | |
| Arrowheads | 39 | 1 | |
| Borers / piercers | 24 | 0.51 | |
| Bifacials | 7 | 0.17 | |
| Burins | 7 | 0.17 | |
| Knives | 4 | 0.10 | |
| Fabricators | 2 | 0.05 | |
| Total assemblage | 3971 | 100 | 9 [374] |

Table 6.7: The intensity of axehead production as a percentage of total published tool assemblages from British flint mines (mines arranged in rough chronological order (cf. Edinborough et al. 2020))

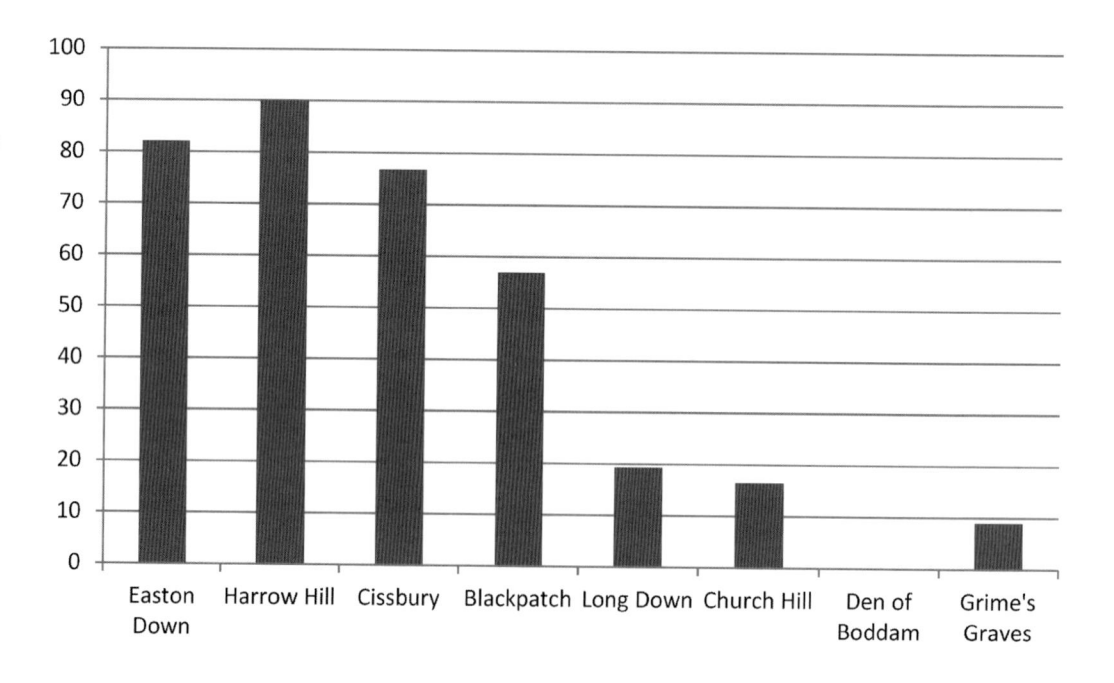

This chronology parallels that of the main upland and island stone quarries at Langdale/Scafell Pike (Cumbria), Graiglwyd (Gwynedd), Lambay Island (Ireland), and Mynydd Rhiw (Gwynedd). On Lambay Island some axeheads remained on-site, with others discovered in hoards and settlement sites, and some mimicked the shape of Cumbrian

Group VI axeheads (Gabriel Cooney pers. comm.). Only the quarries at Creag na Caillich (Perthshire) appear to have been active during the later Neolithic, initially producing traditional axehead forms which was followed by a secondary phase producing shaft-hole axeheads (Edmonds *et al*. 1992). A secondary phase of quarrying may also have occurred at Langdale/Scafell Pike quarries, which could have been the source of 18 Beaker period Group VI stone bracers – unless they were produced from recycled axeheads (Woodward & Hunter 2011). These examples emphasise that certain lithologies held a continuing value to Neolithic communities just as others do for recent/modern traditional peoples.

## The iconography of the axehead …

As Ian Kinnes (1985, 125) once observed: '… stone axes are the most visible and resilient part of the archaeological record. Whatever the circumstances of their deposition, relative quantities are an index of settlement density and their sources an indication of broader cultural and economic contacts.'

The manner in which many axeheads were deposited suggests that they may have been part of social transactions. Good numbers have been found placed in the ditches at causewayed enclosures such as Hambledon Hill (Dorset) (Saville 2002, 98), Etton (Cambridgeshire) (Pryor 1998, 261–8) and especially Windmill Hill (Wiltshire), where 141 complete or fragmented examples were recovered (Smith 1965; Whittle *et al*. 1999; Field 2011c). Undoubtedly, they fulfilled important roles at these sites, that presumably involved some elements of ceremony, before permanent deposition. Certain axeheads from causewayed enclosures exhibit use-wear but others do not, implying a complex relationship between functionality, deposition, and the biography of the artefact (cf. Kopytoff 1986; Fowler 2004, 60–2; Fogelin & Schiffer 2015). At settlements such as Parc Bryn Cegin (Gwynedd), axeheads and axe-working debitage demonstrate Early Neolithic domestic tool production which continued into the Middle–Late Neolithic when pit deposition included burnt axeheads (Kenney 2008).

Axeheads and related items are also recorded in mortuary practices. At West Kennet long barrow a polissoir (Stone 18) was built into the passage, with others in the chambers and passageway, and on Stone 43 in the forecourt blocking (Piggott 1962, 19–21, pl. xiii). Although this may have been coincidental, it is possible that the polissoirs were deliberately used as metonyms for axehead production to associate the activity with the deceased in the tomb. Conversely, axeheads are very rare in early long barrows (Field 2006, 141) and remain comparatively scarce in later Neolithic mounds (Manby 1974; Field 2011b). Apart from burial deposits, axeheads are also discovered in caches of 2–10 finished or roughout implements, many of which appear to have been made by the same person, such as the five axehead cache from Trowse Newton and the seven axehead cache from Knapton, both in Norfolk (Pitts 1996, 339–41). The purpose of caching is unclear but is likely to have encompassed technical reasons connected to knapping (eg, moisture retention in the lithics), for safekeeping, or for symbolic reasons.

The Neolithic quarried axehead became transformative and, in the archaeological literature, epitomised Neolithisation as it cascaded across Europe. Although the axe as metaphor may have represented ideologies and status, it was the mines and quarries from which they emerged that created the springboard to 'being' Neolithic by providing the tools which would symbolise a shift in subsistence practices towards agro-pastoralism. Conceptually, axeheads may have been considered both as 'gifts from the earth' (Whittle 1996) and 'pieces of places' (Bradley 2000, 88), tangible parts of a multi-layered cosmology with a role in maintaining beliefs, and defining identity, status, and prestige (eg, Cooney 1998). The cultural significance of the axehead as *leitmotif* is demonstrated by the fact that they also became memorialised in passage grave art, particularly in French tombs (Shee Twohig 1981; Demoule 2007). In Brittany, of the nine commonest passage grave motifs, three are variations of an axehead (Shee Twohig 1981, 54). Axeheads also appear to have inspired the shaping of certain massive Breton standing stones such as Le Grand Menhir Brisé with its axehead-like side facets (Tilley & Thomas 1993), Le Menhir du Champ Dolent (Giot 1995), the Menhir de Kerloas (Fig. 6.4), or in Britain the Devil's Arrows and Rudston monolith in North Yorkshire – all comprising massive,

*Figure 6.4: The 9.5 m high axehead shaped Menhir de Kerloas at Plouarzel (Brittany) (photo: author)*

in length and perforated for use as pendants, alongside others in clay and bone (Midgley 1992, 290–4). Consequently, through its use in various sizes and in different media, the axehead became a widespread icon across Neolithic Europe.

The symbolic value of the axehead is emphasised by the production of axehead skeuomorphs created from unsuitable materials. Childe (1956, 13) defined skeuomorphs as 'objects aping in one medium shapes proper to another'. The use of soft, non-utilitarian materials is epitomised by two Late Neolithic chalk axeheads discovered buried in postholes at Woodhenge (Wiltshire) (Fig. 6.4); one roughly triangular in shape and 88 mm long, the second tear-drop shaped and 79 mm in length (Cunnington 1929, 112–13; pl. 22, 1–2). Clearly the use of soft chalk as a medium proves these two *ersatz* axeheads were not designed to be functional but rather represent a *bona fide* stone or flint axehead for purposes related to construction ceremonialism during the building of Woodhenge. Other putative chalk axeheads may be represented by a crudely flaked, tear-drop shaped object 160 mm in length discovered in Shaft 1 at Blackpatch, noted by Pye (1968) and Teather (2008, 198–9). At Cissbury two fragments of shaped and possibly polished chalk are axehead-like (less than 110 mm in length), although the provenance is unclear (*ibid.*, 198). A final example of a possible chipped chalk axehead was discovered at Stonehenge (Thomas 1952, 462).

Non-igneous soft lithologies were also used to manufacture axeheads which may have been skeuomorphs. Examples include a silty mudstone axehead from Foumart Knowe (Northumberland) (Clough & Cummins 1988, 229, no. 95), a broken sandstone axehead discovered on the chamber floor of the Orkney-Cromarty tomb of Calf of Eday South-East, (Calder 1938, 204), and a broken and complete sandstone roughout axehead found in the passage of Huntersquoy tomb on Eday (*ibid.*). A narrow, symmetrical polished quartz axehead 210 mm in length was discovered at Ladyflat (Berwickshire), which had little evidence of use-wear damage (*PSAS* 1919).

Stone was not the only medium used for skeuomorphs. At the Drove Site on the Sweet Track (Somerset) an apparent skeuomorph of a hafted axehead was created from two oak slats, the pseudo 'axehead' is 160 m long by 50 mm

axehead-like monoliths situated prominently in the landscape. Some of the Breton axehead-shaped menhirs were also decorated with axehead motifs and some, such as the Table des Marchands, where deliberately broken and incorporated into tomb construction, where axehead motifs were represented within a burial chamber, or at Gavrinis where axehead shapes are incorporated into the entangled designs on the highly decorated orthostats of the passage (Cassen 2012).

At the opposite end of the scale, the north European TRB Culture produced miniature battle axeheads in amber ranging 20–40 mm wide (similar dimensions to many axeheads). This was found lying adjacent to a Neolithic timber trackway built across wetlands (Coles & Coles 1986, 61). The trackway (dated 3807 or 3806 BC by dendrochronology) was also associated with an Alpine jade axehead and an unused flint axehead that was attributed to the South Downs mines by trace element analysis (Coles *et al.* 1973; Craddock *et al.* 1983). These examples suggest that skeuomorphic axeheads possessed the same cultural significance as igneous/flint axeheads, particularly in areas without 'hard' lithologies as seen previously in the ethnographic example of the Hagen and Wiru.

The importance of axehead iconography is also shown by the spatial distribution of axeheads. The ethnography shows that the majority of extraction site products were transported distances of 200+ km from storied sources (see Chapter 2, Table 2.7). Such trends may be reflected in the archaeological record by examples such as the Groups VI and IX axeheads (Clough & Cummins 1988; Cooney & Mandal 1998), Jablines (France) and Spiennes (Belgium) flint axeheads (Collet & Bostyn 2011), the red flint of Heligoland Island (Germany; van Gijn & Raemaekers 2014), flint from the Gargano peninsula in south-eastern Italy (Di Lernia 1997), Alpine jade axeheads (Pétrequin *et al.* 2012a), or Mediterranean obsidian from Sardinia or Lipari (Costa 2007). In Ireland, porphyry axeheads quarried on Lambay Island on the east coast, cluster in coastal regions and along rivers, with major concentrations in Counties Dublin and Antrim (21–40 examples), Meath and West Meath (11–20) and Donegal, Cavan, Kildare, and Limerick (8–10) (Smyth 2014, 136). The fact that Antrim, lying some 150–200+ km north of Lambay Island, had one of the greatest concentrations of porphyry axeheads is particularly noteworthy, as porcellanite was available locally from the quarries at Tievebulliagh in the Glens of Antrim. Significant numbers of porcellanite axeheads (Group IX) found their way throughout Britain and Ireland (Clough & Cummins 1988, 2273; Cooney & Mandal 1998, 62–6, 108). Together, these examples demonstrate that in many cases long-distance distribution was the norm, in the case of jade axeheads huge distances of 2000+ km were covered, while others such as the Jablines/Spiennes axeheads, Gargano flint, Mediterranean obsidian, or those of British and Irish Groups I, VI, and IX, were transported distances of 200–500+ km.

## General trends in pan-European product deposition

The context of extraction site product deposition is fundamental to understanding the role(s) that these artefacts may have played in Neolithic society. Naturally, caution is required in determining whether an archaeological deposit was 'casual discard' or 'deliberate deposition', and ethnography reveals that deposition can range from utilitarian purposes to more esoteric ideological/cosmological reasons. It is often assemblage composition and context which reflect the motivations behind deposition.

*Figure 6.5: The Woodhenge chalk axeheads, now curated at Devizes Museum (photo: author)*

*Table 6.8: Jade axehead hoards by context and number (data from Pétrequin et al. 2012d, 1378)*

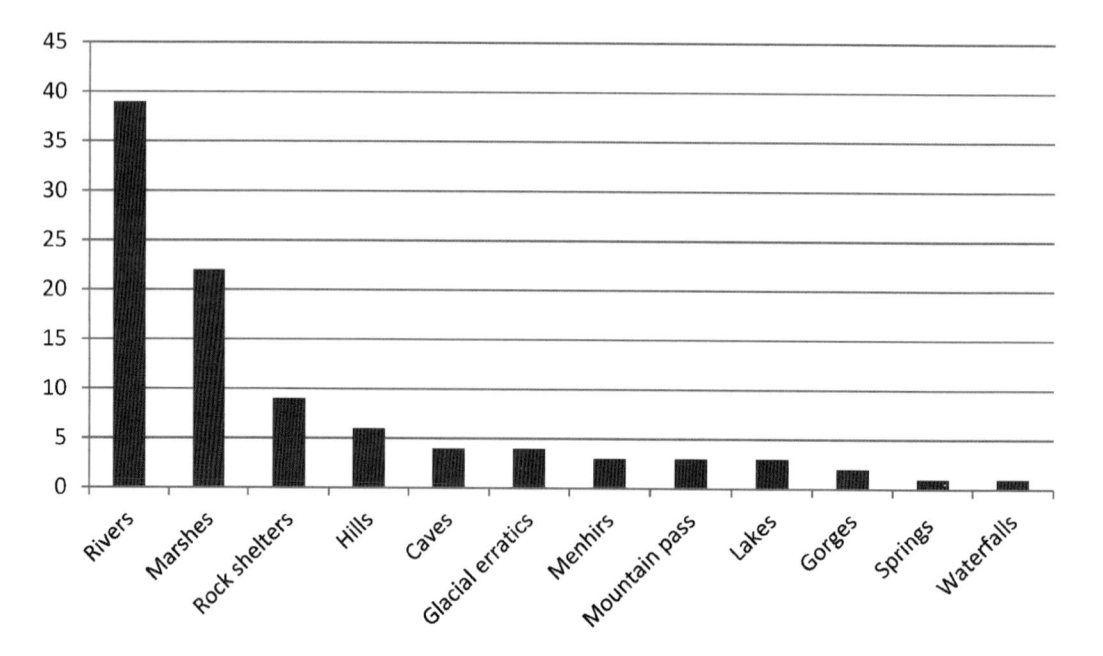

*Table 6.9 General trends in jade axehead hoard deposition (data from Pétrequin et al. 2012d, 1378)*

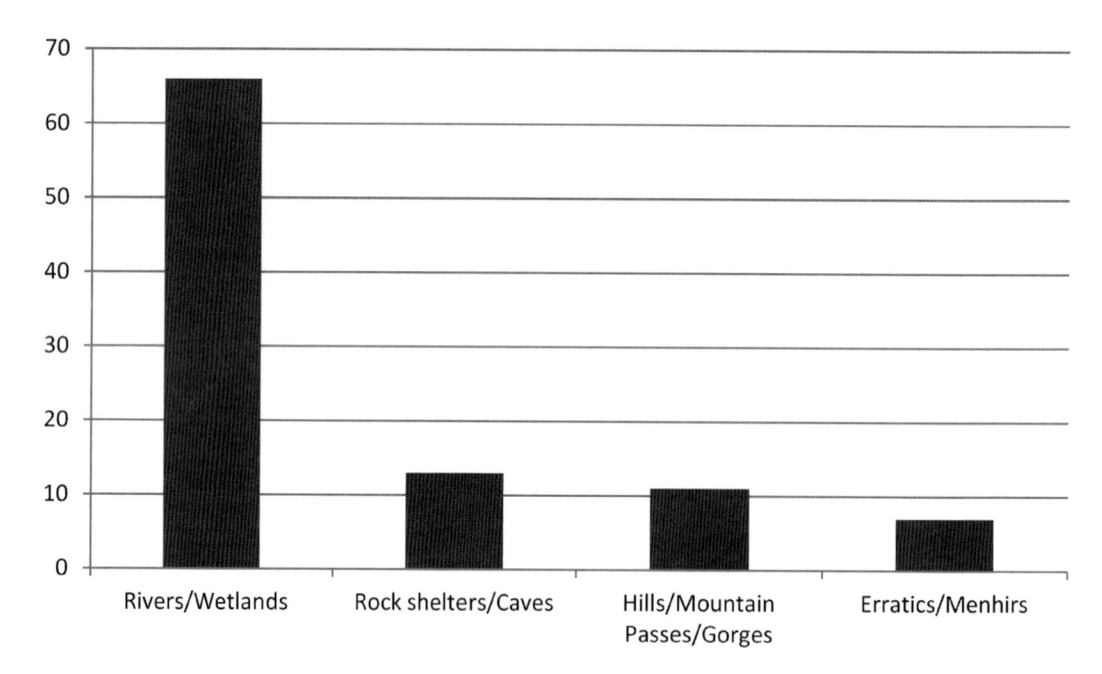

In Europe, broad trends can be seen among large jade axeheads (Tables 6.8 & 6.9) where 79% were deposited in rivers and wetlands compared to only 21% in terrestrial contexts (Petrequin *et al.* 2012d, 1378). A typical hoard discovered at Petit Rohu (Morbihan) comprised two pairs of jade axeheads found 0.3 m apart and set vertically with cutting edges uppermost. These lay close to a stone alignment, with a fifth fibrolite axehead near the southern terminal of the alignment (Cassen *et al.* 2010). Such contexts suggest these iconic Alpine artefacts were created for ritualised purposes. Similar practices occurred in Ireland, where the Malone Road hoard (Belfast) comprised 19 porcellanite axeheads, of which 14 were set vertically with blades uppermost. This hoard was unusually large as most Irish hoards comprise just 2–3 axeheads (Cooney 2015, 526).

In various European contexts paired axeheads may have been significant. At the northern

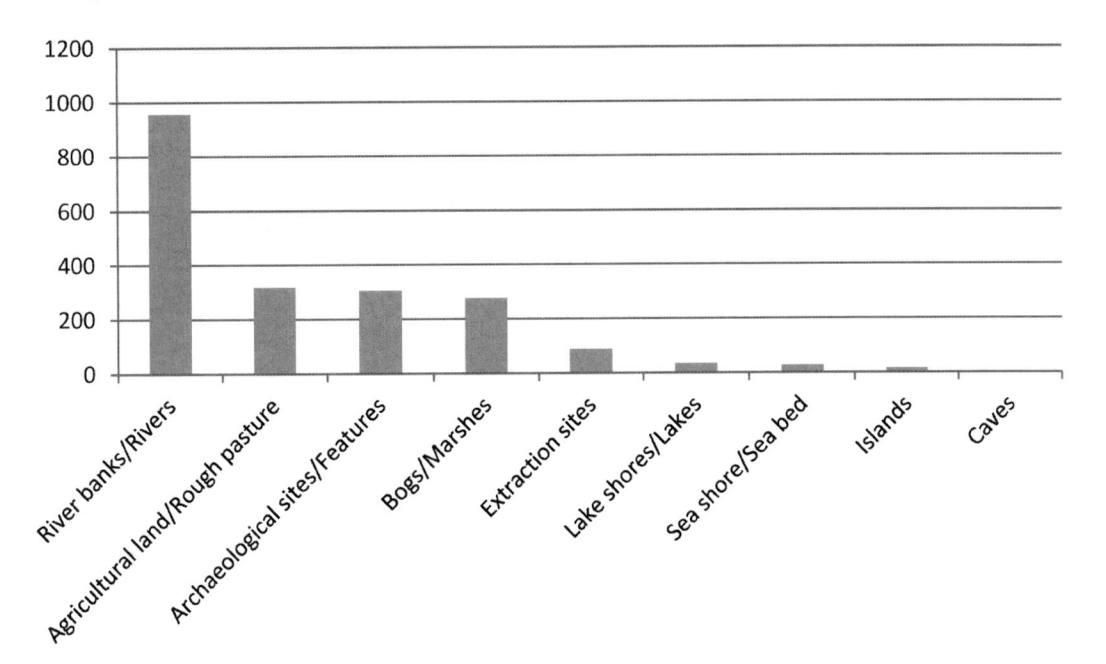

*Table 6.10: The depositional contexts of Irish stone axeheads by number (includes complete axeheads, roughouts, and fragments (based on Cooney & Mandal 1998, 36, table 3.4)*

Chasséen settlement of Les Fondriaux at Bernières-sur-Seine (Upper Normandy), the lithic assemblage included two near identical flint axeheads which had been deliberately burnt and placed together in a deposit. This was not unique, for parallels can be found at Achères (Yvelines) and Vendeuil (Oise) (Prost *et al.* 2017, 32–4). Paired axeheads are also depicted in megalithic art, as at Gavrinis (Morbihan; Shee Twohig 1981, 172–5), where stones L6 and R8 (positioned opposite each other in the passage) both feature paired axeheads. Roughly three-quarters of the way down the passage, stones L9 and R10 (also facing one another) include groups of axeheads; in the case of L9 they comprise seven pairs and four single axeheads. On the back wall of the chamber, facing the passage, an orthostat decorated with two zones of linear or irregular lines had a final pair of upright axeheads in the centre of the design.

Similar deposits also occurred in Sweden. At Svartskylle, Early Neolithic axeheads, scrapers and blades were discovered burnt and placed in four deposits on a prominent hilltop. Fire-damaged lithics comprising 100+ axeheads, tanged arrowheads, projectile points, and debitage along with decorated pottery were deposited in pits at Kverrestad. Other examples include Svågertorp, where six burnt axeheads and a chisel were placed in a pit; and Strandby where 100+ burnt axeheads, chisels, and scrapers were discovered (Larsson 2006, 400–8). These examples record the deliberate destruction of specific artefacts (particularly axeheads), possibly for transformative purposes (*ibid.*, 408), paralleling practices discovered in various European contexts.

Axehead hoards are found in many European countries. In some cases the positioning of axeheads within a hoard may have followed conventions, as suggested by some TRB hoards where at least eight different configurations are recorded (Rech 1979). The distribution of large axeheads associated with the Dutch TRB is centred on the Drenthe Plateau and were made from north German, southern Scandinavian or Heligoland Island flint. These large, thin-butted axeheads show little evidence of use-wear but do retain evidence of ochre smeared over cutting edges and the periodic wrapping and unwrapping in hide covers, suggesting they were used in special practices. These TRB axeheads were generally discovered in wetlands and often accompanied by unmodified flint nodules (some also smeared with ochre) which also originated from the same non-local sources (Wentink 2008; van Gijn 2010a; 2010b). The periodic retrieval and re-deposition of the TRB axehead/nodule hoards demonstrates that wetland assemblages were part of repetitive ceremonialism.

At present one of the clearest views of Neolithic axehead deposition is shown in the

*Table 6.11: The general depositional trends of Irish stone axeheads by number (based on Cooney & Mandal 1998, 36, table 3.4)*

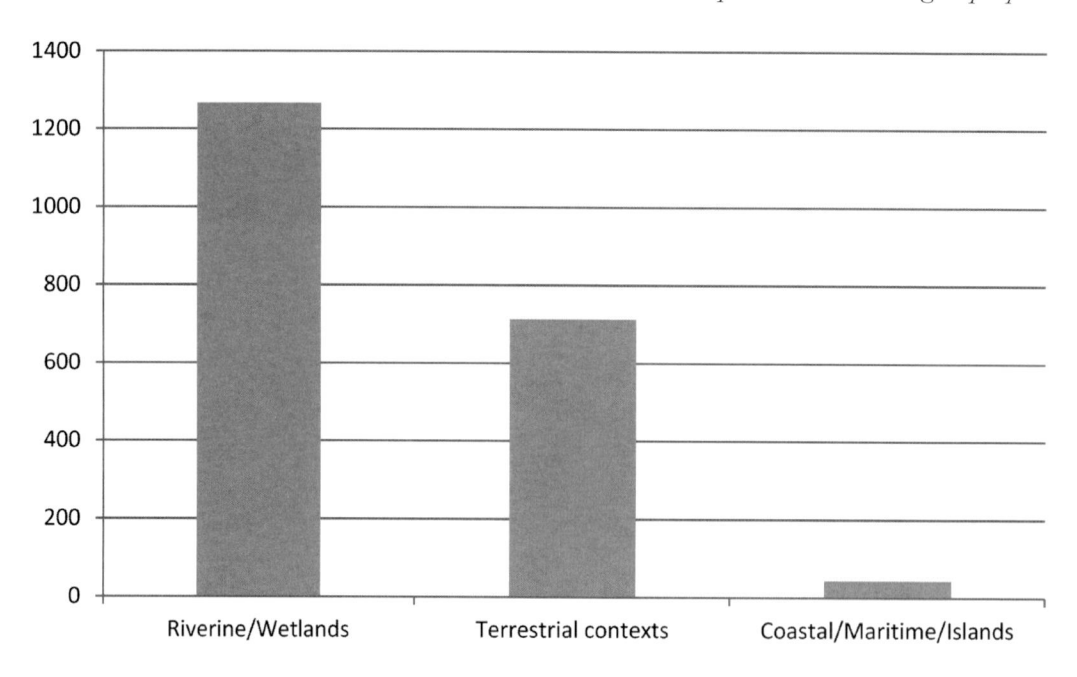

Irish data (Cooney & Mandal 1998). Here, a corpus of 2023 axeheads was recorded from a range of contexts (Table 6.10). By far the greatest number were recovered from rivers and river banks (956), followed by finds on agricultural land and rough pasture (318), archaeological sites (305) and bogs (277). Lesser numbers came from extraction sites (88), lakes and shores (34), the sea shore (28), islands (15) and caves (2). The overall pattern (Table 6.11) records almost twice as many axeheads from riverine or wetland contexts compared to those recovered from Irish terrestrial contexts. This suggests strong parallels with data from the River Thames (Adkins & Jackson 1978) and the European jade axehead corpus (Pétrequin *et al.* 2012a).

The Irish data appears to follow broader European trends with a preference for riverine and wetland deposition. The inescapable conclusion is that stone extraction in Ireland was mainly focused upon axehead production for ritual uses, particularly wetland deposition [63%], with land-based activities [35%] less important; deposits on the seashore and islands [2%] were relatively insignificant, despite some islands being extraction sites (eg, Lambay and Rathlin Islands; Cooney 2005; 2017).

The deposition of imported axeheads in Ireland has a similar pattern to indigenous types (Table 6.12). The small corpus of imported Cumbrian Group VI axeheads [30] have been recovered from well documented contexts, and as a sub-set of the Irish data follow the same general trends: wetland deposition predominates with 60% [18 axeheads], whereas terrestrial contexts produced 40% [12 axeheads] (Cooney & Mandal 1998, 144–6, 172, fig 5.25).

Irish riverine deposition was particularly notable in the rivers Bann, Barrow, Camoge and Shannon (Cooney & Mandal 1998, 144–5). Such practices were clearly part of a wider pan-European tradition which saw Alpine jade axeheads cast into the rivers of the southern Netherlands, especially the Meuse (Schut & Kars 2012, 1004) and Scandinavian flint axeheads were thrown into British rivers (Bradley 1987, 354). Large numbers of exotic axeheads have been dredged from the Thames, including a Durrington Type jade axehead from Barnes (Sheridan & Pailler 2012, 1079–80). Other jade axeheads were found at Vauxhall Bridge, Mortlake (Field & Cotton 1987) and Staines Moor (Field & Wooley 1983), alongside many axeheads of different lithologies, particularly from Cornish sources. The Thames axeheads of all materials were often larger than those found on land in the Thames Valley and were generally unbroken and in a variety of conditions, suggesting some had seen periods of use, whereas others may have been made especially for riverine deposition (Adkins & Jackson 1978; Chappell 1987, 271; Bradley 1990, 67).

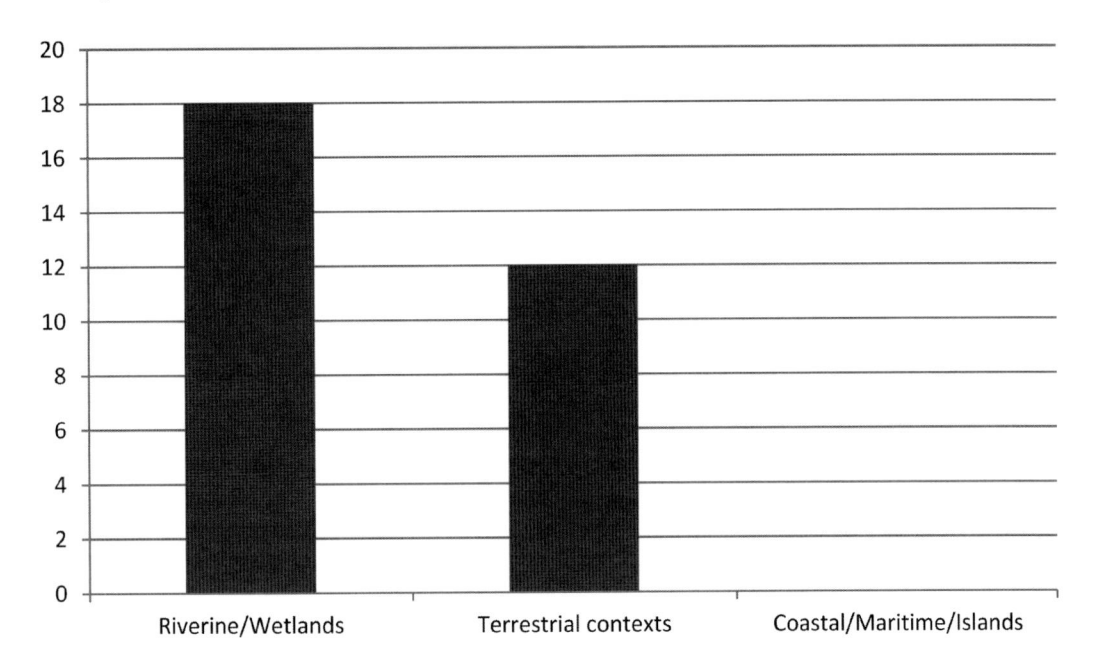

*Table 6.12: The general depositional trends of Cumbrian Group VI axeheads found in Ireland by number (based on Cooney & Mandal 1998, 172, fig 5.25)*

| Context | Number |
| --- | --- |
| Riverine/Wetlands | 18 |
| Terrestrial contexts | 12 |
| Coastal/Maritime/Islands | 0 |

The axeheads in the Scandinavian bogs were also frequently large and apparently unused, suggesting that they too were not everyday tools, but may have been manufactured for wetland deposition (Bradley 1990, 57–60). During the later Dutch Middle Neolithic Funnel Beaker period in the Rhine–Meuse Delta's rivers and bogs, large German and Danish axeheads appear to have been imported specifically for wetland deposition (van Gijn 2010a). The size of these imported axeheads made them impractical for woodland clearance and placing them in bogs suggests that they played a role in the cosmological practices of Dutch communities (van Gijn 2010b, 21–2).

By contrast, lithic assemblages from Dutch TRB megaliths show a marked difference to those from wetlands. Unlike wetland lithics, those from megaliths appear to have been used before deposition and feature edge damage, they are much smaller and produced from locally sourced flint. They are found alongside large quantities of transverse arrowheads, picks, and sickle blades. Use-wear analysis suggests these axeheads had been resharpened following wood-working and the sickle blades had been used for cereal harvesting, all indicative of agricultural activities (van Gijn 2010b, 131–2).

Taken together, the European data suggest that the large unused axeheads recovered from wetlands were reserved for special purposes, and were often sourced from long-distance networks, whereas axeheads from some burial contexts were locally sourced and everyday tools.

## A brief review of British and Irish depositional trends

The ethnographic principles outlined above can be seen in a number of archaeological contexts, some of which are described below.

### Houses

The Neolithic house, as a social construct, has been viewed as encapsulating communal histories and traditions, while incorporating cosmological principles in its structure, dimensions, orientation, and use (Bradley 2001; Coudart 2015; Last 2015). Houses create an arena for the performance and maintenance of common practices, domestic rituals, social transactions, and the maintenance of identity. Some of these activities appear to have incorporated extraction site products.

A number of examples illustrate artefact deposition at house sites. On Mainland (Orkney), during the later phases at Stonehall Farm Structure 1, the building was transformed from domestic use to a repository for the dead and the central hearth was replaced by a cist. The cist produced a lithic assemblage comprising a flaked and ground quartz axehead, four hammerstones, two scrapers, a cortex-backed knife, and 14 flint flakes and chips. A

*Figure 6.6: Part of the hoard from Modesty (Shetland), now curated by the National Museums of Scotland (photo: author)*

pair of finely chipped flint knives was found together, suggesting deposition in a bag, with a large black stone bead buried in the secondary floor surface (Richards & Jones 2016, 136–46, 445–50). A similar sequence occurred at House 2 at Barnhouse (Mainland, Orkney), where the building also featured a cist, and a polished siltstone axe-chisel was buried in the floor near the rear wall (Richards 2005, 129–56, 331). These two examples illustrate some of the ways in which lithics were used in the Northern Isles.

Further north, at Modesty (Mainland, Shetland) an unusually large hoard of nine felsite axeheads and 13 polished Shetland knives, juxtaposed with three steatitic clay pots, were all sealed beneath a layer of birch charcoal up to 130 mm thick, over which lay a deeper layer of peat ash (Sheridan 2012; pers. comm.). This stratigraphic sequence may represent a burnt Neolithic timber house, perhaps with a turf roof, which contained the hoard of undamaged axeheads and knives. The condition of the axeheads suggests that they were probably reserved for special purposes.

At Ronaldsway (Isle of Man) a modest rectangular house contained a large assemblage of pottery, tools, and bones. The lithics included another large hoard of 11 stone axeheads, several miniature flint axeheads and chisels, assorted flint tools, five schist plaques (some decorated), hammerstones, and mauls. Like Modesty, many of these artefacts 'were uniform in character and unweathered', suggesting they too were unused. Most were ranged along the northern and eastern walls, and a pit lay on the eastern side of the central hearth containing ox long bones and a small, unbroken pot, all sealed by a large stone slab (Bruce & Megaw 1947). The fact that many artefacts were unused and distributed around certain walls and the hearth may parallel the ethnography and suggest ritualised deposition relating to the well-being of the house.

As with general axehead deposition, Ireland also provides a large data set of trends within Neolithic houses, particularly in eastern Ireland (Smyth 2014, 25). The majority of houses here have a south-facing long axis (Topping 1996, 161–3; Smyth 2014, 23), and Smyth (*ibid.*, 58) has observed that of roughly 90 sites, '[d]eliberate or purposeful deposition has so far been noted at approximately 20'. Indications had been noted previously by O'Ríordáin (1954) at Site A at Lough Gur, where a greenstone axehead was discovered beneath the north wall of this Early Neolithic structure associated with Carinated Bowl pottery. As noted previously, in the Northern Isles, a number of sites feature foundation deposits of extraction site products: at Corbally the house foundation trench had a mudstone axehead set vertically, blade upright, and partly surrounded by sherds; another mudstone axehead was discovered in a wall trench in Structure 1 at Earlsrath; a deliberately broken porphyry axehead lay amongs stone packing in House B at Monanny, with a second porphyry axehead set blade downwards in a post-hole; the gable wall of House 1 at Ballintaggart produced a burnt flint axehead and a broken porcellanite axehead; a polished axehead was placed in a post-hole in Structure 2 at Kilmainham 1A; at Ballyharry a basalt axehead and an arrowhead were placed in separate central post-holes, both blades downwards.

Most of the axeheads from Irish houses lay in foundation deposits, alongside burnt bones and sherds, and many houses had juxtaposed pits (Smyth 2014, 56–62). However, certain pits were clearly post-abandonment features, as at Ballyharry where they were cut through the footprint of House 1, and contained deposits of worked and retouched porcellanite fragments, flint, greenstone, possible reworked jade roughout axeheads, polished flakes of Cumbrian Group VI tuff, pottery, burnt bone, charred hazelnuts, and cereals (Moore 2003, 158). Other post-abandonment deposits were found at the Balleygalley 1, Corbally 3, Cruicerath, and Richardstown houses (Smyth 2014, 63). In terms of knapping activity, the house sites at Cloghers and Ballyharry provided evidence suggesting axehead production and Townleyhall 2, Ballyglass, and Knocknarea produced large numbers of concave scrapers, suggesting specialist production (*ibid.*, 111). Consequently, in Ireland and elsewhere, extraction site products were placed in foundation deposits during house construction, incorporated into pit deposits during the life of the house, provide evidence for on-site lithic production, and, finally, occur in post-abandonment pit deposits. Houses therefore created a domestic arena for many ritualised activities and social transactions where extraction site products played an important role in objectifying social space.

### Pits

Pit digging was a common practice in Ireland, generally to contain flint implements, debitage, axeheads, complete and broken pottery, burnt hazelnuts, charcoal, animal and human remains, and burnt stone (Smyth 2012; 2014, 112–18). Importantly, pits were also dug at Irish extraction sites. The Early Neolithic porphyry quarry on Lambay Island was embellished with a number of pits containing sequences of Carrowkeel and Goodland styles of pottery, hammerstones, rubbers, flint and porphyry debitage, and some pits were sealed by cairns, similar to those at Goodland (Cooney 1998; 2000; 2004; 2005; Cooney *et al.* 2011). At Goodland (Antrim), a U-shaped segmented ditch enclosed 171 pits containing 6478 Middle–Late Neolithic pot sherds, 13,950 struck flints, and animal remains, all apparently from off-site sources and deliberately buried (Case 1973). On the south-eastern arc of the segmented ditch outcropping flint nodules occurred which were quarried and processed on-site at two knapping floors, creating a conjunction of pit digging and flint extraction practices. These examples highlight the juxtaposition of special pit deposits at quarries and suggest that pit digging was an integral part of extraction at some sites. The absence of pits at British extraction sites may be illusory and the result of excavation bias.

### Causewayed enclosures

Causewayed enclosures may have fulfilled multiple roles, including defence (Crawford 1937), settings for trade and exchange of axeheads (Stone & Wallis 1951), 'liminal' venues for rites of passage (Edmonds 1993), and as places for processing dead bodies before interment in long barrows (Field 2006, 111). Recent research has demonstrated that these enclosures were generally constructed roughly three centuries after the earliest Neolithic mines and quarries were opened in Britain, that they had European antecedents (particularly Chasséen and Michelsberg enclosures), and they were used from 25–300+ years (Whittle *et al.* 2011). They were a key component of the established Neolithic in Britain post-*c.* 3700 cal BC but may have existed earlier in Ireland if the enclosure at Magheraboy is an indication (Danaher 2007).

The ditched layout of causewayed enclosures created boundaries and thresholds (Edmonds 1993, 111) which orchestrated movement via causeways. The assemblages from the ditches comprised lithics, pottery, human remains, animal bones, and carved chalk

Table 6.13: The number of flint implements discovered at English causewayed enclosures from published sources

| Lithic type | HH | Ste | E | WH | BH | Sta | A | MC |
|---|---|---|---|---|---|---|---|---|
| Scrapers | 351 | 240 | 253 | 1399 | 181 | 377 | 166 | 421 |
| Edge-trimmed flakes | 411 | 184 | 410 | 457 | – | – | 370 | – |
| Serrated-edge flakes | 343 | 146 | 219 | 627+ | 83 | 195+ | 272 | 188 |
| Piercers | 86 | 49 | 58 | 68 | 34 | 160 | 5 | 17 |
| Leaf arrowheads | 29 | 9 | 29 | 132 | 18 | 34 | 17 | 28 |
| Axeheads etc | 19 | 15 | 18 | 90 | 3+ | 21 | 11 | 49 |
| Laurel-leaf bifacials | 3 | 3 | 5 | 25 | 1 | 66? | 5 | 2 |
| Knives | 7 | 4 | 1 | 84+ | 11 | 104? | 10 | 12 |
| Fabricators/rods | 7 | 6 | 9 | 2+ | 2 | 12 | 2 | 4 |
| Assemblage totals | 1256 | 656 | 1002 | 2884+ | 333+ | 969+ | 858 | 721 |

*Key*: HH = Hambledon Hill (Dorset); Ste = Stepleton Enclosure, Hambledon Hill (Dorset); E = Etton (Cambridgeshire); WH = Windmill Hill (Wilts); BH = Briar Hill (Northamptonshire); Sta = Staines (Surrey); A = Abingdon (Oxfordshire); MC = Maiden Castle (Dorset). (Based on Saville 2002, 98, table 10.1)

objects, all reminiscent of assemblages found in ditches and forecourts of barrows. The most elaborate deposits were discovered in enclosure ditch terminals, where they were most visible to visitors entering across the causeways. The embellished ditch terminals enhanced key access routes into the interior of the enclosures in the same way as deposits on shaft floors and around gallery entrances did in flint mines.

The presence of lithic assemblages at causewayed enclosures provides empirical evidence of on-site practices (Table 6.13). The prevalence of scrapers and similar processing tools at Etton (Cambridgeshire) (Pryor 1998), Staines (Middlesex) (Robertson-Mackay 1987), Maiden Castle (Dorset) (Sharples 1991) and Windmill Hill (Wiltshire) (Smith 1965; Whittle *et al.* 1999) among others, are often taken as evidence for hide preparation. However, as Saville (2002, 94) has observed, although use-wear analysis can identify the raw materials being processed by implements, it is unable to characterise what that processed raw material was then transformed into. In addition, research has shown that the majority of Neolithic flint implements were used for producing or maintaining everyday equipment and not for subsistence tasks (Jensen 1994, 166). For example, serrated-edged flakes were probably associated with whittling or rope/textile manufacturing rather than food production (Saville 2002, 94–6). Consequently, lithic assemblages from causewayed enclosures may represent the periodic production or maintenance of personal equipment during the cyclical activities enacted at the enclosures, all of which may have been components of overarching renewal rituals.

Despite their traditional association with wood-working and forest clearance, Saville's (2002, 98–9) detailed analysis of axehead use and deposition at causewayed enclosures has shown that although some were cached, complete and intact, far more were deliberately broken and/or burnt, and certain axeheads were reworked (possibly reflecting transformative events at the enclosures). They were 'relatively rarely found intact at causewayed enclosure sites in Britain', with the exception of cached examples at Combe Hill (Sussex), Hambledon Hill (Dorset), and Maiden Castle (Saville 2002, 98). Conversely, these enclosures produced more reworked axeheads, recycled axehead flakes, and deliberately burnt and broken axeheads. At Etton the general lithic assemblage was produced from locally sourced flint (Pryor 1998, 238), supplemented with exotic, non-local stone axeheads, principally sourced from Langdale/Scafell (Group VI, Cumbria) 240 miles/386 km away, and Graiglwyd (Group VII, Gwynedd) lying 220 miles/354 km distant (Table 6.14). The treatment of axeheads at Etton follows the general trend with only a minority intact (Pryor 1998, 260–8). Of 24 finds only two are relatively complete: a small reworked ground axehead of Group VI from a Phase 1 pit (find no. 9), and a miniature flaked axehead roughout from the Phase 2 ditchfill (no. 14). Conversely, the remaining 22 finds are ground flakes or broken axehead fragments, of which four were burnt, suggesting the majority of Etton's axeheads were brought to the site for deliberate destruction and deposition.

6 *The products: an ethnoarchaeological analysis of lithic objects from extraction sites*

| Context & phase | Layer | Finds no. | Description | Identification |
|---|---|---|---|---|
| Subsoil | n/a | 13 | Ground central part of axehead, broken | ?Group VI |
| Buried soil | n/a | 7 | Ground broken flake | Group VII |
| Enclosure ditch; 1A | 3 | 8 | Ground flake | ? |
| Enclosure ditch; 1B | 4 | 20 | Ground axehead fragment, burnt | ?Group VI |
| Enclosure ditch; 1C | 3 | 6 | Ground butt fragment | ?Group VI |
| Enclosure ditch; 1C | 2 | 21 | Ground flake | ?Group VI |
| Enclosure ditch; 1 or 2 | 1 | 10 | Ground fragment | Group VI |
| Small, filled pits; 1 | n/a | 9 | Reworked, ground small axehead | Group VI |
| Small, filled pits; ?1 | 1 | 16 | Ground butt fragment | Group VII |
| Small, filled pits; 1 | 1 | 17 | Ground flake | ? |
| Small, filled pits; 1 | 1 | 18 | Ground central part of axehead, broken | Group VII |
| Scoops; ?1 | n/a | 24 | Ground flake | ?Group VI |
| Enclosure ditch; 2 | – | 1 | Ground flake | Group VII |
| Enclosure ditch; 2 | – | 2 | Ground axehead butt fragment; burnt | Group VII |
| Enclosure ditch; 2 | – | 3 | Ground fragments; burnt | Group VII |
| Enclosure ditch; 2 | – | 4 | Ground fragment; burnt | Group VII |
| Enclosure ditch; 2 | ? | 5 | Ground axehead butt | Altered quartz dolerite |
| Enclosure ditch; 2 | 1 | 11 | Ground butt fragment | Group VII |
| Enclosure ditch; 2 | 1 | 12 | Ground flake | ? |
| Enclosure ditch; 2 | 1 | 14 | Miniature flaked axehead roughout | ?Group VI |
| Enclosure ditch; 2 | 1 | 15 | Ground flake | ? |
| Enclosure ditch; 2 | 2 | 19 | Ground flake | ?Group VI |
| Large pit; 2 | n/a | 22 | Ground flake | Group VII |
| Large pit; 2 | n/a | 23 | Ground fragment | ?Group VII |

(Data from Pryor 1998, 261–6)

*Table 6.14: The contexts of stone axeheads and fragments from Etton (Cambridgeshire) causewayed enclosure*

| Site | \multicolumn{5}{c}{Cornish petrology groups} | \multicolumn{2}{c}{Other sources} |
|---|---|---|---|---|---|---|---|
| | I | IV | IVA | XVI | XVII | Jade | Misc. |
| Carn Brea | 4 | 2 | – | 11–18 | 2 | – | 19 |
| Hambledon Hill (main enclosure) | 2 | 1 | – | 2 | 1 | 2 | 10 |
| Hambledon Hill (Stepleton enclosure) | – | – | – | – | 1 | – | 2 |
| Helman Tor | 2 | – | – | – | 3 | – | 2 |
| Hembury | – | – | 4 | – | 1 | – | 11 |
| Maiden Castle | – | 1 | 6 | 1 | 2 | – | 7 |

(Based on Sharples 1991, 231, table 85).
*Key*: Group I = Mount's Bay area; Group IV = near Callington; Group IVa = south-west England; Group XVI = near Cambourne; Group XVII = near St Austell (Clough 1988)

*Table 6.15: Stone axeheads recovered from Early Neolithic enclosures in south-west England*

Etton was not alone in such practices. At the Maiden Castle enclosure local tertiary gravel flint was used for much of the lithic assemblage including axeheads and large core tools (Sharples 1991, 218), supplemented by imported non-local stone axeheads, particularly Cornish implements (*ibid.*, 230–1). Axeheads were placed in ditches, others in pits, and some were burnt and broken, suggesting parallels with practices seen at Etton (Wheeler 1943, 164–71). Many of the Maiden Castle Cornish axeheads had travelled roughly 170 miles/273 km to the enclosure for on-site deposition, as seen at other enclosures in the south-west (Table 6.15).

The Windmill Hill assemblage, like those from Etton and Maiden Castle, exploited

Table 6.16: The flint axehead and adzehead contextual data from Windmill Hill (Wiltshire)

| Context | Axehead fragments | Adzehead fragments |
|---|---|---|
| *1925–1937 excavations* | | |
| Inner ditch | 28 | – |
| Middle ditch | 31 | 3 |
| Outer ditch | 12 | – |
| Surface | 7 | – |
| Picket barrow | 5 | – |
| Pits | 2 | – |
| *1957–1958 excavations* | | |
| Inner ditch | 2 | – |
| Middle ditch | – | – |
| Outer ditch | 7 | – |
| *1988 excavations* | | |
| Inner ditch | 1 | – |
| Middle ditch | 2 | – |
| Outer ditch | 4 | – |

(From Whittle *et al.* 1999, 333)

local nodular flint, although the axehead fragments may be from a different source (Whittle *et al.* 1999, 318). During the 1988 excavations seven fragments of polished flint axeheads were discovered, all but one from the ditches (*ibid.*, 330). When this is combined with data from previous excavations, the pattern for axehead deposition records 23 fragments in the outer ditch, 33 fragments [plus three adzehead fragments] in the middle ditch, and 31 fragments in the inner ditch. The variable density of this patterning may reflect a relative importance placed upon the innermost segments of the enclosure (Table 6.16). Following practices seen at other sites, axeheads at Windmill Hill seem to have been brought to the site for destruction.

In Ireland, the causewayed enclosure at Magheraboy (Sligo) produced two axehead fragments, one of limestone (possibly a skeuomorph) and one of Antrim porcellanite, placed among a primary midden deposit in one ditch segment. The Antrim axehead had been deliberately broken, paralleling practices at British enclosures (Saville 2002, 98–9), and both axehead fragments had been buried in redeposited subsoil. A third complete mudstone axehead was discovered in another ditch segment, again in a primary midden deposit, but in this case surrounded by 30 fragments of quartz crystal suggesting a structured deposit (Danaher 2007, 113–14).

Overall, the stratigraphy of causewayed enclosure ditches suggests they remained open for only short periods before being deliberately backfilled to bury any deposits, but they could be reopened for the addition of new deposits (Whittle *et al.* 1999, 368). In general, the everyday lithic assemblages from causewayed enclosures are typically made from local lithologies, whereas axeheads (both flint and stone) are normally manufactured from exotic, non-local sources and were often brought to the enclosures to be destroyed and deposited in ditches or pits.

## Conclusions

The importance of 'things' to people can be profound. Artefacts often embody ideologies that can shape individuals and society and this appears to have been the case with certain forms of Early Neolithic axehead, particularly those from extraction sites. These artefacts became aspirational because they carried narratives, had a biography, and represented elements of the cosmographic ordering of agro-pastoral life. As a result, the widespread adoption of deep mining became pivotal to societal change during the transition from foraging to farming.

# 7

# Neolithic extraction: a pan-European phenomenon

The archaeological evidence for the emergence of Neolithic extraction practices across Europe and the influence of Mesolithic precursors were outlined in Chapter 1. Here the ancient DNA (aDNA) data will be discussed briefly to examine the scientific evidence for the migration of Neolithic agro-pastoralists across Europe, their impact upon indigenous communities, and the influence of these indigenes upon emerging extraction practices. Following this, the radiocarbon chronology will be used to chart the spread of Neolithic extraction across the continent. Finally, an overview of European mining will present the evidence for a shared, pan-European practice using the ethnoarchaeological model as an interpretive framework.

## Neolithisation by genome ...

The analysis of aDNA from various prehistoric populations is beginning to provide robust scientific data of population movements to compare with the archaeological evidence. Brace *et al.* (2019) studied genome-wide data from six Mesolithic and 67 Neolithic individuals from Britain, spanning the period 8500–2500 BC. This research found genetic affinities between British Mesolithic individuals and counterparts among western European and Scandinavian hunter-gatherer-fishers, suggesting a shared ancestry. However, this changed dramatically in Britain after *c.* 4000 BC with the appearance of European agro-pastoralists whose ancestry lay in the Aegean/Anatolian region. These early farmers dispersed westwards across Europe following two major routes. The first skirted the Mediterranean coastline and the second passed through Central Europe; in each case genetic footprints recorded the gene flow between nomadic agro-pastoralists and the indigenous populations. Although farming communities reached northern France around 5000 BC, for some unexplained reason they did not cross the Channel for roughly a millennium, despite the fact that it was much narrower than today.

Although radiocarbon chronologies are patchy in places (Consuegra & Díaz-del-Río 2018, 2), the European archaeological data suggests that the dispersal of Neolithic extraction practices broadly corresponds with the two major routes of Neolithisation identified by aDNA – the Mediterranean and the trans-Danubian land routes (Olalde *et al.* 2018; Brace *et al.* 2019; Rivollat *et al.* 2020). Along the Mediterranean coastal route in southern France, for example, indigenous foragers appear to have had continuous interaction with incoming migrant Neolithic groups over a period of 3–4 generations, producing a genetic contribution to the Neolithic gene pool of around 31% and suggesting a degree of stable co-existence between these communities. Occasionally even greater contributions occur in southern France where the Pendimoun (Provence) female skeleton [F2] dated to 5480–5360 cal BC has a 55% genetic contribution from local Mesolithic indigenes. In comparison the ratio in central Europe along the trans-Danubian route was only 3%, and that in the

*Figure 7.1: (opposite) Shaft 27, Cissbury (Sussex), showing the location of the female skeleton lying at the base of the shaft and facing into a gallery (© Worthing Museum and Art Gallery)*

Iberian Peninsula 13% (Rivollat *et al.* 2020). France, Iberia, the Low Countries, Poland, Sweden, Britain, and Ireland, have all produced variable levels of local Mesolithic genes among Neolithic individuals. Despite having a very small local Mesolithic contribution among central European migrant Neolithic groups, they inherited Mesolithic DNA from contact with groups in south-eastern Europe, which suggests a relatively rapid migration into central Europe with limited biological interaction *en route*; the scenario in Iberia was similar.

In Britain, Neolithic individuals show 'a sudden and constant higher hunter-gatherer component at the time of the arrival of the Neolithic in the region' (Rivollat *et al.* 2020, 3), and they shared affinities with Iberian and French populations which had strong Mediterranean antecedents. This aDNA data suggests that the Mediterranean influence among British groups may have arrived from the Atlantic coasts, particularly Normandy and the Paris Basin via the south of France (Rivollat *et al.* 2020, 7–9). A complementary study of Irish aDNA has found little difference between the genomic heritage of British and Irish Neolithic populations, who both appear to share the same northern French genetic markers with a strong Mediterranean ancestry (Cassidy *et al.* 2020). However, as the researchers recognise, more aDNA analysis is needed on both direct testing and dense whole-genome sampling at a regional level to enhance our understanding of the precise origins of migrant Neolithic groups who travelled to Britain and Ireland.

It appears from the aDNA data that the delayed arrival of continental farmers in south-east Britain occurred by *3980–3720* cal BC (95% confidence, modelled date), but slightly earlier in western Britain where there was a rapid dispersal around the Irish Sea and apparently as far north as Orkney (Brace *et al.* 2019, 768; cf. Sheridan 2004; 2007; 2010). Some evidence suggests that migrants using the western routes may represent a single community who traversed Britain eastwards and northwards, intermingling with the indigenous Mesolithic groups to produce a regionalised genomic ancestry. Interestingly, there is data from the west coast of Scotland suggesting the possible co-existence of genetically distinct indigenous populations alongside incomers, although this may only have lasted a few centuries (Brace *et al.* 2019, 770).

One of the most relevant aDNA studies for the present research comes from the established Neolithic some 300-400 years after the appearance of both the first migrants in southern Britain and deep shaft mining on the South Downs. This is the analysis of the female skeleton excavated by John Pull during the 1950s in Shaft 27 at Cissbury (Russell 2001, 178-189; Topping 2005; Fig. 7.1). The skeleton was found buried near the base of the shaft at a depth of 4.57 m [15 feet], and a $^{14}$C determination taken from a tooth provided a date of 3640-3380 cal BC [4775±34 BP; OxA-34470] (Teather 2019, 42-43). However, it is the DNA ancestry of this individual which is important, providing a snapshot of life during the early *mature* Neolithic. The genomic data of this individual recorded an introgression of ±4.1% of Western Hunter Gatherer aDNA, which analysis suggested had largely originated in continental Europe. It would seem that the Cissbury female was strongly related to continental European populations with only an incredibly small amount of indigenous British Mesolithic aDNA in her ancestry, despite the passing of up to *c.* 9-12 generations since first contact (Brace *et al.* 2019, Fig S8; Dr Tom Booth, pers. comm.). Consequently, the Cissbury female may have been associated with a more traditional Neolithic community in southern Britain (or Europe) who retained strong European links and maintained a robust group identity. The Cissbury female may therefore have played a part in cultural interaction between indigenous groups and incomers, possibly representing someone involved in alliance building through arranged marriage. However, what had led to this?

The fact that the early 4th millennium South Downs mines are located in a landscape block between the rivers Arun and Adur which does not contain any distinctively Neolithic monuments (Topping 2005, 82–4), may indicate cultural origins. As we have seen in parts of northern Europe among forager communities such as the Swifterbant and Ertebølle, indigenous peoples often selectively chose to adopt elements of Neolithic practices. Therefore, were the South Downs mines an indigenous phenomenon enhanced by the increasing needs of incoming migrants and ultimately represent a cross-cultural melding

7 *Neolithic extraction: a pan-European phenomenon*

# 1952-1954. PLAN OF FLINT MINE Nº 27. O.M.F.

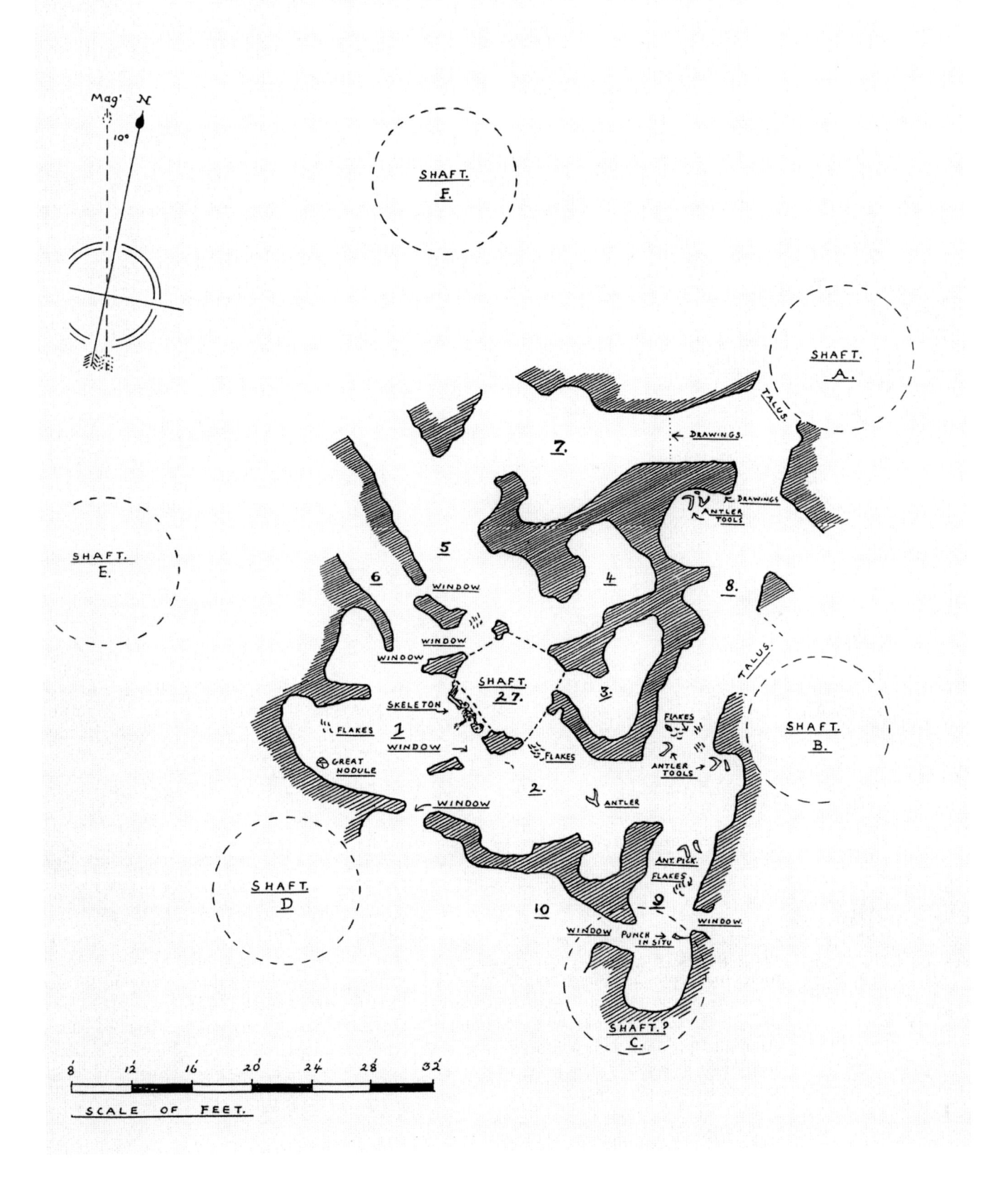

of both Mesolithic and Neolithic practices as seen elsewhere in Europe? Certainly, tranchet axeheads have been found at these sites (see Chapter 6), while the form of Cissbury-type axeheads display Mesolithic traits and may reflect indigenous production (inf. D. Field). In addition, relatively little Early Neolithic pottery has been recovered from these mines compared to other types of contemporary Neolithic sites featuring ditches or pits (Barber *et al.* 1999, 69). It may be that the burial of the Shaft 27 female, several generations after the earliest mines were dug, represents a phase of acculturation between Neolithic practitioners and an indigenous community at a time when long barrows and causewayed enclosures were beginning to appear in surrounding areas. Such a scenario would also help to explain the small amount of British Mesolithic aDNA in the genomic ancestry of the Shaft 27 female.

Taken together, the aDNA data records a complex picture of interaction between indigenous occupants and migrant Neolithic groups around Europe. In terms of Britain and Ireland, clearly France – lying at the junction of the Mediterranean and Danubian routes – played a pivotal role in the Neolithisation process in these countries, lending weight to the suggestion that the mines of the Paris Basin, Normandy, and sites in the Nord-Pas de Calais were the origins of Neolithic deep-shaft mining across the Channel (Sheridan 2010; 2017; 2020; cf. Cassen *et al.* 2019). Importantly, the aDNA data records a survival of significant percentages of hunter-gatherer genes within the biological signature of Neolithic individuals over a number of generations following first contact (eg, Charlton *et al.* 2016). This indicates that a degree of social stability existed which generally allowed Mesolithic and Neolithic communities to be able to interact peacefully and develop communal extraction practices in many parts of Europe.

## Extraction practices at the Mesolithic–Neolithic transition

Following the discussion in Chapter 1 of the evidence for the spread of Neolithic extraction practices across Europe and its Mesolithic forebears, a few observations will provide some archaeological context to the preceding discussion of aDNA data. Chronologically, distinctively Neolithic extraction practices follow the main routes of Neolithisation in central Europe and around the Mediterranean coastlines. In Britain and Ireland the emerging evidence suggests that Neolithic extraction practices were broadly coeval with the appearance of some elements of agro-pastoralism, as Whittle *et al.* (2011, 257–62) discovered regarding the relatively sudden appearance of deep-shaft galleried flint mines in southern Britain. However, the evidence for the introduction of domesticated cereals in Britain is beginning to suggest that they appeared sporadically and, in many regions, did not occur until the more mature Neolithic when monument building occurred, around *c.* 3800 cal BC (cf. Brown 2007; Evans 2018; Griffiths 2018).

This scenario was duplicated in some regions of Europe, where Neolithic extraction and farming practices appeared together during the primary Neolithic (Table 7.1), often before communal enclosures were constructed and, in some cases, before monumental tombs were built. In certain areas Neolithic materiality or elements of the lifeway were selectively adopted before the full shift to Neolithic extraction practices and agro-pastoralism. Consequently, the appearance of semi-mobile, migrant agro-pastoralists must have added to the picture of human movements across many regions, introducing further complexity to community interactions.

This complexity can be seen in the Low Countries and northern Germany, for example. Here, imported lithics and indigenous pottery co-existed amongst the Swifterbant hunter-gatherer-fishers in the Low Countries before the introduction of Neolithic extraction and farming practices (cf. Louwe Kooijmans 2001a; 2001b; 2007; van Gijn 2009; 2010a). In southern Scandinavia and northern Germany the lifeway of the pottery using Ertebølle-Ellerbek foraging communities showed strong elements of continuity over the Mesolithic–Neolithic transition (Gron & Sørensen 2018, 962). However, they did have aspirations towards Neolithic materiality, as shown by the presence of imported Rössen and Michelsberg amphibolite shaft-hole axeheads, implements emblematic of the central European Neolithic. These were used alongside more traditional indigenous bone and antler adornments and implements, some of which were stylistically inspired by farming communities (Price &

Gebauer 2005, 33–5). In addition, LBK pottery was also imported, which may have inspired the production of indigenous ceramics by *c.* 4700 cal BC (Hartz *et al.* 2007). A similar situation existed in central and northern Poland, where communities of forest foragers practised some elements of farming and produced their own varieties of pottery, suggesting conscious aspirations towards the Neolithic lifeway (Nowak 2001).

These examples demonstrate the existence of an often robust hunter-gatherer-fisher cultural tradition in many regions of Europe which was partly resistant to change from external cultural influences, despite the piecemeal adoption of elements of Neolithic materiality and practices. This survival of indigenous culture in many regions during and beyond first contact with Neolithic agro-pastoral communities created the opportunity for cross-cultural fertilisation. This allowed both the adoption of selected Neolithic influences from the east, contrasting with an acceptance of indigenous Mesolithic practices by migrants.

The archaeological record and aDNA data both demonstrate that there was the potential for newcomers to absorb the influence and knowledge of indigenous extraction practitioners as Neolithisation progressed across Europe. Such cross-cultural social interaction would have laid the foundations for increasing collaboration, alliance building, and ultimately acculturation for many. This would explain the presence of later Mesolithic practices within Neolithic extraction repertoire, such as Mesolithic-like placed deposits of raw material or debitage on-site, and the widespread adoption of pre-existing ground stone technology for axeheads. The integration of these Mesolithic practices was generally achieved during the *c.* 1–4 generation window of cross-cultural interaction suggested by the aDNA. However, the archaeological record shows that, in some regions such as the Rhine–Meuse Delta, Neolithisation proceeded at a much slower pace and may have taken around a millennium to complete (van Gijn 2009), once again providing an adequate opportunity for Mesolithic influences to be absorbed by newcomers.

Taken together, the emergent European Neolithic extraction practice must reflect elements of Mesolithic traditions and the cosmological beliefs which underscored their worldview. Consequently, the brave new world of the Neolithic had some of its foundations partly rooted in indigenous culture.

## Chronology

The current radiocarbon chronology suggests the north-westerly spread of Neolithic extraction practices across Europe spanned some two millennia (Table 7.1). The earliest sites occur in the central and western Mediterranean at Defensola 'A' on the Gargano Peninsula in southern Italy, the obsidian quarries on Lipari (Aeolian Islands), and Casa Montero and El Cañaveral in central Spain. Also in this earliest phase of pioneering Neolithic extraction spanning some 7–9 centuries was Krumlovský les (Czechia) associated with LBK extraction, and the iconic jade quarries high in the Italian Alps. Generally, these early sites were coeval with the first appearance of agro-pastoralism in their respective regions, which contrasts with later sites in Poland, the Netherlands, Belgium, France, and Spain where extraction sites often appeared after the introduction of farming practices and during an established Neolithic. This can be seen at the Breton fibrolite quarries which were in use for much of the 5th millennium, beginning around 4800 cal BC (Pailler 2012a; 2012b), some two centuries later than the introduction of farming. Similarly, the variscite mines at Gavà, near Barcelona in south-eastern Spain, were sunk roughly 900 years after farming was established in the region (Borrell *et al.* 2009), and despite the precedent set further inland at the mine complexes of Casa Montero and El Cañaveral. In Poland the major mine complex of Krzemionki appears to have originated around 1300 years after the appearance of agriculture. These examples demonstrate a time-lag between the introduction of farming and the commencement of Neolithic stone extraction in some regions, although caution is needed as this may reflect excavation bias.

After roughly two millennia Neolithic extraction practices had become well established across most of Europe, and a new phase of expansion was inaugurated around the Atlantic façade in Scandinavia, Britain and Ireland. These regions experienced the final stages of European Neolithisation (as demonstrated by aDNA and radiocarbon

*Table 7.1: A crude approximate and selective chronology of the introduction of Neolithic extraction practices at individual sites based upon the excavators' data*

| Country/site | Radiocarbon chronology for the beginning of Neolithic extraction by site, cal BC | Introduction of agro–pastoralism in the same region, cal BC |
| --- | --- | --- |
| *Pioneering Neolithic extraction* | | |
| Italy, Defensola 'A' | 6010–5720 | *c.* 6000 |
| Italy, Lipari | 5900 | *c.* 6000 |
| Spain, El Cañaveral | 5530–5360 | *c.* 5300 |
| Czechia, Krumlovský les [LBK phase] | 5400–5250 | *c.* 5400 |
| Spain, Casa Montero | 5380–5180 | *c.* 5300 |
| Italy, Alpine jade quarries | 5300–4900 | n/a |
| *Extraction amongst established Neolithic communities* | | |
| Poland, Sąspów | 4900–4250 | *c.* 5200 |
| France, Brittany, Plouguin | 4800 | *c.* 5000 |
| France, Normandy, Bretteville-le-Rabet | 4800–3975 | *c.* 5000 |
| Austria, Wien-Mauer/Antonshöhe | 4560 | *c.* 5400 |
| Belgium, Spiennes | 4350 | *c.* 5100 |
| Spain, Catalonia, Gavà | 4320–3780 | *c.* 5800 |
| Netherlands, Rijckholt | 4316–4298 | *c.* 5100 |
| France, Paris Basin | 4300 | *c.* 5100 |
| Germany, Kleinkems | 4150 | *c.* 5400 |
| France, Normandy, Ri | 4100 | *c.* 5000 |
| France, Brittany, Plussulien/Seledin | 3950 | *c.* 5000 |
| Poland, Krzemionki | 3900 | *c.* 5200 |
| *Second pioneering phase of extraction* | | |
| British & Irish extraction sites | 4150–3700 | *c.* 3800 |
| Sweden, Kvarnby-Södra Sallerup mines | 4000–3800 | *c.* 4000 |

(Data from Barber *et al.* 1999; Babel *et al.* 2005; Engel & Siegmund 2005; Högberg 2006; Brown 2007; Borrell *et al.* 2009; Pailler 2009; Baena Preysler *et al.* 2011; de Grooth *et al.* 2011; Lech 2011; Marcigny *et al.* 2011; Tarantini *et al.* 2011; Trnka 2011; Tsobgou Ahoupe & Marcigny 2011; Whittle *et al.* 2011; Muntoni 2012; Pétrequin *et al.* 2012a; 2017; Andersson *et al.* 2016; Collet *et al.* 2016; Giligny & Bostyn 2016; Consuegra & Díaz-del-Río 2018; Edinborough *et al.* 2019, compared with the appearance of farming in the same region, following Gronenborn *et al.* 2019). Although caution is needed, these estimates provide an impression of overall trends

chronology) which saw the introduction of a different extraction technology of deep-shaft galleried mining around *c.* 4150–3700 cal BC (Barber *et al.* 1999; Edinborough *et al.* 2020). However, as discussed in Chapters 1, 5, and 6, the introduction of Neolithic mining practices in these regions occurred alongside the co-existence of indigenous Mesolithic extraction sites and represents a coalescence and enhancement of existing practices. The inauguration of novel deep-shaft galleried mining occurred at a number of sites which had traditionally seen extraction with comparatively shallow pits or quarries. Along with this, the new deeper mines hosted a range of extraction practices which absorbed indigenous practices and redefined them. These included the use of placed deposits comprising debitage, lithics, pottery, carved objects, and graffiti, at times in structured assemblages, alongside the deposition of animal remains. This contrasts with Mesolithic practices which primarily utilised deposits of debitage and raw materials that suggest a focus upon rites of renewal, whereas the richer Neolithic practices encompass renewal but now include aspects of identity and cosmological beliefs. In Britain, such transitional extraction strategies can be seen at sites such as Easton Down and Blackpatch, where shallow forms of extraction were superceded by deeper mines, and assemblages increased in sophistication depending on the type of extraction practised.

This suggests that specific lithic procurement practices became one of the earliest expressions of 'being' Neolithic in Britain and Ireland and an important element of acculturation for indigenous groups, as well as legitimisation for incoming migrants (cf. Sheridan 2010; 2017; 2020; Olalde *et al.* 2018; Brace *et al.* 2019; Cassidy *et al.* 2020; Rivollat *et al.* 2020). This is lent weight by Griffiths (2018) research which has convincingly shown that cereals did not appear before the 38th century cal BC in southern and north-west England and Ireland, and in some regions occurred after the creation of monuments, enclosures, and burials (cf. Whittle *et al.* 2011). Taken together, this evidence implies that the introduction of the Neolithic 'package' into Britain and Ireland was piecemeal and erratic, as seen in other regions of north-west Europe.

At roughly the same time as Neolithic practices were beginning to appear in Britain, further north, in southern Sweden at Kvarnby and Södra Sallerup, small flint quarries and deep shaft mines (2–8 m deep) were sunk when the Funnel Beaker Culture appeared in the region. These sites produced flint for pointed-butt axeheads around 4000 cal BC at a time when some cereals were first grown, closely followed by domesticated animals in *c.* 3800 cal BC (Rudebeck 1998; Andersson *et al.* 2016). Again, extraction sites were being used to underscore the core messages of Neolithisation by producing emblematic artefacts that were associated with the new emergent lifestyle. These examples represent the final flourish of Neolithic extraction practices around the periphery of Europe.

The lengthy pan-European chronology demonstrates that a long-established Neolithic extraction practice existed before Neolithic migrants arrived in southern England and the Irish Sea region. The Paris Basin is one of the potential points of origin of Neolithic extraction in Britain and Ireland. Here deep-shaft flint mining developed roughly 100–300 years earlier than in Britain and Ireland, and the Paris Basin mines were one of the first Neolithic site types created, thus paralleling the sequence in Britain (Giligny 2011; Giligny *et al.* 2011; 2012, 1150–5); they also shared similar practices (Topping 2005; 2019a; 2019b; Wheeler 2008; 2011; Baczkowski 2014). In addition, the aDNA research suggests other areas of northern France, particularly Normandy, were also influential (Olalde *et al.* 2018; Brace *et al.* 2019; Rivollat *et al.* 2020). This aDNA model fits comfortably with the radiocarbon chronology (Table 7.1). Alongside deep-shaft mining, stone quarrying practices in Britain and Ireland may have been influenced by the migration of people from established sites such as Plussulien in the Côte-du-Nord which produced Dolerite A axeheads (Le Roux 1971; 1979; 1998; 1999; 2011), or the Breton fibrolite quarries where large pointed-butt axeheads were manufactured (Pailler 2012a; 2012b). Both areas had easy access to the seaways around the coasts of Britain and Ireland, and the small numbers of imported European axeheads into south-western Britain suggests some level of interaction via exchange networks or the movement of people (Fig. 7.2).

Neolithic practices arrived in southern England via several routes, including those used since the Mesolithic such as the Thames Estuary. Here novel burials appeared at Yabsley Street (Blackwall) where an inhumation was accompanied by plain Carinated Bowl pottery (Coles *et al.* 2008), early 'houses' such as the White Horse Stone structure (Hayden & Stafford 2006), and more permanent constructions such as the Coldrum Stones megalithic tomb was built *3980–3800* cal BC (95% probability, modelled date; Wysocki *et al.* 2013). These new Neolithic sites and practices overlap chronologically with the earliest Neolithic practices at southern British flint mines and build upon long-term traditions of axehead deposition in rivers such as the Thames (see Chapter 6).

The exploitation of some of the South Downs and Wessex groups of flint mines appear to be the earliest manifestations of a Neolithic presence in the Mesolithic landscape (Fig. 7.3), and the early radiocarbon dates juxtaposed with Mesolithic axehead types suggest that this activity probably represents the introduction of Neolithic practices at existing Mesolithic extraction sites (Field 2008; Schulting 2008; Whittle *et al.* 2011; Thomas 2013; Thorpe 2015). It would take another 1–3 centuries before communal monuments such as long barrows or causewayed enclosures were constructed and anchored Neolithic communities to particular places (Bayliss *et al.* 2011; Whittle *et al.* 2011b). Around the same time, *c.* 4100–3700 cal BC, the Graiglwyd axe quarries were established (Williams & Davidson 1998, 18–19). This first pioneering phase of extraction on the South Downs and Graiglwyd was closely followed by Lambay Island (Cooney 2005), possibly Tievebulliagh (Mallory 1990), the Langdale sites, Mynydd Rhiw and the Shetland quarries. All have one thing in common – with the exception of the Wessex mines and Langdale quarries – they are all close to, or intervisible with the sea. This suggests that sea routes facilitated both the movement of people (Cooney 2007; Sheridan

*Figure 7.2: The probable routes of migrant extraction site users, based on radiocarbon chronology of sites ranged around the Irish Sea and Channel coast, and the presence of early jade and fibrolite axeheads in south-western Britain. The map also shows the series of major European extraction sites which were probably the catalysts for British and Irish sites, that had contiguous and overlapping artefact distributions spanning the coastal regions facing Britain (illustration: T. Pearson)*

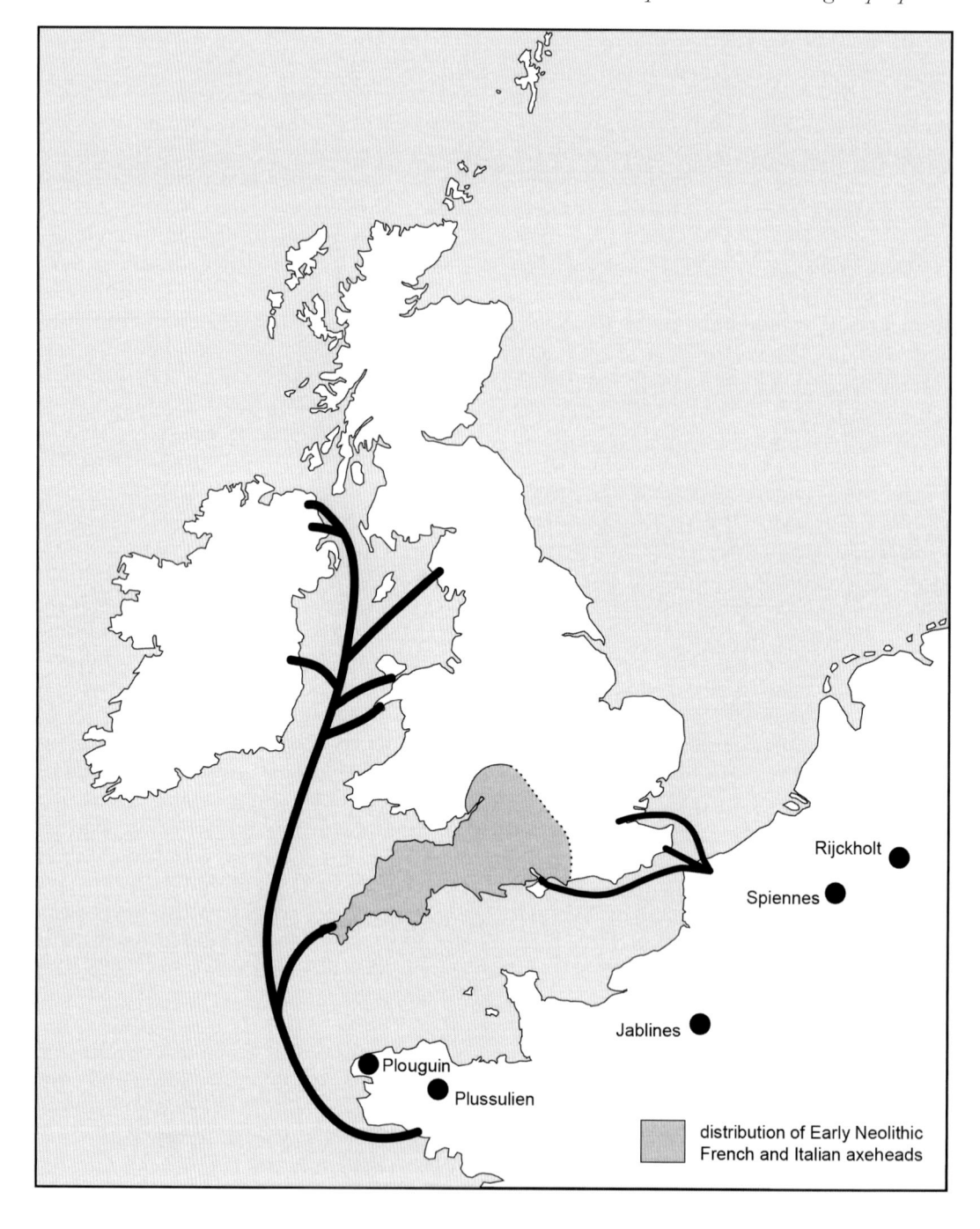

2010) and lithic prospection during the earliest Neolithic of Britain and Ireland, a hypothesis strengthened by the early dates for the South Downs/Wessex mines near the Channel coastline and at Graiglwyd facing the Irish Sea. These early Neolithic extraction dates suggest that stone prospection may have been a greater priority for Neolithic migrants since the mines and quarries are generally located in difficult terrain away from the best agricultural land.

Many upland quarries appear to be abandoned around the Middle Neolithic (c. 3000 BC; Edinborough *et al.* 2020), as were the South Downs/Wessex flint mines. This followed a later 4th millennium phase of social transformations which saw some of the final causewayed enclosures deliberately attacked (eg, Hambledon Hill and Crickley Hill), the introduction of new burial rites and pottery styles (Peterborough Ware, Impressed Ware,

7 *Neolithic extraction: a pan-European phenomenon*

*Figure 7.3: Easton Down (Wiltshire), potentially one of the earliest Neolithic flint mines from current radiocarbon data (Edinborough* et al. *2020), although the presence of smaller pits on-site offers the possibility that some may be Mesolithic in origin and this site might represent a collaborative venture between indigenous foragers and migrant miners (Based on Barber* et al. *1999, 46; illustration: T. Pearson)*

and later Grooved Ware), and the construction of early timber circles, henges, and stone circles. However, extraction restarted at Creag na Caillich, where a second phase of quarrying took place at the end of the Neolithic, coinciding with a final flourish of deep-shaft galleried mining at Grime's Graves (when the technique had all but disappeared in Europe), the surface quarries at Hambledon Hill were used, the last Easton Down mines were sunk, and the Den of Boddam pits were exploited.

The following sections provide a more detailed review of the major trends evident in European Neolithic extraction practices to assess their fit against the ethnoarchaeological model.

## Extraction site locations

While the location of desirable deposits was influenced by geology, the position of the quarries appears to have been determined according to the distinctive nature of the topography. This is shown at the flint mines in southern Britain where surface flint is generally widely available, or from sea or river cliffs and beaches, raising the question of why people chose to dig for raw material at these locations? The situation was similar at many European sites. It appears that it was the cultural cachet given to specific raw materials which created their value to society, becoming as Bradley has suggested 'pieces of places' that were embedded with a deeper symbolism than more easily obtained lithologies, because it was the 'character of the place [which] seemed at least as important as the qualities of the material' (Bradley 2000, 85–90). This is epitomised at Krumlovský les where the mined hornstone was of such poor quality that it prevented the knapping of prestige items such as axeheads or daggers (Oliva 2006, 171). However, despite its flaws the Krumlovský les hornstone was still distributed up to 200 km from the site (Oliva 1997; 2010, 373), which the ethnoarchaeological model would suggest was because it was a culturally valued material for a number of contiguous communities.

It is clear that valley side locations predominated, particularly mid- or upper slope positions and/or prominent landforms where seams may have been exposed that had to be climbed to in order to extract material. This suggests that the visibility of raw material sources may have been an important factor. Many sites overlook rivers or prominent valleys and were located within sight of major routeways or wetland resources. For example, in the Paris Basin the Jablines *Le Haut Château* flint mine complex is located on a locally prominent rise within a U-shaped meander of the River Marne, close to its confluence with the Grand Morin river (Bostyn & Lanchon 1992, 33; Giligny 2011, 188–9). The mines at Flins-sur-Seine are located on a prominent plateau at 100–125 m asl which dominates the south bank of the Seine Valley at its confluence with the Mauldre (Bostyn *et al.* 2008; Giligny 2011, 189–92). The Ri mines overlook the l'Houay, a tributary of the River Orne, from near the summit of rising ground (Giligny & Bostyn 2016, 18–19). In southern France on the south-eastern slopes of the Vaucluse Mountains, Bedoulian flint was extracted from mines and quarries located on small plateaus or in dry coombes overlooking the mouth of the Rhone (De Labriffe *et al.* 2019). Similarly, in north-eastern France the mines of Les Marais de Saint-Gond (Marne) are positioned overlooking the key subsistence resource of the Saint-Gond marshes (Martineau *et al.* 2019). At Spiennes (Belgium) the mines and quarries are ranged around valley sides and rising ground overlooking the Trouille river (Collet *et al.* 2016). The Rijckholt mines are positioned near the upper slopes of the Schone Grub dominating the surrounding countryside (Felder *et al.* 1998). On the Gargano Peninsula in south-eastern Italy the Defensola and Peschici mine complexes are located on the sides of valleys which lead to the nearby coast (Tarantini *et al.* 2011, 254). To the west in the Iberian Peninsula the early mines at Casa Montero (Spain) are positioned on a prominent river bluff overlooking the Jarama Valley, with extensive panoramic views in many directions (Capote *et al.* 2008). Most European valley side and plateaux locations are strongly reminiscent of the southern British flint mine locations on chalk downland crests, which locate extraction sites on or near the horizon.

Similar situations existed at the axe quarries. The Plussulien axehead quarries (Fig. 7.4) are located in the south-eastern Châteaulin Basin on one of the highest points of the Côtes-d'Armor, dominating surrounding low-lying areas (Le Roux 2011). This prominent dolerite outcrop has extensive panoramic views and is prominently located on the skyline. However, the epitome of landscape locations is the jade quarries in the Italian Alps. Here the rugged montane landscape provides a dramatic setting from jagged skylines to steep, glacially impacted valleys, where raw material can be found eroding from mountain sides and jade blocks

# 7 Neolithic extraction: a pan-European phenomenon

litter the upper valley slopes and watershed locations, such as the Alpetto, Vallon Bulè, and Col di Luca catchments (Pétrequin *et al.* 2012a, 214–57). Among those at Oncino is the prominent glaciated terrace known as Porco supérieur, which features the remains of roughly 50 high quality displaced jadeitite boulders which were the source of many British jade axeheads (Fig. 7.5) (Pétrequin *et al.* 2012a, 226–9; Pierre Pétrequin pers. comm.).

Quarry expeditions into the Alps will have encountered extreme weather conditions even during summer months when storms can appear suddenly, fog and mist can envelop and mask the valleys, and overnight temperatures can plummet. The jagged, triangular peak of Mont Viso (3841 m asl) dominates the surrounding ranges and jade sources, creating a heroic landscape of epic proportions where serrated landforms and the climate are juxtaposed to provide an arena where histories, myths, and cosmologies could converge and be experienced at first hand. Such experiences and challenges will have embedded biographies into the jade axeheads which created their cultural value and enabled them to fulfil important roles in social transactions across Europe.

Island based sources presented their own challenges equivalent to those faced by Alpine quarry users, chief of which was sea travel which was equally susceptible to sudden climatic events. Many island stone sources are visible from adjacent coastlines and simply involve line of sight journeys, such as Heligoland, an important source of coloured flint during the TRB which lies 46 km off the north-west German coast. Van Gijn and Raemaekers (2014) have demonstrated the importance of Heligoland flint as part of a package of red materials and substances used

*Figure 7.4: Plussulien (Côte-du-Nord), the Dolerite 'A' quarry (photo: author)*

*Figure 7.5: Porco supérieur, a glacial terrace high in the Mont Viso range (Italy) and the source of many of the jadeitite axeheads discovered in Britain (photo: author)*

to create identity amongst TRB communities. Despite the accessibility of grey granite during the Dutch TRB, rare red/pink granites were sought for megalith construction, querns, and as temper for pottery. Consequently, red Heligoland flint became favoured for important implements as part of this practice. The value of the colour red is highlighted by the hoard from Een, which comprised two Scandinavian-type ground axeheads in grey flint, four flint nodules and one red axehead preform. The largest ground axehead was of Scandinavian flint, all others were from Heligoland but, importantly, both grey Scandinavian-type axeheads and the nodules had been smeared with red ochre – only the red Heligoland preform was not. This hoard follows general TRB practice of using red ochre to recolour large axeheads produced in southern Scandinavia, which were then deposited in rivers in the Netherlands and elsewhere (Midgley 1992; Wentink 2008; van Gijn 2010b).

Heligoland is not an isolated example of important island based lithic resources. Mediterranean islands also played a major role in Neolithisation, particularly through the exploitation of dramatic volcanic mountains. Sources such as Lipari in the Aeolian Islands 30 km north of Sicily distributed obsidian around the coastlines of the western Mediterranean basin (Freund 2017). The obsidian sources on the rugged slopes of Monte Arci (Sardinia) were equally important, as evidenced by the 247 workshops around its flanks. Other island sources on Pantelleria and Palmarola had similar distributions around the western Mediterranean (Costa 2007). These sites show that island based extraction, through its relative isolation, distinctiveness, and degrees of separation

# 7 Neolithic extraction: a pan-European phenomenon

from the mainstream, were influential supra-regional resources underpinning the spread of Neolithisation by material culture across Europe.

In summary, distinctive landforms, unusual lithologies, challenging locations, and/or distant resources all created a cultural value for many European extraction sites and their products.

## Extraction technology

A sample of 88 European sites has provided trends in extraction technology (Kobyliński & Lech 1995; Weisgerber 1999). Structurally, sites can be divided into open air quarries of variable width and depth, open air pits of variable diameter (generally less than 4 m deep), shafts (generally 4+ m deep), and shafts with galleries or chambers.

The European sample comprises 24 quarries, 20 pit complexes, 16 shaft mines, and 28 with galleried shafts. In addition, roughly 25% of sites [21] feature multiple techniques on the same site as pragmatic responses to the variations in the geology. For example, the single Austrian site at Wien/Mauer utilises shafts (Ruttkay 1999), whereas neighbouring Germany predominantly used quarries with only a single example where both pits and shafts occur together. Both Czechia and Hungary used a range of extraction techniques, whereas Italian sites are predominantly stepped quarries extended by adit-like horizontal tunnelling into hillsides, as at Defensola (where galleried shafts also exist). In Spain, Casa Montero used shafts. France has a greater number of sites which used galleried shafts, although quarries, pits, and shafts are juxtaposed at three sites. In Belgium only galleried shafts occur and, in the Netherlands, the two excavated sites both feature quarries and galleried shafts. Switzerland featured quarries exclusively. In northern Europe, Denmark has galleried shafts; Ukraine's single site comprised quarries; Sweden's single site consisted of pits and shafts; Poland utilised all extraction techniques; and the single Belarussian site had multiple techniques.

The most basic form of extraction can be seen on the steep, rugged valley slopes of Valle Lagorara (Italy) (Maggi *et al.* 1995) and Ponte di Veia (Italy) (Barfield 1995), where stepped, linear quarrying had cut work faces into near vertical mountain sides where shafts would have been difficult to sink. Similarly, the important quarries at Grand Pressigny (France), which produced iconic long flint blades, extracted flint from stepped quarries on valley slopes which were supplemented by quarries on the plateau above (Mallet 1999). Stepped quarrying could also be extended by adit-like tunnelling as at Pleigne (Switzerland), where tunnels with supporting pillars followed the flint deposits into the hillside (Schmid 1999). However, a more extreme example can be seen at Defensola 'A' (Italy) where a stepped quarry on the slopes of Intreseglio Hill has been developed into an extensive network of irregular, tunnelled galleries up to 110 m in length (Di Lernia *et al.* 1995; Tarantini *et al.* 2011). Similar techniques were used at Spiennes (Belgium) where some quarries developed short galleries on the Camp-à-Cayaux bank of the River Trouille (Collet *et al.* 2016, 12). In some cases stepped quarrying on smaller landforms led to the complete removal of both the flint and the upper contours, as at Aachen (Germany) (Weiner & Weisgerber 1999). However, where there was a substantial overburden and tunnelling was not an option, then pits, shafts, or galleried shafts were used, and such sites can be found across much of Europe from Iberia to Scandinavia, and eastwards into the Balkans.

At the Tušimice (Czechia) quartzite extraction site irregular shaft-like pits were dug up to 3.25 m deep, and some featured niches or low galleries 3–5 m in length (Lech & Mateiciucová 1995). A similar technique was used at Polany Kolonie II (Poland), where the 2.4 m deep Shaft 1 had extensive undercutting niches (Schild 1995a). Shaft-like pits up to 4.2 m deep were found at Tomaszów (Poland) – where some did not reach flint deposits and may represent prospection (Schild 1995b). However, one of the most elaborate systems occurred at Bjerre (Denmark), where Pits D and E were roughly 3.7 m in depth and featured a series of irregular niches and galleries radiating from the floor of each pit, with some galleries extending 2+ m in length (Becker 1999b).

Shafts were used to reach more deeply buried deposits. Some of the earliest shafts occurred at Casa Montero (Spain), a major complex comprising 3794 shafts and six small open air quarries. Here the shafts were deep,

*Figure 7.6: Spiennes (Belgium), a view of a narrow buttress supporting the roof in the low workings in a 16 m deep mine (photo: author)*

narrow and cylindrical with a mean diameter of 1.15 m, and up to 9.26 m deep. Shafts in area D4 featured rare examples of galleries and chambers which interconnected up to 11 adjacent shafts. Certain shafts had ledges, post-holes, and steps. Interestingly, a series of 23 prospecting pits up to 1.66 m deep were found at the site, demonstrating a high level of technical and strategic competency at this early site (Consuegra *et al.* 2018).

The Krasnaselsky (Belarus) flint mines were similar, with vertical shafts up to 9 m deep which targeted deposits in the shaft walls with irregular niches, but also featured galleries. Linear quarries evolved from conjoined pits, and bell-shaped pits also existed at Krasnaselsky to tackle the changing nature and depth of the deposits (Charniausky 1995). The flint mines at Jablines *Le Haut-Château* (France) followed a similar pragmatic approach to the geology where pits up to 2.2 m deep (some with niches) were used in the northern parts of the site, whereas in southern areas where the overburden was greatest shafts up to 7 m deep with extensive galleries were used to maximise extraction (Bostyn & Lanchon 1992). At Hov (Denmark), expedient strategies are shown by Pit 7 which was 6+ m deep with a series of irregular, radiating galleries, some over 5 m in length, whereas Pit 5, also 6+ m in depth, featured only one short gallery, 2 m in length (Becker 1999a).

The extensive mining complex at Spiennes (Belgium) had various forms of extraction (Fig. 7.6). Pits, some with niches, were used for shallow flint deposits. However, other parts of the complex witnessed some of the deepest mines in Europe. At *Camp-à-Cayaux* the Michelsberg period mines exploited massive flint slabs from galleried shafts up to 16 m in depth, with the flint being prised from gallery ceilings. Other Michelsberg mines at nearby *Petit-Spiennes* were up to 10 m deep and exploited the three uppermost flint seams. Here, the lowest deposits were targeted first with nodules again levered from the ceilings, the tumbled chalk waste then created a rising floor level as the mining progressed upwards towards the higher seams, effectively producing a rising vertical gallery (Collet *et al.* 2016, 15–18). The examples from Spiennes show how innovative miners had become during the mature Neolithic.

Poland had some of the largest mine complexes in Europe, with Krzemionki arguably the most extensive (Barber *et al.* 1999, 58). Here, the workings are spread over a parabola-shaped syncline of Jurassic limestone covering an area 4.5 km long and 785,000 m². An estimated 3500+ mines existed originally, ranging between 2 m and 9 m deep, comprising shallow pits, niche mines, pillar mines, and chamber mines (Bąbel 2008). The epitome of Polish extraction was the chamber mine, where a linear gallery was driven out from the base of a shaft, following which one of the long walls of the gallery formed the working face. Extraction proceeded by cutting back the working face and placing the chalk debris behind the miners, which led to the gallery gradually swinging around the axis of the shaft in a fan-like motion. This enabled the miners to exploit areas of 400+ m² of flint deposits, with the dumped waste being used to retain the ceiling of the workings instead of using pillars or buttresses (Borkowski 1995, 73–7).

Other extensive subterranean workings are found at Rijckholt (Netherlands), where meandering galleries interconnected shafts over great distances, such as Shafts 29 and 45 (Felder *et al.* 1998, 40–1). To maximise extraction, comparatively narrow intervening gallery walls and small buttresses separated these mines (*ibid.*, 34–6).

Fire-setting was discovered at some sites. For example, at Kleinkems (Germany) miners employed fire-setting against the rockface to heat the bedrock, which was then quenched with water to make it friable and easier to shatter. Such practices left behind large quantities of burnt rock and charcoal on-site (Engel & Siegmund 2005). Similar evidence was discovered at the quartz quarries at Lundfors (Sweden) where, at Locus IV, a vein of quartz appears to have been quarried using fire-setting, leaving behind deposits of sooty soil surrounding the vein alongside accumulations of flaked and crushed quartz and four hammerstones (Lindgren 1995, 91–2). The Dolerite A quarry at Plussulien (France) also appears to have used fire-setting (Pétrequin & Rzepecki 2016, 48), and may have been the inspiration for the appearance of the technique at British and Irish sites such as the Langdale quarries through knowledge transmission (Bradley & Edmonds 1993, 128).

Neolithic extraction techniques evolved over some two millennia in Europe, and miners and quarry users had previously developed these specialist skills which allowed them to transplant these new extraction practices into Britain and Ireland, as suggested by the aDNA data. This lengthy gestation in Europe explains the comparatively 'sudden' appearance of deep-shaft galleried mines in the South Downs during the primary Neolithic – it was simply the transfer of an established technique from the continent. Consequently, this knowledge transfer between incoming migrants and indigenous communities allowed miners to now target deeper deposits amongst what were probably the final Mesolithic pits at Easton Down, Cissbury, Harrow Hill, and Blackpatch.

## On-site artefact deposition

European extraction sites display evidence for both casual and deliberate artefact deposition on both the surrounding surface areas and below ground. For example, at the chert extraction site of Stránská Skála (Czechia), a large contiguous Funnel Beaker Culture workshop left behind an assemblage of debitage, scrapers, and blades knapped from on-site material. However, amongst this was a small pottery vessel filled with imported blades (Svoboda 1995, 280), arguably deposited to reference other important lithologies. Another example from Krumlovský les comprised a complete upright Late Lengyel footed bowl among a charcoal deposit discovered in the upper fills of Shaft 4, presumably deliberately deposited during backfilling (Oliva 2006, 165; 2010, 31, 356). The presence of pottery suggests the adoption of Neolithic practices and arguably formed an element of cosmological referencing as part of the creation of identity.

A similar deposit was recorded at Villemaur-sur-Vanne *Les Orlets* (France) where a near complete Michelsberg-type pot was discovered at a depth of 1.0 m in the upper fills of a shaft which appears never to have been used for extraction (de Labriffe *et al.* 1995, 343–5). The nearest Michelsberg settlement lay 30+ km away, reinforcing the observation that many extraction sites lay at a distance from settlements. The fact that this shaft had not been mined may indicate that it had been a prospecting shaft, or perhaps that it was excavated for more symbolic reasons relating to the subterranean elements of a layered cosmos. The inclusion of pottery in extraction practices can also be seen at Spiennes (Belgium), where at *Camp-à-Cayaux* a near complete Michelsberg bottle-shaped vessel was discovered in Pit 7, deliberately broken at a depth of 1.0–1.2 m in the upper fills of the pit. At *Petit-Spiennes*, Shaft 53.2 produced Michelsberg ceramics, with sherds from the same vessel scattered throughout the shaft fills at 2.0–3.7 m depth. Finally, part of a Michelsberg pot was found at the base of an unexcavated mine interconnected with Shaft 1 at *Camp-à-Cayaux* (Collet *et al.* 2011, 173). Clearly pottery deposition played an important role in different stages of extraction practices at European sites.

Lithics were the major component of assemblages found at extraction sites. For example, at Rijckholt (Netherlands) 14,217 flint picks (some unused) were recovered from the galleries and shafts, occasionally found in caches, and formed 97.7% of the overall assemblage (Felder *et al.* 1998). This demonstrates that at some sites an enormous amount of raw material was being transformed into tools and then returned to the mines. At Jandrain (Belgium) caches of unused picks and roughout axeheads were discovered in the galleries (Hubert 1974), as they were in the shafts and galleries at Spiennes (Collet *et al.* 2016), Jablines (Bostyn & Lanchon 1992), and Bretteville-le-Rabet (France; Desloges 1986). If extraction sites had simply been driven by economic motives then it is unlikely that many lithics – other than total rejects – would have remained unused on-site, or been returned underground for deposition. Economic imperatives would simply have forced them into the marketplace. An Alpine jade axehead found at the Spiennes mines and which originated from the Voltri Group source in the Beigua Massif near Genoa (Errera *et al.* 2019), again demonstrates that, like the Stránská Skála (Czechia) pot containing imported blades, exotic artefacts also played a role in Neolithic extraction practices.

The Defensola 'A' (Italy) mine produced a particularly rich assemblage. Here picks, hammerstones, debitage, and obsidian tools were found alongside bone punches. Pottery (complete and decorated vessels, some with organic residues) was found at key locations, particularly at entrances to adjoining galleries. Carved limestone lamps provided artificial lighting and geometric/abstract graffiti was scattered throughout the workings with a cluster of three panels near the entrances. Wood charcoal and faunal remains completed the assemblage (di Lernia *et al.* 1991; 1995; Galiberti 2005; Tarantini *et al.* 2011). Overall, the Defensola assemblage suggests that a range of non-functional activities were practised in these mines, particularly the deposition of curated deposits of pottery and animal remains, and the inscription of graffiti at important locations around the workings.

At Sümeg-Mogyorósdomb (Hungary) antler tools with incised geometric decoration were part of an assemblage of over 500 antler implements (Bácskay 1995, 389–90), suggesting further evidence of deliberate deposition during extraction.

Overall, European sites incorporate a wide range of material culture and art forms as part of extraction practice, including both functional objects and non-functional items. Certain lithics were manufactured and remained on-site, and debitage was often collected and returned to its place of origin below ground, suggesting that renewal rites were an important element of extraction practice. Alongside such activities, lithic deposition could include rare examples of imported exotic artefacts in European, British, and Irish extraction sites. Such practices suggest a shared pan-European tradition.

## Shaft fills

Shaft fills regularly included debitage, artefacts, and animal remains. At Bečov (Czechia) (Lech & Mateiciucová 1995b, 277) and Tomaszów (Poland) (Schild 1995a, 461) large assemblages were recovered from the upper fills, suggesting they were associated with abandonment

# 7 Neolithic extraction: a pan-European phenomenon

rituals. The Krasnaselsky (Belarus) mines featured debitage placed in half-filled shafts (Charniausky 1995, 266), arguably linked to renewal purposes.

At Jablines, sherds of Cerny Culture pottery were discovered in secondary deposits which may be residual from an earlier phase of mining (Bostyn & Lanchon 1995, 309). However, such deposits might equally represent an act of commemoration of the ancestral past through the deposition of 'heirloom' artefacts. Such practices may also have occurred at Shaft 1 at Polany Kolonie II (Poland) (Herbich & Lech 1995, 503). These secondary deposits may have underpinned claims of legitimisation through the use of distinctive cultural artefacts which linked the miners to ancestral practitioners.

The presence of cattle bones from shafts at Serbonnes (France), when there was no evidence for adjacent settlement (de Labriffe & Sidéra 1995, 317), argues against casual domestic discard and suggests these remains were placed deposits or evidence of feasting during or after extraction. A more elaborate assemblage found in the mines at Sümeg-Mogyorósdomb (Hungary) comprised domesticated species (goat, cattle) alongside red deer, horse, aurochs, and roe deer (Bácskay 1995, 390).

The shafts and pit fills of the majority of European extraction sites incorporate extraction debris, debitage, hearths, faunal remains, roughout implements, extraction tools, finished objects, pottery, and human remains. Although some of this evidence represents casual or random discard during extraction, this is less likely in the case of structured deposits of knapping debris, artefact assemblages, hearths, articulated animal remains, or human burials and body parts. The repetitive nature of the contexts of these deposits is noticeable, particularly within shafts and at gallery entrances.

## Burials

Human remains have been discovered at extraction sites in Austria, Belgium, Belarus, Czechia, France, Germany, Hungary, Italy, the Netherlands, and Spain. Although preservation and excavation bias may be distorting this distribution, it nevertheless demonstrates that human interment at extraction sites was a widespread phenomenon.

At Spiennes (Belgium), various Neolithic interments have been discovered. In 1911 excavations uncovered skeletons of an adult and a 12 year old child buried in the upper fill of a shaft at a depth of 1.43 m, with a triangular arrowhead found beneath the adult. The disarticulated remains of a *c.* 10 year old child was discovered in the upper fill of Shaft 3/ Workshop No. III, juxtaposed with six animal bones. In Shaft 79.1 two adult human bones were recovered from the shaft base amongst an erosion deposit but it is not known whether they represent the same individual. The near complete skeleton of a *c.* 45 year old adult was found buried head-down at an angle of 40° at 4.0–5.5 m depth in Shaft ST11, with a separate deposit comprising the fragmentary remains of a newborn from a depth of 4.8–5.2 m. Current excavations in Shaft ST6 have discovered the scattered remains of an adult ?male of *c.* 50 years scattered around the base of the shaft and the upper layers of interconnecting galleries between 5.5 m and 7.9 m depth. The lack of fracturing, bite marks, or signs of trauma suggest these human remains may represent both formal and casual interment, and the absence of grave goods appears to be a local tradition (Toussaint *et al.* 2019).

At Avennes (Belgium), excavations in 1945 in what may have been the upper fills of a mine shaft discovered the articulated skeletons of an adult male with two children. Radiocarbon dating suggests interment took place during the Middle–Late Neolithic transition (Toussaint 2019, 245).

Arguably some of the most important human skeletal evidence has emerged from the variscite mines at Gavà (Spain) (Borrell *et al.* 2015). Here the irregular, meandering workings were dug to a depth of up to 15 m to extract variscite for beads and plaquettes. The production of these variscite objects put Gavà in an extensive exchange network encompassing southern, central, and western France, the Alps, northern Italy, Sardinia and the western Mediterranean. During the most industrious period of activity in the first quarter of the 4th millennium the miners buried some of their dead in the workings (Table 7.2). In Mine 83 the remains of an adult (sex unknown) were discovered in a deep side chamber, sealed by a large rock and accompanied by a rich grave assemblage comprising obsidian and Bédoulien flint lithics, eclogite axeheads, a square pottery

Table 7.2: The changing character of human interment at Gavà (Spain)

| Period | Mine | Location | Burial practice | Skeletal assemblage | Grave goods |
|---|---|---|---|---|---|
| Middle Neolithic | 83 | Deep burial chamber | Primary burial | 1 adult (sex unknown) | Abundant & diverse |
| Middle Neolithic | 84 | Deepest chamber | Primary burial | 1 adult male; 1 adult female | Abundant & diverse |
| Middle Neolithic (by context) | 9 | Gallery | ? | 5 individuals, partial remains | Scarce and unclear |
| Middle Neolithic (end) | 28 | Gallery near mine entrance | ? | 5 individuals, disarticulated | None |
| Final Neolithic | 8 | Chamber | ? | Unclear; MNI of 2 from max. of 14 | Pot sherds ?residual |

(Based on Borrell et al. 2015, 77, table 2)

vessel, a bone chisel, a coral bead necklace, a variscite necklace, variscite fragments, and broken variscite beads. In the deepest part of Mine 84 two burials were found in a chamber at the end of a gallery that was also sealed by stone slabs. Here an adult male and adult female had been interred but seem to have been disturbed in antiquity as suggested by post-mortem fractures. This grave assemblage comprised a square pot, a decorated pot, bone implements, wild boar tusks, Bédoulien flint lithics, and a clam shell; it is unclear whether items were removed when the burials were disturbed. The Gavà interments seem to have occurred immediately after the abandonment of each mine. In addition, the musculoskeletal stress markers and cranial traumas of these Gavà skeletons suggest they were involved in heavy physical activity which necessitated upper body strength, ie, mining, and that these human remains represent the bodies of miners interred in the underground workings. Importantly, the demographic of the skeletal evidence from Gavà demonstrates that mining teams comprised both sexes, offering the possibility that the three female skeletons found in the British flint mines may be representative of this European trend.

Other human remains were discovered at Villemaur-sur-Vanne *Les Orlets* (France), where a putative Chalcolithic child's burial was discovered in an upper shaft fill, lying on its right side and adorned with a necklace (de Labriffe et al. 1995b, 345). A shaft at Krasnaselsky (Belarus) contained a Corded Ware Culture 'miner's burial' juxtaposed with a large bone needle and a decorated pot (Charniausky 1995, 269). Shaft 4 at Krumlovský les contained a sequence of two female skeletons; the lower primary interment was discovered at a depth of 7.0 m and roughly 0.6 m above the shaft floor, comprising an articulated skeleton apparently thrown into the partly backfilled shaft with the head of a new-born infant placed upon her chest and its body lying across her pelvis and juxtaposed with various lithics – the disarticulated skeleton of a small dog was found 0.3 m above this skeleton. The second burial was discovered roughly 0.6 m above the first, may have had a dislocated skull and limbs, and was accompanied by hammerstones and lithics (Oliva 2006, 165–6; 2010, 32, 356–7).

One of the most structured mass burials in an European extraction site was discovered in Chamber A at Valle Sbernia (Italy), where lying upon backfill 'were found about ten skeletons (of adults of both sexes and children) lying in a circle around the furnishings, a flint blade and late Eneolithic ceramics', possibly creating a family crypt (Sisto 1995, 435). Another example at Salinelles (France) comprised 12 crouched or disarticulated skeletons scattered through the middle fills of a shaft and in a gallery leading to an adjoining shaft (Dijkman 1999, 478–9). The upper levels of both shafts appear to have been revetted and formally closed with stone slabs following the interments, thus creating a sealed chamber and converting an extraction site into a communal tomb. At Krasnaselsky (Belarus) the burial of a Corded Ware Culture 'miner's' burial lay in a shaft, accompanied by a large bone needle and a decorated pot (Charniausky 1995, 269), once again recording the coincidence of pottery with interments in extraction sites.

The Kleinkems quarries contained two individuals interred in an extraction chamber, buried beneath mining debris and accompanied by Michelsberg pottery and an antler bowl (Schmid 1999a; Engel & Siegmund 2005). The location of the interments suggests a deliberate referencing of the extraction site by the accompanied burials.

At Wien-Mauer/Antonshöhe (Austria), the abandonment of Late Lengyel period activity at this radiolarite mine led to on-site human burials. In Shaft I the primary burial of a child and infant with a fragmentary pot was followed by a secondary burial of an adult female with a ceramic bowl in the upper layers. Shaft IV also contained a sequence of graves, with the primary burial being an adult female which was superceded by that of an adult male higher up the shaft. To the east of Shaft IV a waste dump was used for Grave 3, where the skeleton of another adult female was interred. A final group of human bones labelled Grave 6 has no context (Trnka 2010; 2011). The burials at Wien-Mauer/ Antonshöhe in both former workings and adjacent waste dumps may represent evidence of social stratification, shown by the different locations used for interment. The site also represents another example of a strong female presence at an extraction site – alongside children – suggesting that during the Neolithic period mixed age and gender teams worked at many sites.

Body part deposition was recorded at Rijckholt (Netherlands), where a skull, mandible fragments, and a right femur were discovered buried amongst 'worked flints' on the slopes of the adjacent *Schoone Grubbe* re-entrant 200 m from the mines (Felder *et al.* 1998, 54–7). To date, these are the only human remains securely dated to the Neolithic period from this site (de Grooth *et al.* 2011).

Certain off-site burials may also have had an association with extraction sites. At Michałowice (Poland) a crouched inhumation of a 'flint knapper' was accompanied by flint implements, a punch, and an anvil stone (Lech 1999, 272). The graves of two Chalcolithic 'flint miners' from the Tiszapolgár-kultur were discovered at Vel'ké Raškovce (Slovakia). Both graves comprised crouched inhumations accompanied by pottery, flint tools, copper artefacts, and a single large flint nodule placed near the feet (Lichardus-Itten 1999, 281). Both interments exhibited an interesting juxtaposition of artefacts relating to both lithic and metal-working technologies.

Many of the formal European burials found within the workings appear to reference the mines by association, possibly commemorating links between an individual and extraction in much the same way as the formal burial in Shaft VI at Cissbury. The presence of human burials demonstrates that on-site human interment was an accepted protocol, and the fact that it is found across Europe demonstrates *selective* burials were part of pan-European extraction practice. The records of females and children at a number of sites suggest that extraction was not an exclusively male activity.

In contrast, however, the two adult female skeletons from Krumlovský les imply a different form of interment, particularly the lower burial where the configuration of the skeleton suggests that the body was thrown into the mines rather than carefully positioned – and the fact that the overlying child's skull was detached from its body. The second burial's dislocated condition also implies rough treatment. This is reminiscent of the head-down burial in Shaft ST11 at Spiennes, the similarly positioned female skeleton found in No.1 Escarp Shaft (Skeleton Shaft) at Cissbury and the skeleton found midway down Pit 2 at Grime's Graves. These examples of unstructured, *ad hoc* interment may imply burial rites which defined the status of the individual, or that these people were deliberately killed as part of abandonment rituals in a similar fashion to the bog bodies in northern Europe. They may also simply represent murder victims.

Overall, the human remains found at European extraction sites, if indicative of the composition of extraction teams, suggests that extraction was not age or gender specific (cf. Gero 1991).

## Hearths

The presence of hearths in English flint mines has been seen as significant for some time (cf. Barber *et al.* 1999, 61–7), and their existence in European mines has also been noted. Examples include a hearth discovered on the basal silts of Shaft 5 at Tušimice (Lech & Mateiciucová 1995a, 274), and another in Shaft 28 at Wierzbica 'Zele' (Poland; Lech & Lech 1999, 472–7). At the latter site, Shafts 28 and 19 produced sequences of hearths (juxtaposed with lithics and mining debris) within shaft fills, demonstrating the repetitious nature of deposition and backfilling events within the mines. In Shaft 1 at Polany Kolonie II (Poland), another sequence of hearths was recorded, the

*Figure 7.7: Krzemionki (Poland), charcoal graffito of a possible human figure (photo: author)*

first on the shaft floor, a second on top of a dump of backfill, followed by a third comprising redeposited *older* material (demonstrated by radiocarbon dates), all superseded by a final hearth higher in the shaft (Schild 1995b, 484). This sequence emphasises the importance of fire in repetitious abandonment practices at some European mines. A less complex sequence was found in Shaft 1 at Polany II, where a small hearth built on basal deposits was juxtaposed with flint nodules, which was followed by a final hearth surrounded by nodules and worked lithics on the upper fills (Herbich & Lech 1995, 503). The conjunction of hearths with mined raw materials and lithics may have been part of abandonment practice focussed upon mitigation, renewal, and commemoration.

In Denmark at Bjerre, the shallow workings contained a small hearth located on a gallery floor between Shaft D and Shaft J which was juxtaposed with unspecified animal bones and pot sherds (Becker 1999b, 464–8). It is unclear whether this hearth was part of ritualised practice, or used for more utilitarian purposes, although the fact that it lay in a gallery with severely restricted space suggests that it may have had a special purpose.

At Stránská Skála (Czechia) a pit located at a workshop adjacent to an extraction site included a hearth on its floor, juxtaposed with Moravian Painted Ware Culture type lithics (Svoboda 1995, 281). Clearly this pit-enclosed hearth was paralleling practices found in abandoned mine shafts but on a much smaller scale.

This brief review demonstrates that hearths were an integral part of extraction practice in Europe, preceding the examples found in Britain and Ireland amongst the South Downs flint mines, Grime's Graves, Ballygalley Hill, Graiglwyd, Lambay Island, Le Pinacle, and the Langdale quarries.

## Graffiti

Rock art is comparatively rare in Europe. At Defensola 'A', the mines contained five graffiti panels scattered throughout the workings in galleries and in a chamber, while a sixth was scratched onto a limestone block near the entrance to the workings (di Lernia *et al.* 1995, 428). This incised graffiti comprises linear motifs of irregular lattice patterns, curvilinear aggregations, coalescing striations, and pseudo-geometrical images (Galiberti 2005), and it suggests that artworks may have added a further level of complexity to ritualised extraction practises through the use of visual imagery.

At Krzemionki (Fig. 7.7), a series of four amorphous charcoal pictographs were recorded in the underground workings, interpreted as a 'bull's head', 'bull's horns', a 'pair of human feet', and a possible human figure of either a man or a woman giving birth (Babel 1999, 594). Although these motifs appear ambiguous, it is possible they are representational art, which is a relatively rare phenomenon in European extraction sites. Overall, artworks are more common amongst the later extraction sites on the periphery of Europe.

## Exchange networks and artefact distribution

One of the key observations in the ethno-archaeological model concerning the cultural value of extraction sites was the scale of product distributions. Put crudely, the ethnography suggests that the further an object travelled from its source the greater its value was to the producer and consumer/user. By implication, this correlation can be used to identify culturally important archaeological extraction sites by the presence of extensive product distributions (Topping 2017, 94–100).

The objectification of extraction site products created their value to society, as Godelier (1999, 167–70) has observed 'it is when the object … is used to reactivate this imaginary and symbolic relationship with the origin, that it becomes sacred and acquires an even greater value … [and] … bearing on the places they occupy in a social and cosmic order'. Such objectification sets the social parameters for the object's use-life through to final deposition, entangling objects in transactions which could transport them across great distances through regional and pan-European networks.

The scale of extraction site product distributions in Europe is variable. For example, at Stránská Skála (Svoboda 1995), Flintsbach-Hardt (Germany) (Weißmüller 1995) and Wierzbica 'Zele' (Lech & Lech 1995) the sites all appear to have had a relatively localised distribution of up to 100 km from the source. In contrast, the epitome of long-distance distribution is the jade axeheads from the Italian Alps which spanned the European continent from Scandinavia to the Black Sea, and the Iberian Peninsula to Britain and Ireland. During the second half of the 5th millennium the Carnac region of Brittany became an important centre for these Alpine jade products. Here, jade axeheads and ring-disk armlets were collected in large numbers for both local deposition in extravagant hoards comprising 2–28 axeheads (particularly in graves around the Gulf of Morbihan), and for reworking into different axehead types. The reshaped Alpine axeheads were then redistributed as far as northern Iberia, northern Germany, and Laterza in southern Italy – the latter a total journey of around 2800 km (Pétrequin et al. 2012a; 2012b; 2017). Significantly, 'the number of large axeheads does not diminish with distance from the source of the raw material' (Pétrequin et al. 2015, 87).

Other long-distance networks existed in the western Mediterranean. The variscite (or callaïs) mines at Gavà were part of a complex network which exchanged variscite for Alpine jade axeheads (Pétrequin et al. 2012b), flint from the lower Rhone Valley around Vaucluse (France) (De Labriffe et al. 2019), shells from Tarragona (Spain), Mediterranean obsidian, Mediterranean red coral jewellery, pottery, and salt from mines lying 70 km inland at Cardona (Borrrell & Bosch 2012; Weller & Fíguls 2012). As a result of this exchange network, variscite jewellery was found in distant contexts such as the Morbihan tombs (France; Querré et al. 2019), roughly 1120 km away, where it was used in rich grave assemblages. In return, Carnac-type reshaped jade axeheads (which had travelled roughly 1900 km from Italy to Brittany and then to Spain) were transported to north-east Spain. Gavà variscite was also distributed across northern Iberia.

Within the western Mediterranean region other lithologies were similarly exploited. Sardinia was a major source of obsidian, where extraction centred upon Monte Arci in the volcanic massif in the west-central part of the island. Here four varieties of obsidian were found distributed over an area of some 270 km$^2$ and processed at 247 workshops (Costa 2007; Lugliè 2012). Only certain types of obsidian were targeted, notably smaller blocks up to 100 mm thick, despite more accessible material being available from secondary sources, paralleling the selectivity practised at the Langdale quarries in Britain (Bradley & Edmonds 1993). During the Early Neolithic only small quantities of obsidian left Sardinia but, by the Middle Neolithic, specialised blade and bladelet production coincided with the introduction of elaborate funerary rituals associated with rich grave assemblages which resulted in a change to the distribution pattern of the obsidian. By the Final Neolithic, extraction of Monte Arci obsidian appears to have increased and it became abundant in neighbouring Corsica, but less so in Italy and southern France (Costa 2007; Lugliè 2012). However, considering the close proximity of the Palmarola island source to northern Italy and southern France, the presence of Monte Arci obsidian in these areas suggests it was probably the most valued raw material around the north-western Mediterranean.

The island of Lipari, 30 km north-east of Sicily, was the major obsidian source for Sicily and much of southern Italy, but less so for northern Italy and southern France (Costa

*Table 7.3: The size range of axeheads from Dutch TRB graves and wetland deposits by number (data from Wentink 2008, 155, fig 3)*

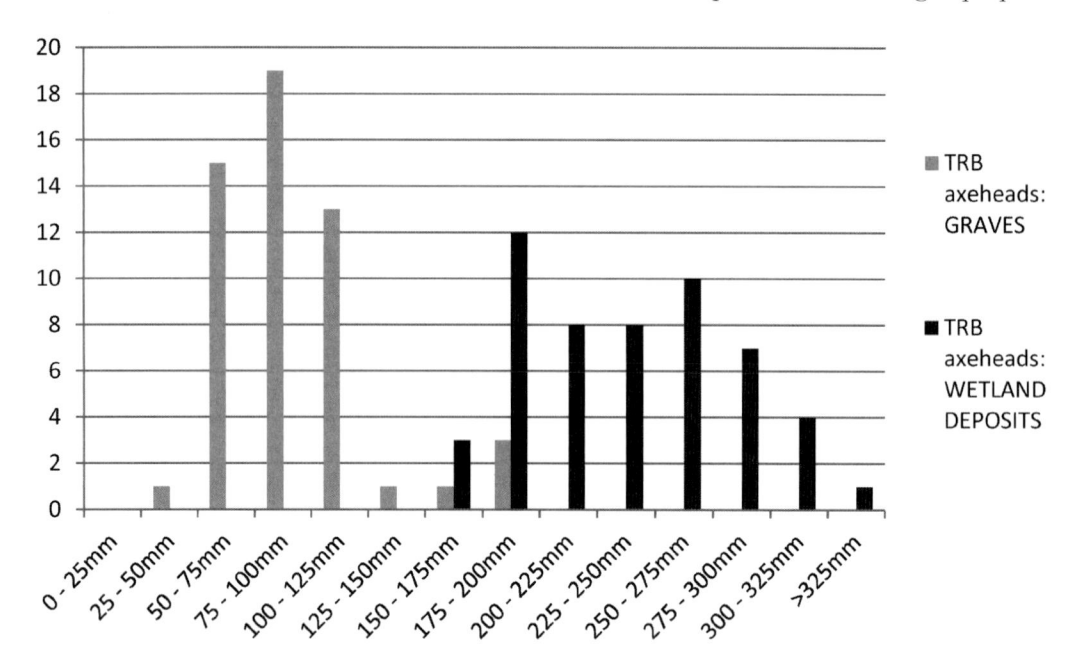

2007; Muntoni 2012). Nested within this lithic exchange network were the Gargano Peninsula flint mines, which specialised in the production of long blades and axeheads for numerous villages up to 120 km west of the mines (Guilbeau 2012; Muntoni 2012). At present it is unclear how much obsidian from Palmarola Island was quarried or distributed from its east coast location, although its products are found up to 350+ km from the source (Muntoni 2012, 409). However, there is no evidence of Neolithic settlement on Palmarola, so it appears that these quarries were exploited on a seasonal basis. The Pantellaria source is located on the eponymous island lying between Sicily and Tunisia and was not colonised before the Bronze Age (Costa 2007). Overall, these island based obsidian sources appear to have been held in high regard by Neolithic communities around the western Mediterranean, as suggested by the quantity and distribution of their products.

Northern regions of Europe also participated in long-distance networks. In Poland the Świeciechów mines on the banks of the River Wisla produced a grey flint with white flecks which was distributed up to 400+ km during the Funnel Beaker Culture. In contrast the nearby grey banded flint from Krzemionki, 30 km to the east, was distributed only 300 km or so during the same Funnel Beaker phase. However, by the slightly later Globular Amphora phase, the distribution of Krzemionki banded flint had eclipsed Świeciechów flint and was transported over 600 km as far north as the Baltic coastline and west to the River Oder and beyond (Balcer 1999). The unusual, almost psychedelic, patterning on ground and polished banded flint implements would have lent itself to objectification, thus increasing its cultural value over time.

In the Netherlands the Trichterbecherkultur (TRB) imported axeheads from northern Germany and Denmark for wetland deposition (often in hoards) and these were generally larger than the functional examples recovered from graves which had evidence of use-wear (Table 7.3). Conversely, the axeheads deposited in wetlands produced no evidence of hafting or use which, combined with their comparatively larger size, suggests that these imported axeheads were not made for everyday purposes but were destined for careful deposition in major wetlands such as the Drenthe Plateau (Wentink 2008). The fact that these unused, large axeheads had been imported 200+ km specifically for wetland deposition, demonstrates again the importance placed upon non-local, exotic extraction site products for depositional practices in various European regions.

In central Europe during the earliest Neolithic, the LBK, Stroked Pottery Culture, and Lengyel communities in Moravia and eastern

Austria imported lithics from sources up to 700+ km away, including Carpathian obsidian, Bavarian striped cherts, Bohemian quartzites, and Transdanubian radiolarite (Mateiciucová & Trnka 2015). These imports occurred despite having access to abundant local lithic resources. Once again, it was exotic imported lithologies which were most valued by these communities, presumably through storied associations, and local lithologies appear to have been reserved for mundane purposes.

However, it was the Atlantic façade, the Channel, and North Sea coastlines which provide the most informative data regarding long distance networks and their influence on the introduction of Neolithic extraction practices in Britain and Ireland. A contiguous series of extraction site networks existed stretching from Brittany in the west, through to Normandy, the Paris Basin, into Belgium, the Netherlands and beyond. In Brittany, the major Plussulien source of metadolerite 'A' (Group X), located upon the north-facing summit outcrop of Roch Pol Hill, provided raw material for roughly 40% of all Breton axeheads. However, they are also found more distantly as far south as the Pyrenees and Rhone Valley, and east to the Rhine Valley and beyond (Le Roux 2011). Recent research has found that metadolerite axeheads were imported into the eastern TRB Group, as evidenced by three polished adzeheads discovered at Plemięta (Poland) that appear to be of Breton origin and had travelled some 1500+ km. Others have been recognised in northern Germany, Denmark, southern Scandinavia, and southern Britain. Interestingly, the form of the Plemięta hoard adzeheads may have been inspired by Bégude-type jade axeheads. These Polish metadolerite adzeheads occur coincidentally at the north-eastern limit of jade axehead distribution, demonstrating that it was not just jade objects which travelled considerable distances across Europe (Pétrequin & Rzepecki 2016). However, one of the most significant discoveries regarding metadolerite 'A' distribution is the occurrence of seven axeheads in southern Britain, including a particularly fine polished example from Pulborough (Sussex) with a distinctive button-shaped butt.

As would be expected of material evidence of European contact, this small corpus of axeheads are scattered around the nearest points of contact on the Channel coast, the Bristol Channel, and northwards to Bredon Hill (Walker 2015, 104–10), lending weight to the Sheridan model of Neolithisation (eg, 2010; 2017) and the human migration data provided by the aDNA evidence. In addition, the typo-chronology of the jade axeheads suggests that some of the examples discovered in southern Britain (eg, the Sweet Track axehead from Somerset) may pre-date *c.* 4000 cal BC, and thus may have been brought across the Channel before, or during, the primary Neolithic, suggesting that Trans-Manche contacts were longstanding and complex (Sheridan 2007; 2010; Pétrequin *et al.* 2008; 2012a; 2017; Sheridan & Pailler 2012)

Alongside Plussulien, the fibrolite sources located in the north-western tip of Finistère (Brittany), such as the Plouguin quarries, produced raw material for highly polished flat-profiled axeheads found in the Carnacéen tombs such as Tumulus St-Michel and Mané er Hroëck (Pailler 2012a). It is also possible that some fibrolite implements were imported into Brittany from Spanish sources along with the variscite beads found in certain tombs (Cassen *et al.* 2012). Nevertheless, indigenous Breton fibrolite implements were transported eastwards into Basse-Normandie and the Paris Basin, south-west to Loire Atlantique (Pailler 2012a; 2012b), and two Breton fibrolite axeheads were discovered across the Channel at Saint Buryan in Cornwall (Cassen *et al.* 2012, 926; Walker 2015, 110), providing further evidence of cross-Channel contacts during the primary Neolithic in Britain. To date no fibrolite axeheads have been discovered in Ireland (Walker 2015, 137).

The next contiguous network lay in the Paris Basin. During the Early Neolithic Villeneuve-Saint-Germain Culture, lithology often determined the form of an artefact. Consequently, local flint was used for everyday flake production, whereas better quality Bartonian flint was favoured for long (>200 mm) regular blades which were distributed widely from the Armorican massif in the west, to the Ardennes in the east, suggesting these blades were more valued than artefacts chipped from local materials (Bostyn 1997; Giligny 2011). In addition, small numbers of Alpine or Armorican axeheads have also been recovered, alongside LBK shoe-last adzeheads and perforated wedges (Giligny &

*Figure 7.8: A typical Spiennes axehead (photo: author)*

Bostyn 2016, 276), demonstrating that exotic axeheads were also imported into the region at this time. In contrast, a separate adjacent regional network centred on the Île-de-France focused on the production of quartzite sandstone axeheads in workshops on the Stampian Hills. However, this network also imported axeheads of Alpine jade [roughly 20%], Armorican dolerites, metadolerites and hornfels [45%], and small numbers of flint axeheads from the Caen Plain (Giligny & Bostyn 2016, 278), suggesting that different material practices may have existed between near neighbours, as seen previously in the ethnographic case study of the Hagen and Wiru discussed in Chapter 6.

It was not until Middle Neolithic II, and the Chasséen and Michelsberg phases in the Paris Basin and Normandy, that many of the important flint mines such as Jablines (Bostyn & Lanchon 1992) and Ri (Marcigny *et al.* 2011) began operating. At this time locally produced flint axeheads began to appear in assemblages alongside imported axeheads. The largest number of axeheads were recovered from flint mines themselves [18%] (suggesting they may have played a role in renewal rites), followed by workshops [11%], settlements [3%], and burials [1%] (Giligny & Bostyn 2016, 276). The Paris Basin mines distributed products over distances of 200+ km, thus overlapping with both the Breton sources and the Belgian mines to the east (Collet & Bostyn 2011; Bostyn 2015). Despite exporting products, the Paris Basin region also imported axeheads from Brittany, Normandy, the Vosges, the Massif Central, the Ardennes, and the Alps (Manolakakis & Giligny 2011). Clearly during the more mature Neolithic the demand for exotic items had increased in the Paris Basin.

The distribution of Jablines products overlaps with those from Spiennes located to the north-east and the Breton sites in the west, creating contiguous networks (Collet & Bostyn 2011; Bostyn 2015; Collett *et al.* 2016). The Spiennes and Rijckholt mines appear to have been the main lithic resources for many Michelsberg sites (Manolakakis & Giligny 2011, 49), whereas Breton dolerite axeheads are also found distributed throughout the Jablines/Spiennes network (Bostyn & Collet 2011, 343) and northwards into Poland (Pétrequin & Rzepecki 2016), producing a complex picture of lithic preferences.

The users of the Michelsberg mines at Spiennes (Belgium) appear to have carefully managed the distribution of their material, thus nodules, roughout axeheads, and blades occur up to 50 km from the mines; flake tools, axeheads, and blades were distributed 50–80 km; and around 160 km only blades and axeheads are recovered (Fig. 7.8). Spiennes also appears to have specialised in the production of long blades (Collet *et al.* 2008; Collet & Bostyn 2011; Bostyn 2015, 80; H. Collet pers. comm.).

It was also during the Michelsberg period that deep-shaft, galleried mining was introduced at Rijckholt, Lousberg, and Valkenburg (Netherlands), forming the hub in the next contiguous network which overlapped with the Paris Basin mines to the west, and those lying to the east in northern Germany and Poland. Rijckholt flint was extensively distributed, being transported 200–300 km to the Dutch coastal sites and Westphalia, but also roughly 550 km south as far as Lake Constance (southern Germany) and Lake Zürich (Switzerland); the northerly limit was northern Germany. The largest quantities of Rijckholt lithics are found in the Michelsberg, Hazendonk Group, and Stein Group sites lying to the north and east of the mines (de Grooth 2015).

Around the turn of the 4th millennium BC it was precisely the networks described above, ranged along the Channel and North Sea coasts of Europe, which appear to have been the springboard for the introduction of Neolithic extraction practices into Britain and Ireland, which led to the open-air quarries of indigenous Mesolithic groups gradually being replaced by the new deep mining techniques. The spread of Neolithic extraction practices, built upon those of indigenous peoples, may have been spurred on by the iconography of the exotic imported axeheads which appeared around Europe and even its periphery – some apparently before other aspects of the Neolithic lifeway were adopted. The role of long distance networks in the distribution of these extraction site products, alongside the appearance of Neolithic extraction practices themselves during the earliest Neolithic in a number of regions around Europe (see Table 7.1), demonstrates that stone extraction was often at the forefront of Neolithisation in many places.

## Conclusions

This review of Neolithic extraction in continental Europe demonstrates that many sites and their assemblages had common elements, suggesting a shared practice developed around the introduction of a new method of flint extraction using deep-shaft, galleried mines. Much of the new technique was mediated by ritualised practices which must reflect belief systems combining elements of indigenous culture. Many of these ritualised practices involved the use of assemblages of objects which were not always functional or associated with the extraction process *per se*, but rather formed meaningful deposits placed within specific areas in the workings:

- Pottery is found in galleries and upper shaft fills.
- Human remains were interred in galleries and chambers as well as upper shaft fills.
- Hearths occur on shaft floors or in shaft fills.
- Graffiti is rarely found, but can occur within workings and/or sign-posting them locally.
- Redeposited axeheads/picks, rejected tools, and debitage can be found throughout the workings in contexts which were not working floors.

Much of this European evidence is focused on access routes into the workings, both when active and abandoned. The prevalence of such evidence suggests that the Neolithic extraction sites shared common practices, which had developed over some two millennia in Europe and these were transplanted across the Channel as part of Neolithisation. Neolithic extraction had built upon Mesolithic traditions and beliefs with the use of distinctive locations or raw materials, placed deposits and ground stone technology, and augmented these earlier practices by developing deeper mining techniques and a wider range of material deposits to enhance ritualised extraction. Much of this activity must have been undertaken for purposes of mediation with controlling supernatural forces (spirits/ancestors/deities) who presided over the raw materials. As a result, the products which emerged from many mines and quarries appear to have been highly valued and will have underscored many aspects of social interaction and ideologies, as shown by their long-distance distributions, use-life, and the context of their final deposition.

# 8

# Neolithic stone extraction in Britain and Europe

> ... it is important to challenge the 'utilitarian' interpretation of some of these finds.
> Bradley (1990, 66)

Traditionally, prehistoric mines and quarries have been studied from technological and quantitative perspectives, focusing on the scale and engineering of the workings, the quantities of raw material extracted, and the estimated numbers of objects produced, and/or the chronology of this activity (eg, Borkowski 1995; Longworth *et al.* 2012). Such basic interpretive paradigms suggest that technology is perceived as being more easily understood because the potentially irrational impediment of the social context of extraction is ignored (Warren 2006, 15). Consequently, the interpretation of mines and quarries has often become mired in self-perpetuating economic determinism, characterised in such loaded terminology as 'flint-axe factories' which participated in 'an industrial system ... of long-range communications between the factories and their buyers' (Piggott 1954, 36), all creating an 'axe trade' complete with its associated 'middle-men' (Houlder 1961, 136–9). This trend has continued to be explored in some detail, for example investigating such themes as 'monopoly or direct access', 'production and exchange' (Torrence 1984; 1986) and 'supply and demand' (Shennan *et al.* 2017). However, such economic paradigms fail to address the important issue of social context – why and how was an object sourced, produced, and used, and what led to its final deposition.

The over-arching question is what *initiated* extraction? Was it economic imperative, ideology, cosmological beliefs, or a complex amalgam of reasons? In many cases the answer was superficially practical – the winning of raw materials for artefact production, personal adornment, artworks, or construction purposes (Fig. 8.1). However, both ethnographic and pre-industrial historical accounts document contexts where ideological or cosmological beliefs underpin functional, economic, or cultural drivers, and are often in the foreground of extraction and production activities (Topping 2017, 45–109). This is particularly true where mining was (and is) practised with certain rituals because the raw material has a deep cultural significance and is used to reinforce social conventions, cultural beliefs, power relations, or interaction with supernatural forces.

Such values can be readily seen at the Native American Pipestone quarries in Minnesota. Here, extraction spanning more than a millennium has produced tobacco pipes for symbolic and ceremonial purposes which are emblematic of tribal identity and personify spiritual beliefs (Hughes 1995; Hughes & Stewart 1997; Scott *et al.* 2006). Similar cultural imperatives buttress much Aboriginal Australian procurement where considerable journeys of more than 1000 km are regularly undertaken to visit quarries to obtain particular types of stone or minerals which are believed to embody the essence of Ancestral Beings of the Dreamtime. They are essential for ritual performances, maintaining social networks, or strengthening group identity (Gould 1977, 164). Maori communities often made perilous journeys through hostile territory to obtain jade for important artefacts (Best

*Figure 8.1: A reconstruction of Neolithic mining activities at Spiennes, from a display in the Interpretation Centre for the Neolithic Flint Mines of Spiennes (photo: author)*

1912, 179; Field 2012, 58). In some cases male competition lies behind axe-making in New Guinea, demonstrating that status, wealth, and identity also feature in procurement strategies (Pétrequin & Pétrequin 2011; 2020). At the medieval Wieliczka salt mines (Poland; which had Neolithic precursors), the galleries and tunnels were decorated with religious iconography as a metaphysical support mechanism to counter safety concerns. Throughout Europe examples of otherworldly beings are recorded in historical extraction sites that needed to be appeased to ensure success. Examples include the 'knockers', mythical creatures associated with post-medieval Cornish tin mines, or the malevolent 'demons of ferocious aspect', Germanic dwarves, and the Greek *cabalos* who inhabited mines and quarries in Europe and were described by Georgius Agricola in the 16th century (Agricola 1556, 217). This provides evidence of a widespread mythologised dimension to historical European extraction to stand alongside the ethnography. Taken together, this suggests that extra-functional perspectives need to be considered during the analysis of the rich assemblages and structures contained in the archaeological record to achieve a more critical understanding of the social context of extraction practice.

## The emergence of Neolithic extraction practices

Neolithic extraction practices developed from the convergence of two cultural traditions, one held by indigenous Mesolithic foraging groups and the other by migrant farming communities as they spread across Europe. One fed into the other to create a suite of

Neolithic practices when the two communities intermingled (as shown by aDNA), which provided an opportunity for a cross-cultural fertilisation of ideologies. However, initially there were a number of differences between the two traditions in terms of technique, on-site practices, the use of material culture, and the use-life of products. Over time these procedures merged to create the new Neolithic practice (Table 8.1).

The principal difference between the two traditions was technical – deep-shaft galleried mines did not exist among Mesolithic groups whose *modus operandi* was the open-air pit or quarry (with the possible exception of Krumlovský les (Czechia); Oliva 2010). Such techniques may have suited the Mesolithic lifeway, where journeys to quarries were part of a range of seasonally exploited resources (cf. Zvelebil 1994; Milner 2006). Consequently, the technique of relatively rapid quarrying of exposed igneous outcrops or the pit extraction of shallow flint deposits fulfilled the needs of the indigenous population, much as it did among well-documented Native American communities (eg, Holmes 1919). In contrast, the Neolithic deep-shaft galleried mines were both a technical and cultural innovation which was predicated upon a greater logistical commitment to a more time-consuming form of extraction. The introduction of deep mining allowed the exploitation of deposits previously unavailable to quarry and pit users and must reflect an ideological shift towards targeting more deeply buried strata. Clearly the easily won lithologies favoured by Mesolithic quarry teams did not meet the requirements of the Neolithic communities during a time of social transformation and land-use intensification. The cultural contacts between indigenous people and migrant agro-pastoralists in many regions led to a comingling of both extraction traditions, resulting in the development of the more elaborate ritualised practices found at many Neolithic sites and ultimately a widespread adoption of deep-shaft mining.

On-site assemblages are another major difference between Mesolithic and Neolithic sites. During the Mesolithic, practices focused almost exclusively on on-site placed deposits of raw material and debitage, arguably reflecting animistic beliefs associated with rites of renewal. Although the final Mesolithic populations in north-western Europe may have had a comparatively simpler technological repertoire compared with Neolithic communities, they did have a rich ritual life, as demonstrated by their burial ceremonialism comprising carefully positioned inhumations accompanied by grave goods including lithics, bone artefacts, ochre, and selected animal/bird bones. Such burial practices can be seen at Téviec and Hoëdic in Brittany (Schulting 1996) through to the Ertebølle cemeteries at Vedbaek (Denmark) (Albrethsen & Brinch Petersen 1976) and Skateholm (Sweden) (Larsson 1993) in Scandinavia. These grave assemblages suggest the commemoration of status and identity, while undoubtedly conforming to cosmological beliefs. These assemblages find parallels in Neolithic flint mines where carved chalk objects, pottery, axeheads, lithics/debitage, human and animal remains, etc, were placed in various contexts in and around the workings, which must also reflect aspects of identity and contemporary beliefs. Consequently, the fusion of Mesolithic extraction and ritual practices with the developed deep mining tradition expressed itself through the on-site deposition of increasingly more complex assemblages, particularly featuring the use of pottery. These practices reflected the changing world view which had emerged from the conjunction of foraging and agro-pastoral cultural traditions. In addition, the assemblages found at established British and Irish Neolithic extraction sites parallel those discovered at causewayed enclosures and long barrows, for example, thus linking deposits found at extraction sites with practices seen at other forms of communal monument (Topping 2005, 68).

There is no evidence of built structures at Mesolithic extraction sites. However, natural features such as niches amongst boulder fields

|  | Mesolithic | Neolithic |
|---|---|---|
| Storied/mythologised locations | ● | ● |
| Open-air quarries | ● | ● |
| Deep shaft galleried mines | ? | ● |
| Placed deposits | ● | ● |
| Structures in workings |  | ● |
| Human burials in workings |  | ● |
| Animal remains in workings |  | ● |
| Long distance product distributions [200+ km] | ● | ● |

Table 8.1: The similarities and differences between Mesolithic and Neolithic extraction practices, demonstrating increased elaboration over time following opportunities for acculturation between indigenous foragers and migrant agro-pastoralists

or rock shelters were used as locations for significant on-site deposits of raw material. In contrast, developed Neolithic sites saw the construction of chalk platforms in many mine workings, used for the display of extraction tools, lithics, and pottery, or as a setting for carved chalk objects and human and animal remains. Rare so-called 'caves' were built from chalk blocks in one mine at Cissbury and an artificial cave-like tunnel was quarried into the flanks of Pike of Stickle adjacent to South Scree at Langdale, with other tunnels quarried into Top Buttress. These examples illustrate the range of small-scale constructions and quarried features which formed part of Neolithic extraction practice.

Human burials and deposits of animal remains do not appear to form part of Mesolithic extraction practice, although they do occur at many Neolithic extraction sites. Caution is needed, as taphonomic processes may have affected Mesolithic open-air sites where these deposits could have been lost to erosion, acidification, weathering, or animal predation, unlike Neolithic assemblages which have survived because they were buried deep below ground. However, the pan-European Mesolithic practice of interring disarticulated human bones in a range of sites, particularly caves (Conneller 2006, 158), may have led to the practice being adopted in Neolithic flint mines, where body parts and occasionally complete skeletons were placed in similar but man-made subterranean contexts. In addition, the incorporation of animal/bird remains in Mesolithic burials such as Vedbaek and Skateholm demonstrates the use of faunal remains in such contexts, and when seen through the lens of the ethnographic data suggests they were an expression of personhood, articulating the life and afterlife status of the individual through their juxtaposition with animal remains.

The Mesolithic practice of animal/bird deposition generally used only parts of the animal, such as a swan's wing or a roe deer's foot, only rarely was a complete skeleton interred, such as the dog burials at Skateholm, which may find a Neolithic parallel discovered in a gallery lying between Greenwell's Pit and Shaft A at Grime's Graves where a canine was found carefully buried (Longworth & Varndell 1996, 9–33). The pseudo-Mesolithic practice of selective animal bone deposition is most common at flint mines where domesticated species are regularly represented as body parts and skulls, whereas complete skeletons, such as the ox discovered in Shaft 27 at Cissbury, was a relatively rare occurrence. The cultural messages behind such deposits were fundamental. As Fowler (2004, 135) has observed, '[t]he beginnings of ... structured deposition also suggests that the retention of animal body parts was important, and that the deposition of humans and animals might be thought of in equivalent ways' (cf. also Ingold 2000). Accordingly, the cultural significance of deposits of human/animal/bird bones at extraction sites must have lain in the juxtaposition of these remains with other forms of artefact to create relational assemblages which incorporated meaningful referents to cultural traditions or beliefs.

One of the key aspects of Neolithic extraction practice was the long-distance distribution (200+ km) of certain products by established Neolithic communities. Such activity is presently obscured during the later Mesolithic and first contact periods, with the exception of some axehead distributions in north-western Europe centred around Germany, Poland, and Scandinavia, and the circulation of flint tranchet axeheads in Britain. This suggests that more evidence may come to light in the future regarding long-distance artefact movements during the final Mesolithic and first contact periods. However, in comparison, during the earlier European Neolithic there were many examples of long-distance product dispersals beyond the obvious Alpine jadeitite axeheads, such as Breton fibrolite, Group X dolerite, variscite, Bartonian flint, Polish banded flint, Group I greenstones, Group VI tuff, Group VII granophyre, and Group IX porcellanite. Such distributions were defining aspects of extraction sites, and the often pan-European scale of circulation demonstrates that raw material from particular sites was highly valued in many regions, with products generally used in quite specific ways in non-functional contexts. The ethnoarchaeological model suggests that long-distance movements imply that the cultural value of these products indicates that they originated from important storied/mythologised sources and were destined to play particular roles in society. Such products became part of an entangled meshwork of social and cosmological narratives which helped to centre people within their cultural landscape, maintain social networks, and anchor them materially to their beliefs.

A major trend seen at many Mesolithic extraction sites was a focus on prominent landforms, and/or the exploitation of visually distinctive raw materials, which continued throughout the 4th millennium. This enabled site users to conceptualise extraction sites as mythologised places which could be linked to beliefs and origin stories. Once anchored within a cultural landscape, storied extraction sites provided an arena where people could interact directly with their cosmography and develop strategies for legitimisation, status, and communal identity. These storied extraction sites provided lithologies which carried a biography that spoke to society. The potency of the objectified product became a societal metaphor, symbol, and icon, which ensured the importance and legacy of significant extraction sites at a regional or supra-regional level. This cultural importance was reflected in the long-distance circulation of lithics by established Neolithic communities, who introduced Neolithisation to the Mesolithic regions of Europe by building on indigenous practices while advancing the new technology and ideology behind Neolithic deep-shaft mining.

## The social context of Neolithic extraction sites

The characterisation of extraction sites can now be more confidently addressed using the aggregated ethnoarchaeological model presented here. The use of a comparatively large body of aggregated ethnography provides a more rounded, statistically robust model which overcomes earlier flawed attempts that used smaller data sets.

The ethnoarchaeological model has drawn upon non-westernised ethnographic data to analyse the traditional methods and processes used at extraction sites and, in particular, to assess material culture patterning to provide comparators for the evidence recorded in the archaeological record. As Fogelin and Schiffer (2015, 818) have observed, '... ethnographic and archaeological accounts can supply hints as to possible patterns' in formation processes which might explain their underlying social context.

It is clear from the ethnography that many traditional extraction sites fulfilled specialised roles within society. However, not every extraction site was considered extraordinary, some produced materials for domestic or subsistence activities. Nevertheless, the aggregated ethnographic data records that a high percentage of traditional extraction sites were storied/mythologised places [93%] and linked to the worldview of the community, where ritualised practices [92%] were followed to ensure successful outcomes and objectify the raw material or products. These observations offer fresh perspectives with which to interpret archaeological sites and their products and infer their cultural value to Neolithic society.

In terms of the social context of extraction site users, the ethnography records that extraction teams predominantly consist of men, with a minority of them comprising mixed gender teams with children, and women only teams are exceedingly rare. In contrast, the landscape and raw material is often conceptually embodied as a female entity, or is protected by female spirits, producing a male/female dichotomy in extraction practice. The male quarry teams are often specialists who have been brought together by relatives or clan/kinship affiliates, and many undergo apprenticeships or initiations. Political power and status can rest upon access to, or ownership of, the symbolic power embodied in extraction site products. In addition, although some objects may be produced initially for functional uses, they can often be ritually transformed into sacred or wealth/status objects at a later time. Also, certain societies believe in a connection between some products and bodily symbolism (eg, Battaglia 1990; Hall 1997). Overall, extraction practices are repeatedly intertwined with social networks and transactions which allow the users to establish and maintain identity, status, and power relations.

The combined ethnoarchaeological data suggests that Neolithic extraction sites operated at two levels of intensity and social complexity: (1) to satisfy everyday domestic requirements from local or accessible sources; and (2) more specialised sites which were often located in distant areas and exploited for rare, distinctive materials which were more highly valued than those used in the domestic sphere. The ethnography suggests that it was the topographic setting and distinctiveness of sites which generally created their ideological value to society, and that objects from distant sites were often the most valued. In a number of cases the journey/pilgrimage to a site was an important feature of extraction practice.

How did the cultural value of extraction sites develop? The ethnography provides many examples of societies whose worldview is dominated by animistic beliefs, typified by a conviction that supernatural entities inhabit or control access to the various elements of the cultural landscape, and in particular lithic resources embedded within it. Consequently, these entities need to be appeased by some form of ritualised mediation before, during, and after extraction. In addition, a society's worldview is generally used to construct cosmologies to legitimise a society's place in the landscape through its origin stories, thus establishing communal identity through mythologised locations – particularly those of important extraction sites. As a result, the act of lithic extraction was/is often viewed as a human–supernatural interaction, accompanied by strategic ritual acts of exchange generally designed to ensure not only access and the appeasement of supernatural forces but mitigation to ensure the ongoing supply of the raw material.

These ritual acts of appeasement comprise both offerings and/or sacrifices of burnt, broken, or consumed objects, materials, or foodstuffs – precisely the types of evidence found at many Neolithic extraction sites. The presence of certain animal remains in and around many Neolithic extraction sites may also represent totemism, used to symbolise the site users in their placatory interactions with the spirit entities who controlled access to the sites and raw material. Other remains represent the deliberate killing of animals which the ethnography suggests was linked to renewal practices and ritualised feasting (eg, Ingold 1986, 246–50). Extraction ritualisation can therefore be viewed as a 'basic mechanism for the proper operation of the 'socio-cosmic' universe, relating social and supernatural domains' (Verhoeven 2012, 13). Over time extraction practices and material deposition increased in sophistication, and the incoming Neolithic practices (building upon those of the Mesolithic period) included the deposition of a wider range of objects and materials. In addition, they paralleled those found at other forms of communal monument, thus linking extraction to practices experienced at enclosures, burial monuments, and other significant places in the landscape.

The evidence of ritualised practices appears to be strongly represented at Neolithic mines and quarries. Assemblages recorded at British and Irish extraction sites generally occur in distinct contexts depending upon the type of material or object involved (see Chapter 6), and this appears to have been influenced by practices discovered previously at European sites. Many assemblages are found at access routes into the workings, particularly the shafts and gallery entrances, suggesting that the first and last places experienced by site users were being deliberately enhanced by contact with meaningful deposits. Among these assemblages, lithics and debitage was deliberately redeposited in various subterranean contexts where they had not been manufactured, suggesting links to rites of renewal. The episodic backfilling of shafts and galleries also appears to have been accompanied by the deposition of artefacts and human or animal remains, implying staged rituals as part of abandonment practices. Ethnography records that for many societies this form of structured activity was generally socially sanctioned, symbolic in nature, and designed to control human affairs, particularly the on-site interactions with the supernatural controllers of the site and its raw material (cf. Firth 1951; Bourdieu 1977; 1990; Hampton 1997; Godelier 1999; Pétrequin *et al.* 2012a; 2015; 2017; etc).

Evidence of potentially ritualised extraction and assemblages can be found at European sites (see Chapters 1 & 7) such as Jablines (Bostyn & Lanchon 1992) and those of the Paris Basin (eg, Giligny & Bostyn 2016) in France, at Spiennes in Belgium (Collet *et al.* 2016), at Rijkholt in the Netherlands (de Grooth 2015), Defensola in Italy (Tarantini *et al.* 2011), Mont Viso and Mont Beigua in the Italian Alps (Pétrequin *et al.* 2012a), and at Hov and Bjerre in Denmark (Becker 1999a; 1999b). Similar evidence occurs in Britain and Ireland at the flint mines and quarries at Ballygalley Hill, Black Mountain, Blackpatch, Church Hill, Cissbury, Durrington, Easton Down, Goodland, Grime's Graves, Harrow Hill, Stoke Down, and the quarries at Creag na Caillich, Graiglwyd, Lambay Island, Langdale, Le Pinacle, Mynydd Rhiw, Shetland, and Tievebulliagh.

The question of the cultural value of extraction site products is equally illuminating. Some of the evidence for the scale and nature of European long-distance networks has been presented previously, particularly regarding the distributions of jade, fibrolite, dolerite 'A', and the various distinctive Polish types of flint. Similar evidence has been recorded in Britain and Ireland, where the distribution of stone axeheads of petrological Groups I, IV, V–IX, XI–XX, XXIII, XXIV, and XXVII all exhibit circulation up to 200+ km from their source. In the case of axeheads of British Group VI and the Irish Group IX, they had been taken across the Irish Sea in opposite directions, and Breton dolerite 'A' axeheads of Group X were transported across the Channel into Britain (data from Clough & Cummins 1988; Cooney & Mandal 1998; Walker 2015; Schauer et al. 2020). Unfortunately, the same precision is not available for the analysis of flint implements because of the difficulties of provenancing the raw material. However, generalised distributions do emerge from a small sample of implements which suggests that regionalised flint axehead groups can be identified across southern Britain (Craddock et al. 1983; 2012). This data tentatively hints that the most heavily represented group was from the South Downs mines (arguably reflecting their early start date and comparatively large numbers), which can be found in southern Britain ranging from East Anglia and the south-east across to the south-west peninsula. The second largest group was from the Wessex mines, distributed over the same areas but in smaller numbers. In contrast, a far smaller number was identified from East Anglian sources in most of these areas, but unusually not the south-east. However, the overall small sample size and the fact that, in some regions such as East Anglia, up to 40%+ of the implements tested could not be assigned to any source, suggests that this data has to be treated with caution. Nevertheless, the extensive distributions of so many stone axehead Groups, and the suggestion that at least in southern Britain some flint mine products also circulated widely, indicates that certain extraction sites and their products were as, or more, important to many Neolithic communities than locally available material.

The final deposition of many extraction site products in non-domestic contexts, particularly wetlands, rivers, and hoards, strongly suggests roles rooted in cosmology, social networks, identity, status, power relations, and obligations. Examples of deposition can be drawn from Sweden where potlach-like events (cf. Mauss 1954, 17–45) of conspicuous consumption and deliberate destruction at Svartskylle witnessed Early Neolithic axeheads, scrapers, and blades being burnt and left in four deposits on a prominent hilltop. At Kverrestad, fire-damaged flint implements and decorated pottery were deposited in pits, including 100+ axeheads, tanged arrowheads, projectile points, and debitage – stone axeheads were also burnt and deposited. Other examples include Svågertorp where six burnt axeheads and a chisel were placed in a pit; Øster Nibstrup where two Late Neolithic flint daggers (one burnt) were placed in a house post-hole; and at Strandby where 100+ burnt axeheads, chisels, and scrapers were discovered (Larsson 2006, 403–8). This evidence suggests that the deliberate destruction of large assemblages of artefacts was a significant cultural event, which ethnography suggests was designed to maintain social networks, transactions, and power relations.

These examples were not alone. In the Carnac tombs of Brittany, the rich grave assemblage at Mané er Hroëck included 90 fibrolite axeheads with the majority appearing to have damaged butts, and 13 jadeitite axeheads of which ten were broken. The vast tomb of Saint-Michel contained 11 jadeitite axeheads, three of which were broken, alongside 26 smaller fibrolite axeheads which included at least 16 with damaged butts. The Mané Hui tomb (Fig. 8.2) included two broken jadeitite axeheads, and one axehead and a chisel of fibrolite (Cassen et al. 2012). Alternative practices can be seen with some TRB axeheads in the Netherlands which were removed from circulation, smeared with ochre, wrapped in hides, and deliberately buried or submerged in wetlands. Microwear analysis suggests some were retrieved periodically, demonstrating that they had an ongoing role in society despite being hidden from view (Wentink 2006; 2008; Wentink & van Gijn 2008; van Gijn 2010a; 2010b).

A further perspective on deposition practices is recorded in New Guinean ethnography, where some Highland tribes use Langda-Sela adzeheads as 'power stones' at harvest time or

*Figure 8.2: Part of the Mané Hui (Carnac) tomb assemblage, comprising deliberately broken jade axeheads amongst ceramics and other lithics, now curated in the National Museum, Paris Saint Germain (photo: author)*

during the opening of new gardens, and small Yeineri and Tagime style adzeheads and stone knives can be planted with crops to encourage growth (Hampton 1997, 649). The latter example could explain the social context of some isolated axehead discoveries which are often considered accidental losses but could actually be explained as deliberate deposits in significant places to symbolically encourage fertility amongst plant or animal resources. Although clearly some isolated finds must have been accidentally lost, the purposeful burial of single axeheads in non-domestic contexts could explain their occurrence among the Irish data where 318 were buried on agricultural land or pasture, 34 on lake shores or in lakes, and 28 on the sea shore (Cooney & Mandal 1998, 36, table 3.4). Similarly, the *c.* 5% of jade axeheads discovered in 'context-free' locations in the wider landscape (Pétrequin *et al.* 2012a, 1378) may also have been associated with practices surrounding fertility or renewal rites.

That the axehead was held in high regard by Neolithic society is shown by the fact that the truly iconic examples, such as rare Alpine jade axeheads, were carefully curated, and the typology and colouration were imitated in a number of European regions using local lithologies. Consequently, Carnac style axeheads were copied in flint in the Paris Basin, Denmark, and northern Germany, and also using silimanite in Iberia. In the Paris Basin quartzite was also used to fashion imitations of Durrington and Bégude style axeheads and dolerite was used for fake Bégude style axeheads near the Armorican Massif. In Switzerland serpentinite was utilised to create Zug type *ersatz* Alpine axeheads, whereas flint was favoured in the upper Rhine Valley and Switzerland. In Britain,

Chenoise type flint was employed to create Tumiac style roughouts found in Kent and the green epidotized tuff of the Langdale/Scafell massif may have been deliberately chosen as a visually close approximation to jade (Giligny et al. 2012; Pétrequin et al. 2012c; Sheridan & Pailler 2012). This Neolithic fixation with rare green lithologies also led to the rise of variscite exploitation in the Iberian Peninsula at Gavà and elsewhere. These examples lend weight to the hypothesis that the axehead had become a powerful metonymic 'tool' used for mediation and the maintenance of social structures and power relations. As Pétrequin et al. (2015, 84) have suggested, citing the work of Mauss and Godelier and their own fieldwork in Irian Jaya (Pétrequin & Pétrequin 2020 'in order to understand the force and power that was associated with the objects that were given and received as gifts, it was necessary to escape from considerations of market exchange and instead explore the imaginary and ideal functions that people attributed to these "signs"', highlighting the key issue of the potential non-functional, symbolic role(s) of objects in the Neolithic. Such observations are borne out by complimentary research in other ethnographic regions (eg, Topping 2017). Consequently, the weight of archaeological and ethnographic evidence strongly suggests that certain axeheads, notably those circulating in long distance networks, were never designed to be functional implements, instead being destined for elaborate gift-giving, social transactions, structured deposition, or burial ceremonialism.

Ritualised extraction practices were a fundamental stage in the objectification of artefacts from mines and quarries. Across Europe extraction ritual had developed to ensure success, safety, and sustainability in the dangerous environs of mines and quarries. Nascent ritualised extraction had emerged during the Mesolithic and was adopted and elaborated upon during the course of Neolithisation. As Fowler (2004, 41) has suggested, such '[p]atterns in practices … [were] … the means through which identities are shaped and perpetuated'. Ritualised extraction was thus entangled in personhood and identity, while functioning as a coping mechanism to counter supernatural issues surrounding the act of digging into the earth. Extraction produced 'gifts from the earth'

| *Expedient artefacts* | *Extraction site products* |
|---|---|
| Everyday tools for all | Objectified artefacts for the few |
| Expedient production, needs driven | Craft specialist production of artefacts |
| Quick production time | Considerable investment in production, grinding & polishing |
| Local/regionally available lithologies | Rare exotic rocks from distant storied/ mythologised sources |
| Local/regional distribution >200 km | Regional/supra-regional distribution 200+ km |
| Used | Generally unused |
| Accidental breakages and re-use | Often complete. Some deliberately broken/burnt |
| Casual discard, generally in domestic contexts | Special deposition in significant landscape contexts, especially rivers, wetlands & hoards |

(Based on Pétrequin *et al.* 2012d, 1434, with additions)

*Table 8.2: The 'sacred and profane' binary oppositions associated with the origins and use of lithic assemblages from expedient sources compared to those from extraction sites*

(cf. Whittle 1995), and in return extraction teams reciprocated with 'gifts to the earth' in the form of placed deposits and respectful ceremonialism to mitigate their impact upon what was probably an embodied cultural landscape.

The final deposition of the majority of products in rivers, wetlands, and sometimes in hoards, often pristine and unused, indicates that they were considered extraordinary by Neolithic society (Table 8.2). Consequently, Neolithic extraction sites were not a pivotal element in the supply chain of a market economy that serviced a growing population fixated upon systematic forest clearance (*contra* Shennan *et al.* 2017). Although tree removal was undoubtedly of importance to the process of Neolithisation and the establishment of an agro-pastoral economy, it does not appear to have generally been predicated upon the supply of axeheads from extraction sites, which conversely seem to have fulfilled more symbolic, non-functional roles in society. The mines and quarries provided Neolithic communities with 'socially-valourised' objects (eg, Pétrequin *et al.* 2015), emblematic of the origins of the raw material and ritualised extraction. Such artefact biographies ensured they carried a narrative into various social transactions and cultural institutions, underpinning the creation

**Group VI Distribution**

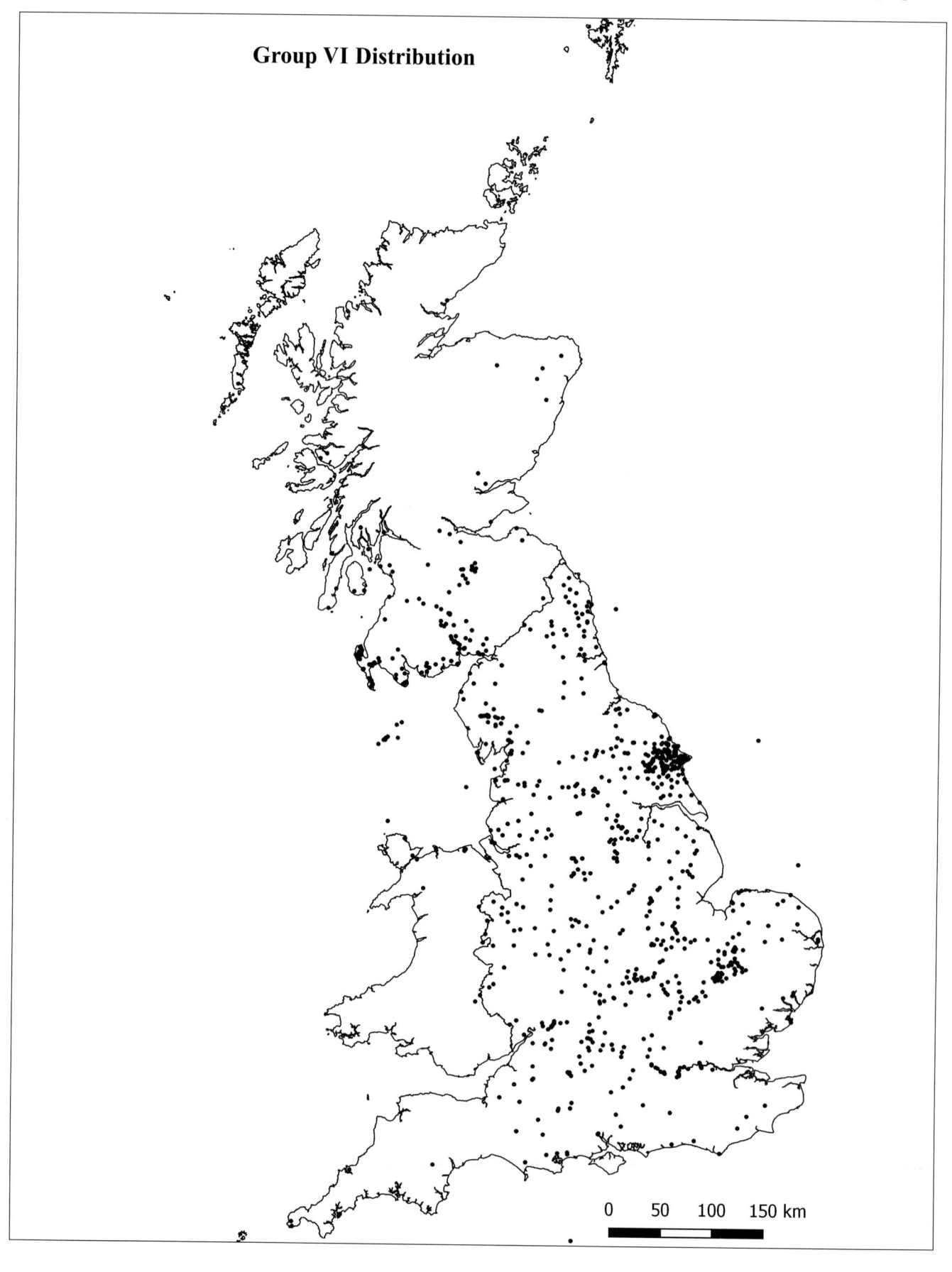

of identity, the maintenance of beliefs, and demonstrating materially a person's status in life and death.

One further perspective is illuminating. The cultural value of extraction site products may have been based upon rarity. It has been suggested that the production of large jade axeheads was around 12 per year at the peak of production, 4600–4000 cal BC (Pétrequin *et al.* 2012a, 1432). This estimate is founded upon the survival of 1800 examples catalogued around Europe, which would produce an average figure of only three axeheads per year. So the figure of 12 per year has taken into account losses to the archaeological record. This figure corresponds well with the ethnographic accounts of Yeineri quarry groups (comprising 5–10 men) who spend around 3 days securing enough stone to fashion 10–15 oversized Ye-yao axeheads during a quarry expedition (Hampton 1997, 698–718). Although the biases inherent in the formation of the archaeological record need to be considered, the jade example is not alone and the numbers of other provenanced Neolithic axehead types are also relatively small. For example, one of the most visible axehead groups in Britain and Ireland is Group VI, sourced around the Langdale Pikes. Here again, the number of provenanced Group VI axeheads found in the Implement Petrology Group's (IPG) Masterlist is currently just 1661 (from a total of 8138 petrologically assigned implements), thus representing 20.4% of all sourced axeheads (inf. Mik Markham) (Fig. 8.3). However, if we consider this number against the latest radiocarbon chronology, which suggests these quarries operated over a period of 250–750 years (Edinborough *et al.* 2019, 20–7) and a similar timespan to the peak production at the jade sources, the approximate annual axehead production figure based on provenanced examples alone could be somewhere between just 2–7 implements. So, using the formula of the jade/New Guinea estimate, the annual production figure of the Langdale quarries could have been as small as 8–28 axeheads.

Similarly, the early quarries at Graiglwyd in Gwynedd operated between *c.* 4100–3800 and 3400–2800 cal BC (Edinburgh *et al.* 2019), and produced 387 provenanced axeheads (Clough 1988, 4), which averages fewer than one axehead per year. Consequently, the formulaic estimate could be around four axeheads per year. The miniscule number of 33 identified axeheads from the Mynydd Rhiw quarries (Clough 1988, 4) almost disappears when averaged over some *c.* 700 years of quarrying (*c.* 3800–3100 cal BC; Edinburgh *et al.* 2019). Taken together, the overall trend appears to be for the annual production of comparatively small numbers of axeheads at many extraction sites. This despite the potential impact of unidentified axeheads curated in collections, the unknown numbers destroyed in antiquity, or those yet to be discovered, all of which cannot be accurately quantified at present.

These examples lend weight to the proposed model of targeted, small scale operations at most extraction sites, a situation far from the economic determinism, mass production, and market economies suggested by some commentators. Although we have to recognise that these estimates are undoubtedly under-representations, nevertheless, the underlying quantative trend appears to be one of low production figures, emphasising the fact that most extraction sites were exploited in a small-scale way despite the monumental quantities of debris and debitage at some, such as South Scree at Langdale. The fact that so many rejects, roughouts, and debitage remained behind at all extraction sites, such as the 33 roughout axeheads placed in Shaft III at Harrow Hill (Holleyman 1937, 239), suggests that extraction and production was highly selective. This process of selection resulted in comparatively small numbers of products and/or amounts of raw material being allowed off-site and into the wider community, thus maintaining the rarity and importance of extraction site products and creating the relatively limited quantative distributions found in the archaeological record. A rarity value which was then reflected in the ways these artefacts were used within Neolithic society.

Overall, the ethnoarchaeological evidence presented here demonstrates that Neolithic extraction sites do not fit simplistic economic models often used by archaeologists. There is irrefutable evidence for the ritualisation of extraction practices, while the use-life and deposition of many extraction site products is often demonstrably non-functional in nature. The special axeheads and other objects which emerged from extraction sites clearly contained a symbolic dimension that transcended the

*Figure 8.3: (opposite) The distribution of Group VI Langdale axeheads in Britain from the Implement Petrology Group Masterlist (Illustration: M. Markham)*

mundane world, incorporating cosmological beliefs which determined their role in society. They were, as Brumm (2011) has characterised them 'power tools', implements that had emerged from ritualised performances at storied locations in a mythologised landscape. It was these objects which carried some of the first messages of Neolithisation across Mesolithic Europe and into the nascent agro-pastoral communities.

# Bibliography

Adkins, R. & Jackson, R. 1978. *Neolithic Stone and Flint Axes from the River Thames*. London: British Museum Occasional Paper 1

Affleck, T., Edwards, K.J., & Clarke, A. 1988. Archaeological and palynological studies at the Mesolithic pitchstone and flint site of Auchareoch, Isle of Arran. *Proceedings of the Society of Antiquaries of Scotland* 118, 37–59

Agricola, G. 1556. *De Re Metallica* (trans. H.C. & L.H. Hoover 1912). New York: Dover Publications (reprinted 1986)

Albrethsen, S. & Brinch Petersen, E. 1976. Excavation of a Mesolithic cemetery at Vedbaek, Denmark. *Acta Archaeologica* 47, 1–28

Allard, P., Bostyn, F., Giligny, F. & Lech, J. (eds), 2008. *Flint Mining in Prehistoric Europe: Interpreting the archaeological records*. Oxford: British Archaeological Report S1891

Allen, M.J. & French, C. 2020. Investigations of the buried soil beneath the mound of Amesbury 42. In M. Parker Pearson, J. Pollard, C. Richards, J. Thomas, C. Tilley & K. Welham, *Stonehenge for the Ancestors, Part 1*, 106–15. Leiden: Sidestone Press

Allen, M.J. & Gardiner, J. 2012. Not out of the woods yet: some reflections on Neolithic ecological relationships with woodland. In A.M. Jones, J. Pollard, M.J. Allen & J. Gardiner (eds), *Image, Memory and Monumentality*, 93–107. Oxford: Prehistoric Society Research Papers 5

Allen, M.J., Chan, B., Cleal, R., French, C., Marshall, P., Pollard, J., Pullen, R., Richards, C., Ruggles, C., Robinson, D., Rylatt, J., Thomas, J., Welham, K. & Parker Pearson, M. 2016. Stonehenge's Avenue and 'Bluestonehenge', *Antiquity* 90, 991–1008

Andersson, M., Artursson, M. & Brink, K. 2016. Early Neolithic landscape and society in South-West Scania – new results and perspectives. *Journal of Neolithic Archaeology* 18, 23–114 [doi: 10.12766/jna.v18i0.118, accessed 26/04/18]

Armstrong, A.L. 1923. Discovery of a new phase of early flint mining at Grime's Graves, Norfolk. *Proceedings of the Prehistoric Society of East Anglia* 4(1), 113–25

Armstrong, A.L. 1924. Percy Sladen Memorial Fund Excavations. Grime's Graves, Norfolk, 1924: (1) further researches in the primitive flint mining area; (2) discovery of an early Iron Age site of Hallstat Culture. *Proceedings of the Prehistoric Society of East Anglia* 4(2), 186–7

Armstrong, A.L. 1932. The Percy Sladen Trust excavations, Grime's Graves, Norfolk. Interim Report 1927–1932. *Proceedings of the Prehistoric Society of East Anglia* 7(1), 57–61

Armstrong, A.L. 1934. Grime's Graves, Norfolk: report on the excavation of Pit 12. *Proceedings of the Prehistoric Society of East Anglia* 7, 382–94

Arthur, K.W. 2010. Feminine knowledge and skill reconsidered: women and flaked stone tools. *American Anthropologist* 112(2), 228–43

Babel, J., Braziewicz, J., Jaskóła, A., Kretschmer, W., Pajek, M., Semaniak, J., Scharf, A. & Uhl, T. 2005. The radiocarbon dating of the Neolithic flint mines at Krzemionki in central Poland. *Nuclear Instruments and Methods in Physics Research* 240, 539–43

Baena Preysler, J., Baréz, S., Pérez-González, A., Roca, M., Lázaro, A., Márquez, R., Rus, I., Manzano, C., Cuartero, F., Ortiz, I., Rodríguez, P., Pérez, T., González, I., Polo, J., Rubio, D., Alcaraz, E. & Escobar, A. 2011. Searchers and miners: first signs of flint exploitation in Madrid's region. In Capote *et al.* (eds) 2011, 203–220

Ballin, T.B. 2015. Arran pitchstone (Scottish volcanic glass): new dating evidence. *Journal of Lithic Studies* 2(1), 5–16

Ballin, T.B. & Ward, T. 2013. Burnetland Hill chert quarry: a Mesolithic extraction site in the Scottish Borders. *The Quarry* 9, 3–23

Ballin, T.B., Ellis, C. & Baillie, W. 2018. Arran pitchstone – different forms of exchange at different times? *Chartered Institute for Archaeologists Scottish Group Newsletter (Spring)*, 1–6

Ballin, T., Topping, P., & Cooney, G. 2017. *The Grut Wells Hoard. Making an Island World: Neolithic Shetland. North Roe Felsite Project Report 3*. Dublin: University College Dublin, School of Archaeology

Barber, M. 2005. Mining, burial and chronology: the West Sussex flint mines in the Late Neolithic and Early Bronze Age. In Topping & Lynott (eds) 2005, 94–109

Barber, M. & Dyer, C. 2005. Scouting for shafts: aerial reconnaissance and the Neolithic flint mines at Stoke Down, West Sussex. In Topping & Lynott (eds) 2005, 30–50

Barber, M., Field, D. & Topping, P. 1999. *The Neolithic Flint Mines of England*. Swindon: RCHME/English Heritage

Battaglia, D. 1990. *On the Bones of the Serpent: person,*

*memory, and materiality in Sabarl Island society*. Chicago IL: University of Chicago Press

Bayliss, A. & Woodman, P.C. 2009. A new Bayesian chronology for Mesolithic occupation at Mount Sandel, Northern Ireland. *Proceedings of the Prehistoric Society* 75, 101–23

Becker, C.J. 1999a. DK 1 Hov, Gem. Sennels, Amt Thisted, Jütland. In Weisgerber (ed.) 1999, 457–64

Becker, C.J. 1999b. DK 2 Bjerre, Gem. Vigsö, Amt Thisted. In Weisgerber (ed.) 1999, 464–8

Bell, C. 1997. *Ritual: Perspectives and Dimensions*. Oxford: Oxford University Press

Bell, R. & Bennett, S.A. 1923. A recently discovered prehistoric site in Co. Antrim. *Annual Reports and Proceedings of the Belfast Naturalists Field Club*, Ser 2, 8 (1918–1928), 242–55

Best, E. 1912. *The Stone Implements of the Maori*. Wellington NZ: AR Shearer

Blinkhorn, E., Lawton-Matthews, E. & Warren, G. 2017. Digging and filling pits in the Mesolithic of England and Ireland: comparative perspectives on a widespread practice. In N. Achard–Corompt, E. Ghesquière & V. Riquier (eds), *Digging in the Mesolithic: Actes de la séance de la Société préhistorique française de Châlons-en-Champagne (29–30 mars 2016)*, 211–23. Paris: Société Préhistorique Française

Bloxam, E. 2015. 'A place full of whispers': socializing the quarry landscape of the Wadi Hammamat. *Cambridge Archaeological Journal* 25, 789–814

Boas, F. & Hunt, G. 1921. *Ethnology of the Kwakiutl*. Washington DC: American Bureau of Ethnology, 35th Annual Report

Boivin, N. 2004. From veneration to exploitation: human engagement with the mineral world. In Boivin & Owoc (eds) 2004, 1–29

Boivin, N. & Owoc, M.A. (eds). 2004. *Soils, Stones and Symbols: Cultural perceptions of the mineral world*. London: University College London Press

Boivin, N. 2008. *Material Cultures, Material Minds*. Cambridge: Cambridge University Press

Booth, A. St J. & Stone, J.F.S. 1952. A trial flint mine at Durrington, Wiltshire. *Wiltshire Archaeological and Natural History Magazine* 54, 381–8

Borrell, F. & Estrada, A. 2009. Elements ornamentals Neolítics de variscite trobats a les mines 83 I 85 de Gavà. *Rubricatum* 4, 165–74

Borrell, F., Bosch, J. & Majó, T. 2015. Life and death in the Neolithic variscite mines at Gavà (Barcelona, Spain). *Antiquity* 89, 72–90

Borrell, F., Bosch, J. & Vincente, O. 2009. Datacions per radiocarbon a les mines Neolítiques de la serra de les ferreres de Gavà. *Rubricatum* 4, 241–6

Bostyn, F. 1997. Characterization of flint production and distribution of the tabular Bartonian Flint during the early Neolithic (Villeneuve-Saint-Germain period) in France. In Schild & Sulgostowska (eds) 1997, 171–83

Bostyn, F. & Lanchon, Y. 1992. *Jablines, Le Haut Château (Seine-et-Marne): Une minière de silex au Néolithique*. Paris: Editions de la Maison des Sciences de l'Homme, Documents d'Archéologie Française 35

Bottrell, W. 1873. *Traditions and Hearthside Stories of West Cornwall*, Vol. II. Penzance: Beare and Sons

Bourdieu, P. 1977. *Outline of a Theory of Practice*. Cambridge: Cambridge University Press

Bourdieu, P. 1990. *The Logic of Practice*. Cambridge: Polity Press

Bourke, J.G. 1984. *Snake-Dance of the Moquis*. Tucson AZ. University of Arizona (originally published in 1884)

Bowers, A.W. 1950. *Mandan Social and Ceremonial Organisation*. Chicago IL. University of Chicago Press

Bowers, A.W. 1992. *Hidatsa Social and Ceremonial Organisation*. Lincoln NE: University of Nebraska Press, Bison Books

Brace, S., Diekmann, Y., Booth, T.J., Faltyskova, Z., Rohland, N., Mallick, S., Ferry, M., Michel, M., Oppenheimer, J., Broomandkhoshbacht, N., Stewardson, K., Walsh, S., Kayser, M., Schulting, R., Craig, O.E., Sheridan, A., Parker Pearson, M., Stringer, C., Reich, D., Thomas, M.G., & Barnes, I. 2018. *Population Replacement in Early Neolithic Britain* [http://dx.doi.org/10.1101/267443, accessed 18/02/18]

Brace, S., Diekmann, Y., Booth, T.J., van Dorp, L., Faltyskova, Z., Rohland, N., Mallick, S., Olalde, I., Ferry, M., Michel, M., Oppenheimer, J., Broomandkhoshbacht, N., Stewardson, K., Martiniano, R., Walsh, S., Kayser, M., Charlton, S., Hellenthal, G., Armit, I., Schulting, R., Craig, O.E., Sheridan, A., Parker Pearson, M., Stringer, C., Reich, D., Thomas, M.G. & Barnes, I. 2019. Ancient genomes indicate population replacement in Early Neolithic Britain. *Nature Ecology & Evolution* 3, 765–71 [https://doi.org/10.1038/s41559-019-0871-9, accessed 25/05/19]

Brady, J.E. & Rissolo, D. 2006. A reappraisal of Ancient Maya cave mining. *Journal of Anthropological Research* 62(4), 471–90

Bradley, R. 1987. Stages in the chronological distribution of hoards and votive deposits. *Proceedings of the Prehistoric Society* 53, 351–62

Bradley, R. 1990. *The Passage of Arms: an archaeological analysis of prehistoric hoards and votive deposits*. Cambridge: Cambridge University Press

Bradley, R. 1998. *The Significance of Monuments: on the shaping of human experience in Neolithic and Bronze Age Europe*. London: Routledge

Bradley, R. 2000. *An Archaeology of Natural Places*. London: Routledge

Bradley, R. 2001. Orientations and origins: a symbolic dimension to the long house in Neolithic Europe. *Antiquity* 75, 50–6

Bradley, R. 2010. Dead stone and living rock. In O'Connor *et al*. (eds) 2010, 1–8

Bradley, R. & Edmonds, M. 1988. Fieldwork at Great Langdale, Cumbria, 1985–1987: preliminary report. *Antiquaries Journal* 68, 181–209

Bradley, R. & Edmonds, M. 1993. *Interpreting the Axe Trade: production and exchange in Neolithic Britain*. Cambridge: Cambridge University Press

Bradley, R. & Ford, S. 1986. The siting of Neolithic stone quarries – experimental archaeology at Great Langdale, Cumbria. *Oxford Journal of Archaeology* 5(2), 123–8

Bradley, R. & Suthren, R. 1990. Petrographic analysis of hammerstones from the Neolithic quarries at Great Langdale. *Proceedings of the Prehistoric Society* 56, 117–22

Bradley, R., Watson, A. & Style, P. 2019. After the axes? The rock art at Copt Howe, North–west England, and the Neolithic sequence at Great Langdale. *Proceedings of the Prehistoric Society* 85, 177–92

Brophy, K. & Barclay, G. 2009. *Defining a Regional Neolithic:*

*the evidence from Britain and Ireland*. Oxford: Neolithic Studies Group Seminar Papers 9

Brown, A. 2007. Dating the onset of cereal cultivation in Britain and Ireland: the evidence from charred cereal grains. *Antiquity* 81, 1042–52

Brown, F., Dickson, A. & Evans, H. 2019. Crossing the divide: raw material use in the north–west of the British Isles in the late Mesolithic and Neolithic. In Teather *et al.* (eds) 2019, 149–62

Bruce, J.R. & Megaw, E.M. 1947. A Neolithic Site at Ronaldsway, Isle of Man. *Proceedings of the Prehistoric Society* 13, 139–60

Bryan, K. 1950. *Flint Quarries – the Sources of Tools and, at the Same Time, the Factories of the American Indians*. Cambridge MA: Harvard University Peabody Museum Papers 17(3)

Brumm, A. 2004. An axe to grind: symbolic considerations of stone axe use in Ancient Australia. In Boivin & Owoc (eds) 2004, 143–63

Brumm, A. 2010. 'The falling sky': symbolic and cosmological associations of the Mt William greenstone axe quarry, central Victoria, Australia. *Cambridge Archaeological Journal* 20(2), 179–96

Brumm, A. 2011. Power tools: symbolic considerations of stone axe production and exchange in 19th century south–eastern Australia. In Davis & Edmonds (eds) 2011a, 85–97

Burrow, S. 2011. The Mynydd Rhiw quarry site: recent work and its implications. In Davis & Edmonds (eds) 2011a, 247–60

Burrow, S., Jackson, H. & Blackamore, N. 2011. New discoveries at the Mynydd Rhiw axehead production site. In Saville (ed.) 2011a, 107–115

Burton, J. 1984. Quarrying in a tribal society. *World Archaeology* 16, 234–47

Calder, C.S.T. 1938. Excavations of three Neolithic chambered cairns – one with an upper and a lower chamber – in the islands of Eday and Calf of Eday in Orkney. *Proceedings of the Society of Antiquaries of Scotland* 72, 193–216

Capote, M., Consuegra, S., Díaz-del-Río, P. & Terradas, X. (eds). 2011. *Proceedings of the 2nd International Conference of the UISPP Commission on Flint Mining in Pre- and Protohistoric Times (Madrid, 14–17 October 2009)*. Oxford: British Archaeological Report S2260

Care, V. 1979. The production and distribution of Mesolithic Axes in southern England. *Proceedings of the Prehistoric Society* 45, 93–102

Case, H. 1973. A ritual site in north-east Ireland. In G. Daniel & P. Kjaerum (eds), *Megalithic Graves and Ritual*, 173–96. Copenhaven: Jutland Archaeological Society

Cassen, S. 2012. L'objet possédé, sa representation: mise en contexte general avec stele et gravures. In Pétrequin *et al.* 2012a, 1310–53

Cassen, S., & Grimaud, V. 2020. Resolution of a sign (1). Regarding a Neolithic slab in the Petit Mont passage grave (Arzon, France). *Camera praehistorica* 2(5), 25–41 [doi: 10.31250/2658-3828-20202-25-41, accessed 26/08/20]

Cassen, S., Boujot, C., Errera, M., Menier, D., Pailler, Y., Pétrequin, P., Marguerie, D., Veyrat, E., Vigier, E., Poirier, S., Dagneau, C., Degez, D., Lorho, T., Neveu-Derotrie, H., Obeltz, C., Scalliet, F. & Sparfel, Y. 2010. Un dépôt sous–marin de lames polies néolithiques en jadéitite et sillimanite, et un ouvrage de stèles submergé sur la plage dite du Petit Rohu près Saint-Pierre-Quiberon (Morbihan). *Bulletin de la Société préhistorique française* 107(1), 53–84

Cassen, S., Boujot, C., Dominguez Bella, S., Guiavarc'h, M., Le Pennec, C., Prieto Martinez, M.P., Querré, G., Santrot, M.-H. & Vigier, E. 2012. Dépôts bretons, tumulus carnacéens et circulations à longue distance. In Pétrequin *et al.* (eds) 2012b, 918–95

Cassidy, L.M., Ó Maoldúin, R., Kador, T., Lynch, A., Jones, C., Woodman, P.C., Murphy, E., Ramsey, G., Dowd, M., Noonan, A., Campbell, C., Jones, E.R., Mattiangeli, V. & Bradley, D.G. 2020. A dynastic elite in monumental Neolithic society. *Nature* 582, 384–8

Chappell, J. 1966. Stone axe factories in the Highlands of East New Guinea. *Proceedings of the Prehistoric Society* 32, 96–121

Chappell, S. 1987. *Stone Axe Morphology and Distribution in Neolithic Britain*. Oxford: British Archaeological Report 177

Chatterton, R. 2006. Ritual. In Conneller & Warren (eds) 2006, 101–20

Cherry, J. & Cherry, P.J. 1973. Mesolithic habitation sites at St Bees, Cumberland. *Transactions of the Cumberland and Westmorland Antiquarian and Archaeological Society* 173, 47–66

Cherry, J. & Cherry, P.J. 1983. Prehistoric habitation sites in West Cumbria: part 1, the St Bees area and north to the Solway. *Transactions of the Cumberland and Westmorland Antiquarian and Archaeological Society* 183, 1–14

Cherry, P.J. 2009. Flint and tuff in prehistoric Cumbria. *Internet Archaeology* 26 [https://doi.org/10.11141/ia.26.3, accessed 27/08/19]

Childe, V.G. 1956. *Piecing Together the Past*. London: Praeger

Childs, S.T. & Killick, D. 1993. Indigenous African metallurgy: nature and culture. *Annual Review of Anthropology* 22, 317–37

Clark, C.P. & Martin, S.R. 2005. A risky business: late Woodland copper mining on Lake Superior. In Topping & Lynott (eds) 2005, 110–22

Clark, J.G.D. & Rankine, W.F. 1939. Excavations at Farnham, Surrey (1937–38): the Horsham Culture and the question of Mesolithic dwellings. *Proceedings of the Prehistoric Society* 5(1), 61–118

Clarke, W.G. (ed.) 1915. *Report on the Excavations at Grime's Graves, Weeting, Norfolk, March–May 1914*. London: Prehistoric Society of East Anglia

Clason, A.T. 1981. The Flintminer as a Farmer, Hunter and Antler Collector. In F.H.G. Engelen (ed.), *Third International Symposium on Flint, 24–27 Mei 1979, Maastricht*, 119–25. Maastricht: Nederlandse Geologische Vereniging

Cleal, R. 2004. The dating and diversity of the earliest ceramics of Wessex and south west England. In R. Cleal & J. Pollard (eds), *Monuments and Material Culture*, 164–92. Salisbury: Hobnob Press

Cleghorn, P.L. 1984. An historical review of Polynesian stone adze studies. *Journal of the Polynesian Society* 93(4), 399–422

Clough, T.H. McK. 1973. Excavations on a Langdale axe chipping site in 1969 and 1970. *Transactions of the Cumberland & Westmorland Antiquarian & Archaeological Society*, NS 78, 25–46

Clough, T.H. McK. 1988. Introduction to the regional

reports: prehistoric stone implements from the British Isles. In Clough & Cummins (eds) 1988, 1–11

Clough, T.H. McK. & Cummins, W.A. (eds). 1979. *Stone Axe Studies*. London: Council for British Archaeology Research Report 23

Clough, T.H. McK. & Cummins, W.A. (eds). 1988. *Stone Axe Studies, Volume 2*. London: Council for British Archaeology Research Report 67

Clutton-Brock, J. 1984. *Excavations at Grimes Graves, Norfolk, 1972–1976, Fascicule 1: Neolithic antler picks from Grimes Graves, Norfolk, and Durrington Walls, Wiltshire: a biometrical analysis*. London: British Museum Press

Coles, B. & Coles, J. 1986. *Sweet Track to Glastonbury: the Somerset Levels in prehistory*. London: Thames & Hudson

Coles, J.M., Hibbert, F.A. & Orme, B.J. 1973. Prehistoric roads and tracks in Somerset: 3. the Sweet Track. *Proceedings of the Prehistoric Society* 39, 256–93

Coles, J.M., Orme, B., Bishop, A.C. & Wooley, A.R. 1974. A jade axe from the Somerset Levels. *Antiquity* 48, 216–20

Collet, H. & Bostyn, F. 2011. Diffusion du silex de Spiennes et du silex Bartonien du Bassin parisien dans le Nord de la France et en Belgique de la fin du 5e millénaire au début du 4e millénaire BC: une première approche. *Revue Archéologique de Picardie* 28, 331–48

Collet, H., Lavachery, P., & Woodbury, M. 2016. Raw material exploitation strategies on the flint mining site of Spiennes (Hainaut, Belgium). *Journal of Lithic Studies* 3(2) [doi: 10.2218/jls.v3i2.1821, accessed 26/04/17]

Collins, A.E.P. 1978. Excavations on Balleygalley Hill, County Antrim. *Ulster Journal of Archaeology* 41, 15–32

Collins, T. & Coyne, F. 2003. Fire and water … Early Mesolithic cremations at Castleconnell, Co. Limerick. *Archaeology Ireland* 64, 24–7

Conneller, C. 2006. Death. In Conneller & Warren (eds) 2006, 139–64

Conneller, C. & Warren, G. (eds) 2006. *Mesolithic Britain and Ireland: new approaches*. Stroud: Tempus

Consuegra, S. & Díaz-del-Río, P. 2018. Early prehistoric flint mining in Europe: a critical review of the radiocarbon evidence. In D.H. Werra & M. Woźny (eds), *Between History and Archaeology:pPapers in honour of Jacek Lech*, 1–9. Oxford: Archaeopress Archaeology

Consuegra, S., Castañeda, N., Capdevila, E., Capote, M., Criado, C., Casas, C., Nieto, A. & Díaz-del-Río, P. 2018. The Early Neolithic flint mine of Casa Montero (Madrid, Spain), 5350–5220 cal BC. *Trabajos de Prehistoria* 75(1), 52–66

Cooney, G. 1998. 'Breaking stones, making places: the social landscape of axe production sites'. In A. Gibson & D. Simpson (eds), *Prehistoric Ritual and Religion*, 108–18. Stroud: Sutton

Cooney, G. 2000. *Landscapes of Neolithic Ireland*. London: Routledge

Cooney, G. 2004. Neolithic worlds; islands in the Irish Sea. In V. Cummings & C. Fowler (eds), *The Neolithic of the Irish Sea: materiality and traditions of practice*, 145–59. Oxford: Oxbow Books

Cooney, G. 2005. Stereo porphyry: quarrying and deposition on Lambay Island, Ireland. In Topping & Lynott (eds) 2005, 14–29

Cooney, G. 2009. The role of islands in defining identity and regionality during the Neolithic: the Dublin coastal group. In Brophy & Barclay (eds) 2009, 106–18

Cooney, G., Mandal, S. & O'Keefe, E. 2011. The Irish Stone Axe Project: reviewing progress, future prospects. In Davis & Edmonds (eds) 2011a, 427–42

Cooney, G. 2015. Stone and flint axes in Neolithic Europe. In Fowler *et al.* (eds) 2015, 515–34

Cooney, G. 2017. The role of stone in Island societies in Neolithic Atlantic Europe: creating places and cultural landscapes. *Arctic* 69(1), 1–12 [doi: https://doi.org/10.14430/arctic4666, accessed 24/06/17]

Cooney, G. & Mandal, S. 1998. *The Irish Stone Axe Project: monograph 1*. Bray: Wordwell

Cooney, G., Mandal, S. & O'Keefe, E. 2011. The Irish stone axe project: reviewing progress, future prospects. In Davis & Edmonds (eds) 2011a, 427–42

Cooney, G., Ballin, T., Davis, V., Sheridan, A. & Megarry, W. 2014. *Making and Island World: Neolithic Shetland. 2013 field season report North Roe Felsite Project Newsletter 1*. Dublin: University College Dublin School of Archaeology

Cooney, G., Gaffrey, J., Gilhooly, B., Megarry, W., O'Neill, B. & Sands, R. 2017. *NRFP 2014 and 2016 Field Seasons. Making an Island World: Neolithic Shetland. North Roe Felsite Project Report 4*. Dublin: University College Dublin, School of Archaeology

Costa, L.J. 2007. *L'Obsidienne: un témoin d'échanges en Méditerranée préhistorique*. Paris: Editions Errance

Costa, L.J., Sternke, F. & Woodman, P.C. 2005. Microlith to macrolith: the reasons behind the transformation of production in the Irish Mesolithic. *Antiquity* 79, 19–33

Coudart, A. 2015. The Bandkeramik Longhouses: a material, social, and mental metaphor for small-scale sedentary societies. In Fowler *et al.* (eds) 2015, 309–25

Coutts, P.J.F. 1971. Greenstone: the prehistoric exploitation of bowenite from Anita Bay, Milford Sound. *Journal of the Polynesian Society* 80(1), 42–73

Craddock, P.T., Cowell, M.R. & Hughes, M.J. 2012. The provenancing of flint axes by chemical analysis and the products of the Grimes Graves mines: a reassessment. In Longworth *et al.* 2012, 145–57

Craddock, P.T., Cowell, M.R., Leese, M.N. & Hughes, M.J. 1983. The trace element composition of polished flint axes as an indicator of source. *Archaeometry* 25(2), 135–64

Crawford, O.G.S. 1937. Causewayed settlements. *Antiquity* 11, 210–12

Crothers, G.M. 2012. Early Woodland ritual use of caves in eastern North America. *American Antiquity* 77(3), 524–41

Cunnington, M.E. 1929. *Woodhenge*. Devizes: George Simpson

Curwen, E. & Curwen, E.C. 1926. Harrow Hill flint-mine excavation 1924–5. *Sussex Archaeological Collections* 67, 103–38

Danaher, E. 2007. *Monumental Beginnings: the archaeology of the N4 Sligo Inner Relief Road*. Dublin: National Roads Authority

Darbishire, R.D. 1874. Notes on discoveries at Ehenside Tarn, Cumberland. *Archaeologia* 44, 273–92

Darvill, T. 2019. Carn Menyn and the stones of southwest Wales. In Teather *et al.* (eds) 2019, 115–32

Darvill, T. & Wainwright, G. 2014. Beyond Stonehenge: Carn Menyn Quarry and the origin and date of

## Bibliography

bluestone extraction in the Preseli Hills of south-west Wales. *Antiquity* 88, 1099–14

David, A. 2007. *Palaeolithic and Mesolithic Settlement in Wales with Special Reference to Dyfed*. Oxford: British Archaeological Report 448

David, A. & Walker, E. 2004. Wales during the Mesolithic period. In A. Saville (ed.) *Mesolithic Scotland and its Neighbours: The Early Holocene prehistory of Scotland, its British and Irish context, and some North European perspectives*, 299–338. Edinburgh: Society of Antiquaries of Scotland

Davis, L.B., Aaberg, S.A., Schmitt, J.G. & Johnson, A.M. 1995. *The Obsidian Cliff Plateau Prehistoric Lithic Source, Yellowstone National Park, Wyoming*. Denver OH: National Park Service, Rocky Mountain Region, Selections from the Division of Cultural 6

Davis, V. & Edmonds, M. (eds), 2011a. *Stone Axe Studies III*. Oxford: Oxbow Books

Davis, V. & Edmonds, M. (eds), 2011b. A time and place for the Belmont Hoard. In Davis & Edmonds (eds) 2011a, 167–86

Dean, C. 2010. *A Culture of Stone: Inka perspectives on Rock*. Durham NC & London: Duke University Press

DeCory, S. & DeCory, J. 1989. The gift of the sacred pipe. *Coteau Heritage* 2(1), 18–19

Demoule, J.-P. (ed) 2007. *La révolution néolithique en France*. Paris: La Découverte

DeRegnaucourt, T. & Georgiady, J. 1998. *Prehistoric Chert Types of the Midwest*. Arcanum OH: Occasional Monographs Series of the Upper Miami Valley Archaeological Research Museum 7

Di Lernia, S. 1997. Local and mid-range exchange in the south-eastern Neolithisation process in Italy: the problem of lithic raw material distribution. In Schild & Sulgostowska (eds) 1997, 217–23

Di Lernia, S., Fiorentino, G., Galiberti, A. & Basili, R. 1995. The Early Neolithic mine of Defensola 'A' (I 18): flint exploitation in the Gargano area in Southern Italy. *Archaeologia Polona* 33, 119–32

Domínguez-Bella, S., Ramos Muñoz, J. & Martínez, J. 2011. Prehistoric flint exploitation in Loma de Enmedio-Realillo (Tarifa coast, Cadiz, Spain). In Capote *et al.* (eds) 2011, 193–202

Dubois, C. 1935. Wintun thnography. *University of California Publications in American Archaeology and Ethnology* 28(5), 279–403

Edinborough, K., Shennan, S., Teather, A., Baczkowski, J., Bevan, A., Bradley, R., Cook, G., Kerig, T., Parker Pearson, M., Pope, A. & Schauer, P. 2019. New radiocarbon dates show early Neolithic date of flint-mining and stone quarrying in Britain. *Radiocarbon* 62(1), 75–105 [doi:10.1017/RDC.2019.85, accessed 26/04/20]

Edmonds, M. 1993. Interpreting causewayed enclosures in the past and the present. In C. Tilley (ed.), *Interpretative Archaeology*, 99–142. Oxford: Berg

Edmonds, M. 1995. *Stone Tools and Society*. London: Batsford

Edmonds, M. 2012. Axes and mountains: a view from the West. In Pétrequin *et al.* 2012a, 1194–207.

Edmonds, M., Sheridan, A. & Tipping, R. 1992. Survey and excavation at Creag na Caillich, Killin, Perthshire. *Proceedings of the Society of Antiquaries of Scotland* 122, 77–112

Edmonds, M., Johnston, R., La Trobe-Bateman, E.,
Roberts, J.G. & Warren, G. 2004. Bardsey Island (SH117224). *Archaeology in Wales* 44, 146–7

Ellaby, R. 1987. The Upper Palaeolithic and Mesolithic in Surrey. In J. Bird & D.G. Bird (eds), *The Archaeology of Surrey to 1540*, 53–69. Guildford: Surrey Archaeological Society

Emerson, T.E. & Hughes, R.E. 2000. Figurines, flint clay sourcing, the Ozark Highlands, and Cahokian acquisition. *American Antiquity* 65, 79–101

Engel, F. & Siegmund, F. 2005. Radiocarbon dating of the Neolithic flint mine at Kleinkems (near Efringen-Kirchen, District Lörrach, Baden-Württemberg, Germany). *Antiquity* Project Gallery 79(306) [doi: http://www.antiquity.ac.uk/projgall/siegmund306/, accessed 06/09/20]

Felder, P.J., Rademakers, P.C.M. & de Grooth, M.E.Th. 1998. *Excavations of Prehistoric Flint Mines at Rijkholt-St. Geertruid (Limburg, The Netherlands)*. Bonn: Archäologische Berichte 12

Fell, C. 1951. The Great Langdale stone-axe factory. *Transactions of the Cumberland and Westmorland Antiquarian and Archaeological Society* 50, 1–14

Fell, C.I. & Davis, R.V. 1988. The petrological identification of stone implements from Cumbria. In Clough & Cummins (eds) 1988, 71–77

Field, D. 1989. Tranchet axes and Thames picks: Mesolithic core tools from the West London Thames. *Transactions of the London and Middlesex Archaeological Society* 40, 1–26

Field, D. 2006. *Earthen Long Barrows: the earliest monuments in the British Isles*. Stroud: Tempus

Field, D. 2008. *Use of Land in Central Southern England during the Neolithic and Early Bronze Age*. Oxford: British Archaeological Report 458

Field, D. 2011a. The origins of flint extraction in Britain. In Capote *et al.* (eds) 2011, 29–34

Field, D. 2011b. Seamer axeheads in southern England. In Saville (ed.) 2001a, 153–78

Field, D. 2011c. Neolithic ground axe–heads and munuments in Wessex. In Davis & Edmonds (eds) 2011a, 325–32

Field, D. 2012. Porourangi: a Maori symbol of war, peace and identity. In J. Trigg (ed.), *Of Things Gone But Not Forgotten: essays in archaeology for Joan Taylor*, 55–61. Oxford: British Archaeological Report S2434

Field, D. & Cotton, J. 1987. Neolithic Surrey: a survey of the evidence. In J. Bird & D.G. Bird (eds), *The Archaeology of Surrey to 1540*, 71–96. Guildford: Surrey Archaeological Society

Field, D. & McOmish, D. 2016. *Neolithic Horizons: monuments and changing communities in the Wessex landscape*. Fonthill: Fonthill Media

Field, D. & Wooley, A.R. 1983. A jadeite axe from Staines Moor. *Surrey Archaeological Collections* 74, 141–5

Firth, R. 1951. *Elements of Social Organisation*. London: Watts

Fischer, A. 2002. Food for feasting? An evaluation of explanations of the Neolithisation of Denmark and southern Sweden. In A. Fischer & K. Kristiansen (eds), *The Neolithisation of Denmark: 150 Years of Debate*, 343–93. Sheffield: JR Collis

Flood, J. 1995. *The Archaeology of the Dreamtime* (rev. edn). London: Collins

Flood, J. 1997. *Rock Art of the Dreamtime*. London: Harper Collins

Fogelin, L. & Schiffer, M.B. 2015. Rites of passage and other rituals in the life histories of objects. *Cambridge Archaeological Journal* 25(4), 815–27

Fowler, C. 2004. *The Archaeology of Personhood.* Abingdon: Routledge

Fowler, C., Harding, J. & Hofmann, D. (eds). 2015. *The Oxford Handbook of Neolithic Europe.* Oxford: Oxford University Press

French, C., Lewis, H., Allen, M., Green, M., Scaife, R. & Gardiner, J. 2007. *Prehistoric Landscape Development and Human Impact in the Upper Allen Valley, Cranborne Chase, Dorset.* Cambridge: McDonald Institute

Gell, A. 1998. *Art and Agency: an anthropological theory.* Oxford: Clarendon

Gero, J. 1989. Assessing social information in material objects: how well do lithics measure up? In R. Torrence (ed.), *Time, Energy and Stone Tools*, 92–105. Cambridge: Cambridge University Press

Gero, J. 1991. Genderlithics: women's roles in stone tool production. In J. Gero & M. Conkey (eds), *Engendering Archaeology: women and prehistory.* 163–93. Oxford: Blackwell

Gijn, A. van 2009. The use of exotic flint and the Neolithisation of the Lower Rhine Basin (NL). *Internet Archaeology* 26 [doi: https://doi.org/10.11141/ia.26.35, accessed 04/06/19]

Gijn, A. van 2010a. The ideological significance of flint for Neolithic and Bronze Age communities in the Rhine/Meuse Delta of the Netherlands. In O'Connor *et al.* (eds) 2010, 127–37

Gijn, A. van 2010b. *Flint in Focus.* Leiden: Sidestone Press

Gijn, A. van & Raemaekers, D.C.M. 2014. Choosy about stone – the significance of the colour red in the Dutch Funnel Beaker Culture. *Settlement and Coastal Research in the Southern North Sea Region* 37, 195–202

Giligny, F. 2011. Neolithic territories and lithic production: some examples from the Paris Basin and neighbouring regions. In Saville (ed.) 2011a, 179–195

Giligny, F. & Bostyn, F. 2016. *La hache de silex dans le Val de Seine: production et diffusion des haches au Néolithique.* Leiden: Sidestone Press

Giligny, F., Bostyn, F. & Le Maux, N. 2012. Production et importation de haches polies dans le Bassin parisien: typologie, chronologie et influences. In Pétrequin *et al.* 2012a, 1136–67

Giot, P.-R. 1995. *Bretagne des Mégalithes.* Rennes: Éditions Ouest-France

Godelier, M. 1999. *The Enigma of the Gift.* Oxford: Polity Press

Gosden, C. & Marshall, Y. 1999. The cultural biography of objects. *World Archaeology* 31(2), 169–78

Gould, R.A. 1977. Ethno-archaeology; or, where do models come from? In R.V.S. Wright (ed.) *Stone Tools as Cultural Markers*, 162–77. Canberra: Australian Institute of Aboriginal Studies

Green, R.C. 1974. A review of the portable artifacts from Western Samoa. In R.C. Green & J.M. Davidson (eds) *Archaeology in Western Samoa, Volume II.* Auckland: Bulletin of the Auckland Institute and Museum

Green, M. & Allen M. 1997. An early prehistoric shaft on Cranborne Chase. *Oxford Journal of Archaeology* 16(2), 121–32

Greenwell, W. 1870. On the opening of Grime's Graves in Norfolk. *Journal of the Ethnological Society of London* NS 2, 419–39

Grinnell, G.B. 1923. *The Cheyenne Indians: their history and ways of life.* New Haven CO: Yale University Press

Gronenborn, D. Horejs/Börner/Ober 2019 (RGZM/OREA). The 2019.3 version from Hofmann, D., Banffy, E., Gronenborn, D., Whittle, A. & Zimmermann, A. 2019. Als die Menschen sesshaft wurden: Die Jungsteinzeit in Süd– und Mitteldeutschland. In E. Bánffy, K.P. Hofmann & P. von Rummel (eds), *Spuren des Menschen: 800 000 Jahre Geschichte in Europa*, 110–133. Darmstadt: wbg Theiss in Wissenschaftliche Buchgesellschaft (Web Based Graphic)

Grooth, M.E.Th. de 1997. Social and economic interpretations of the chert procurement strategies of the Bandkeramik settlement at Hienheim, Bavaria. *Analecta Praehistorica Leidensia* 29, 91–8

Grooth, M.E.Th. de 2015. The 'Rijckholt' connection: Neolithic extraction and circulation of Lanaye flints. In Kerig & Shennan (eds) 2015, 24–41

Grooth, M.E.Th. de, Lauwerier, R.C.G.M. & ter Schegget M.E. 2011. New $^{14}$C dates from the Neolithic flint mines at Rijckholt-St. Geertruid, the Netherlands. In Capote *et al.* (eds) 2011, 77–89

Gunnerson, J.H. 1998. Mountain lions and pueblo shrines in the American southwest. In N.J. Saunders (ed.), *Icons of Power: feline symbolism in the Americas*, 228–57. London: Routledge

Hall, R.L. 1997. *An Archaeology of the Soul.* Chicago IL: University of Illinois Press

Hammond S. 2005. *Pipeline Route: Mercers Quarry, Merstham to North Park Farm Quarry, Godstone, Surrey. An Archaeological Evaluation.* Reading: Thames Valley Archaeological Services, unpublished excavation report *05/29*

Hampton, O.W. 1997. Rock Quarries and the Manufacture, Trade, and Uses of Stone Tools and Symbolic Stones in the Central Highlands of Irian Jaya, Indonesia: Ethnoarchaeological Perspectives. Unpublished DPhil thesis, Texas A&M University

Harding, P. 1988. The Chalk Plaque Pit, Amesbury. *Proceedings of the Prehistoric Society* 54, 320–6

Harrell, J.A. & Storemyr, P. 2009. Ancient Egyptian quarries – an illustrated overview. In N. Abu-Jaber, E.G. Bloxam, P. Degryse, & T. Heldal (eds), *QuarryScapes: ancient stone quarry landscapes in the Eastern Mediterranean*, 7–50. Trondheim: NO–7491: Geological Survey of Norway Special Publication 12

Hazzeldine Warren, S. 1919. A Stone-axe factory at Graig-Lwyd, Penmaenmawr. *Journal of the Royal Anthropological Institute of Great Britain and Ireland* 49, 342–65

Hazzeldine Warren, S. 1921. Excavations at the stone-axe factory of Graig-Lwyd, Penmaenmawr. *Journal of the Royal Anthropological Institute of Great Britain and Ireland* 51, 165–99

Hazzeldine Warren, S. 1922. The Neolithic stone axes of Graig Lwyd, Penmaenmawr. *Archaeologia Cambrensis* 77(1), 1–32

Healy, F., Bayliss, A., Whittle, A., Allen, M.J., Mercer, R., Rawlings, M., Sharples, N. & Thomas, N. 2011a. South Wessex. In Whittle *et al.* (eds) 2011a, 111–206

Healy, F., Bayliss, A. & Whittle, A. 2011b. Sussex. In Whittle *et al.* (eds) 2011b, 207–62

Healy, F., Marshall, P., Bayliss, A., Cook, G., Bronk Ramsey,

C., Plicht, J. van der & Dunbar, E. 2014. *Grime's Graves, Weeting-with-Broomhill, Norfolk. Radiocarbon dating and chronological modelling.* Portsmouth: English Heritage Research Report Series 27-2014

Healy, F., Marshall, P., Bayliss, A., Cook, G., Bronk Ramsey, C., Plicht, J. van der & Dunbar, E. 2018. When and why? the chronology and context of flint mining at Grime's Graves, Norfolk, England. *Proceedings of the Prehistoric Society* 84, 277–301

Hodder, I. 1982. *Symbols in Action: ethnoarchaeolgical studies in material culture.* Cambridge: Cambridge University Press

Hodder, I. 2012. *Entangled: an archaeology of the relationships between humans and things.* London: Wiley

Hoebel, E. A. 1960. *The Cheyenne: Indians of the Great Plains.* New York: Holt, Rinehart & Winston

Högberg, A. 2006. A technological study of flake debitage attributes from the production of Neolithic Square-Sectioned Axes from Scania South Sweden. In Körlin & Weisgerber (eds) 2006, 387–94

Holleyman, G. 1937. Harrow Hill excavations, 1936. *Sussex Archaeological Collections* 78, 230–51

Holmes, W.H. 1919. *Handbook of Aboriginal American Antiquities, Part 1, Introductory, The Lithic Industries.* Washington DC: Smithsonian Institution, Bureau of American Ethnology Bulletin 60

Houlder, C.H. 1961. The Excavation of a Neolithic Stone Implement Factory on Mynydd Rhiw in Caernarvonshire. *Proceedings of the Prehistoric Society* 27, 108–43

Hughes, D.T. 1995. *Perceptions of the Sacred: A review of selected Native American groups and their relationships with the Catlinite Quarries.* Omaha NE: Report produced for the National Park Service, Midwest Region, Omaha, Nebraska

Hughes, D.T. & Stewart, A.J. 1997. *Traditional Use of Pipestone National Monument: Ethnographic Resources of Pipestone National Monument.* Omaha NE: Report produced for the National Park Service, Midwest Region, Omaha, Nebraska

Ingold, T. 1990. Society, nature and the concept of technology. *Archaeological Review from Cambridge,* 9(1) (Technology in the Humanities), 5–16

Ingold, T. 2000. *The Perception of the Environment. essays on livelihood, dwelling and skill.* London: Routledge

Insoll, T. 2004. *Archaeology, Religion, Ritual.* New York: Routledge

Insoll, T. 2011. *The Oxford Handbook of the Archaeology of Ritual and Religion.* Oxford: Oxford University Press

Jacobi, R.M. 1987. Misanthropic miscellany: musings on British early Flandrian archaeology and other flights of fancy. In P. Rowley-Conwy, M. Zvelebil & H.P. Blankholm (eds), *Mesolithic Northwest Europe: recent trends,* 163–8. Sheffield: Department of Archaeology & Prehistory, University of Sheffield

Jensen, H.J. 1994. *Flint tools and Plant Working.* Åarhus: Åarhus University Press

Jones, K.L. 1984. Polynesian quarrying and flaking practises at the Samson Bay and Falls Creek argillite quarries, Tasman Bay, New Zealand. *World Archaeology* 16(2), 248–66

Jope, E.M. 1952. Porcellanite axes from factories in north-east Ireland: Tievebulliagh and Rathlin. *Ulster Journal of Archaeology* 15, 31–55

Karsten, P. 1994. Att Kasta Yxan i Sjön. Stockholm: *Acta Archaeologica Lundensia* 8(23).

Kerig, T, Edinborough, K., Downey, S & Shennan, S. 2015. A radiocarbon chronology of European flint mines suggests a link to population patterns. In Kerig & Shennan (eds) 2015, 116–64

Kennedy, R. 1934. Bark-cloth in Indonesia. *Journal of the Polynesian Society* 43, 229–43

Kenney, J. 2008. Recent excavations at Parc Bryn Cegin, Llandygai, near Bangor, North Wales. *Archaeologia Cambrensis* 157, 9–142

Kerig, T. & Shennan, S (eds), 2015. *Connecting Networks: characterising contact by measuring lithic exchange in the European Neolithic.* Oxford: Archaeopress

Kinnes, I.A. 1985. Circumstances not context: the Neolithic of Scotland as seen from outside. *Proceedings of the Society of Antiquaries of Scotland* 115, 15–57

Klassen, L. 2002. The Ertebølle Culture and Neolithic continental Europe. In A. Fischer & K. Kristiansen (eds), *The Neolithisation of Denmark: 150 Years of Debate,* 305–17. Sheffield: JR Collis

Klassen, L. 2004. *Jade und Kupfer. Untersuchungen zum Neolithisierungsprozess im Westlichen Ostseeraum Unter Besonderer Berücksichtigung der Kulturentwicklung Europas 5500–3500 BC.* Moesgård: Jutland Archaeological Society

Knowles, W.J. 1903. Stone axe factories near Cushendall, County Antrim. *Journal of the Anthropological Institute of Great Britain and Ireland* 33, 360–6

Kopytoff, I. 1986. The cultural biography of things: commodities as process. In A. Appadurai (ed.), *The Social Life of Things,* 64–91. Cambridge: Cambridge University Press

Körlin, G. & Weisgerber, G. (eds). 2006. *Stone Age – Mining Age.* Bochum: Deutsches Bergbau-Museum

Kucharek, A. 2012. Gebel el-Silsila. In W. Wendrich (ed.), *UCLA Encyclopedia of Egyptology.* Los Angeles: UCLA [doi: http://digital2.library.ucla.edu/viewItem.do?ark=21198/zz002c2fj3, accessed 24/10/19]

Lane Fox, A.H. 1876. Excavations in Cissbury Camp, Sussex; being a report of the Exploration Committee of the Anthropological Institute for the year 1875. *Journal of the Anthropological Institute of Great Britain and Ireland* 5, 357–90

Larsson, L. (ed.). 1988. *The Skateholm Project I: Man and Environment.* Stockholm: Almqvist & Wiksell

Larsson, L. 1993. The Skateholm project: late Mesolithic coastal settlement in southern Sweden. In P. Bogucki (ed.), *Case Studies in European Prehistory,* 31–62. London: CRC Press

Larsson, L. 2006. Flint and fire – destruction of wealth. In Körlin & Weisgerber (eds) 2006, 403–12

Last, J. 2015. Longhouse lifestyles in the Central European Neolithic. In Fowler *et al.* (eds) 2015, 273–89

Leary, J., Field, D. & Campbell, G. 2013. *Silbury Hill: the largest prehistoric mound in Europe.* Swindon: English Heritage

Lech, J. 2011. Danubian organization of flint mining in the southern part of the Polish Jura: a study from Sąspów near Cracow. In Capote *et al.* (eds) 2011, 117–28

Legge, A.J. 1992. *Excavations at Grimes Graves, Norfolk, 1972–1976, Fascicule 4: Animals, environment and the Bronze Age economy.* London: British Museum Press

Le Rouzic, Z. 1932. *Tumulus du Mont St Michel.* Vannes: Lafoyle & Lamarzelle

Lewis, J. & Pine, J. 2008. Pendell Farm, Bletchingley, Surrey: an archaeological evaluation, phase 1. Reading:

Thames Valley Archaeological Services, unpublished excavation report 08/13
Lewis-Williams, D. & Pearce, D. 2005. *Inside the Neolithic Mind*. London: Thames & Hudson
Little, A., Gijn, A. van, Colluns, T., Cooney, G., Elliot, B., Gilhooly, B., Charlton, S. & Warren, G. 2017. Stone dead: uncovering early Mesolithic mortuary rites, Hermitage, Ireland. *Cambridge Archaeological Journal* 27(2), 223–43
Lødøen, T. 2013. Concepts of *rock* in Late Mesolithic western Norway. In J. Goldhahn, I. Fuglestvedt & A. Jones (eds), *Changing Pictures: rock art traditions and visions in Northern Europe*, 35–47. Oxford: Oxbow Books
Longworth, I. & Varndell, G. 1996. *Excavations at Grimes Graves, Norfolk, 1972–1976, Fascicule 5: Mining in the deeper mines*. London: British Museum Press
Longworth, I., Varndell, G. & Lech, J. 2012. *Excavations at Grimes Graves, Norfolk, 1972–1976, Fascicule 6: Exploration and excavation beyond the deep mines*. London: British Museum Press
Lothrop, J.C., Burke, A.L., Winchell-Sweeney, S. & Gauthier, G. 2018. Coupling lithic sourcing with least cost path analysis to model Paleoindian pathways in Northeastern North America. *American Antiquity* 83(3), 462–84
Louwe Kooijmans, L.L. 2001a. *Hardinxveld–Giessendam Polderweg. Een mesolithisch jachtkamp in het riviergebied (5500–5000 v. Chr.)*. Amersfoort: Rijksdienst vor het Oudheidkundig Bodemonderzoek
Louwe Kooijmans, L.L. 2001b. *Hardinxveld–Giessendam De Bruin. Een kampplaats uit het Laat–Mesolithicum et het begin van de Swifterbant–vultuur (5500–4450 v. Chr.)*. Amersfoort: Rijksdienst vor het Oudheidkundig Bodemonderzoek
Louwe Kooijmans, L.L. 2007. The gradual transition to farming in the Lower Rhine Basin. In Whittle & Cummings (eds) 2007, 225–42
MacDonald, D.H., Horton, E.A. & Surovell, T.A. 2019. Cougar Creek: quantitative assessment of obsidian use in the Greater Yellowstone ecosystem. *American Antiquity* 84(1), 158–78
Malinowski, B. 1922. *Argonauts of the Western Pacific*. London: Routledge
Mallory, J.P. 1990. Trial excavations at Tievebulliagh, Co. Antrim. *Ulster Journal of Archaeology*, 3 Ser. 53, 15–28
Malo, D. 1951. *Hawaiian Antiquities (Moolelo Hawaii)* (2nd edn). Honolulu: BP Bishop Museum Special Publication 2
Manby, T.G. 1974. *Grooved Ware Sites in the North of England*. Oxford: British Archaeological Report 9
Marcigny, C., Ghesquière, E., Giazzon, D., Tsobgou Ahoupe, R., Charraud, F., Juhel, L. & Giazzon, S. 2011. The flint mine of Ri «Le Fresne». In Capote et al. (eds) 2011, 67–76
Marshall, Y. 2008. Archaeological possibilities for feminist theories of transition and transformation. *Feminist Theory* 9(1), 25–45
Matthiessen, P. (ed) 1989. *George Catlin: North American Indians*. New York: Penguin Books
Mauss, M. 1954. *The Gift: forms and functions of exchange in archaic societies*. London: Routledge (1988 reprint)
Mauss, M. 1979. The notion of body techniques. In M. Mauss, *Sociology and Psychology. Essays 1979*, 97–123. London: Routledge & Keagan Paul
Mauss, M. 1954. *The Gift: Forms and Functions of Exchange in Archaic Societies*. London: Routledge (1988 Reprint)
McBryde, I. 1979. Petrology and prehistory: lithic evidence for exploitation of stone resources and exchange systems in Australia. In Clough & Cummins 1979, 113–126
McBryde, I. 1984. Kulin greenstone quarries: the social contexts of production and distribution for the Mount William site. *World Archaeology* 16, 267–85
McOmish, D., Field, D. & Brown, G. 2010. The Late Bronze Age and Early Iron Age midden site at East Chisenbury, Wiltshire. *Wiltshire Archaeological and Natural History Society Magazine* 103, 35–101
McCoy, M.D., Ladefoged, T.N., Graves, M.W. & Stephen, J.W. 2011. Strategies for constructing religious authority in ancient Hawai'i. *Antiquity* 85, 927–41
McPherson, R.S. 1992. *Sacred Land, Sacred View; Navajo perceptions of the Four Corners region*. Salt Lake City UT: Brigham Young University, Charles Redd Monographs in Western History 19
Mercer, R.J. 1976. Grime's Graves Norfolk – an interim statement on conclusions drawn from the total excavation of a flint mine shaft and a substantial surface area in 1971–2. In C. Burgess & R. Miket (eds), *Settlement and Economy in the Third and Second Millennia B.C.*, 101–12. Oxford: British Archaeological Report 33
Mercer, R.J. 1981a. *Grimes Graves, Norfolk, Excavations 1971–72. Volume I*. London: HMSO
Mercer, R.J. 1981b. *Grimes Graves, Norfolk, Excavations 1971–72. Volume II*. London: HMSO
Midgeley, M. 1992. *TRB Culture: The first farmers of the North European Plain*. Edinburgh: Edinburgh University Press
Miller, D. 2010. *Stuff*. Cambridge: Polity Press
Mills, W.C. 1921. Flint Ridge. *Ohio Archaeological and Historical Publications* 30, 91–161
Milner, N. 2006. Subsistence. In Conneller & Warren (eds) 2006, 61–82
Moore, D.G. 2003. Neolithic houses in Ballyharry townland, Islandmagee, Co. Antrim. In I. Armit, E. Murphy, E. Nelis & D. Simpson (eds), *Neolithic Settlement in Ireland and Western Britain*, 156–63. Oxford: Oxbow Books
Morphy, H. 1995. Landscapes and the reproduction of the Ancestral Past. In E. Hirsch & M. O'Hanlon (eds), *The Anthropology of Landscape*, 184–209. Oxford: Clarendon
Muntoni, I.M. 2012. Circulation of raw materials, final products or ideas in the Neolithic communities of southern Italy: the contribution of archaeometric analyses to the study of pottery, flint and obsidian. *Rubricatum* 5, 403–11
Murray, R.A. 1983. A brief survey of the pipes and smoking customs of the Indians of the Northern Plains. *Minnesota Archaeologist* 42(1 & 2), 81–100
Murray, R.A. 1993. *Pipes on the Plains*. Pipestone MI: Pipestone Indian Shrine Association
Needham, S., Parker Pearson, M., Tyler, A., Richards, M. & Jay, M. 2010. A first 'Wessex 1' date from Wessex. *Antiquity* 84, 363–373
Negrino, F., Martini, S., Ottomano, C. & Del Lucchese, A. 2006. Palaeolithic evidence for quarrying activity at 'I Ciotti' (Mortola Superiore, Ventimiglia, Imperia, Italy). In Körlin & Weisgerber (eds) 2006, 153–62
Nilsson, M., Ward, J., Almásy, A. & Doherty, S. 2015. Gebel el Silsila: field report from the Main Quarry.

*Journal of Intercultural and Interdisciplinary Archaeology* (2), 147–92

Nyland, A. 2015. Humans in Motion and Places of Essence: variations in rock procurement practices in the Stone, Bronze and Early Iron Ages, in southern Norway. Oslo: unpublished PhD Thesis, University of Oslo

Nyland, A. 2017. Quarrying as a socio-political strategy at the Mesolithic–Neolithic transition in southern Norway. In T. Pereira, X. Terradas & N. Bicho (eds), *The Exploitation of Raw Materials in Prehistory: sourcing, processing and distribution*, 30–45. Newcastle upon Tyne: Cambridge Scholars Publishing

Nyland, A. 2019. Being 'Mesolithic' in the Neolithic: practices, places and rock in contrasting regions in South Norway. In Teather *et al.* (eds) 2019, 67–82

Nyland, A.J. 2020. In search of cloudstones? The contribution of charismatic rocks towards an understanding of Mesolithic and Neolithic communities in the montane regions of south Norway. *Proceedings of the Prehistoric Society* 86, 43–64

Oakley, K.P., Rankine, W.F. & Lowther, A.W.G. 1939. *A Survey of the Prehistory of the Farnham District (Surrey)*. Guildford: Surrey Archaeological Society

O'Connor, B., Cooney, G. & Chapman, J. (eds), 2010. *Materialitas: working stone, carving identity*. Oxford: Prehistoric Society Research Papers 3

Olalde, I., Bracc, S., Allentoft, M.E., Armit, I., Kristiansen, K., Booth, T., Rohland, N., Mallick, S., Szecsenyi-Nagy, A., Mittnik, A., Altena, E. *et al.* 2018. The Beaker phenomenon and the genomic transformation of northwest Europe. *Nature* 555, 190–196 [doi:10.1038/nature25738, accessed 10/04/18]

Oliva, M. 2010. *Prehistoric Mining in the 'Krumlovský les' (Southern Moravia): origin and development of an industrial-sacred landscape*. Brno: Moravské Zemské Muzeum

Ono, A., Shimada, K., Hashizume, J., Yoshida, A. & Kumon, F. (eds), 2016. *An Anthropology of the Prehistoric Central Highlands of Japan: the 2011–2013 excavation seasons at the Hiroppara Site Group, Nagano Prefecture*. Tokyo: Meiji University, Center for Obsidian and Lithic Studies, Materials and Reports 1

O'Ríordáin, S. 1954. Lough Gur excavations: Neolithic and Bronze Age houses on Knockadoon. *Proceedings of the Royal Irish Academy* 56C, 297–459

O'Sullivan, A. 1998. *The Archaeology of Lake Settlement in Ireland*. Dublin: Royal Irish Academy

Otake, S., Yajima, K. & Ohta, A. 2020. *Takayama site cluster, Volume VIII. Study of obsidian mine and quarry sites at the Hoshikuso Pass in the central highlands of Japan: a report of archaeological investigations, 2016–2019*. Nagawa, Japan: Obsidian Museum of Archaeology

Pailler, Y. 2009. Neolithic fibrolite working in the west of France. In O'Connor *et al.* (eds) 2010, 113–26

Pailler, Y. 2012a. La fibrolite, un matériau pour façonner des haches, mais encore? Le travail de la fibrolite au Néolithique dans l'Ouest de la France. In P.A. de Labriffe & E. Thirault (eds), *Produire des Haches au Néolithique: de la Matière Première à l'Abandon*, 121–36. Paris: Société Préhistorique Française

Pailler, Y. 2012b. L'exploitation des fibrolites en Bretagne et ses liens avec les productions alpines. In Pétrequin *et al.* 2012a, 1168–93

Park Harrison, J. 1877a. On marks found upon chalk at Cissbury. *Journal of the Anthropological Institute* 6, 263–71

Park Harrison, J. 1877b. Report on some further discoveries at Cissbury. *Journal of the Anthropological Institute* 6, 430–42

Park Harrison, J. 1878. Additional discoveries at Cissbury. *Journal of the Anthropological Institute* 7, 412–33

Patton, M. 1991. An Early Neolithic axe factory at Le Pinacle, Jersey, Channel Islands. *Proceedings of the Prehistoric Society* 57(2), 51–60

Patton, M. 1993. *Statements in Stone: monuments and society in Neolithic Brittany*. London: Routledge

Patton, M. 2001. Le Pinacle, Jersey: a reassessment of the Neolithic, Chalcolithic and Bronze age horizons. *Archaeological Journal* 158, 1–61

Peake, A.E. 1919. Excavations at Grime's Graves during 1917. *Proceedings of the Prehistoric Society of East Anglia* 2(2), 268–319

Pennington, W. 1991. Palaeolimnology in the English Lakes – some questions and answers over fifty years. *Hydrobiologia* 214, 9–24

Pennington, W. & Tutin, T.G. 1964. Pollen analysis from the deposits of six upland tarns in the Lake District. *Philosophical Transactions of the Royal Society of London, Series B, Biological Sciences* 248, 746, 205–44

Pétrequin, P. & Pétrequin, A.-M. 1993. *Ecologie d'un outil: La hache de pierre en Irian Jaya (Indonesie)*. Paris: CNRS Editions

Pétrequin, P. & Pétrequin, A.-M. 2011. The twentieth-century polished stone axeheads of New Guinea: why study them? In Davis & Edmonds (eds) 2011, 333–49

Pétrequin, P. & Pétrequin, A.-M. 2012. Chronologie et organisation de la production dans le massif du Mont Viso. In Pétrequin *et al.* 2012a, 214–57

Pétrequin, P. & Pétrequin, A.-M. 2020. *Ecology of a Tool: The ground stone axes of Irian Jaya (Indonesia)*. Oxford: Oxbow Books

Pétrequin, P., Gauthier, E., & Pétrequin, A.-M. 2017. *Jade: Objets-signes et interpretations sociales des jades alpins dans l'Europe néolithique*. Bésancon: Presses universitaires de Franche–Comté 379, Collection << Les Cahiers de la MSHE Ledoux >> 27, Série Dynamiques territoriales 10

Pétrequin, P., Sheridan, A., Cassen, S., Errera, M., Gauthier, E., Klassen, L., Le Maux, N. & Pailler, Y. 2008. Neolithic Alpine axeheads, from the Continent to Great Britain, the Isle of Man and Ireland. *Analecta Praehistorica Leidensia* 40, 261–79

Pétrequin, P., Cassen, S., Errera, M., Klassen, L., Sheridan, A. & Pétrequin, A.M. 2012a. *JADE. Grandes haches alpines du Néolithique européen, V$^e$ au IV$^e$ millénaires av. J.–C.* Bésancon: Presses Universitaires de Franche–Comté 1224, Collection Les cahiers de la MSHE Ledoux 17, Série Dynamiques territoriales 6

Pétrequin, P., Errera, M., Martin, A., Valcarce, R.F. & Vaquer, J. 2012b. Les Haches en jades Alpins pendant les Ve et IVe millénaires, l'exemple de l'Espagne et du Portugal dans une perspective Européenne. *Rubricatum* 5, 213–22

Pétrequin, P., Cassen, S., Klassen, L. & Valcarce, R.F. 2012c. La circulation des haches carnacéennes en Europe occidentale. In Pétrequin *et al.* 2012a, 918–95

Pétrequin, P., Cassen, S., Errera, M., Klassen, L., & Sheridan, A. 2012d. Des choses sacrées … fonctions idéelles des jades alpins en Europe occidentale. In Pétrequin *et al.* 2012a, 1354–423

Pétrequin, P., Sheridan, A., Gauthier, E., Cassen,

S., Errera, M. & Klassen, L. 2015. *Project Jade 2. 'Objects-signs' and social interpretations of Alpine jade axeheads in the European Neolithic: theory and methodology.* In Kerig & Shennan (eds) 2015, 83–102

Piggott, S. 1954. *The Neolithic Cultures of the British Isles.* Cambridge: Cambridge University Press

Piggott, S. 1962. *The West Kennet Long Barrow: Excavations 1955–56.* London: HMSO

Pitts, M. 1996. The stone axe in Neolithic Britain. *Proceedings of the Prehistoric Society* 61, 311–71

Plomley, N.J.B. (ed) 1966. *Friendly Mission: the Tasmanian journals and papers of George Augustus Robinson, 1829–1834.* Hobart: Tasmanian Historical Research Association 904

Popper, K. 2002. *Conjectures and Refutations: the growth of scientific knowledge.* London: Routledge

Pratt, S. & Troccoli, J.C. 2013. *George Catlin: American Indian Portraits.* London: National Portrait Gallery

Price, T.D. & Gebauer, A.B. 2005. *Smakkerup Huse: A Late Mesolithic Coastal Site in Northwest Zealand, Denmark.* Aarhus: Aarhus University Press

PSEA = Proceedings of the Society 1919. No title. *Proceedings of the Society of Antiquaries of Scotland* 53, 118–19

Prost, D., Biard, M., Deloze, V., Gosselin, R. & Lepinay, D. 2017. L'industrie lithique chasséenne de Bernières–sur–Seine « Les Fondriaux » (Eure). *Gallia Préhistoire* 57, 3–27

Pryor, F. 1998. *Etton: Excavations at a Neolithic causewayed enclosure near Maxey Cambridgeshire, 1982–7.* London: English Heritage

Pull, J.H. 1932. *The Flint Miners of Blackpatch.* London: Williams & Norgate

Pye, E. 1968. The Flint Mines at Blackpatch, Church Hill and Cissbury. Unpublished MA Thesis, University of Edinburgh

Rankine, W.F. 1956. *The Mesolithic of Southern England.* Guildford: Research Papers of the Surrey Archaeological Society 4

Rathje, W.L. 1979. Modern material culture studies. In M.B. Schiffer (ed.), *Advances in Archaeological Method and Theory* 2. 1–37. New York: Academic Press

Rech, M. 1979. *Studien zu Depotfunden der Trichterbecher– und Einzelgrabkultur des Nordens.* Neumünster: Offa–Bücher

Renfrew, C. 1975. Trade as action at distance: questions of integration and communication. In J.A. Sabloff & C.C. Lomberg-Karlovsky (eds), *Ancient Civilisation and Trade*, 3–59. Albuquerque NM: University of New Mexico

Renfrew, C. 1993. Trade beyond the material. In C. Scarre & F. Healy (eds), *Trade and Exchange in European Prehistory*, 5–16. Oxford: Oxbow Books

Richards, C. (ed.). 2005. *Dwelling Among the Monuments: the Neolithic village of Barnhouse, Maeshowe passage grave and surrounding monuments at Stenness, Orkney.* Cambridge: McDonald Institute for Archaeological Research

Richards, C. & Jones, R. 2016. *The Development of Neolithic House Societies in Orkney: investigations in the Bay of Firth, Mainland, Orkney (1994–2014).* Oxford: Windgather

Richards, J. 1990. *The Stonehenge Environs Project.* London: English Heritage

Rivollat, M., Jeong, C., Schiffels, S., Küçükkalıpçı, İ., Pemonge, M.-H., Benjamin, A., Rohrlach, A.B., Alt, K.W., Binder, D. *et al.* 2020. Ancient genome–wide DNA from France highlights the complexity of interactions between Mesolithic hunter–gatherers and Neolithic farmers. *Science Advances* 2020 (6) [doi: http://advances.sciencemag.org/, accessed 09/06/20]

Robb, J. 2015. Prehistoric art in Europe: a deep-time social history. *American Antiquity* 80(4), 635–54

Robbins, L.H., Murphy, M.L., Campbell, A. & Brook, G.A. 1996. Excavations at the Tsodilo Hills Rhino Cave. *Botswana Notes and Records* 28, 23–45

Robertson-Mackay, R. 1987. The Neolithic causewayed enclosure at Staines, Surrey: excavations 1961–63. *Proceedings of the Prehistoric Society* 53, 23–128

Robinson, D. 2004. The mirror of the sun: surface, mineral applications and interface in California rock-art. In Boivin & Owoc (eds) 2004, 91–105

Robinson, G., Town, M., Ballin, T.B., Clarke, A., Dunne, J., Evershed, R.P., Gardiner, L.F., Gibson, A. & Russ, H 2020. Furness's first farmers: evidence of Early Neolithic settlement and dairying in Cumbria. *Proceedings of the Prehistoric Society* 86, 165–98

Ross, H.M. 1970. Stone adzes from Malaita, Solomon Islands: an ethnographic contributuion to Melanesian archaeology. *Journal of the Polynesian Society* 79(4), 411–20

Rowley-Conwy, P. & Legge, T. 2015. Subsistence practices in Western and Northern Europe. In Fowler *et al.* (eds) 2015, 429–46

Rudebeck, E. 1998. Flint extraction, axe offering, and the value of cortex. In M. Edmonds & C. Richards (eds), *Understanding the Neolithic of North-Western Europe*, 312–27. Glasgow: Cruithne Press

Russell, M. 2001. *Rough Quarries, Rocks and Hills: John Pull and the flint mines of Sussex.* Oxford: Oxbow Books

Ryan, M. 1980. An Early Mesolithic site in the Irish midlands. *Antiquity* 54, 46–7

Salisbury, E.F. 1961. Prehistoric Flint Mines on Long Down, Eartham. *Sussex Archaeological Collections* 99, 66–73

Saunders, N.J. 2004. The cosmic earth: materiality and minerology in the Americas. In Boivin & Owoc (eds) 2004, 123–141

Saville, A. 1977. Two Mesolithic implement types. *Northamptonshire Archaeology* 12, 3–8

Saville, A. 1995. Prehistoric exploitation of flint from the Buchan Ridge Gravels, Grampian Region, north-east Scotland. *Archaeologia Polona* 33, 353–68

Saville, A. 2002. Lithic artefacts from Neolithic causewayed enclosures: character and meaning. In Varndell & Topping (eds) 2002, 91–106

Saville, A. 2005. Prehistoric quarrying of a secondary flint source: evidence from north–east Scotland. In Topping & Lynott (eds) 2005, 1–13

Saville, A. (ed.) 2011a *Flint and Stone in the Neolithic Period.* Oxford: Oxbow Books.

Saville, A. 2011b Residues at the Neolithic flint extraction site at Den of Boddam, Aberdeenshie, Scotland. In Capote *et al.* (eds) 2011, 19–28

Schiffer, M.B. 1972. Archaeological context and systemic context. *American Antiquity* 37, 156–65

Schiffer, M.B. 1988. The structure of archaeological theory. *American Antiquity* 53, 461–85

Schild, R. & Sulgostowska, Z. (eds). 1997. *Man and Flint.* Warsaw: Institute of Archaeology and Ethnology, Polish Academy of Sciences

Schulting, R.J. 1996. Antlers, bone pins and flint blades:

the Mesolithic cemeteries of Téviec and Hoëdic, Britanny. *Antiquity* 70, 335–50

Scott, L.G. & Calder, C.S.T. 1952. Notes on a chambered cairn, and a working gallery, on the Beorgs of Uyea, Northmaven, Shetland. *Proceedings of the Society of Antiquaries of Scotland* 86, 171–7

Scott, D.D., Thiessen, T.D., Richner, J.J. & Stadler, S. 2006. *An Archeological Inventory and Overview of Pipestone National Monument, Minnesota*. Lincoln NE: United States Department of the Interior, National Park Service, Midwest Archeological Center, Occasional Studies in Anthropology 34

Shaeffer, J.B. 1958. The Alibates flint quarry, Texas. *American Antiquity* 24(2), 189–91

Sharpe, K.E. 2008. Rock art and roughouts. Exploring the sacred and social dimensions of prehistoric carvings at Copt Howe, Cumbria. In A. Mazel, G. Nash & C. Waddington (eds), *Art as Metaphor: the prehistoric rock-art of Britain*, 151–73. Oxford: Archaeopress

Sharpe, K.E. 2015. Connecting the dots: Cupules and communications in the English Lake District. *Expression* 9, 109–16

Sharples, N.M. 1991. *Maiden Castle: excavations and field survey 1985–6*. London: English Heritage

Shaw, G.J. 2014. *The Egyptian Myths*. London: Thames and Hudson

Shee Twohig, E. 1981. *The Megalithic Art of Western Europe*. Oxford: Clarendon

Shennan, S., Bevan, A., Edinborough, K., Kerig, T., Parker Pearson, M. & Schauer, P. 2017. Supply and Demand in Prehistory? Economics of Neolithic Mining in NW Europe (NEOMINE). *Archaeology International* 20, 74–9 [https://doi.org/10.5334/ai-358, accessed 10/12/17]

Sheridan, A. 2004. Neolithic connections along and across the Irish Sea. In V. Cummings & C. Fowler (eds), *The Neolithic of the Irish Sea: materiality and traditions of practice*, 2–9. Oxford: Oxbow Books

Sheridan, A. 2007. From Picardie to Pickering and Pencraig Hill? New information on the 'Carinated Bowl Neolithic' in northern Britain. In Whittle & Cummings (eds) 2007, 441–92

Sheridan, A. 2010. The Neolithisation of Britain and Ireland: the 'big picture'. In B. Finlayson & G.M. Warren (eds), *Landscapes in Transition*, 89–105. Oxford: Council for British Research in the Levant Supplementary Series 8

Sheridan, A. 2012. Neolithic Shetland: a view from the 'mainland'. In D.L. Mahler (ed.), *The Border of Farming and the Cultural Markers*, 6–36. Copenhagen: National Museum of Denmark

Sheridan, A. & Pailler, Y. 2012. Les haches alpines et leurs imitations en Grande–Bretagne, dans l'île de Man, en Irlande et dans les îles Anglo–Normandes. In Pétrequin *et al.* 2012a, 1046–87

Shimada, K., Yoshida, A., Hashizume, J. & Ono, A. 2017. Human responses to climate change on obsidian source exploitation during the Upper Palaeolithic in the Central Highlands, central Japan. *Quaternary International* 442, 12–22

Sillitoe, P. 1988. *Made in Niugini. Technology in the Highlands of Papua New Guinea*. London: British Museum Publications

Simek, J.F., Franklin, J.D. & Sherwood, S.C. 1998. The context of Early Southeastern prehistoric cave art: a report on the archaeology of 3rd Unnamed Cave. *American Antiquity* 63(4), 663–77

Smith, S.P. 1892. Stone implements from the Chatham Islands. *Journal of the Polynesian Society* 1(2), 80–2

Smith, I.F. 1965. *Windmill Hill and Avebury: Excavations by Alexander Keiller 1925–1939*. Oxford: Clarendon

Smith, M.E. 2015. How can archaeologists make better arguments? *SAA Archaeological Record* 15(4), 18–23

Smyth, J. 2012. Breaking ground: an overview of pits and pit-digging in Neolithic Ireland. In H. Anderson-Whymark & J. Thomas (eds), *Regional Perspectives on Neolithic Pit Deposition: beyond the mundane*, 13–29. Oxford: Neolithic Studies Group Seminar Papers 12

Smyth, J. 2014. *Settlement in the Irish Neolithic: new discoveries at the edge of Europe*. Oxford: Prehistoric Society Research Papers 6

Spielmann, K.A. 2002. Feasting, craft specialization, and the ritual mode of production in small-scale societies. *American Anthropologist* 104(1), 195–207

Stanley, L.A. 1999. The Sacred Rock Petroglyph Site & the Seven Sacred Stones. *Abstracts of the 64th Annual Meeting, Chicago, Illinois*, 271. Washington DC: Society for American Archaeology

Stone, J.F.S. 1931. Easton Down, Winterslow, S. Wilts, flint mine excavation, 1930. *Wiltshire Archaeological Magazine* 45, 350–66

Stone, J.F.S. 1933. Excavations at Easton Down, Winterslow 1931–32. *Wiltshire Archaeological Magazine* 46, 225–42

Stone, J.F.S. & Wallis, F.W. 1951. Third report of the Sub-Committee of the South-Western group of Museums and Art Galleries on the petrological identification of stone implements. *Proceedings of the Prehistoric Society* 17, 99–158

Stout, D. 2002. Skill and cognition in stone tool production: an ethnographic case study from Irian Jaya. *Current Anthropology* 43(5), 693–722

Strassburg, J. 2000. *Shamanic Shadows: One Hundred Generations of Undead Subversion in Southern Scandinavia, 7000–4000 BC*. Stockholm: Stockholm University Press

Strathern, M. 1969. Stone axes and flake tools: evaluations from two New Guinea Highlands Societies. *Proceedings of the Prehistoric Society* 35, 311–29

Svoboda, J. 1995. CZ3 Stránská Skála, Brno District. *Archaeologia Polona* 33, 278–81

Taçon, P.S.C. 1991. The power of stone: symbolic aspects of stone use and tool development in western Arnhem Land, Australia. *Antiquity* 65, 192–207

Taçon, P.S.C. 2004. Ochre, clay, stone and art: the symbolic importance of minerals as life-force among Aboriginal Peoples of Northern and Central Australia. In Boivin & Owoc (eds) 2004, 31–42

Tanimoto, S., Stacey, R., Varndell, G. & Sweek, T. 2011. Grimes Graves revisited: a new light on chalk 'lamps'. *British Museum Technical Research Bulletin* 5, 39–47

Tarantini, M., Galiberti, A. & Mazzarocchi, F. 2011. Prehistoric flint mines of the Gargano: an overview. In Capote *et al.* (eds) 2011, 251–63

Teather, A.M. 2008. Mining and Materiality in the British Neolithic. Unpublished PhD thesis, Sheffield University

Teather, A., Topping, P. & Baczkowski, J. (eds), 2019. *Mining and Quarrying in Neolithic Europe: A Social Perspective*. Oxford: Neolithic Studies Group Seminar Papers 16

Thomas, N. 1952. A Neolithic chalk cup from Wilsford in the Devizes Museum: and notes on others. *Wiltshire Archaeological and Natural History Magazine* 57, 452–62

Thompson, M., Bush, P. & Ferguson J. 1986. Flint source determination by plasma spectrometry. In GdeG Sieveking & MB Hart (eds), *The Scientific Study of Flint and Chert*, 243–247. Cambridge: Cambridge University Press

Thorpe, N. 2015. The Atlantic Mesolithic–Neolithic transition. In Fowler *et al.* (eds) 2015, 215–29

Tilley, C. & Thomas, J. 1993. The axe and the torso: symbolic structures in the Neolithic of Brittany. In C. Tilley (ed.), *Interpretative Archaeology*, 225–324. Oxford: Berg

Tipping, R., Edmonds, M. & Sheridan, A. 1993. Palaeo-environmental investigations directly associated with a Neolithic axe 'quarry' on Beinn Lawers, Near Killin, Perthshire, Scotland. *New Phytologist* 123(3), 585–97

Topping, P. 1996. Structure and ritual in the Neolithic house: Some examples from Britain and Ireland. In T. Darvill & J. Thomas (eds), *Neolithic Houses in Northwest Europe and Beyond*, 157–70. Oxford: Neolithic Studies Group Seminar Papers 1

Topping, P. 2005. Shaft 27 Revisited: an ethnography of Neolithic flint extraction. In Topping & Lynott (eds) 2005, 63–93

Topping, P. 2011. The evidence for the seasonal use of the English flint mines. In Capote *et al.* (eds) 2011, 35–43

Topping, P. 2017. The Social Context of Prehistoric Extraction Sites in the UK. Unpublished PhD thesis Newcastle University

Topping, P. 2019a. The social context of lithic extraction in Neolithic Britain and Ireland. In Teather *et al.* (eds) 2019, 179–92

Topping, P. 2019b. The social context of Neolithic flint and stone extraction in Britain and Ireland. *Anthropologica et Præhistorica* 128, 209–225

Topping, P. & Lynott, M. (eds). 2005. *The Cultural Landscape of Prehistoric Mines*. Oxford: Oxbow Books

Torrence, R. 1984. Monopoly or direct access? Industrial organisation at the Melos obsidian quarries. In J.E. Ericson & B.A. Purdy (eds), *Prehistoric Quarries and Lithic Production*, 49–64. Cambridge: Cambridge University Press

Torrence, R. 1986. *Production and Exchange of Stone Tools*. Cambridge: Cambridge University Press

Trnka, G. 2011. The Neolithic radiolarite mining site of Wien-Mauer-Antonshöhe (Austria). In E. Violának (ed.), *Papers in Honour of Viola T. Dobosi*, 287–96. Budapest: Hungarian National Museum

Tsobgou Ahoupe, R., & Marcigny, C. 2011. A new approach for analysing mining production and management combining geomorphological, geological and physical approaches: the case of Ri/Fresne Neolithic flint mine, France. In Capote *et al.* (eds) 2011, 51–66

Varndell, G. & Topping, P. (eds), 2002. *Enclosures in Neolithic Europe*. Oxford: Oxbow Books

Vecsey, C. 1983. *Traditional Ojibwa Religion and its Historical Changes*. Philadelphia PA: American Philosophical Society.

Verhoeven, M. 2011. The many dimensions of ritual. In Insoll (ed.) 2011], [doi: 10.1093/oxfordhb/9780199232444.013.0010, accessed 06/08/18]

Vermeersch, P.M., Paulissen, E., & Van Peer, P. 1995. Palaeolithic chert mining in Egypt. *Archaeologia Polona* 33, 11–30

Vial, L.G. 1941. Stone axes of Mount Hagen, New Guinea. *Oceania* 11, 158–63

Waddington, C., Beswick, P., Brightman, J., Bronk Ramsey, C., Burn, A., Cook, G., Elliot, L., Gidney, L., Haddow, S., Hammon, A., Harrison, K., Mapplethorpe, K., Marshall, P., Meadows, J., Smalley, R., Thornton, A. & Longstone Local History Group 2012. Excavations at Fin Cop, Derbyshire: an Iron Age hillfort in conflict? *Archaeological Journal* 169(1), 159–236

Wade, A.G. 1923. Ancient flint mines at Stoke Down, Sussex. *Proceedings of the Prehistoric Society of East Anglia* 4(1), 82–91

Walderhaug, E.M. 1998. Changing art in a changing society: the hunters' rock-art of western Norway. In C. Chippendale & P.S. Taçon (eds), *The Archaeology of Rock-Art*, 285–301. Cambridge: Cambridge University Press

Walker, D. 1965. The post–glacial period in the Langdale Fells, English Lake District. *New Phytologist* 64(3), 488–510

Walker, K. 2015. Axe-heads and Identity: an investigation into the roles of imported axe-heads in identity formation in Neolithic Britain. Unpublished PhD thesis, University of Southampton

Ward, T. 2012. A Mesolithic chert quarry at Burnetland Farm. The Biggar Gap Project. http://www.biggararchaeology.org.uk/pdf_reports/BURNETLAND_CHERTMINE_REPORT2012.pdf

Warren, S.H. 1921. Excavations at the stone-axe factory of Graig–Lwyd, Penmaenmawr. *The Journal of the Royal Anthropological Institute of Great Britain and Ireland* 51, 165–99

Warren, G. 2006. Technology. In Conneller & Warren (eds) 2006, 13–34

Warren, G. 2007: An archaeology of the Mesolithic of eastern Scotland. Deconstructing culture, constructing identity. In C. Waddington & K. Pedersen (eds), *Mesolithic Studies in the North Sea Basin and Beyond*, 137–50. Oxford: Oxbow Books

Weir, D.A. 1993. Pollen analysis of a small basin deposit, Tievebulliagh, Co. Antrim. *Ulster Journal of Archaeology* 56, 18–24

Weisgerber, G. (ed.). 1999. *5000 Jahre Feuersteinbergbau: Die Suche nach dem Stahl der Steinzeit*. Bochum: Deutschen Bergbau-Museum

Weisler, M.I. 2008. Tracking ancient routes across Polynesian seascapes with basalt artefact geochemistry. In B. David & J. Thomas (eds), *Handbook of Landscape Archaeology*. 536–43. Blue Ridge Summit PA: Altamira Press

Wentink, K. 2006. *Ceci n'est pas une hache: Neolithic depositions in the northern Netherlands*. Leiden: Sidestone Press

Wentink, K. 2008. Crafting axes, producing meaning. Neolithic axe depositions in the northern Netherlands. *Archaeological Dialogues* 15(2), 151–73

Wentink, K. & Gijn, A. van. 2008. Neolithic depositions in the northern Netherlands. In C. Hamon & B. Quilliec (eds), *Hoards from the Neolithic to the Metal Ages: technical and codified practices*, 29–43. Oxford: British Archaeological Report S1758

Werra, D.H. & Kerneder-Gubała, K. 2021. 'Chocolate' flint mining from Final Palaeolithic up to Early Iron

# Bibliography

Age – a review. In F. Bostyn, F. Giligny & P. Topping (eds), *From Mine to User: production and procurement systems of siliceous rocks in the European Neolithic and Bronze Age*, 42–56. Oxford: Archaeopress Archaeology

Wheeler, R.E.M. 1943. *Maiden Castle, Dorset*. London: Report of the Research Committee of the Society of Antiquaries of London 12

Whittle, A. 1996. *Europe in the Neolithic: the creation of new worlds*. Cambridge: Cambridge University Press

Whittle, A. 2003. *The Archaeology of People: dimensions of Neolithic life*. London: Routledge

Whittle, A. & Cummings, V. (eds), 2007. *Going Over: the Mesolithic–Neolithic transition in north-west Europe*. Oxford: Oxford University Press/Proceedings of the British Academy 144

Whittle, A., Pollard, J. & Grigson, C. 1999. *The Harmony of Symbols: the Windmill Hill causewayed enclosure*. Oxford: Oxbow Books

Whittle, A., Healy, F. & Bayliss, A. 2011. *Gathering Time: dating the Early Neolithic enclosures of southern Britain and Ireland*. Oxford: Oxbow Books

Wickham-Jones, C.R. 1990. *Rhum: Mesolithic and later sites at Kinloch, Excavations 1984–86*. Edinburgh: Society of Antiquaries of Scotland Monograph 7

Willet, E.H. 1880. On flint workings at Cissbury, Sussex. *Archaeologia* 45, 337–48

Williams, J.Ll.W. & Davidson, A. 1998. Survey and excavation at the Graig Lwyd Neolithic axe factory, Penmaenmawr. *Archaeology in Wales* 38, 3–21

Winchell, N.H. 1983. Indian pictographs at the Pipestone Quarry. *Minnesota Archaeologist* 42 (1 & 2), 15–18 (reprinted from Winchell, N.H. 1884. *The Geology of Minnesota, Vol 1*, 556–9. Minneapolis MI: Johnson, Smith & Harrison)

Woodman, P.C. 1978. *The Mesolithic in Ireland*. Oxford: British Archaeological Report 58

Woodman, P.C. 1985. *Excavations at Mount Sandel, 1973–77, County Londonderry*. Belfast: HMSO, Northern Ireland Archaeological Monograph 2

Woodman, P.C., Anderson, E. & Finlay, N. 1999. *Excavations at Ferriter's Cove, 1983–85: Last foragers, first farmers in the Dingle Peninsula*. Bray: Wordwell

Woodward, A. & Hunter, J. 2011. *An Examination of Prehistoric Stone Bracers from Britain*. Oxford: Oxbow Books

Wymer, J. 1977. *Gazetteer of Mesolithic sites in England and Wales*. London: Council for British Archaeology Research Report 20

Yakushige, M. & Sato, H. 2014. Shirataki obsidian exploitation and circulation in prehistoric northern Japan. *Journal of Lithic Studies* 1(1), 319–42

Zimmermann, A. 1995. *Austauschsysteme von Silexartefakten in der Bandkeramik Mitteleuropas*. Bonn: Habelt

Zvelebil, M. 1994. Plant use in the Mesolithic and its role in the transition to farming. *Proceedings of the Prehistoric Society* 60, 35–74

Zvelebil, M., Moth, E. & Peterson, J. 1989. 1989:096 – Monvoy, Waterford [doi: https://excavations.ie/report/1989/Waterford/0000930/ , accessed 23/07/19]

# Appendix

## *References to excavation reports and archives, listed alphabetically by site*

Entries are listed by: mine/quarry; excavator; excavation; dates of excavation [brackets] where known; primary archive location; references.

At Grime's Graves there were a number of excavations which were not fully published so have not been used in this study and some confusingly have the same numbering system as certain sites listed below; references to what little has been published about these sites is listed in Longworth and Varndell (1996).

BALLYGALLEY HILL; Collins; Surface Quarry: Collins 1978

BLACK MOUNTAIN; Bell & Bennett; Quarry pits: Bell & Bennett 1923

BLACKPATCH; Pull; Shaft 1 [1923]: Pull Archive, Worthing Museum; Pull 1932, 34–40; Russell 2001, 27–34, 203–204

BLACKPATCH; Pull; Shaft 2 [1923]: Pull Archive, Worthing Museum; Pull 1932, 40–4; Russell 2001, 34–8, 204

BLACKPATCH; Pull; Shaft 3 [1924]: Pull Archive, Worthing Museum; Pull 1932, 44; Russell 2001, 38

BLACKPATCH; Pull; Shaft 3A [1924]: Pull Archive, Worthing Museum; Russell 2001, 38

BLACKPATCH; Pull; Shaft 4: Pull Archive, Worthing Museum; Pull 1932, 44; Russell 2001, 39

BLACKPATCH; Pull; Shaft 5 (see Barrow No. 3) [1927]: Pull Archive, Worthing Museum; Russell 2001, 39–40

BLACKPATCH; Pull; Shaft 6 [1928]: Pull Archive, Worthing Museum; Pull 1932, 44–5; Russell 2001, 41

BLACKPATCH; Pull; Shaft 7 [1930]: Pull Archive, Worthing Museum; Pull 1932, 44; Russell 2001, 41–4

BLACKPATCH; Pull; Shaft 8 (see also Barrow No.12): Pull Archive, Worthing Museum; Pull 1932, 84–7; Russell 2001, 44, 204–6

BLACKPATCH; Pull; Chipping Floor 1: Pull Archive, Worthing Museum; Pull 1932, 49–50; Russell 2001, 45

BLACKPATCH; Pull; Chipping Floor 2 [1928]: Pull Archive, Worthing Museum; Pull 1932, 58–62; Russell 2001, 45–7; Barber 2005, 102

BLACKPATCH; Pull; Chipping Floor 3 [1930]: Pull Archive, Worthing Museum; Pull 1932, 50–1; Russell 2001, 48, 205

BLACKPATCH; Pull; Chipping Floor 4: Pull Archive, Worthing Museum; Pull 1932, 51; Russell 2001, 48, 205

BLACKPATCH; Pull; Barrow No. 1 [1924]: Pull Archive, Worthing Museum; Pull 1932, 64–7; Russell 2001, 48–54

BLACKPATCH; Pull; Barrow No. 2 [1927]: Pull Archive, Worthing Museum; Pull 1932, 67–9; Russell 2001, 54–8

BLACKPATCH; Pull; Barrow No. 3 (see Shaft 5) [1927]: Pull Archive, Worthing Museum; Pull 1932, 69–72; Russell 2001, 58–63; Barber 2005, 100–1

BLACKPATCH; Pull; Barrow No. 4 [1927]: Pull Archive, Worthing Museum; Pull 1932, 72–4; Russell 2001, 63–6

BLACKPATCH; Pull; Barrow No. 5 [1928]: Pull Archive, Worthing Museum; Pull 1932, 74–6; Russell 2001, 66–9

BLACKPATCH; Pull; Barrow No. 6 [1928]: Pull Archive, Worthing Museum; Pull 1932, 76–7; Russell 2001, 69–71

BLACKPATCH; Pull; Barrow No. 7 [1929]: Pull Archive, Worthing Museum; Pull 1932, 77–9; Russell 2001, 71–3; Barber 2005, 102

BLACKPATCH; Pull; Barrow No. 8 [1929]: Pull Archive, Worthing Museum; Pull 1932, 79–80; Russell 2001, 73–5

BLACKPATCH; Pull; Barrow No. 9: Pull Archive, Worthing Museum; Pull 1932, 80–2; Russell 2001, 75–7; Barber 2005, 99

BLACKPATCH; Pull; Barrow No. 10: Pull Archive, Worthing Museum; Pull 1932, 82–83; Russell 2001, 77–78; Barber 2005, 102

BLACKPATCH; Pull; Barrow No. 11: Pull Archive, Worthing Museum; Pull 1932, 83–4; Russell 2001, 78; Barber 2005, 102

BLACKPATCH; Pull; Barrow No. 12 [1930]: Pull Archive, Worthing Museum; Pull 1932, 84–7; Russell 2001, 79–81; Barber 2005, 101–2

CHURCH HILL; Pull; Shaft 1 [1933]: Pull Archive, Worthing Museum; Russell 2001, 87–94; Barber 2005, 102–3

CHURCH HILL; Pull; Shaft 2: Pull Archive, Worthing Museum; Russell 2001, 94

CHURCH HILL; Pull; Shaft 3: Pull Archive, Worthing Museum; Russell 2001, 94

CHURCH HILL; Pull; Shaft 4 [1946–1948]: Pull Archive, Worthing Museum; Russell 2001, 94–102; Barber 2005, 103–4

CHURCH HILL; Pull; Shaft 5A [1948]: Pull Archive, Worthing Museum; Russell 2001, 102–8

CHURCH HILL; Pull; Shaft 6 [1950–1952]: Pull Archive, Worthing Museum; Russell 2001, 108–21

CHURCH HILL; Pull; Shaft 7 [1950–1952]: Pull Archive, Worthing Museum; Russell 2001, 108–21

CHURCH HILL; Pull; Pit A [1934]: Pull Archive, Worthing Museum; Russell 2001, 122–5

CHURCH HILL; Pull; Pit B [1948–1949]: Pull Archive, Worthing Museum; Russell 2001, 125–8

CHURCH HILL; Pull; Pit C [1949]: Pull Archive, Worthing Museum; Russell 2001, 129

CHURCH HILL; Pull; Chipping Floors 1–11: Pull Archive, Worthing Museum; Russell 2001, 132–3

CHURCH HILL; Pull; Chipping Floor 12 [1949]: Pull Archive, Worthing Museum; Russell 2001, 133–6

CHURCH HILL; Pull; Chipping Floor 13 (see also Shafts 6 & 7) [1950–1952]: Pull Archive, Worthing Museum; Russell 2001, 137

CHURCH HILL; Pull; Chipping Floor 14 [1950–1952]: Pull Archive, Worthing Museum; Russell 2001, 137–8

CHURCH HILL; Pull; Chipping Floor 15: Pull Archive, Worthing Museum; Russell 2001, 138

CHURCH HILL; Pull; Barrows 1–10: Pull Archive, Worthing Museum; Russell 2001, 138–49; Barber 2005, 103

CISSBURY; Willett [1873], Tindall [1874]: Willett 1880
CISSBURY; Willett [1874]: Willett 1880
CISSBURY; Lane Fox [1875]: Lane Fox 1876
CISSBURY; Park Harrison; Cave Pit: Park Harrison 1877b; 1878
CISSBURY; Park Harrison; Shaft V: Park Harrison 1878
CISSBURY; Park Harrison; Shaft VI [1877–1878]: Park Harrison 1878
CISSBURY; Pull; Shaft 24 [1955]: Pull Archive, Worthing Museum; Russell 2001, 176–7
CISSBURY; Pull; Shaft 27 [1953]: Pull Archive, Worthing Museum; Russell 2001, 178–89; Topping 2005

CREAG NA CAILLICH; Edmonds *et al.*; East Quarry (Site 1) [1989]: Edmonds *et al.* 1992; Tipping *et al.* 1993

CREAG NA CAILLICH; Edmonds *et al.*; West Quarry (Site 2) [1989]: Edmonds *et al.* 1992; Tipping *et al.* 1993

CREAG NA CAILLICH; Edmonds *et al.*; East Working Floor (Site 3) [1989]: Edmonds *et al.* 1992; Tipping *et al.* 1993

CREAG NA CAILLICH; Edmonds *et al.*; West Working Floor (Site 4) [1989]: Edmonds *et al.* 1992; Tipping *et al.* 1993

DEN OF BODDAM; Saville; Quarry pits: Saville 1995; 2005; 2011b

DURRINGTON; Booth & Stone; Small galleried shafts: Booth & Stone 1952

EASTON DOWN; Stone; Pit B1 (Floor B1) [1930]: Stone 1931

EASTON DOWN; Stone; Pit B1(A) (Floor B2) [1930]: Stone 1931

EASTON DOWN; Stone; B19, B45 & B67 [1931–1932]: Stone 1933

EASTON DOWN; Stone; Pit B49 [1931–1932]: Stone 1933

GOODLAND; Case; Surface Quarrying, pits and segmented ditch enclosure: Case 1973

GRAIGLWYD; Hazzeldine Warren; Floor B [1920–1921]: Hazzeldine Warren 1919; 1921; 1922

GRAIGLWYD; Williams & Davidson; Trench 3 [1992]: Williams & Davidson 1998, 3–21

GRAIGLWYD; Williams & Davidson; Trench 5 [1992]: Williams & Davidson 1998, 9–10

GRAIGLWYD; Williams & Davidson; Site F, Cairn 65 [1993]: Williams & Davidson 1998, 17–18

GRAIGLWYD; Williams & Davidson; Site F, Cairn 67 [1993]: Williams & Davidson 1998, 18–19

GRAIGLWYD; Williams & Davidson; Site F, Mound 3077 (Trench M) [1993]: Williams & Davidson 1998, 15

GRAIGLWYD; Williams & Davidson; Site F, Mound 3078 (Trenches J & R) [1993]: Williams & Davidson 1998, 14–16

GRAIGLWYD; Williams & Davidson; Site F, Mound 3079 (Trench K & Test Pit P) [1993]: Williams & Davidson 1998, 16

GRAIGLWYD; Williams & Davidson; Site F, Test Pits B & F [1993]: Williams & Davidson 1998, 16

GRAIGLWYD; Williams & Davidson; Site F, Test Pit C [1993]: Williams & Davidson 1998, 14

GRAIGLWYD; Williams & Davidson; Site F, Test Pit E [1993]: Williams & Davidson 1998, 12–13

GRAIGLWYD; Williams & Davidson; Site F, Test Pit G [1993]: Williams & Davidson 1998, 14

GRAIGLWYD; Williams & Davidson; Site F, Test Pit H [1993]: Williams & Davidson 1998, 14

GRAIGLWYD; Williams & Davidson; Site F, Test Pit I [1993]: Williams & Davidson 1998, 14–15

GRAIGLWYD; Williams & Davidson; Site F, Test Pit L [1993]: Williams & Davidson 1998, 17

GRAIGLWYD; Williams & Davidson; Site F, Test Pit N [1993]: Williams & Davidson 1998, 16

GRAIGLWYD; Williams & Davidson; Site F, Test Pit O [1993]: Williams & Davidson 1998, 16–17

GRAIGLWYD; Williams & Davidson; Site F, Test Pit Q [1993]: Williams & Davidson 1998, 16

GRAIGLWYD; Williams & Davidson; Site F, Test Pit S [1993]: Williams & Davidson 1998, 16

GRAIGLWYD; Williams & Davidson; Site F, Test Pit 550e/570n [1993]: Williams & Davidson 1998, 17

GRIME'S GRAVES; Greenwell; Greenwell's Pit [1868–1870]: Greenwell 1870; Longworth & Varndell 1996, 9–33

GRIME'S GRAVES; Prehistoric Society of East Anglia; Pit 1 [1914]: Clarke 1915; Longworth & Varndell 1996, 61–3

GRIME'S GRAVES; Prehistoric Society of East Anglia; Pit 2 [1914–1915]: Clarke 1915; Longworth & Varndell 1996, 35–7

GRIME'S GRAVES; Armstrong; Pit 3 [1923]: Armstrong 1923; Longworth & Varndell 1996, 35–39

GRIME'S GRAVES; Armstrong; Pit 4 [1923]: Armstrong 1923; Longworth & Varndell 1996, 63–5

GRIME'S GRAVES; Armstrong; Pit 5 [1924]: Armstrong 1924; Longworth & Varndell 1996, 65–6

*Appendix*

GRIME'S GRAVES; Armstrong; Pit 6 [1924]: Armstrong 1924; Longworth & Varndell 1996, 65–7

GRIME'S GRAVES; Armstrong; Pit 7 [1924]: Armstrong 1924; Longworth & Varndell 1996, 65–6

GRIME'S GRAVES; Armstrong; Pit 8 [1924]: Armstrong 1924, 1927, 1932; Longworth & Varndell 1996, 65, 69–70

GRIME'S GRAVES; Armstrong; Pit 9 [1927]: Armstrong 1932; Longworth & Varndell 1996, 69, 71

GRIME'S GRAVES; Armstrong; Pit 10 [1928]: Armstrong 1932; Longworth & Varndell 1996, 69–73

GRIME'S GRAVES; Armstrong; Pit 11 [1928–1930; 1973]: Armstrong 1932; Longworth & Varndell 1996, 45–9

GRIME'S GRAVES; Armstrong; Pit 12 [1928–1933]: Armstrong 1932; 1934; Longworth & Varndell 1996, 73–5

GRIME'S GRAVES; Armstrong; Pit 13 [1934]: Armstrong 1934; Longworth & Varndell 1996, 73

GRIME'S GRAVES; Armstrong; Pit 14 [1934]: Armstrong 1934; Longworth & Varndell 1996, 73–77

GRIME'S GRAVES; Armstrong; Pit 15 [1937–1939]: Longworth & Varndell 1996, 50–9

GRIME'S GRAVES; Mercer; 1971 and 1972 Shafts [1971–1972]: Mercer 1976; 1981a; 1981b; Longworth & Varndell 1996, 73–8

HARROW HILL; Curwen & Curwen; Pit No. 21 [1924–1925]: Curwen & Curwen 1926

HARROW HILL; Holleyman; Shaft III [1936]: Holleyman 1937

LAMBAY ISLAND; Cooney; Quarry, pits and cairns: Cooney 1998; 2000, 196–197; 2004; 2005; Cooney *et al.* 2011

LANGDALE; Fell; South Scree Cave and Top Buttress [1949]: Fell 1951

LANGDALE; Pennington & Tutin; Blea Tarn and Red Tarn Pollen Sampling: Pennington & Tutin 1964

LANGDALE; Walker; Mickleden and Langdale Combe Pollen Sampling: Walker 1965

LANGDALE; Clough; Thunacar Knott [1969–1970]: Clough 1973

LANGDALE; Bradley & Edmonds; Dungeon Ghyll [1985–1987]: Bradley & Edmonds 1988, 192–4, 198; 1993, 108–12, 119–22

LANGDALE; Bradley & Edmonds; Harrison Stickle [1985–1987]: Bradley & Edmonds 1988, 194–6; 1993, 115–18

LANGDALE; Bradley & Edmonds; Stake Beck [1985–1987]: Bradley & Edmonds 1988, 194–8; 1993, 112–15

LANGDALE; Bradley & Edmonds; Pike of Stickle Site 95 [1985–1987]: Bradley & Edmonds 1988, 198–203; 1993, 122–5

LANGDALE; Bradley & Edmonds; Pike of Stickle Site 98 [1985–1987]: Bradley & Edmonds 1988, 198–203; 1993, 122–5

LANGDALE; Bradley & Edmonds; Loft Crag Site DS87 [1985–1987]: Bradley & Edmonds 1993, 118–19

LANGDALE; Bradley & Edmonds; Langdale Combe Pollen Sampling [1985–1987]: Bradley & Edmonds 1993, 96–7, 139

LANGDALE; Bradley & Edmonds; Stake Beck Pollen Sampling [1985–1987]: Bradley & Edmonds 1993, 139

LANGDALE; Bradley & Edmonds; Loft Crag Site DS87 Pollen Sampling [1985–1987]: Bradley & Edmonds 1993, 139–40

LE PINACLE; Godfray & Burdo; 1930–1936 Excavations [1930–1936]: Patton 1991; 1993; 2001

MYNYDD RHIW; Houlder; Site B [1958–1959]: Houlder 1961

MYNYDD RHIW; Houlder; Site G [1958–1959]: Houlder 1961

MYNYDD RHIW; Burrow *et al.*; Trench 1 and 2 [2005–2006]: Burrow 2011; Burrow *et al.* 2011

RATHLIN ISLAND; Jope; Galleries 1 and 2: Knowles 1903, 360; Jope 1952; Cooney 2000, 192–193

SHETLAND; Scott & Calder; Beorgs of Uyea Working Gallery: Scott & Calder 1952

SHETLAND; Cooney *et al.*; Beorgs of Uyea and Grut Wells [2014–2016]: Cooney *et al.* 2017

STOKE DOWN; Wade; Pit D1: Wade 1923; Barber & Dyer 2005

STOKE DOWN; Wade; Shaft No.1: Wade 1923; Barber & Dyer 2005

STOKE DOWN; Wade; Shaft No.2: Wade 1923; Barber & Dyer 2005

STOKE DOWN; Wade; Shaft No.3: Wade 1923; Barber & Dyer 2005

TIEVEBULLIAGH; Mallory; 1984 Excavations [1984]: Mallory 1990

TIEVEBULLIAGH; Weir; Pollen Sampling: Weir 1993

# Index

Entries in italics denote pages with images, entries suffixed t indicate pages with tables

abandonment and renewal 16, 30, 33, 45, 46, *48*, 58t, 69, 70–1, *72*, 75, *76*, 81–4, 85, 109, 110, 118, 120, 128–9, 131, 132, 137, 141, 144, 146
abundance of products 32, 96–100t
adzehead/production of 3, 4, 5–6, 9, 10, 11, 12, 13, 19, 41, 46, 48, 49, 50, 51, 84, 92, 93, *94*, 95, 135, 145, 146
    shaft-hole 19
    shoe-last 18, 95, 135
Africa 28, 29, 31, 33, 56
    Konso 28, 49
    metallurgy/metal working 30, 33
agriculture, *see* farming
ancestors, supernatural beings/power and spirits 25, 26–7, 30, 37, 40, 41, 43, 44–6, 47–9, 69, 85, 90, 92, 93, 129, 137 139, 140, 143, 144, 147
    *Alim Yongnum* 27, 45
    *Apu* 40
    *Atiswin* 26
    Big bird 26, 40, 69
    *Buffalo Calf Woman* 27, 39
    *Elogor* 26, 43, 44, 46
    Great Spirit 39
    *Hine-tchu-wai-wanga* 46
    *Huaca* 37
    *Mishebeshu* (Underwater Manitou) 40
    *Mondong* 27, 40, 44
    Mother of Axes 27, 41
    *Murbilik Kue* 27, 45
    *Pachamama* 25–6, 27, 37
    *Sweet Medicine* 46
ancient DNA 1, 113–16, 119, 127, 141
    dispersal of Neolithic communities 113, 135, 141
animal
    domestic 6, 7, 13, 18, 19, 43, 45, 72, 119, 129, 142
    migratory 69–70, 72, 82
    wild 7, 18, 72, 129, 130, 142
animal bone/remains/deposits 11, 13, 15, 21, 65, 69, 71, 72, 74, 75, 79, 81, 82, 84, 85, 93, 108, 109, 116, 118, 128, 129, 130, 132, 141, 142, 144
    artefacts 3, 11, 14, 79, 128, 130, 141; *see also* human remains
    burnt 15, 17
    feasting and fasting 41, 42, 71, 81, 84, 129, 144
animism 40, 41, 44, 96, 141, 144
antler/antler object 12, 14, 19, *58*, 75, 76, 77, 82, 116, 128
    pick 71, 72, *72*, 75, 76–7, *76*, 80, 81, 82
art 1, 132, 139

    depictions of axes/adzes 95, *95*, 101, 105
    portable 80, 108, 118, 128
    *see also* rock art/graffiti/idols
artefact biographies, *see* object and material biography
Australia 27, 28, 29, 31, 33, 40, 42–3, 56, 71, 80
    Aboriginal tribes 25, 29, 33, 41, 42, 47, 50, 75, 79, 139
    Dreamtime 40, 41, 47, 50, 139
    extraction sites
        Flinders Range 43
        Mount William 41, 42, 47, 50, 56, 57
        Ngilipitje, Arnhem Land 26, 41, 49–50
        Wilgie Mia 26–7, 40, 42, 50, 71, 75, 77
    Tasmanian Tiwi 28, 29, 49
axe/axehead (general) 1, 9, 13, 15t, 41, 70
    bride-price 48, 93
    cache 13, 93, *94*, 100–1, 104t, 105, 108, 110, 128, 133
    ceremonial/over-sized 31, 47, 48, 59, 91, 92, 93–4, 97, 134, 135
        jade 104, 104t, 148
        'Ye-Yao' 42, 43, 47, 48–9, 51, 92, 93, 149
    ground/grinding and polishing of 6, 10, 11, 12–15, 50, 117
    deposition of 12–18, 74, 75, 80, 84, 85, 101–2, 137, 142
        at causewayed enclosures 101, 110–12, 110t, 111t, 112t
        burnt/deliberate breakage 17, 81–2, 104, 109, 110, 111, 112, 145–6, *146*
        in burials/mortuary practices 81, 95, 101, 129, 133
        in Ireland 12–13, 103, 104–5, 105t, 106, 106t, 107t, 108–9, 149
        in pairs 104–5
        in pits 3, 101, 105, 109, 145
        in settlements/houses 101, 107–8
        in wetlands/rivers 12–13, *13*, 17–18, 103, 104, 106–7, 134, 134t
    distribution 4, 6 *13*, 17, 18–19, 50–1, 56, 57, 72, 92, 93, 94, 95, 96, 103, 105, 134–7, 134t, 142–3, 145, *148*
    embodiment/objectification 25, 30, 48, 51, 57, 92, 133, 147
    exotic, imported 17, 95, 106, 110, 112, 136, 137
    flint 6, 13, 18, 81, 95, 96, 97, 100t, 102, 103, 105, 106, 109, 112, 112t, 119, 124, 130, 136, 145, 146
    iconography of 101–3, 137, 140, 146
    miniature/pendant 102, 110
    quarries *9*, 18, 42, 65, *66*, 67, 71, 72, 74, 75, 77, 80, 85, 87–8t, 90, 119, 122; *see also* individual extraction sites
    production debitage 10, 78, 101
    reworked/recycled 17, 109, 110, 133

roughouts and preforms 10, 43, 46, 50, 74, 75, 78, 80, 81, 82, 84, *94*, 96, 101, 109, 149
skeuomorphs and imitations 102–3, *103*, 112
symbolism 13, 48, 76, 93, 96, 101, 102, 146, 149
typology 3
    Glastonbury type 17
    Limnhamnøkse 11
    Michelsberg 14, 116
    Rössen 14, 116
    shaft-hole 101, 116
    tranchet 12, 19, 97, 114, 142
    Trindørkse 11
value/relative value 1–2, 17, 48, 50, 74, 94–101, 102, 123
axe-shaped menhir/monolith 101–2, *102*

Balleygalley Hill, Ireland, flint mines 19, 65, 71, 75, 85, 86, 132, 165
  extraction tools 75
  hearths 71, 132
bead/bead necklace 17, 18, 93, 108, 130
Belgium, flint mines
  Jandrain 128
  Spiennes, Belgium, flint 18, 96, 103, 125, 126–7, *126*, 128, 129, 131, *136*, 136–7, 144
belief system/religion 6, 25, 30, 39, 40, 41, 42, 47, 49, 67, 68, 69, 74, 85, 96, 97, 101, 107, 118, 137, 139, 141, 142, 143, 144, 149, 150
Beorgs of Uyea, Shetland, extraction quarries 75, 76, 86
  offerings 74
  special deposits 75
  structures 78
Black Mountain, Co. Antrim, flint mines 19, 144, 165
  extraction tools 75
Blackpatch, Sussex, flint mines 6, 65, 71, 85, 86, 89, 98, 118, 127, 144, 165
  abandonment practices 81
  chalk objects/platform 71, 72, 77, 81, 102, 141
  chipping floors 72
  extraction tools 75
  hearths and charcoal 71, 72, 81
  human remains/burials 79, 81
  mounds ('barrows') 62, 68, 79
  offerings 72
  special deposits, lithics 74, 81
bone, *see* animal bone *and* human remains
Brittany (inc. Morbihan) 14, 17, *17*, 89, 101, 133, 135, 136, 141, 145
  alpine jade axes 17, 133, 135, 146
  megalithic tombs and menhirs 102, *102*, 145, *146*
    Gavrinis, Brittany 102, 105
    Tumulus St Michel 17, 135, 145
Bronze Age 2, 20, 73, 75, 81, 82, 83, 86, 87t, 134
Buckenham Toft, Norfolk, flint mines 19
burial/burial customs 1, 3, 7, 11, 12, 25, 27, 28, 29, 30, 33–4, 35, 35t, 48, 49, 54, 56, 57, 61–2, 63, 69, 72, 79–80, 93, 95–6, 96t, 101, 107, 109, 114, 116, 119, 120, 129, 136, 141, 144, 147
  monuments 33, 44–2, 61–2, 68, 69, 95, 101–2, 107, 119, 144
  *see also* human remains

cache/caching/hoard 3, 12, 13, 15, 30, 43, 44, 46, 60, *60*, 61, 74, 92–3, 94, *94*, 95, 96, 100–1, 104, 104t, 105, 108, *108*, 110, 124, 128, 133, 134, 135, 145, 147
Catlin, George 39, 42, 51
causewayed enclosure 20, 21, 79, 109–12, 110t, 111t, 112t, 116, 119, 120
  Combe Hill, Sussex 110
  Crickley Hill, Gloucestershire 120
  Etton, Cambridgeshire 82, 101, 110–11
  Hambledon Hill, Dorset 101, 110, 120, 122
  Magheraboy, Co. Sligo 112
  Maiden Castle, Dorset 110, 111
  Staines, Middlesex 110
  Whitehawk, Sussex 79
  Windmill Hill, Wiltshire 73, 82, 101, 110, 111–12
caves and swallow holes 3, 9, 15, 26, 40, 41, 54, 71, 75, 77, *78*, 142
ceremonial sites 33, 34, 47, 101
chalk 81
  axeheads 102, *103*
  objects 56, 71, 72–4, *73*, 73t, 79, 81, 82, 109–10
  platforms 54, 73, 75, 142
charcoal 3, 10, 11, 65, 71–2, 74, 75, 79, 81, 82, 84, 108, 109, 127, 128, 132, *132*; *see also* hearths
charred plant remains 109
Chassèen culture 95, 105, 109, 136
children 28, 31, 40, 42, 44, 80, 129–30, 131, 143
  sacrifice of 44
Church Hill, Sussex, flint mines 19, 65, 85, 86, 89, 98, 144, 165–6
  chalk object 74
  extraction tools 75
  graffiti 80
  human remains 79
  special deposits 74
  wooden bowl 74
Cissbury, Sussex, flint mines 19, 54, 65, 69, 71, 72, 77, 85, 86, 89, 97, 127, 166
  abandonment practices 81
  burials 57, 72, 79, 81, 114, *115*, 116, 131, 142
    DNA evidence 114
  chalk objects/platforms/'cave' 72, 75, 77, 79, 81, 102, 142
  extraction tools 75
  graffiti 80
  hearths and charcoal 71, 72, 79, 81
  special deposits 71, 72, 74, 75, 81
community history/biography and identity 3, 14, *14*, 16, 18, 23, 24, 25, 30, 34, 35, 37, 39, 40, 41, 46, 49, 51, 59, 61, 70, 76, 93, 94, 97, 99, 101, 114, 118, 124, 127, 139, 140, 141, 143, 144, 145, 147, 149
cosmology/cosmography 3, 23, 24, 25, 27, 29, 34, 37, 40, 68, 71, 80, 85, 90, 101, 103, 107, 112, 117, 118, 123, 127, 139, 141, 142–3, 144, 145, 150
craft specialisation 6, 25, 27, 28, 29, 31, 32t, 34, 35, 45, 46, 49–50, 54, 56, 57, 59–60, 61, 62, 63, 95, 127, 133, 143
  apprentices 35, 42, 43, 49, 50, 143
  initiates 44, 49, 143
Creag na Caillich, Perthshire, Group XXIV quarries 20, *54*, 57, 61, 65, 67, 68, 72, 74, 75, 80, 84, 85, 86, 101, 121, 144
  abandonment/renewal 84
  charcoal 74, 84
  extraction tools 75
  special deposits 74
curation 27, 30, 45, 46, 47, 48, 75, 82, 84, 92, 93, 94, 128, 146

deliberate breakage of objects 17, 58, *59*, 81–2, 102, 104, 109, 110, 111, 112, 128, 145–6, *146*
demography (age/sex) of extraction site users and processes 25, 28–9, 31, 35, 42, 43, 49, 50, 57, 80, 130, 131, 143
dendrochronology 17–18
Denmark 6–7, 13–14, *14*, 15t, 19, 125, 132
  extraction sites 6, 19, 126, 132, 144
Den of Boddam, Aberdeenshire, flint mines 19, 20, 65, 74, 99, 122, 165
  extraction tools 75
  special deposits 74
deposition 57, 65, 69, 71–7, *72–3*, *76*, 127–9, 137, 144–50
  of axeheads, *see under* axeheads

# Index

caches/hoards 3, 12, 13, 15, 30, 43, 44, 46, 60, *60*, 61, 74, 92–3, 94, *94*, 95, 96, 100–1, 104, 104t, 105, 108, *108*, 110, 124, 128, 133, 134, 135, 145, 147
    closing/abandonment and renewal 16, 17, 30, 33, 45, 46, *48*, 58t, 69, 70–1, *72*, 75, *76*, 81–4, 85, 104, 109, 110, 111, 112, 118, 120, 128–9, 131, 132, 137, 141, 144–6, *146*
        extraction tools 71, 75, 77, 81, 82, 84, 129
    in burials/mounds/tombs/cists 1, 3, 7, 11, 12, 17, 95, 96, 96t, 101–2, 107–8
    in houses 107–8
    in pits 1, 3, 11, 12, 15, 16, 70, 83, 84, 109, 145
    Mesolithic 1, 3, 4, 5, 6, 11–14, *13*, 21, 116, 118, 141–2
    on settlements 11, 12, 96, 100–1, 108–9
    wetlands and rivers 1, 12–13, *13*, 16, 17–18, 96, 134, 134t, 145, 147
distribution of materials and products 2, 4, 5–6, 5t, 13, 14, 15–16, 17, 18, 19, 21, 25, 31–2, 32t, 33, 34, 35, 42, 50–1, 54, 56, 57, 59, 60, 61, 63, 65, 69, 89, 91, 95, 96, *120*, 122, 124, 132–7, 134t, 149
    Adze/axeheads 4, 6 *13*, 17, 18–19, 50–1, 56, 57, 72, 92, 93, 94, 95, 96, 103, 105, 134–7, 134t, 142–3, 145, *148*
    'down-the-line' 32
    Supra-regional/long distance 2, 11, 15, 19, 21, 25, 27, 28, 29, 31–2, 32t, 33, 34, 35, 50–1, 54, 56, 57, 59, 60, 61, 63, 69, 93, 94, 96, 103, 105, *120*, 122, 124, 133–8, 142–3, 145, *148*
domestic practices and structures 1, 48, 69, 71, 93, 96, 101, 107, 109, 129, 143
Durrington, Wiltshire, flint mines 19, 65, 144
    extraction tools 75
    special deposits 74

Easton Down, Hampshire, flint mines 19, 65, 71, 72, 82, 97, 118, *121*, 122, 127, 144, 166
    abandonment/renewal 82
    extraction tools 75, 82
    hearths and charcoal 71, 82
Egypt 35–7, *36*
    cosmology 37
    dynastic period quarries 37
    Palaeolithic quarries 2
    Tutankhamun's burial chamber 37
embodiment/objectification
    axeheads 25, 30, 48, 51, 57, 92, 133, 147
    objects 30, 35, 45, 46, 49, 51, 57, 92, 93, 133, 134, 143, 147
    rocks/landscapes/material resources 25, 27, 40, 41, 133, 143
engendering 25–6, 27, 35, 37, 40, 45, 47, 49, 92
Ertebølle culture 7, 13, 14t, 19, 114, 116, 141
ethnographic models/studies 23–37, 26t, 28–31t, *36*, 139, 142, 143, 147, 149
excavations (extraction sites)
    Ballygalley Hill, Ireland 65, 71, 75, 85, 86, 132, 165
    Blackpatch, Sussex 71, 72, 74, 75, 77, 79, 81, 102, 144, 165
    Church Hill, Sussex 79, 165–6
    Cissbury, Sussex 71, 72, 77, 79, 81, 166
    Creag na Caillich, Scottish Borders 72, 84, 80, 85, 86, 101, 121, 144, 166
    Den of Boddam 74, 99, 122, 166
    Durrington, Wiltshire 144, 166
    Easton Down, Hampshire 71, 75, 82, 97, 118, *121*, 122, 127, 144, 166
    Goodland, Ireland 75, 77, 80, 83, 85, 86, 109, 144, 166
    Graiglwyd, Wales 10–11, 70, 71, 74, 78, 84, 85, 86, 101, 11, 144, 166
    Grime's Graves, Norfolk 71, 72, *72*, 75, 76–7, 79, 99, 121, 132, 144, 166–7
    Harrow Hill, Sussex 71, 73, 74, 75, 80, 81–2, 86, 98, 127, 144, 167
    Lambay Island, Ireland 70, 71–2, 74, 75, 78, 83, 84, 85, 86, 100, 103, 106, 109, 119, 132, 144, 167
    Langdale, Cumbria 70, 71, 72, 74, 75–6, 78, 80, 84, 86, 89, 94, 100, 101, 110, 119, 127, 132, 133, 142, 144, 147, *148*, 149, 167
    Le Pinnacle, Jersey 71, 75, 78, 86, 132, 144, 167
    Mynydd Rhiw, Wales 72, 75, 76, 100, 119, 144, 149, 167
    Rathlin island, Ireland 106, 167
    Shetland 74, 75, 76, 78, 86, 119, 144, 167
    Stakalleneset, Norway 4
    Stoke Down, Sussex 74, 75, 82, 144, 167
    Tievebulliagh, Ireland 75, 103, 144, 167
    Ynys Enlli (Bardsey Island), Wales 11
    *see also* individual sites
exchange/procurement/social networks 3, 7, 11, 14, 17–18, 24, 32, 42, 43, 47, 48, 50–1, 57, 58, 59, 90–1, 91t, 94–5, 101–2, 109, 119, 129, 132–7, 134t, 134–7, 139, 143, 144, 147
    bride-wealth/price 48, 49, 59, 93
    ceremonial/ritual 50–1, 59, 93
    gift giving 24, 90, 147
    Kula 24, 90
    potlatch 24, 90, 145
    reciprocal 50–1, 90
exotic materials/objects 2, 10, 17, 18, 48, 61, 93, 95, 96, 97, 106, 110, 112, 128, 134, 135, 136, 137
    axeheads 17, 95, 106, 110, 112, 136, 137
expeditions/journeys to extraction sites 42–3, 50, 69, 139–40, 144
    by sea 43, 50, 68, 119
extraction and lithic technology 1, 3, 11, 12, 13, 16, 18, 19, 40, 59, 117, 118, 125–7, *126*, 137, 139, 143
extraction practices 19, 21, 23, 24, 35, 39–51, 65, 71, 72–3, 75, 78, 81, 82, 84, 86, 109, 113–22, 118t, 119, 122, 128, 131, 132, 140, 141–5
    at Mesolithic–Neolithic transition 5, 19, 21, 113–17, 135, 137, 140–1, 144, 151t
    *chaîne opératoire* 24, 59
    changes in 18, 19, 72–4, 113–17, 127, 137, 141–5, 141t
    dispersal/chronology of 113, 117–22, 118t, 127, 137
    Mesolithic 3, 4, 5, 6, 16, 141–2, 141t
    *see also* ritual, ceremonial and ritualised extraction practices/ deposition
extraction tools 71, 75–7, 81, 82, 129, 142
    abandoned at extraction sites 71, 75, 77, 81, 82, 84, 129
    imported 75–7, 134–6

farming/agro-pastoralism 1, 6, 7, 10, 14, 18, 19, 21, 43, 50, 96, 97, 101, 107, 112, 113–16, 117, 141, 141t, 147, 150
    cereals 116, 118, 119
feasting and fasting 41, 42, 71, 81, 84, 129, 144
fertility/birth 26, 27, 30, 37, 41, 78–9
    soil/harvest 48, 92–3, 145–6
finishing of implements off-site 4, 8, 31, 50
fire/fire-setting 3, 4, 8, 41, 71, 84, 97, 127
flint 6, 18, 21, 39–40, 46–7, 53, 96–7, 105, 110t, 125, 131
    axeheads 6, 13, 18, 81, 95, 96, 97, 100t, 102, 103, 105, 106, 109, 112, 112t, 119, 124, 130, 136, 145, 146
    Bartonian 18, 95, 96, 135, 142
    Bédoulien 129, 130
    burnt 9, 109
    gunflints 53
    imported 6, 7, 18–19, 96, 123, 124, 133
    mines (general) 4, 6, 19, 69, 75, 85, 110, 116, 119, 122, 131–2
    nodules 6, 74, 81, 106, 109, 124, 131, 132
    provenancing of 18, 76–7, 89, 97, 145
    raw material 6, 10, 11, 89, 95, 107, 110, 111, 122, 125, 126–7, 134, 135, 131, 142, 146–7
    tools/flakes 13, 19, 74, 81, 85, 89, 96, 107–8, 110, 125, 128, 130, 131, 142, 145
    *see also* individual mine and extraction sites

flint clay 26
foragers/foraging 1, 7, 14, 112, 113, 116, 117, 141
France
    Flins-sur-Seine, France, flint mines 18, 97
    Grand Pressigny, flint quarries 18, 96, 125
    Jablines, flint mines 18, 95, 96, 97, 103, 126, 128, 129, 136, 144
    Paris Basin
        flint mines 18, 95, 116, 119, 122, 135, 136, 137, 144
        Neolithic cultures and networks 95, 114, 116, 135–6, 146
    Plussulien/Sélèdin, Group X quarries 5, 119, 127, 135
        Ri, flint mines 95, 136
    Villemaur-sur-Vanne, flint mines 130
functionality of products 1, 6, 13, 25, 28, 30, 34, 46–9, 57, 59, 71, 92, 97, 101, 134, 137, 142, 147, 149
    empowered objects/power stones 46–9, 90–3, 91t, 145–6, 147, 150
    non-functional objects 7, 24, 30, 48, 57, 71, 73, 74, 93, 102, 128, 149
    ritual/functional duality 28, 30, 35, 47, 48, 49, 50, 59, 90, 92, 93, 128, 140, 143, 147
Funnel Beaker culture, *see* TRB

Gavrinis, Brittany 102, 105
Goodland, Co. Antrim, flint mines 19, 65, 72, 77, 85, 86, 109, 144, 166
    abandonment/renewal 83
    extraction tools 75, 80
    special deposits 74
    structures 77, 83, 109
graffiti, *see* rock art/graffiti, idols
Graiglwyd, Wales, Group VII quarries 10–11, 20, 56, 65, 68, 70, 71, 74–5, 78, 84, 85, 86, 100, 110, 119, 120, 144, 149, 166
    abandonment/renewal 84
    extraction tools 75, 76
    hearths and charcoal 71, 72, 74, 75, 84, 132
    offerings 74, 84
    special deposits 74–5, 84
    stone plaque, decorated 80, 84
    structures 78
Grand Pressigny, France 18, 96, 125
Grave goods, *see* burials *and* human remains
Grime's Graves, Norfolk, flint mines 19, 20, *20*, 65, 68, *68*, 69, 85, 86, 89, 99, 121
    abandonment/renewal 82–3, *83*
    antlers/antler picks 71, 72, *72*, 75, 76–7, *76*
    Bronze Age activity and deposition 75, 82–3
    burials and human remains 79, 82, 83, 131, 142
    chalk objects/platforms 72–4, 75, 77, 82
    extraction tools 75, 76, 77, 82
    graffiti 76, 80, *80*
    Grooved Ware pottery 71, 73, 77
    hearths and charcoal 71, 72, *72*, 77, 79, 82, 132
    periglacial stripes 68
    special and placed deposits 71, 72–4, *72*, 75, *76*, 82–3
grinding and polishing 3, 6, 10, 11, 17, 43, 46, 50, 137
ground stone tools 3, 6, 10, 11–15, 16, 17, 18, 19, 51, *51*, 76, 80, 96, 97, 107, 110, 117, 124, 134, 137
    Mesolithic 11–15, 16, 117

Harrow Hill, Sussex 6, 54, 65, 67, 71, 73, 74, 75, 80, 81–2, 86, 98, 127, 144, 167
    abandonment/renewal 81–2
    chalk object 73
    extraction tools 75
    graffiti 80
    hearths 71, 73
    special deposits 74, 81–2

hearths 11, 13, 33, 46, 48, 56, 65, 69, 71–2, *72*, 74, 78, 79, 80, 81, 82, 84, 85, 93, 108, 129, 131–2, 137
    *see also* charcoal *and* fire/fire-setting
human remains
    burials and burial/funerary practices 25, 27, 28, 29, 30, 33–4, 35, 35t, 48, 49, 54, 56, 57, 61–2, 63, 69, 72, 79–80, 83, 95–6, 96t, 101, 107, 109, 114, 116, 119, 120, 129, 136, 141, 144, 147
    children 129–30, 131
    cremation deposits 11, 12, 72, 79
    grave goods 61, *61*, 95–6, 129–30, 133, 134, 141
    in mine shafts/at extraction sites 21, 56, 57, 72, 79–81, 82, 83, 95, 114, *115*, 116, 129–31, 130t, 133, 137, 142
    Mesolithic 12, 21, 141, 142
    monuments 33, 44–2, 61–2, 68, 69, 95, 101–2, 107, 119, 144
    Saxon 79
    *see also* ancient DNA
hunter-gatherers(-fishers) 2, 3, 7, 114, 117; *see also* foragers

identity 16, 18, 35, 3, 48, 58, 59, 70, 93, 94, 96, 97, 107, 118, 127, 141, 143, 145, 148
    community 3, 14, *14*, 16, 18, 23, 24, 25, 30, 34, 35, 37, 39, 40, 41, 46, 49, 51, 59, 61, 70, 76, 93, 94, 97, 99, 101, 114, 118, 124, 127, 139, 140, 141, 143, 144, 145, 147, 149
ideology 1, 27, 37, 39, 41, 47, 101, 103, 112, 138, 139, 141, 144
Indonesia, To Onda'e 46
Ireland 2, 3, 4, 11, 12–13, 19–20, 54, 65, 66, 80, 86, 89, 90, 103, 104–5, 109, 112, 118, 119–20, *120*, 132, 133, 135, 137, 144, 149
    ancient DNA evidence 114, 116, 117, 127
    axehead deposition 12–13, 103, 104–5, 105t, 106, 106t, 107t, 108–9
    Belderrig, Co. Mayo 3, 15
    Ferriter's Cove, Co. Kerry 13
    Hermitage, Co Limerick 3, 11–12
    houses 108–9
    Lough Gur, Ireland 108
    Magheraboy, Co. Sligo 112
    Mesolithic 3, 11
    *see also* individual extraction sites
Iron Age 3–4
iron pyrites 81
Italy/Italian alps 1, 19, 89–90, 93, 117, 125, 133
    extractions sites
        I Ciotti 2
        Defensola A/Gargano Peninsula 16, 73, 117, 125, 128, 132, 134, 144
        Mont Beigua 16–17, 144
        Mont Viso 16–17, *56*, 144
        Ponte di Veia 125
        Val Sbernia 54, 130
        Valle Lagorara 125
    jade/jadeitite 1, 16–17, *16*, 18, 19, 32, 56, *56*, 95, 103, 104t, 106, 128, 133, 135, 142, 144, 146, *146*, 147, 149

jade/jadeitite 1, 16–18, *16*, 18, 19, 32, 56, *56*, 57, 61, 90, 94, 95, 103, 104t, 106, 109, *120*, 128, 133, 135, 136, 139, 142, 144, 145, 146, *146*, 147, 149
    jewellery 133
Japan, obsidian quarries 2, 54, 56, 58–9
jewellery
    beads/necklaces 17, 18, 93, 108, 130
    coral 133
    jade 133

kinship networks/affiliation 35, 42, 43, 58, 59, 90, 143

# Index

Knapper/knapping 3, 11, 31, 40, 46, 49–50, 65, 74, 85, 107, 109, 122, 127, 129, 131
Krasnaselsky, Belarus, flint mines 126, 127, 129, 130
Krumlovský les, Czechia, chert mines 7, 56, 117, 127, 131
    Mesolithic 2, 6, 7, 15, 141
Krzemionki, Poland, flint mines 117, 127, 132, *132*, 134

Lambay Island, Co. Dublin, porphyritic andesite quarries 20, 54, 65, 68, 70, 71–2, 75, 78, 83, 84, 85, 86, 100, 103, 106, 109, 119, 132, 144
    abandonment/renewal 84
    extraction tools 75
    hearth 71–2, 78, 84
    offerings 74
    special deposits 75, 83, 109
    structures 78, 83, 84
lamps 73, 128
Langdale/Scafell, Cumbria extraction quarries 6, *9*, 10–11, *10*, 15, 18, 19–20, 54, 56, 57, 61, 65, 67, 68, 71, 72, 74, 80, 84, 86, 89, 94, 100, 101, 110, 119, 127, 133, 142, 144, 147, *148*, 149, 167
    abandonment/renewal 84
    extraction tools 75–6, 84
    hearths and charcoal 71, 72, 132
    offerings 74
    Pike of Stickle 6, *9*, 54, 67, *67*, 70, 75, *78*, 84, 85, 142
    special deposits 75, 84
    structures 78, 84
Le Pinacle, Jersey, extraction quarries 65, 68, 86, 144, 167
    extraction tools 75
    hearths 71, 132
    midden material 71, 78
Lengyel culture 127, 134–5
Linearbandkeramik/LBK 7, 18, 19, 95, 117, 134–5
Lipari, Island 133
lithics
    anvil 75, 78, 131
    arrowhead/projectile point 74, 93, 105, 107, 145
    Bann flakes 11
    bifacial implements 4, 56, *60*
    blades/bladelets/blade tools 4, 5, 6, 8, 11, 13, 16, 17, 18, 19, 42, 43, 49, 74, 95, 96, 105, 125, 127, 128, 130, 133, 134, 135, 137, 145
    bracers 101
    burins 8, 10
    burnt 9, 105, 109, 145; *see also under* axeheads
    chisel 48, 51, 92, 96, 105, 108, 145
    Clovis points 2
    cores/core-tools 4, 5, 9, 11, 74, 111
    daggers 18, 122, 145
    debitage 4, 5, 6, 8, 9, 10, 11, 13, 15, 65, 69, 71, 72, 73, 74, 75, 77, 78, 81, 82, 83, 84, 85 101, 105, 107, 109, 117, 118, 127, 128, 129, 137, 141, 144, 145, 149
    flaked tools 5, 108, 110, 137
    flakes 3, 4, 6, 7, 8, 11, 18, 19, 74, 75, 81, 82, 84, 107, 109
    grinders 50, 84
    hammerstones 3, 4, 8, 10, 44, 74, 75, 76, 78, 81, 82, 84, 107, 108, 109, 124, 127, 128, 130
    knapping debris 3, 4, 11, 129
    knives 42, 46, 48, 51, 74, 81, 92, 93, *94*, 107, 108, 146
    maceheads 78
    mauls 108
    microliths/microblades 4, 10, 11, 12, 15, 44
    nodules 6, 10, 18, 19, 25, 26, 41, 74, 79, 81, 82, 83, 96, 105, 109, 131, 132, 137
    picks 9, 12, 82, 107, 128
    polissoirs 78, 101
    punch 131
    rod 99
    rubbers 75, 109
    saddle quern 82
    serrated-edged flakes 110
    sickle 96, 107
    scrapers/end- /concave- 6, 8, 11, 18, 31, 74, 81, 105, 107, 109, 110, 127, 145
    spearhead 49–50
    strike-a-light 96
    tanged points 6
    *Tchamajillas* (hoe) 47
    waste/dumps of 3, 4, 45, *55*, 74, 79, 81, 84, 127, 131
    wedges 95, 135
    'Ye-Yao' axeheads/blades 42, 43, 47, 48–9, 51, 92, 93, 149
    *see also* cache, *and* abandonment
Long Down, Sussex, flint mines 19, 99

mammoth hunters 2
market 37, 128, 147, 149
Martin's Clump, Hampshire, flint mines 19, 68
material wealth 24, 43, 48, 59, 90, 140, 143
megalithic sites/tombs 17, 107, 116, 119, 124, 133, 145, *146*
    axe-shaped menhirs/monoliths 101–2, *102*
    Gavrinis, Brittany 102, 105
    Petit Mont, Arzon, France, decorated orthostat 95, *95*
    *see also* long barrows and burials
Mesolithic 1–21, 5t, 41
    Denmark 6–7
    deposition 1, 3, 4, 5, 6, 11–14, *13*, 21, 116, 118, 141–2
    extraction practices 3, 4, 5, 6, 16, 141–2, 141t
    extraction sites
        Bjerre, Denmark, flint 6, 132, 144
        Bloodstone Hill, Isle of Rhum, bloodstone 10
        Burnetland Hill, Scottish Borders, chert 8–9, 15
        Carn Menyn, Pembrokeshire, meta-mudstone 8, *8*, 15
        Fin Cop, Derbyshire, chert 9
        Halsane, Norway, quartzite 4, 5, 6
        Hespriholmen, Norway, greenstone 3, 4, 6, 19
        Hov, Denmark, flint 6, 144
        Kjølskarvet, Norway, quartzite 4, 5, 6
        Krumlovský les, Czechia, chert 2, 6, 7, 15, 141
        Langdale/Scafell, Cumbria, tuff 6, 10–11, *10*, 15
        Monvoy, Co. Waterford, rhyolite 11
        Nautøya, Norway, jasper 6
        Rijkholt, Netherlands, flint 7
        Rivenes, Norway, dolerite 4
        Sallerup-Tullston, Sweden, flint 7, 19, 119
        Scottish Borders 8–9
        Skjervika, Norway, jasper 6
        Stakalleneset, Norway, dolerite 3, 4, 5, 6
        Stegahaugen, Norway, greenstone 3–4
    ground stone tools 11–15, 16, 117
    in Europe 1, 3–5, 5t, 2–13, 5t, *13*, *14*
    pits 3, 8, *8*, 9, 11, 12, 13, 118, 121, 141
    settlements/camps 10–15, 15t
    Sweden 7
Mesolithic–Neolithic transition 1, 6, 7, 16–21, 97, 101, 112–17, 121, 137, 144, 150
    ancient DNA evidence 113–16, 117, 119, 127, 135, 141
    contact period 2, 7, 8, 18, 19, 21, 85, 140–1, 142
    extraction practices 5, 19, 21, 113–17, 135, 137, 140–1, 144, 151t
    impact and spread of agro-pastoralists 6, 7, 14, 19, 97, 113–17, 140–1, 141t
    Neolithisation 7, 10, 11, 14, 17, 113–18, 119, 120, 135, 137, 150

metal/metal ores/metallurgy 24, 30, 34, 37, 91
    copper 40, 61, 131
    tin 44
methodology 23–4
Michelsberg culture 7, 18, 95, 109, 126–7, 128, 136–7
microwear *see* use-wear
midden 7, 12, 13, 71, 112
minerals 25, 26, 27, 34, 37, 40, 41, 139
MINES
    Britain and Ireland, flint *66*
        Ballygalley Hill 19, 65, 71, 75, 85, 86, 132, 165
        Black Mountain, Co. Antrim 19, 75, 144
        Blackpatch, Sussex 6, 62, 65, 67, 71, 72, 74, 75, 77, 79, 81, 102, 144
        Buckenham Toft, Norfolk 19
        Church Hill, Sussex 19, 65, 74, 75, 79, 80, 85, 86, 89, 98, 144, 165–6
        Cissbury, Sussex 9, 54, 57, 65, 69, 71, 72, 74, 75, 77, 79, 80, 81, 85, 86, 89, 97, 114, *115*, 116, 127, 131, 142
        Den of Boddam, Aberdeenshire 19, 20, 65, 74, 75, 99, 122, 144, 166
        Durrington, Wiltshire 19, 65, 74, 75, 144
        Easton Down, Hampshire 19, 65, 71, 72, 97, 118, *121*, 122, 127, 144, 166
        Goodland, Co. Antrim 19, 65, 72, 74, 75, 77, 83, 85, 86, 109, 144, 166
        Grime's Graves, Norfolk 19, 20, *20*, 65, 68, *68*, 69, 71, 72–4, *72*, 75, 76–7, *76*, 77, 79, 80, *80*, 82–3, *83*, 85, 86, 89, 99, 121, 131, 132, 142, 144, 166–7
        Harrow Hill, Sussex 6, 54, 65, 67, 71, 73, 74, 75, 80, 81–2, 86, 98, 127, 144, 167
        Long Down, Sussex 19, 99
        Martin's Clump, Hampshire 19, 68
        Nore Down, Sussex 19
        Skelmuir Hill, Scottish Borders 19
        South Downs (general) 18, 19, 20, 68, *73*, 73, 82, 85, 89, 103, 114, 119–20, 132, 145
        Stoke Down, Sussex 19, 65, 74, 75, 82, 144, 67
        Wessex (general) 19, 20, 119–20, 145
    European
        Aachen, Germany, flint 125
        Avennes, Belgium, flint 129
        Bjerre, Denmark, flint 6, 132, 144
        Casa Montero, Madrid, Spain, flint 16, 117, 125–6
        Defensola A, Gargano Peninsula, Italy, flint 16, 73, 103, 117, 125, 128, 132, 134, 144
        El Cañaveral, Spain, flint 117
        Flins-sur-Seine, France, flint 18, 97
        Gavà, Barcelona, Spain, varicite 18, 117, 129–30, 130t, 133, 147
        Hov, Denmark, flint 126
        Jablines, France, flint 18, 95, 96, 97, 103, 126, 128, 129, 136, 144
        Jandrain, Belgium, flint 128
        Iberian peninsula 16, 19
        Kleinkems, Germany, chert 127, 130–1
        Krasnaselsky, Belarus, flint 126, 127, 129, 130
        Krumlovský les, Czechia, chert 2, 6, 7, 15, 56, 117, 127, 131, 141
        Krzemionki, Poland, flint 117, 127, 132, *132*, 134
        Kvarnby-Södra, Sweden flint 119
        Lousberg, Netherlands, flint 137
        Orońsko II, Poland, flint 2
        Polany Kolonie II, Poland, flint 125, 129, 131–2
        Paris Basin, France, flint 18, 95, 119, 135, 136, 137, 144
        Ri, France, flint 95, 136
        Rijckholt, Netherlands flint 7, 18, 54, 95, 97, 127, 128, 131, 136–7, 144
        Sallerup-Tullstop, Sweden, flint 7, 19
        Spiennes, Belgium, flint 18, 96, 103, 125, 126–7, *126*, 128, 129, 131, *136*, 136–7, 144
        Stránská Skála, Czechia, chert 127, 128, 132, 133
        Sümeg-Mogyorósdomb, Hungary, flint 128, 129
        Świeciechó, Poland, flint 134
        Tomaszow, Poland, flint 125, 128–9
        Tušimice, Csechia, Quartzite 125, 131
        Valkenburg, Netherlands, flint 137
        Villemaur-sur-Vanne, France, flint 130
        Wien-Mauer/Antonshöhe, Austria, radiolarite 131
        Wierzbica 'Zele', Poland, flint 131, 133
    rest of world
        Gold and silver (South America) 37
        Wilgie Mia, Australia, ochre 26–7, 40, 42, 50, 71, 75, 77
mining (general)
    adits and tunnels 2, 125, 142
    dating and chronology 17, 18, 19–20, 97–101, 112, 116, 117–22, 118t, 134–7
    deep shaft galleried 1, 2, 15, 19, 20–1, 85, 112, 113, 116, 118, 119, 121, 125–7, *126*, 137, 141, 143
    earliest Neolithic 16, 19, 117, 119
    possible Mesolithic 2, 7, 19, 97, 121, 127
    shaft fills 72, 74, 79, *83*, 128–9, 130, 131, 137
    *see also* abandonment and renewal *and* human remains
mobility and movement of people 1, 3, 7, 21, 97, 113–14, 116, 119–20, *120*, 135
    sea-travel 2, 43, 50, 68, 119
    to extraction sites 2
Modesty, Shetland *60*, 93, 108, *108*
motivation for lithic procurement and use 23, 24, 34, 37, 54, 65, 67, 89, 103
Mynydd Rhiw, Wales, extraction quarries 11, 20, 72, 75, 76, 100, 119, 144, 149
    extraction tools 75, 76
    hearths and charcoal 75
    special deposits 75
mythology/mythological/storied sites and sources 24, 25–7, 26t, 28, 29, 32, 34, 35, 37, 39–41, *39*, 41, 47, 49, 54
    caves and rock shelters (entrances to underworld) 26, 40, 41, 54
    offerings 26, 40, 43, 44–5, *45*, 46, 51, 144
    origin myths 25, 35, 37, 41
    *see also* site/deposit location

New Guinea 24, 26, 27, 28, 29, 31, 41, 43, 44–5, 48, 50, 69, 90–2, 140, 145–6
    *Alim Yongnum* 27, 45
    Dani 25, 27, 29, 41, 42, 43, 48, 92
    Dismal Swamp 42, 90
    *Elogor* 26, 43, 44, 46
    Hagen 90–2, 103, 136
    Highland tribes 29, 42
    *Mother of Axes* 27, 41
    *Murbilik Kue* 27, 45
    sacred objects 90–3, 91t
    Sentani 48
    Tungei 29, 45
    Una 27, 29, 41, 42, 45, 48, 92
    Wano 27, 29, 41, 42, 43, 44, 46
    Wiru 90–2, 103, 136
    'Ye-Yao' axeheads/blades 42, 43, 47, 48–9, 51, 92, 93, 149
New Zealand 28
    Anati Bay quarries 43
    Chatham Islands, *Hine-tchu-wai-wanga* 46
    Maori 26, 41, 43, 49, 50, 139–40
Neolithic (general)
    appearance of extraction 5, 19, 21, 113–22, 118t, 127, 135, 137, 140–1, 144, 151t

*Index*

Causewayed enclosures 20, 21, 73, 79, 82, 93, *94*, 101, 109–12, 110–12, 110t, 111t, 112t, 116, 119, 120, 122, 144
    houses 93, 107–8, 119
    long barrows 20, 21, 68, 69, 79, 101, 109, 110, 116, 119, 141
    monuments 2, 114, 116, 119, 121, 141, 144
    pottery 6, 7, 10, 17, 18, 19, 56, 58, *59*, 71, 72, 73, 74, 75, 77, 78, 79, 82, 85, 93, 105, 108, 109, 116, 117, 118, 119, 120, 121, 127, 128, 129–30, 131, 132, 133, 137, 141, 145, *146*
    settlements 7, 18, 95, 100, 101, 136
Neolithisation 7, 10, 11, 14, 17, 113–18, 119, 120, 135, 137, 150
Netherlands 7, 18, 96, 96t, 105, 106, 107, 125, 134, 145
    Brandwijk, Netherlands 7, 18
    Hardinxveld, Netherlands 7, 18
    Lousberg flint mines 137
    Rijckholt, Netherlands flint mines 7, 18, 54, 95, 97, 127, 128, 131, 136–7, 144
    Valkenberg flint mines 137
non-functional objects 7, 24, 30, 48, 57, 71, 73, 74, 93, 102, 128, 149; *see also* functionality
Nore Down, Sussex, flint mines 19
North America 28, 33, 41–2, 56, 79, 80, 90, 141
    Big bird 26, 40, 69
    *Buffalo Calf Woman* 27, 39
    effigy mounds 46
    extraction sites
        3rd Unnamed Cave, Tennessee, chert 54, 61
        Alibates, Texas 54
        Crescent Hills, Missouri 54, 61
        Kaolin, Illinois 54, *60*
        Mammoth, Kentucky 54
        Mill Creek, Illinois 54
        Obsidian Cliffs, Wyoming 54
        Pipestone quarries, Minnesota 27, 31, 33, 41–2, 43–4, 45, *44–6*, 49, 57, 61, 69, 74, 139
        Wyandotte, Indiana 54
        Yellowstone, Wyoming 2
    Great Spirit 39
    Hidatsa 39–40, 46, 49, 69
    Hopewell grave goods 61, *61*
    Lakota/Dakota 25, 27, 29, 33, 42, 46
    *Mishebeshu* (Underwater Manitou) 40
    Navajo 27, 29, 43
    Ojibwe 39–40, 46
    Plains tribes 27, 29, 33–4, 39–40, *39*, 42, 46, 49, 79
    Puebloan Indians 46
    Three Maidens shrine, Minnesota 43, 51, *51*
    *Sweet Medicine* 46
Norway 3–7, 5t, 11, 12, 19
    extraction sites 3–4, 5, 6, 19
    rock art 4

object and material biography 13, 27, 30, 42, 48, 49, 50, 59, 60, 90, 95, 101, 112, 133, 138, 141, 147
objectification and embodiment 40, 41, 133
    axeheads 25, 30, 48, 51, 57, 92, 133, 147
    objects 30, 35, 45, 46, 49, 51, 57, 92, 93, 133, 134, 143, 147
    rocks/landscapes/material resources 25, 27, 40, 41, 133, 143
obligation 47, 90, 93, 145
offerings 26, 40, 43, 44–5, *45*, 46, 51, 68, 71, 72–4, *73*, 81, 84
origin myths 25, 35, 37, 41, 90, 143
Orkney 107–8
ownership of/restricted access to sites/raw material sources/objects 25, 27, *28t*, 28, 35, 41–3, 56–7, 62, 85, 92, 93
    Big Man 41, 42, 43, 44, 51

*Ngurungaetas* 42
quarrymen/leaders/custodians 42, 43, 44, 45, 56, 57, 62

Palaeoindian extraction quarries, Texas 2
Palaeolithic extraction sites 2
Palmarola Island 134
Pantellaria Island 134
Pendell Farm, Surrey 3, 15
periglacial stripes 68, *68*
personal adornment 24, 116, 139
petrological/chemical analysis and provenancing 50, 60, 89, 97, 145
    pXRF 89–90
Pike of Stickle, Cumbria, *see* Langdale
pits 1, 3, 70, 77, 78, 83, 109, 132, 141, 145
    axeheads in 3, 101, 105, 109, 145
    Mesolithic 3, 8, 9, 11, 12, 13, 118, 121, 141
    objects in 1, 3, 11, 12, 15, 16, 70, 83, 84, 109, 145
Poland, flint extraction sites
    Krzemionki, mines 117, 127, 132, *132*, 134
    Polany Kolonie II, mines 125, 129, 131–2
    Świeciechó, mines 134
    Wierzbica 'Zele', mines 131, 133
    Tomaszow, quarries 125, 128–9
Polynesia 50
    Cook islands 27, 50
    Hawai'i 46, 50, 54, 56
pottery 6, 7, 17, 56, 58, *59*, 71, 72, 74, 75, 78, 82, 85, 93, 105, 108, 109, 116, 117, 118, 127, 128, 129–30, 131, 132, 133, 137, 141, 145, *146*
    Beaker 79
    Carinated bowl 10, 18, 108, 119
    Cerny culture 129
    Collared Urn 79
    Corded Ware 130
    Ertebølle 19
    Grooved Ware 71, 73, 77, 121
    Impressed Ware 120
    Lengyel 127
    LBK 7, 117
    Michelsberg 128, 130
    Peterborough Ware 120
    Steatitic clay 108
    Swifterbant 7
prestige power, power relations and status 24, 25, 27, 30, 35, 43, 47, 48, 49, 50–1, 58, 59, 90, 93, 97, 101, 139, 140, 143, 145, 147
procurement strategies 10, 68, 77, 140
Pull, John 114, 165–6
purification rituals 43–4, 57, 71

QUARRIES
    Britain and Ireland
        Balleygalley Hill, Co. Antrim, flint 19, 65, 71, 75, 85, 86, 132, 144, 165
        Bloodstone Hill, Isle of Rhum, bloodstone 10
        Burnetland Hill, Scottish Borders, chert 8–9, 15
        Carn Menyn, Wales, meta-mudstone 8, *8*, 15
        Creag na Caillich, Perthshire, Group XXIV, hornfels 20, *54*, 57, 61, 65, 67, 68, 72, 74, 75, 80, 84, 85, 86, 101, 121, 144
        Fin Cop, Derbyshire, chert 9
        Graiglwyd, Wales, Group VII tuffaceous 10–11, 20, 56, 65, 68, 70, 71, 74–5, 76, 78, 80, 84, 85, 86, 100, 110, 119, 120, 132, 144, 149, 166
        Lambay Island, Co. Dublin, porphyritic andesite 20, 54, 65, 68, 70, 71–2, 75, 78, 83, 84, 85, 86, 100, 103, 106, 109, 119, 132, 144

Langdale/Scafell, Cumbria, Groups VI and IX epidotized tuff 6, 10–11, *10*, 15, 18, 19–20, 56, 57, 61, 65, 67, 68, 71, 72, 74, 75–6, 78, 80, 84, 86, 89, 94, 100, 101, 110, 119, 127, 132, 133, 142, 144, 147, *148*, 149, 167
    Le Pinacle, Jersey, dolerite 65, 68, 71, 75, 86, 132, 144, 167
    Monvoy, Co. Waterford, rhyolite 11
    Mynydd Rhiw, Wales, Group XXI rhyolitic tuff 11, 20, 72, 75, 76, 100, 119, 144, 149
    Pike of Stickle, Cumbria, Groups VI and IX, epitorised tuff 9, 10, 6, 54, 67, *67*, 70, 75, *78*, 84, 85, 142
    Rathlin Island, Co. Antrim, Group IX, porcellanite 54, 57, 65, 68, 106, 167
    Scottish Borders, cherts 8–9
    Shetland 54, 65, 74, 75, 76, 86, 89, 119, 144, 167
        Beorgs of Uyea, felsite 75, 76, 86, 167
    Tievebulliagh, Co. Antrim, Group IX, porcellanite 20, 54, 56, 65, 67, 68, *68*, 75, 103, 144
  European
    Bømlo (Mount Siggjo) Norway, rhyolite 3–4, 6, 19
    Grand Pressigny, France, flint 18, 96, 125
    Halsane, Norway, quartzite 4, 5, 6
    Heligoland Island, Germany, flint 54, 57, 103, 105
    Hespriholmen, Norway, greenstone 3, 4, 6, 19
    Hov, Denmark, flint 6, 144
    I Ciotti, Italy, flint and quartzite 2
    Kjølskarvet, Norway, quartzite 4, 5, 6
    Kozu-Onbase Island, Japan obsidian 2
    Lundfors, Sweden, quartz 127
    Mont Beigua, Italy, jade/jadeitite 16–17, 144
    Mont Viso, Italy, jade/jadeitite 16–17, *56*, 144
    Monte Arci, Sardinia, obsidian 124, 129, 133
    Nautøya, Norway, jasper 6
    Pleigne, Switzerland, crystal quartz 125
    Ponte di Veia, Italy, flint 125
    Plussulien/Sélèdin, France, Group X metadolerite 5, 119, 127, 135
    Rivenes, Norway, dolerite 4
    Sallerup-Tullstop, Sweden, flint 7, 19
    Skjervika, Norway, jasper 6
    Stakalleneset, Norway, dolerite 3, 4, 5, 6
    Stegahaugen, Norway, greenstone 3–4
    Val Sbernia, Italy, flint 54, 130
    Valle Lagorara, Italy, jasper 125
  rest of world
    3rd Unnamed Cave, Tennessee, chert 54, 61
    Abiamp, New Guinea 47, 92
    Alibates, Texas, flint 54
    Anita Bay, New Zealand, greenstone 43
    Awigobi, New Guinea greenschist/amphibolitic schist 49, 93
    Crescent Hills, Missouri, chert 54, 61
    Flinders Range, Australia 43
    Flint Ridge, Ohio, flint 54, *55*, 56, 61, *62*
    Henderson Island, Pacific 54, 57
    Hoshikuso Pass, Japan, obsidian 54, *58–9*
    Hokkiado: Japan, Shirataki, obsidian 2, 56
    Honshu, Japan, obsidian 2, 56
    Kaolin, Illinois, chert 54, *60*
    Langda, New Guinea 27, 42, 45, 46, 50, 51, 145–6
    Mammoth Cave, Kentucky, flint 54
    Manau Kea, Hawai'i, basalt 54, 56
    Mill Creek, Illinois, chert 54
    Mount William, Australia, greenstone 41, 42, 47, 50, 56, 57
    Naslet Safaha and Naslet Khater, Egypt, flint 2
    Ngilipitje, Arnhem Land, Australia, quartzite 26, 41, 49–50
    Obsidian Cliffs, Wyoming, obsidian 54
    Ormu, New Guinea 44
    Pipestone quarries, Minnesota 27, 31, 33, 41–2, 43–4, 45, *44–6*, 49, 57, 61, 69, 74, 139
    Sela, New Guinea 42, 50, 51, 145–4
    Tagime, New Guinea 42, 43, 44–5, 46, 50, 51, 92, 146
    Wyandotte, Indiana, chert 54
    Yeineri, New Guinea 26, 42, 43, 44, 48, 50, 51, 92, 146, 148
    Yellowstone, Wyoming, obsidian 2
quarries/quarrying (general) 1, 2, 19 5t, 19
  axe *9*, 18, 42, 65, *66*, 67, 71, 72, 74, 75, 77, 80, 85, 87–8t, 90, 119, 122
  Palaeolithic 2
  quarrymen/leaders/custodians 42, 43, 44, 45, 56, 57, 62
  workshops 3, 4, 6, 31, 65, 95, 127, 129, 132, 136, 141
radiocarbon date 1, 7, 8, 11, 12, 16, 17, 18, 19, 97, 99, 113, 114, 117–18, 118t, 119, 129, 132, 149
Rathlin Island, Co. Antrim, Group IX extraction quarries 54, 57, 65, 68, 106, 167
RAW MATERIALS
  general 1, 2, 3
    exotic 2, 10, 17, 18, 48, 61, 93, 95, 96, 97, 106, 110, 112, 128, 134, 135, 136, 137
    local 1, 3, 4, 5, 50, 76, 90, 95, 96, 103, 107, 110, 111, 112, 135, 143, 145, 146, 147t
    redeposition 2, 74, 82, 84, 85, 132, 137, 141
    relative quality/status/value 2, 6, 7, 9, 10, 13, 15, 18, 27, 41, 43, 54, 67, 95, 96, 111, 122, 124, 125, 132, 133, 134, 135, 137, 141, 142, 143–4
    significance of colour 10, 42, 93, 146
    green 18, 147
    toolstone 26, 27, 41, 45, 46, 48, 50, 51, 67, 90, 91, 93
  extracted, non-lithic
    copper 40, 61, 131
    ochre 28, 40–1, 42, 49, 50, 105, 141, 145; *see also* Wilgie Mia
    tin 44
  lithic
    agatized dolomite 2
    amphibolite 14, 95, 116
    amphibolitic schist 49, 93
    augite granophyre (Group VII) 110, 142, 145
    basalt 49, 50, 109
    beach deposits/cobbles 6, 10, 76
    bloodstone 10
    chert 2, 6, 7, 8, 9, 10, 59, 95, 135
        dolerite (inc. 'A' dolerite and Group X)/metadolerite 4, 12, 76, 95, 119t, 127, 135, 136, 137, 142, 145, 146
    drift deposits 9, 10
    epidotized tuff (Group VI) 10, 18, 32, 56, *94*, 101, 103, 106, 107t, 109, 110, 142, 145, 147, *148*, 149
    felsite 108
    fibrolite/Breton fibrolite 17, *17*, 56, 104, 117, 119, *120*, 135, 142, 145
    flint 6, 10, 11, 89, 95, 107, 110, 111, 122, 125, 126–7, 134, 135, 131, 142, 146–7
        Bartonian 18, 95, 96 135, 142
    granite 75–6
    greenschist 49, 93
    greenstone (inc. Group I) 3, 6, 18, 32, 74, 75, 76, 82, 111, 142, 145 3, 6, 18, 43, 47, 50, 73, 74, 75, 76, 82, 108, 109, 142
    hornfels (inc. Group XXIV) 20, *55*, 95, 136, 145
    jade/jadeitite/Alpen 1, 16–18, *16*, 18, 19, 32, 56, *56*, 57, 61, 90, 94, 95, 103, 104t, 106, 109, *120*, 128, 133, 135, 136, 139, 142, 145, 146, *146*, 147, 149
    jasper 6
    meta-mudstone 8, *8*

*Index*

mudstone 102, 109, 112
nephrite 41
obsidian 2, 26, 42, 44, 47, 49, 56, 57, 58, 103, 117, 128, 129, 133
pitchstone (Arran) 9, 10
porcellanite (inc. Group IX) 20, 103, 104, 109, 112, 142
porphyry 103, 109
quartz 127
quartzite 4, 7, 26, *39*, 135, 146
quartzite sandstone 95, 136
radiolarite 131, 135
red pipestone (Catlinite) 26, 27, 31, 33, 39, *39*, 41–2, 43–4, *45–7*, 49, 51
riebeckite felsite (Group XXII) *60*
rhyolite 4, 6, 11, 19
rhyolitic tuff Group XXI 11
schist 108
serpentine 146
siltstone 47, 108
slate 47
stream-bed deposits, gravel and river cobbles 2, 42, 76, 111
surface deposits 6, 18
variscite 18, 117, 129, 133, 135, 142, 147
Wommersom quartzite 7, 18
Rhine–Waal–Maas delta 7, 18, 107, 117
ritual, ceremonial and ritualised extraction practices/deposition 24, 25, 26, 27, 28, 29–30, 30t, 32, 33, 33t, 34, 35, 37, 40, 41, 43–9, *44–5*, *47–8*, 50, 54, 57–8, 58t, *58–60*, 61, 62, 68, 69, 74, 75–7, 81, 82–3, 84, 85–6, 87–8t, 93, 101, 102, 104, 105, 108, 109, 112, 132, 137, 139, 141, 143–50, 147t, 149
ceremonial sites 33, 34, 47, 101
feasting and fasting 41, 42, 71, 81, 84, 129, 144
purification 43–4, 57, 71
renewal 30, 33, 45, 46, *46*, 57, 58, *60*, 69, 71, 74–5, 78, 81–4, 85, 110, 118, 128, 132, 136, 141, 144, 146
ritual specialists 26, 41, 45, 46, 48
Shaman 45, 48
River Shannon, axeheads associated with 12–13, 16, 106
River Thames, axeheads from 12, *13*, 16, 106, 119
rock art/graffiti/idols 2–3, 4, 5, 11, 21 25, 26, 27, 28, 29, 33, 34, 34t, 35, 37, 40, 41, 43, 46, 51, 54, 56, 60–1, 63, 65, 68, 69, 71, 76, 80, *80*, 84, 85, 118
Ronaldsway, Isle of Man 93, 108

sacred 34, 50
bundle 40, 46, 49
landscape features/sites 40, 41, 42, 43, 69
objects and raw materials 35, 37, 40, 44, 46–9, 90–3, 91t, 133, 143, 147t
tobacco pipes and smoking rituals 39, 43, 46–7, *47*, 139
tree (*Yeli*) 49, 93
weapon 49
sacrifice 44, 71
salt 133
mines 140
Sardinia 124, 129, 133
seasonality 25, 27, 28, 29t, 33, 34, 35, 40, 42–3, 56–7, 62, 69–71
settlements associated with extraction 42, 45
on-site 42, 43, 65, 68–9
permanent 27, 28, 43
shells and molluscs 43, 44, 46, 48, 51, 72, 82, 93, 130, 133
Shetland 54, 65, 89, 119, 144, 167
Beorgs of Uyea, extraction site 75, 76, 78, 86
hoards 93, *94*, 108, *108*
Silbury Hill, Wiltshire 77

Single Grave Culture 96
site/deposit location 3, 25, 26, 27, 37, 39, 40, 41, 44, 54–5, 57, 60, 62, 63, 65, 66–9, *67–9*, 122–5, *123*, *125*, 137, 143–4
caves/swallowholes 26, 40, 54, 71, 75, 142
coastal/island 4, 6, 7, 11, 13, *15*, 19, 54, 68, 119, 134
mythologised 8, 24, 25, 26, 28, 29, 34, 35, 49, 54, 56, 62, 63, 67, 69, 93, 144
prominent/distinctive 6, 8, *8*, 9–11, *9*, 15, 19, 21, 26, 27, 37, 41, 54–6, 57, 62, 63, 65, 66–7, *67–9*, 69, 122–5, *123–4*, 137
visibility to/from 67, 80, 81, 119, 122, 123
Skelmuir Hill, Scottish Borders, flint mines 19
skeuomorphs and copies/imitations 102–3, *103*, 112, 146–7
social context of extraction 23–4, 28, 28t, 63, 65, 90–1, 91t, 139–40, 143–50
social and exchange networks 24, 43, 47, 48, 49–51, 58, 59, 90–1, 91t, 94–5, 101–2, 109, 119, 129, 134–7, 139, 143, 144, 147
bride-wealth/price 48, 49, 59, 93
ceremonial/ritual 50–1, 59, 93
gift giving 24, 90, 147
Kula 24, 90
potlatch 24, 90, 145
reciprocal 50–1, 90
South America 29, 33, 37, 56, 61, 80
Inka 25–6, 27, 37, 40
*Apu* 40
*Huaca* 37
*Pachamama* 25–6, 27, 37
Spain 117, 125, 129, 133
extraction sites
Casa Montero, Madrid, flint mines/quarries 16, 117, 125–6
El Cañaveral, flint mines 117
Gavà, Barcelona, Spain, varicite mines 18, 117, 129–30, 130t, 133, 147
Spiennes, Belgium, flint mines 18, 96, 103, 125, 126–7, *126*, 128, 129, 131, *136*, 136–7, 144
Stoke Down, Sussex, flint mines 19, 65, 74, 75, 82, 144, 67
abandonment/renewal 82
extraction tools 75, 82
special deposits 74
Stonehenge 68, 102
storied sites, *see* mythology
structures associated with extraction sites 56–7, 62, 77–9, *77*, 84
buildings 78
cairns and mounds 62, 68, 70, 77, 78, 79, 83, 84
chalk platform/'cave' 54, 71, 77, 142
enclosure with pits 83, 109
shrines 56, 57, 62, 84
stone setting 78
*see also* pits
subsistence/subsistence strategy 1, 3, 18, 57, 97
swallow holes, *see* caves
sweat lodge 33, 43, *44*, 45
Sweden 6–7, 11, 12 *12*, 105, 125, 145
extraction sites 7, 19, 119
Sweet Track, Somerset 17–18, 135
Swifterbant 7, 18, 114
symbolism 1, 12, 25, 28, 30, 35, 39, 40, 45, 48, 69–70, 75, 78–9, 80, 82, 84, 92, 101, 122, 128, 133, 139, 143, 144, 147, 149
axeheads 13, 48, 76, 93, 96, 101, 102, 146, 149

taboo 43, 44, 47, 48, 69, 71, 92
technology 3, 13, 18, 19
burnishing 11
grinding/polishing 3, 6, 11, 137

177

Tievebulliagh, Co. Antrim, Group IX extraction quarries 24, 54, 56, 65, 67, 68, *68*, 103, 144
    extraction tools 75
    special deposits 75
tin, Cornish modern 44
    'knockers' 140
trend data 25–37, 26t, 28–31t, 53, 53t, 69, 85, 87–8t
    themes 63, 63–4t
TRB/Funnel Beaker culture 96, 102, 105, 107, 119, 127, 134, 134t, 135, 145
Tumulus St Michel, Carnac, Brittany 17, 135, 145

use-wear/micro-wear 7, 12, 18, 30, 59, 101, 102, 105, 107, 110, 134

value/relative value 6, 18, 25, 27, 31, 43, 51, 57, 69, 90, 93, 94–101, 132–3, 138, 143–4, 145, 149
    axeheads 1–2, 17, 48, 50, 74, 94–101, 102, 123

raw materials 2, 7, 10, 27, 41, 43, 54, 122, 124, 125, 133, 134, 135, 141, 142, 143
Villeneuve-Saint-Germain culture 95, 135

warfare 50, 51
warriors 46, 48, 49, 92
wetlands 1, 7, 18, 103
    deposits in 1, 12–13, *13*, 17–18, 96, 103, 104, 106–7, 134, 134t, 145, 147
wooden objects 74, 91, 102–3
woodland/forest 67–8
    clearance 20, 97, 107, 110, 147
woodworking 110
workshops, debitage and products 3, 4, 6, 31, 65, 95, 127, 129, 132, 136, 141

XRF 2